Knowledge and Values
in Social and
Educational Research

Knowledge and Values in Social and Educational Research

Edited by

ERIC BREDO *and*
WALTER FEINBERG

Temple University Press
PHILADELPHIA

85-2596

Temple University Press, Philadelphia 19122

© 1982 by Temple University. All rights reserved

Published 1982

Printed in the United States of America

Library of Congress Cataloging in Publication Data

Main entry under title:
  Knowledge and values in social and educational research.
  Includes bibliographical references.
    1. Sociology—Research. 2. Social sciences—Research.
  3. Educational Research. 4. Positivism. 5. Hermeneutics.
  6. Criticism (Philosophy) I. Bredo, Eric, 1944–. II. Feinberg,
  Walter, 1937–
  HM24.K589 1982   301'.072   82-10371
  ISBN 0-87722-242-8
  ISBN 0-87722-245-2 (pbk.)

TO

ANNEKE BREDO,

NATHAN FEINBERG,

ARLENE FEINBERG,

and the memory of

ADELINE FEINBERG

Contents

Contents

Acknowledgments

We wish to thank the following people for their help with various parts of the manuscript: Elizabeth Hansot, Ernest Kahane, Gabriele Lakomski, Steven Tozer, David Tyack, Hans Wagemaker, and David Yick. We would also like to thank the students who have taken our seminar, Modern Theories of Education, for their response to much of the material presented in the book. Our special appreciation goes to Anneke Bredo, who read the entire manuscript in various drafts and provided important criticisms and suggestions.

Throughout the book we have edited spelling, grammatical forms, and note style to provide a semblance of continuity to materials published in several countries and various disciplines. In a few cases we have edited the articles slightly to omit references to material not found in this volume. In Chapter 20, we have regretfully made some cuts in order to shorten the article.

Knowledge and Values
in Social and
Educational Research

Introduction: Competing Modes of Social and Educational Research

Eric Bredo *and* Walter Feinberg

The present time appears to be the latest in a series of major historical turning points in the methodological foundations of educational research and of the social sciences generally.[1] While some methodological debate is a more or less constant feature of work in these areas, the last two decades have seen this debate reach rare levels of intensity, signaling a period of unusual self-reflection. As a result this period is particularly exciting intellectually, since what was previously taken for granted is becoming visible and held up for active reconsideration. At the same time it is a relatively confusing period, since methodological standards are largely up for grabs. The purpose of this volume is to introduce the rationale and assumptions underlying the principal competing traditions involved in this debate by bringing together some of the important essays in the different traditions, along with research examples applied to education. It also seeks to highlight a synthesis that may be emerging from the present normative confusion.

The Present Situation

The sixties began with the relatively clear dominance of a methodological paradigm in which the social sciences were seen as best modeled after the natural sciences, at least as these were understood in terms of logical positivism.[2] The emphasis was on increased logical and methodological rigor, on greater mathematical sophistication and better experimental or correlational control. What was wrong with previous research in the social sciences, it was held, was primarily that it was not sufficiently rigorous or precise or well controlled. The social sciences were still young and immature, but with enough time and resources, it was felt, they could become like their more sophisticated natural science counterparts.

Opposition to such a program in the social sciences came primarily from advocates of interpretive or qualitative approaches such as symbolic interactionists or phenomenologists, whose status was clearly subordinated to those taking the dominant approach. Rather than arguing for more of the same, advocates of these approaches suggested that there should be an openness to the conceptions and understandings of those people or groups whom one studies and much more tentativeness in the way the researcher holds or applies his or her own concepts, particularly because their correct usage depends upon the conceptions of those being studied. At first, this opposition was not only subordinated but in general relatively loyal. Some who held interactionist theoretical ideas adopted a positivistic methodology, thus splitting their theory from the methodological approach that would seem to be consistent with it. A division of labor also developed. Interpretive theory and methods were deemed more useful in micro contexts of face-to-face interaction while macro structural issues were to be approached from the standpoint of a different (functionalist) theory and positivistic methodology. Furthermore, it was often tacitly agreed that while interpretive methods were helpful in a preliminary way, such as for generating hypotheses, they were out of place when truly tested knowledge had to be produced.

This arrangement began to come to an end in the mid to late sixties. In the light of the social movements of the time, positivistic research began to appear to many either as irrelevant to concrete issues and sentiments or as actually manipulative and repressive. As Gouldner has suggested, theoretical change in social science often occurs when the domain assumptions or infrastructure of a theory are dissonant with shared sentiments and interests.[3] A theory that implies that certain distinctions are absolute, logical ones, and hence serves to justify a particular set of authorities, will not sit well with those who have more egalitarian sentiments for example. This seems to have been what happened in the sixties and seventies, when critics called into question not only the dominant substantive theoretical orientation (e.g., structural functionalism) but also the positivistic theory of knowledge that went along with it.[4] Since following the dominant tradition apparently meant that one had to be systematically deaf to some of the major events of one's time, the conclusion that many drew was that the whole prior approach was wrong.[5] What was needed was not achieving greater precision and rigor in the use of existing ideas but rather keeping a closer ear to the ground and attempting a more sensitive interpretive understanding. The fact that many reached these conclusions served to strengthen opposition in the research community and to question the legitimacy of its subordination.

Did all social research perhaps depend in fundamental ways on understanding the way events are construed by those being studied? If so, was not interpretation primary rather than merely preliminary?

The present situation in the research community appears to be characterized by a standoff between these two approaches. Although positivistic understanding of research in these areas is still dominant in terms of institutional support, its legitimacy has been damaged. As a result many people continue to conform to its norms, but without firm belief in them. Interpretive or qualitative approaches, on the other hand, seem to have more vitality and to generate more whole-hearted belief even though they get much less tangible support. In the various training institutions, standards for research methodology are often in disarray or there are competing clusters of researchers who hold opposing standards. Where tolerant individuals do agree that there is something to be granted to each approach, they remain unsure of what or how much should be granted. Overall, the situation is very nearly one in which "anything goes" so that the anarchic position adopted by some at least honestly reflects the contemporary state of affairs, even if it resolves little.

Given the debate between "hard" and "soft," or positivistic and interpretive, approaches and the apparent standoff between them, it is not surprising that there has been growing interest in approaches that attempt to mediate or possibly transcend the dichotomy between these two poles. The problem is to find an approach that avoids both the implicit absolutism of positivism and the implicit relativism of interpretivism, one that is open to questioning its own categorical distinctions, but not open at both ends. Attempts at synthesis are emerging in some evolutionary approaches to the philosophy of the natural sciences[6] and in "critical theory" in the social sciences.[7] Both of these approaches, whatever their other differences, view knowledge in a long-term social evolutionary perspective that allows for critical reflection on the adequacy of current paradigms or approaches. Our concern here will be mostly with critical theory, though arguments drawn from work in the natural sciences will be discussed briefly in the introduction to Part One.

Positivism, Interpretivism, and Critical Theory

So far we have discussed the three methodological orientations that this volume is concerned with as though all three—positivism, interpretivism, and critical theory—were already familiar. Some further introduction to them may be helpful. Since each of the three orientations is discussed in more detail in later introductory essays, our concern here is merely with giving an intuitive sense of the orientations and their inter-relations.

One way in which to facilitate this initial understanding is to consider the relation between knower and known that is presupposed in each theory. The positivistic approach assumes a strict subject-object dichotomy in which the knower is uninvolved with the known. In positivism, all knowledge, or at least all valid or legitimate knowledge, is that which is consistent with this detached point of view. The person or collectivity that is known is treated as a system to be studied by noting relations between perturbations in the state of one of its elements and changes in the states of other elements. By observing associations between these changed states the researcher seeks to infer the "laws" according to which the system operates. From this point of view there is no difference, at least in principle, between studying persons (or social phenomena) and studying natural phenomena. Each can be studied as a type of closed system.

In contrast to this, an interpretive approach views knower and known as being much more closely involved with one another. The way we find out about another's character or about another culture is through the consistency of their characterological or cultural patterns and our own. The way we learn that others behave according to different presuppositions is by having our expectations of them violated. In other words, we use our own expectations as a sounding board, with the interaction between the two patterns making us aware of the ways in which our own pattern contrasts with that of others.[8] Seen in this way, knower and known are inevitably involved with one another since one must use oneself or one's culture to understand others. The positivist then becomes metaphorically equivalent to a person who only follows his or her own score and does not listen to the jointly created melody.

For the critical theorist knower and known are even more mutually involved, though both may fail to recognize this fact. From this viewpoint the knowledge generated is a part of a process of mutual growth or evolution on the part of both parties. The researcher is inevitably an agent of change or a reinforcer of the status quo. This is because the very conceptual and methodological framework within which the research is conducted allows certain things to be questioned while it places others outside the bounds of legitimate discourse. Thus the researcher serves to legitimize certain kinds of questions or policies and to delegitimize others. On the other hand, changes in social structure result in new social priorities and new patterns of research relevance and support. These can then affect research foci and the frameworks within which legitimate, institutionally supported research is conducted. By having been mutually shaped by each other, knower and known find independent positions for judgment difficult to attain. Critical theory suggests that, like it or not, knower and known are involved in just this way. Defining knowledge only in "objective" terms or only in involved but nonevolving terms does not lessen the researcher's social responsibility but only serves to hide it. As Robert Penn Warren has said, "The recognition of complicity is the beginning of innocence." The critical theorist suggests that this recognition is just what is needed if social or educational research is to be at least more "innocent."

The Orientations in Institutional Context

Another way to get perspective on the three methodological approaches we have been discussing is to consider them in the light of their relations to current practices and institutions. We will consider them in relation to the system of formal education, but a similar perspective could be gained from other institutional standpoints.

Certain tendencies in the field of education are highly compatible with the positivistic temper. Behavioral objectives, behavior modification, minimal competency testing, and concern for accountability (as this is usually understood) are all efforts in which the principal focus is on instrumental rationality. These tendencies align well with positivism because of its implicit orientation towards prediction and control. Since positivistic knowledge seeks to find how change in one variable will produce change in another, it nicely fits the attempt to get more output for one's input that is the practical concern of rationalizers in education. Of course, one may share this concern when it is in the service of other values, but in educational settings, as in others, the search for efficiency sometimes becomes an overriding end in itself.

Most educational research has served to bolster just this sort of effort. In educational psychology most research has been directed towards efforts to find which "treatments" produce the greatest increase in individual achievement. Similarly, in educational sociology most research has been in the "school effects" tradition, which seeks to find the school or classroom factors that predict achievement. In the economics of education the dominant tradition has been the analysis of educational "production functions," in which schools are seen as analogous to factories in which one seeks the most efficient combination of inputs to produce a unit of (achievement) output. Each of these fields has at times been virtually defined by this type of research interest, resulting in a strong confluence of academic research with rationalizing, efficiency-oriented management techniques.

Other forces in education pull in a contrary direction. Rationalism in education has commonly been more limited than in many other spheres, at least in the United States. Schools may have all the formal trappings of bureaucracies, but they often remain "structurally loose" in practice.[9] An authority hierarchy exists, but the control of superior over subordinate is relatively limited; there is a division of labor but it often involves merely separate, segmented activities rather than truly interdependent ones; there are rules and procedures but they often operate more as general guidelines than as detailed specifications for action.[10] The particularistic influences that limit rationalization include the diversity of student clients who have different relevancies and interests, the diversity of cultural groups served by the schools (each of which wants its children treated in ways that are sensitive to their varying heritages), a tradition of decentralized local control, and the limited legitimizing power or plausibility of pedagogical science. These countervailing tendencies and interest groups suggest a need for attention to substantive rather than merely procedural rationality, and a desire by some to see that students are treated equitably in more than name only.

Research in the interpretive tradition aligns well with these efforts. Psychological research emphasizing the importance of cognitive schemata for learning supports the idea that teachers should be sensitive to the particular expectations and assumptive framework in which the child is working, just as sociological research in a phenomenological tradition emphasizes the importance of the way actors define the situation. Similarly, the concern of educational anthropologists with differences in communicative codes serves to underline the need to take social conventions and background assumptions into account. Such research would seem to bolster just those practical efforts towards attaining increased educational equity and relevance already mentioned.

Still other forces in education arise in response to the very fact that there is such a divergence between formal and substantive rationality, between bureaucratic form and situated practice, between head and heart. Most of the time this divergence is greatest for those who are the least privileged, who are told that they are (formally) equal but are treated in ways that ensure their practical inequality. Their reactions are evident in school violence, malaise, and related problems of discipline and control. At other times, systemic irrationality affects even those who are the system's most legitimate clients, thereby throwing the system generally into question. Such times of legitimation crisis, such as the late 1960s to 1970s, raise doubts not only about the technical rationality or efficiency of the system, and its relevance to the lives of its (more favored) clients, but about the legitimacy of institutional authority itself.

Critically oriented research focuses on just these types of phenomena—that is, on the contradiction between the formal and the substantive—and the meaning or explanation of this disjunction. As we have suggested, most American educational research has not been in this vein, though much of it can be seen as tacitly related to this problem of divergence. The "school effects" or "production function" literature mentioned earlier suggests, in effect, that the way to deal with the issue is to impose the formal more fully and carefully over the informal through more efficient management and control. Interpretively oriented research suggests that the way to handle the problem is to soften the formal to bring it more in line with the informal, to make teaching more "relevant." And critically oriented research suggests that the problem is neither with the formal nor with the informal but rather with the power relations and self-interest that maintain such divergence beyond what is technically or socially necessary.

Conclusion and Plan of the Volume

In this introduction we have tried to give an intuitive feel for the three theories of knowledge that are considered in the essays that follow by appealing, first, to a sense of where the social, scientific, and educational research communities are at present; second, to an examination of the image of the knower and the known that underlies each approach; and, third, to an understanding of present conditions in formal education. Each of these discussions presents a very similar set of contrasting positions in the hope that these will be clarified by discussing them in different contexts. However, the discussion of the three theories of knowledge has some additional implications that bear further discussion.

Each of the three theories of knowledge invites one to define its object domain differently from the others. The positivistic social scientist typically examines "behavior"—that is, units that are constituted by his or her own conceptual scheme and not by that of the actor. The interpretivist studies "actions"—units that are constituted by the culture and related conceptual schemes of those being studied. And the critical theorist studies "ideological distortion"—the relation and possible contradiction between the way people behave in practice and the way they understand themselves to be acting. It is easily possible for each of these object domains to become reified or objectified so that they become no more than substantively different "things" to study. One can treat "behavior" or "meanings" or "ideological distortion" in a positivistic mode as things that can be known from a value-neutral, objective position. This is in fact what frequently happens when these methodological orientations become institutionalized. However, the point of a theory of knowledge is that it should apply to the knower as well as to the known (if the latter is also a knower). What is involved is not merely a theory of knowledge for others but also for oneself. This means that the behaviorist, to be consistent, should be able to account for his own knowing strictly in behavioral terms. And the structuralist should acknowledge the fact that his own knowledge of others' cultures or cognitive structures is itself constituted by some cognitive structure or set of structures. Finally, the critical theorist, if he or she is also to be consistent, must confront the fact that his or her own knowledge may derive from an ideologically distorted understanding. From the standpoint of critical theory, ideological distortion is a result of the failure to be reflective and to apply one's theory of knowledge to oneself in order to consider what one could know using one's own theory and, in particular, what one's approach hides as well as what it reveals. It is the failure to be adequately self-reflective in this way that presumably contributes to the frequent divergence between theory and practice (in dogmatic anti-dogmatism, for instance). However, it is one thing to have a reflective theory of knowledge and another to employ it successfully. In fact, it is clear that one can never be fully successful. In this sense the present volume should also be seen as self-limited. For instance, the categorization of approaches in terms of which it is organized serves to hide certain types of distinctions between approaches even as it reveals others.

This volume is organized in three parts around each of the three methodological orientations we have been discussing. Each part contains several types of essays. The first chapter or two is usually a philosophical statement of the position being considered. This is followed by other statements of the position that discuss it in terms of its implications for one of the social sciences. After this a set of chapters exemplify the approach as applied in actual research. In order to make comparison clearer, these research applications all explore the same general issue: the differences in educational outcomes experienced by students from different social origins. By bringing together essays discussing the philosophical aspects of an orientation with examples of its practical application in research we hope to steer a course that avoids the extremes of abstract philosophical discussion without application on the one hand and cook-book discussions of methods without theoretical basis on the other.

A final caveat: while we have selected articles that we feel are good examples of each type of approach, no author or article *is* a pure type. They exemplify the categorical distinctions to different degrees.

Notes

1. For an excellent discussion of a previous historical turning point for the social sciences that bears great similarity to the most recent one, see H. Stuart Hughes, *Consciousness and Society* (New York: Vintage, 1958).
2. Richard Bernstein, The *Restructuring of Social and Political Theory* (Philadelphia: University of Pennsylvania Press, 1978).
3. Alvin Gouldner, *The Coming Crisis in Western Sociology* (New York: Basic Books, 1970). For a similar discussion of theory change in the sociology of education, see Jerome Karabel and A. H. Halsey, *Power and Ideology in Education* (New York: Oxford University Press, 1977), "Introduction." A related analysis of theory change in sociology is offered by Norbert Wiley, "History and the Chicago School of Sociology," paper presented at the Annual Convention of the Organization of American Historians, Detroit, Mich., April 3, 1981. Wiley discusses theory change in terms of Weber's concept of "elective affinity" between practical interests and theoretical rationale.
4. See Stephen Toulmin, *Human Understanding* (Princeton, N.J.: Princeton University Press, 1972), for a discussion of changes in disciplinary selection procedures.
5. Charles Taylor's chapter, "Interpretation and the Sciences of Man," in Part Two of this volume suggests the limitations of a positivistic approach in studying this type of phenomenon.
6. See Frederick Suppe, ed., *The Structure of Scientific Theories* (2nd ed.; Urbana: University of Illinois Press, 1977); Russell Keat and John Urry, *Social Theory as Science* (London: Routledge and Kegan Paul, 1975); and Toulmin, *Human Understanding*.
7. Jürgen Habermas, *Knowledge and Human Interests* (Boston: Beacon, 1971).
8. Gregory Bateson, *Mind and Nature: A Necessary Unity* (New York: E. P. Dutton, 1979).
9. Charles Bidwell, "The School as a Formal Organization," in *Handbook of Organizations*, ed. James G. March (New York: Rand McNally, 1965).
10. Dan Lortie, "The Balance of Control and Autonomy in Elementary School Teaching," in *The Semi-Professions and Their Organization*, ed. Amitai Etzioni (New York: Free Press, 1969).

PART ONE

The Positivistic Approach to Social and Educational Research

Eric Bredo *and* Walter Feinberg

In the current climate in which positivism is being attacked as a rigid orthodoxy it is important to remember that it was initially perceived as liberating from the traditions that preceded it. The term "positivism" was coined in the last century by the French philosopher-sociologist Auguste Comte as a way of referring to his "positive philosophy," which represented a particular understanding of the nature and growth of knowledge in the natural sciences and the application of this understanding to issues of social progress. In this view, science represented an evolutionary advance over prior stages in the development of knowledge, such as religious myths or metaphysical systems. Scientific knowledge was grounded in the facts of sensory experience, which, at least at their simplest, were thought to be indubitable. These facts could be related to and explained by general laws, and sets of laws integrated into coherent theoretical systems such that, as science progressed, more and more facts could be explained by fewer, more general laws. Because scientific knowledge was empirically testable, it was open to rational modification and could develop in a way that these prior systems would not.

Comte suggested that the application of the scientific method to society, a "social physics" and an applied "social engineering," could provide intellectual grounds for a new, more rational social order that could emerge from the apparent intellectual and political anarchy of the time. Social changes could be tried out on a limited basis, like scientific experiments, to determine which ones worked, and the knowledge gained would then suggest how one could rationally change conditions for the better, or, in the case of circumstances that could not be changed, which conditions must be endured. Science would thus provide the rational basis for a social order that was neither static, like those based on tradition, nor anarchic, but rather one in which change itself could be orderly. As Gouldner puts it:

> *Vis-à-vis* the old traditionalism and the emerging bourgeoisie, the new positivistic sociology at first had a liberative and rational function. It brought into question the self-understanding of all elites, so far as these could not be given an "empirical" grounding. Definitions of social reality advanced by any of the elites, old or new, could now be subject to systematic questioning, to examination, to a demand for justification. *En principe*, pronouncements were now no longer credited by virtue of being affirmed by persons of authority. . . . A man's social position or political allegiance no longer sufficed to credit his discourse.[1]

Considered politically, Comte's approach thus represented a hopeful, forward-looking liberalism, one that served to undermine traditional bases of authority, even as it also undercut the idea of revolutionary change.

The contemporary form of positivism, "logical positivism," does not come to us directly from Comte. It derives from the work in the early decades of this century of Alfred Ayer in England, and of the "Vienna Circle" philosophers, such as Mortiz Schlick and Rudolf Carnap. These scholars refined and elaborated earlier positivism by bringing together the fundamental work on the logical foundations of mathematics of the British analytic philosophers, such as Bertrand Russell, with other work in the foundations of the physical sciences such as that of Ernst Mach. Logical positivism thus served to bring together elements of two very powerful bases for knowledge: an empiricism that based knowledge on sensory or observational experience and a rationalism that based knowledge on self-evidently clear and consequential arguments. Logic became the scaffolding on which one modeled the world, while the facts of sensory or observational experience provided the constraints to which the logical model had to conform. By basing knowledge on these twin pillars, logic and sensory experience, especially as these had been developed in the most advanced work in the foundations of mathematics and science at the time, logical positivism was in a strong position to legitimize itself as *the* paradigm for true knowledge of the world.

One of the main concerns of the logical positivists was to develop clear criteria for meaningful statements and adequate explanations. This concern was based on the desire to eliminate knowledge claims that were presented in the form of explanations but that either did not truly explain anything or were imune to being put to empirical test. Statements that proposed to explain why people go to sleep under the influence of opium in terms of opium's "dormative powers," for example, were discounted as meaningless because they merely restate what happens rather than explain it logically. Similarly, explanations in terms of entities, whether God, Devil, or human spirit, that cannot be put to empirical test were also rejected. The positivists wanted to eliminate metaphysical statements from the domain of science, and to do so they proposed rigorous standards of cognitive relevance.

Only analytic or synthetic statements were accepted as meaningful. The first, analytic statements, were said to be true by definition. These were often illustrated by statements such as "all bachelors are unmarried" and were thought to be most clearly represented by mathematical truths. The second, synthetic statements, like "there are no bachelors in this room," were said to be true or false by virtue of experience. Such synthetic statements formed the basis for the empirical sciences. All other statements, such as "peace is good" or "the painting is beautiful," were outside of the realm of verification and were termed meaningless since their truth could not be established either by definition or by experience (as conceived by the positivists). By limiting the domain of valid knowledge to that of analytic or synthetic truth, the positivists sought to define clearly the line between scientific and unscientific explanation and in this way eliminate seemingly irresolvable and unproductive moral and metaphysical arguments.

The distinction between analytic and synthetic statements provided grounds for a related distinction between theory and observation. If one can logically distinguish between analytic and synthetic statements, one can, by implication, distinguish between the logical relations that are "inside" a theory and the external observations that are "outside" of it. This distinction was important for the positivistic program because in that program theories must be tested by independent observational facts. If these observations are to serve as the grounds on which theories are tested, then they must be logically independent of the theory being tested, for otherwise the "test" becomes merely tautologous and not a true independent test of the theory. For the positivist, then, there is always a logical gap between theoretical and observational statements. Critics of positivism, as we will see, have challenged this assumption of a *logical* distinction between theory and observation, though they would agree that the two may be relatively independent in some other way.

A final distinction that was important in the positivistic program, especially in education and the social sciences, was the distinction between fact and value. Fact and value were assumed to be logically heterogeneous in positivism like the other distinctions between analytic and synthetic or theoretical and observational statements. The positivist sought to describe things as they are, not as they are seen or judged to be. From a purely logical point of view the meaning of a statement can be seen as what it denotes rather than as its practical connotations. Recognizing this, the positivists sought to adopt a purified language that was purged of as much connotative import as possible so that his or her statements could be seen as the purely technical or descriptive statements that they were intended to be. In short the positivists assumed a logical distinction between fact and value, viewing empirical generalizations as a map describing the connections between what is and values as determining where one wants to go.

Many of these concerns and distinctions are apparent in the chapter by Michael Martin in this part of the present volume. Martin clearly articulates a notion of scientific explanation that has been developed in great detail by philosophers such as Carl Hempel and Ernest Nagel. Accordingly, our discussion of the positivistic view of explanation in this introduction will draw primarily on Hempel, whose work has often been cited by social scientists in support of their own research. However, it is well to remember that a broad range of contemporary research practice can be seen as consistent with what Bernstein has termed the "positivistic temper" even if it is not self-consciously guided by the technical precepts of logical positivism proper.[2]

Positivistic Explanation

Knowledge, for the positivist, exists at three levels of generality or abstraction: (1) particular observations, (2) laws, or empirical generalizations, and (3) theoretical statements and definitions. We will discuss the positivistic view of explanation in terms of the relation between the first two, laws and particular observations, and then consider what positivism has to say about the nature of theories. It is important to bear in mind, however, that theoretical principles explain lower-level laws in the same way that such lower-level laws or generalizations explain particular observations.

For the positivist, explanation consists of showing that a particular event is an instance of an established regularity,[3] or, as Hempel puts it, "The explanation fits the phenomena to be explained into a pattern of uniformities." To take an example from elementary physics, imagine that the pressure in a closed container filled with a gas is 10 lbs./sq. inch and the temperature is 50° K, at time one, while at time two the pressure is 20 lbs./sq. inch and the temperature is 100° K. Both of these events or facts are "explained" by a law stating that "pressure is directly proportional to temperature." This law explains the two events in the sense that the events are particular instances of the general relation between variables that it states. One could visualize this form of explanation by imagining a line going through the two points representing these two events in the pressure-temperature plane. The equation specifying the line would be equivalent to a law in that all the points that fall on the line are instances of the general relation stated in the equation. Each point is explained by the equation for the line in the sense that, given any temperature, we can logically deduce that the pressure must be, assuming the law (or equation) to be true. To make the example a little more specific, imagine that the law is "pressure equals five times temperature" ($P = 5T$). If this is an accepted law, and we know that the antecedent condition is that the temperature in a vessel is 100°, then we can deduce that the pressure in the vessel must be 500 lbs./sq. inch. If this is indeed what we observe, then this observation is "explained" by the law in conjunction with the antecedent condition.

Law:	Pressure equals five times temperature.
Antecedent condition:	Temperature equals 100° K.
Observational implication:	Pressure equals 500 lbs./sq. inch.

The explanation of the event (the pressure in the vessel) is thus equivalent to logically deducing it from some accepted statement of regularity along with a correct statement of initial condition. This is what Hempel and Martin refer to as the Deductive-Nomological (or D-N) model of explanation, a term that derives from the fact that the explanation of the observations consists of their being deducible from a universal (i.e., nomological) statement.

However, Hempel points out there must be more to (positivistic) explanation than this, for otherwise we would be unable to differentiate between accidental generalizations and laws. For example, the line going through the two points just discussed must be more than a mere summary of what was observed on those two occasions, or on any number of occasions. If our general statement merely summarizes what has previously occurred, then this gives us no logical basis for expecting things to be different should conditions change. A law must allow us to anticipate how things will be (or would have been) if antecedent conditions are (or were) different. A law must go "beyond the information given" and not merely summarize what has been observed to date. However, it is one thing to argue that laws must have this property of being able to generate what are called counter-factual or subjunctive conditionals and another to determine what it is about some laws that enables them to do this successfully. Hempel suggests that this depends upon whether the law is consistent with the accepted scientific theories, for whether a statement in the form of a universal will be counted as a law will depend in part upon theories accepted as scientific at the time. In fact, the issue seems to be more difficult than Hempel suggests although we shall not pursue it further here.[4]

Both of the previously cited examples of positivistic explanation are drawn from the natural sciences rather than from the social sciences or education because it is difficult if not impossible to find relationships in the latter fields that take the universal and determinate form of the laws just considered. The problem with laws of this type with respect to the social sciences is that any one event that does not conform to them invalidates them. But in social science there are exceptions to every rule, so adopting a strict Deductive-Nomological model of explanation would virtually rule out social science from the beginning.

Hempel has been instrumental in arguing that a positivistic form of explanation can be liberalized or generalized to include statements that include probabilistic or statistical terms as well as those of the determinate type just considered. In discussing these he introduces a second model of explanation, the Inductive-Statistical (I-S) model or, as Martin calls it in Chapter 1, the statistical probabilistic model of explanation. One can visualize the way this model works by imagining a line drawn through a set of points (e.g., a set of readings of temperature and pressure, as before) in which the points are scattered about the line rather than falling exactly on it, and in which the scatter is thought to be due to more than measurement error. The scientist first observes the scatter representing all his observations. He then tries to find a general *probabilistic* relationship that would account for the scatter of points. Of course, he must again state a relationship that applies beyond the samples used for his observation and not just summarize his existing data, for otherwise he would again have only a summary and not an explanation. By proceeding inductively in this way the scientist may develop "law-like" generalizations that allow him or her to explain particular events as instances of a more embracing generalization in much the same way as in the deterministic case, but with the difference that it is understood that the particulars only conform to the generalization in a statistical rather than in a deterministic sense. Hempel suggests that while this form of explanation is less strict, it has strong similarities with the D-N case and should also be accepted as an adequate form of explanation.

In both of these related models explanation and prediction are viewed (although with some controversy) as symmetrically related. That is, given the law or law-like statement and some initial conditions, one can predict the consequent conditions that must occur if the law is true. On the other hand, given some consequent conditions—that is, some outcomes that one has observed—and some initial conditions, the law can then be used to explain these. In other words, one can equally well work "up" to the explanation of a set of observed facts by a law or "down" from established laws to the predicted outcomes. Of course, given an established law, one can also work "sideways" from a set of consequent conditions to a conclusion as to what the initial conditions must have been. The main point for our purposes, however, is that the very same knowledge allows one both to explain prior events and to predict or know how to control and bring about future events, assuming the law to be correct.

An issue that is closely related to the issue of explanation is that of causation. The view of causation usually adopted by positivists is essentially a Humean one[5] in which cause is seen as regular sequential conjunction, other theoretically admissible factors being held constant. Certainly the way in which causal inferences are made in positivistic research is by seeing which event regularly precedes another, with relevant confounding influences held constant or randomized.[6]

Theories in Positivism

A set of laws may function in a larger deductive system or theory when they are themselves explained by some higher-level theoretical principles. In fact, functioning in an accepted theory is what differentiates "laws" from empirical generalizations. These higher-level theoretical statements deductively explain the lower-level laws in much the same way that the laws (or law-like statements) explain factual observations. Theoretical statements are often seen as referring to the properties of unobservable hypothetical entities or mechanisms lying "behind" the observable events. For instance, both Skinner and Homans (in Chapters 2 and 3 of this volume) appeal to "reinforcement" as a principle that can explain a set of empirical generalizations. Abstract concepts such as this are removed from direct observation or what would be considered direct

19

observation, but are acknowledged as necessary in most positivistic accounts of knowledge. One of the crucial reasons they are necessary is that without an underlying theory one cannot distinguish between events that are spuriously related and those that are causally related to one another (given the positivistic view of causation). That is, two types of events may be correlated merely because both are "caused" by some third type of event, but without knowing their relation to the third event, one might erroneously conclude that the first two were causally related. An underlying theory serves to suggest the relevant confounding influences, which can then be controlled or randomized in the attempt to observe causal rather than merely spurious or symptomatic relations.

However, since theoretical laws or definitions are not put in terms that are directly observable, one must at least partially translate (or interpret) the implications of these laws in terms of observable quantities. This partial interpretation is performed using correspondence rules, where these rules state the way in which the abstract terms used in the higher-level laws can be put in terms of observables. The kinetic theory of gases, which Hempel refers to, can be used as an example. The theoretical statements postulate a certain conception of gases—for example, that they are made up of noninteracting molecules that can be characterized as symmetrical point masses. A set of correspondence rules serves to relate this idealized conception to observable conditions such as the pressure, temperature, and volume of the gas (e.g., by postulating that temperature is a function of the average kinetic energy of the molecules). The various gas laws (e.g., that pressure is proportional to temperature) are derivable from the initial theory along with the correspondence rules. These laws may then be related to particular observations via statements of initial conditions. In this way, the whole theory forms an integrated deductive system.

While positivists may acknowledge the necessity of theoretical terms and statements, such terms have often had a troublesome and ambiguous status in positivistic thought. This is because statements using such terms are not analytically true nor (directly) synthetically true. They are not analytically true because they are not derived from higher-level principles. And they are not synthetically true because no one has ever directly observed "reinforcement" or "cognitive balance" or "intelligence." Thus the very mention of these terms may put the positivists in a quandary since by using them they seem to be engaging in the very form of metaphysical speculation that proponents of positivism have sought to eliminate.

One proposed solution to this problem has been to regard theoretical terms and principles as mere hypothetical postulations, as logical constructions rather than as real entities. This accounts for the fact that this approach to theories has been called the Hypothetical-Deductive (H-D) view of theories. In this view theoretical terms are merely useful fictions, which although they have no direct deductive relation to observables do have an indirect one. That is, by explaining a set of laws—and in fact aiding in the derivation of new laws—theoretical statements are seen as indirectly related to observational facts.

In considering these different levels of abstraction in the positivistic approach it is well to keep in mind that what is a theoretical statement in one theory may be an observed fact in another. In other words, the lowest-level "atoms" out of which the theory is constructed may be of different sorts such that what is at the atomic level in one theory is at a "molecular" level in another. Theories are only logically "higher" relative to the laws that can be derived from them, just as laws are only logically "higher" relative to a certain set of observations.

Varieties of Positivistic Research

A variety of types of actual research efforts may be seen as consistent with a positivistic approach. One way of distinguishing between these has to do with the stage of theoretical development in an area of research. Some of the more prominent stages would be (1) initial clarification of theoretical concepts, (2) the formalizing of empirical generalizations, and (3) self-conscious theory construction. Berger, Cohen, Snell, and Zelditch refer to three related types of formalizing activity as explication, representation, and theory-construction.[7]

The first type of endeavor, explication, has to do with developing formal representations of theoretical concepts. An example would be the application of mathematical graph theory to intuitive notions of cognitive balance in order to clarify the initual concept.

The second type of effort, representation, has as its goal the representation of a particular set of empirical results in a simple and precise way. It amounts to a formalized summary of existing empirical relationships. For instance, one might attempt to fit data to mathematical models like exponential curves and Markov models that are particularly easy to handle. Some of Coleman's work (not included here) has been of this type, in which he takes abstract equations having to do with diffusion or contagion and fits them to data on the acceptance of innovations by physicians. Simon's use of differential equations to summarize some of Homans' earlier generalizations about social interaction is a further example.[8] What these have in common is the restatement of a set of empirical generalizations in terms that are simpler and more precise than previously. If one can "explain" a set of data in terms of an equation that is mathematically simple and that also yields a better fit with the data than some other equation, than one has achieved a certain sort of progress.

The third form of inquiry, theory-construction, seeks to test or elaborate a theory itself, rather than just explicating its concepts or formalizing empirical generalizations. At this stage the theory must be very explicit so that various laws can be derived from it and put to empirical test, and the theory falsified or modified.

Another way of distinguishing between types of positivistic research efforts is between theoretical and applied studies, or what Berger, Zelditch, and Anderson (in Chapter 4 in this section) refer to as "generalizing" versus "historical" strategies. These efforts also differ in aim, with the former aiming at developing explanations that hold universally—that is, in all times and places—while the latter attempt to develop those that apply to only a particular case. Those adapting the first would want to explain warfare or conflict in general, while those adapting the second would want to explain the Civil War in particular. Among the studies included in this volume, Homans' and Webster's work may be seen as directed towards general theory while the Campbell and Coleman chapter summarizing the "Coleman Report" shows the result of an applied study in which theory played little or no part until used for *post hoc* interpretation of the data.

Problems with Positivism

In recent years the positivistic understanding of science has been subjected to a range of attacks whose effects have been so devastating that one authoritative philosophical account suggests "positivistic philosophy of science has gone into near total eclipse."[9] While virtually all the fundamental tenets of positivism have been criticized, we would like to limit our consideration to two critical areas: (1) the positivistic understanding of the relation between theory and observation and (2) the positivistic account of explanation.

Objections to positivism can be seen—in retrospect, at least—as coming from two positions. Chronologically the first objections came primarily from a "conventionalist"[10] perspective, or what Suppe refers to as "weltanschauung views,"[11] an approach that is roughly the natural science equivalent of the interpretative approach that is discussed in Part Two of this volume. Thomas Kuhn's *The Structure of Scientific Revolutions* was a particularly important work in this attack on positivism because of the rich suggestiveness of its description of scientific practice.[12] In Kuhn's view one has to look at the scientific community the way a sociologist or anthropologist would look at other communities to determine the conventions and presuppositions—the culture—of the community that allow scientists to communicate with one another and to reach agreed-upon judgments. Seen in this way scientific theories become "paradigms" or ways of seeing rather than logical models.

The principal challenge that this and related work presents to a positivistic account of science is to undermine the absolute logical distinction positivists make between theory and observation. If theories are, or are based on, paradigms, then observations are always constructed according to the pattern or gestalt involved in the paradigm. What you see depends upon how you look. If this is true, then the notion that observations are logically independent of theories and thus constitute an independent test of them has to be rejected, and along with it the positivistic view of science. This is not to say that under this conventionalist account theories and observations are the same, for it is one thing to be looking for a certain pattern and another thing to see instances of it, but it is a denial of the *logical* independence of the two. From this standpoint theories and observations probably appear to be independent to positivists because, during times of "normal" science, the standards making up the paradigm are relatively fixed and taken for granted and so invisibly organize observations. However, this independence is only apparent, not real, as becomes evident during times of "revolutionary" science, when what was previously taken for granted is called into question.

The positivistic view of explanation was also challenged on related grounds from this position. Basically the challenge suggested that positivism focused on formal rationality to the exclusion of substantive rationality. For the positivists explanation consisted of making an argument that supported the (observed) conclusion, with acceptable explanations being logical arguments. However, it is often possible to offer logical arguments that are not satisfactory on other grounds. The argument may not be convincing or plausible; it may be trivial, labored, or irrelevant to the purpose at hand. Neither in everyday nor in scientific life are all logical arguments accepted as correct arguments. As Nelson Goodman puts it:

> Truth, far from being a solemn and severe master, is a docile and obedient servant. The scientist who supposes that he is single-mindedly dedicated to

the search for truth deceives himself. He is unconcerned with the trivial truths he could grind out endlessly; and he looks to the multifaceted and irregular results of observations for little more than suggestions of overall structures and significant generalizations. He seeks system, simplicity, scope; and when satisfied on these scores he tailors truth to fit. . . . He as much decrees as discovers the laws he sets forth, as much designs as discerns the patterns he delineates.[13]

   In this expanded view explanation does not merely consist of "covering" oneself, that is, with logically justifying a conclusion, but in the riskier business of offering an account that is plausible and illuminating and thereby truly enhances understanding. A variety of criteria other than logical truth enters into the evaluation of a scientific theory and its acceptance, modification, or rejection, for a "correct" theory is something more than one that is merely logically true. In fact, even the use of logical criteria depends upon broader judgment of correctness of application. On this account, then, the positivistic view of the nature of explanation and of the grounds on which even the most rigorous sciences accept or reject theories is much too narrow. Taken together, these two objections strike at the heart of the positivistic account of science, questioning its assumptions about the nature of theories and of explanations.
   A second set of objections to positivism comes from a "realist" position,[14] which some see as related to critical theory, discussed in Part Three of this volume. According to this interpretation, the realist position can be seen as the natural science analog of critical theory, just as the conventionalist position is the natural science analog of the interpretative approach. In general, the realist approach can be seen as an attempt to get beyond the positivist-conventionalist dichotomy and to correct some of the excesses of the conventionalist position.
   The realist seeks explanations primarily in terms of an appeal to underlying structures or mechanisms that are postulated as "really" existing rather than as mere hypothetical fictions although it is acknowledged that there is no unmediated knowledge of these mechanisms. In other words, the realist introduces, as real, some of the nonobservational entities that positivists sought to eliminate. The positivistic understanding of the relation between theory and observation may then be criticized from a realistic position as follows: For the realist the relevant distinction is not that between theory and observation, as for the positivist, or between normal and revolutionary science, as for the conventionalist, but rather between direct and nondirect observation.[15] Direct observation occurs when information about some theoretical entity is received with-

out interruption or interference; nondirect observation is approximate and depends on idealizations or simplifications or involves models or theories that are not yet established. What makes knowledge direct or indirect is the accepted background knowledge—in particular, knowledge about causal structures or entities. Thus, at a certain state of knowledge, viewing something with an electron microscope would count as direct observation and as basically no different from seeing it with the naked eye, whereas, before the principles of the electron microscope were adequately understood, such observation might be considered highly indirect and inferential. Thus, what counts as a direct observation changes with the state of knowledge and technology and so is subject to historical change. The point with respect to the positivistic theory/ observation dichotomy is that theory is involved in both direct and nondirect observations so that "it is not a contrast between two different sorts of concepts, one 'observational' and the other 'theoretical.' "[16] Instead, the distinction is practical, one that is relative to existing technology and experience. Thus, the positivist's dichotomy is again denied and seen not as a logical but as a practical matter.

The criticism of the positivistic view of explanation that a realist would offer is, again, that positivists accept many explanations that are not adequate explanations. To the realist, an adequate explanation is one that (correctly) explains the phenomenon in terms of causal necessity, not merely by seeing it as an instance of an established regularity. Some positivistic accounts might be adequate because they are based on a correct understanding of the underlying structures or mechanisms, but others that a positivist would accept would be unacceptable to a realist because although logically correct they were based on a misconception of these structures. Thus the positivist is again found wanting for having an account that is simultaneously too restrictive—because it sees explanation only in narrow logical terms—and not restrictive enough—because it admits too many explanations that are inadequate.

Conclusion

If positivism began as a liberating force from old orthodoxies, it later itself became an overly restrictive orthodoxy. Like the person who is compulsively logical in everyday life, positivism is too rigid to provide an adequate way of understanding how all correct or adequate knowledge is gained. The criticisms of positivism should not lead one to deny that the development of logical, integrated theoretical systems are possible and have their uses. They do, however, lead one to deny that such systems should be a universal ideal or that this ideal represents an adequate basis for a theory of the nature of scientific knowledge.

The discussion of some of the arguments against positivism draws primarily on the positivistic understanding of the natural sciences and not on the social or human sciences. Analogous arguments have been raised in the social sciences and in education, but in these cases the issue gains additional complexity. When one is studying human beings one must suppose that any theory of knowledge and learning that one holds for oneself might—to be consistent—also be held by those whom one studies. The problem then becomes how to understand or explain others' actions or behavior when they are themselves using similar types of capabilities for explaining and understanding themselves and others. Once the positivist ideal is discarded, for example, how is it possible to say that another person's view is wrong and ours is right, given this similar capacity? The issue becomes especially prominent when fundamentally different views exist about the nature of the world. Since the problems that this condition raises are relatively unique to the social and human sciences, we feel justified in considering the other methodological orientations—interpretivism and critical theory—under names that differentiate them from related conventionalist or realist approaches to natural science. As we will see in both interpretive and critical approaches, a set of objections to positivism are raised that, while related to those arising within the philosophy of natural science, also present some new twists.

Notes

1. Alvin W. Gouldner, *The Dialectic of Ideology and Technology* (New York: Seabury, 1976), p. 17.
2. Richard J. Bernstein, *The Restructuring of Social and Political Theory* (Philadelphia: University of Pennsylvania Press, 1978).
3. Russell Keat and John Urry, *Social Theory as Science* (London: Routledge and Kegan Paul, 1975), p. 9.
4. Nelson Goodman, *Fact, Fiction, and Forecast* (Indianapolis: Hackett, 1965).
5. Keat and Urry, *Social Theory*.
6. One other view of causations, for instance, sees it in terms of structural determinants or necessary conditions.
7. Joseph Berger, Bernard Cohen, Laurie Snell, and Morris Zelditch, *Types of Formalization in Small Group Research* (Boston: Houghton Mifflin, 1962).
8. Herbert Simon, *Models of Man* (New York: Wiley, 1957).
9. Frederick Suppe, ed., *The Structure of Scientific Theories* (2nd. ed. Urbana: University of Illinois Press, 1977).
10. Keat and Urry, *Social Theory*.
11. Suppe, *Structure*.

12. Thomas Kuhn, *The Structure of Scientific Revolutions* (Chicago: University of Chicago Press, 1962).
13. Nelson Goodman, *Ways of Word Making* (Indianapolis: Hackett, 1978), p. 18.
14. Keat and Urry, *Social Theory*.
15. See the discussion of Shapere's work in Suppe, *Structure*, pp. 689–96.
16. Shapere, quoted in ibid., p. 692.

CHAPTER 1

Explanation

Michael Martin

The Ambiguity of "Explanation"

The word "explanation" and its cognates are used to refer to various things in science. We will distinguish two stands. First, "explanation" may refer—among other things—to (1) clarification of words or phrases, (2) justification of beliefs or actions, (3) causal accounts of events, states, or processes, (4) theoretical derivations of laws, (5) functional accounts of organs or institutions. Secondly, and cutting across these distinctions, "explanation" may refer to (1') the actions of people who are engaged in explaining something to someone, (2') the discourse of such people, (3') the success of those who are engaged in seeking explanations, (4') the discourse of such people, (5') certain linguistic expressions which stand in certain semantical, epistemological, and logical relations to the events, states, laws, words, etc., being explained.

(1) A scientist may explain some expression, such as "tidal wave," i.e., he may *clarify* what "tidal wave" means in some particular context or how it is normally used in scientific contexts. This may involve giving a definition, but it need not, since giving a definition is not the only way to clarify meaning. . . .* However, it is important to realize that an explanation in this sense does not explain the *phenomenon* of tidal waves but only the phrase "tidal wave." One might understand the phrase yet not understand the phenomenon.

(2) A scientist may explain some belief or action, e.g., his acceptance of a theory rejected by his colleagues or his refusal to engage in a research project that is popular among his fellow scientists. That is, he may *justify* his belief in the theory or his refusal to engage in research.

From *Concepts of Science Education: A Philosophical Analysis* by Michael Martin. Copyright © 1972 by Scott, Foresman and Company. Reprinted by permission.
*Editors' deletion.

Normally justification is not called for unless there is some apparent discrepancy between a belief or action and what is commonly accepted. In justifying his belief or action, the scientist is not giving a causal account, nor is he clarifying the meaning of terms. He is, rather, citing evidence or reasons that purport to make his belief or action reasonable, or at least not unreasonable.

(3) A scientist may explain some event, state, or process, such as the extinction of the dinosaurs; he may give a causal account of dinosaurs becoming extinct. In doing so, he would be neither explaining the meaning of the word "dinosaurs" nor justifying his belief that dinosaurs became extinct, but rather citing factors he takes to be causally responsible for the extinction of dinosaurs, such as changes in temperature or vegetation.

(4) A scientist may explain why some law holds. Here causal factors would not be cited, for presumably laws are not caused. Rather, some theory would be cited to explain the law. Thus Kepler's laws are explained by Newton's theory, from which close approximations to the laws can be deduced.

(5) A scientist may explain the operation of something, e.g., the heart or a social institution in society, by explaining its function. (Whether in fact the operation of a thing is explained by its function is a question we will consider later.)

In each of the five types of explanation discussed above there is still an ambiguity.[1]

(1') By "explanation" we could mean the *activity* of someone explaining something to someone. Thus:

(a) Smith explained "tidal wave" to Jones. (Clarifying the meaning of a term for someone.)
(b) Marion explained his refusal to engage in the research project to Jones. (Justifying an action to someone.)
(c) Smith explained the extinction of the dinosaurs to Jones. (Giving a causal account of an event to someone.)

(2') "Explanation" can also refer to the *discourse* used in the activity of explaining something to someone. For example:

(a) "You see, Smith, 'tidal wave' in its ordinary use is roughly equivalent to . . ."
(b) "Jones, to be frank with you, I refuse to engage in the project for basically the following reasons . . ."

(c) "The causal factors responsible for the extinction of the large reptiles of antiquity—commonly known as dinosaurs—are . . ."

(3') "Explanation" can also refer to the success of certain research, deliberation, or study:

(a) Smith explained "tidal wave," i.e., he successfully clarified the phrase.
(b) Marion explained his refusal to work on the project, i.e., he successfully justified his action.
(c) Smith explained the decline of the dinosaurs, i.e., he produced a correct causal account.

It is obvious, of course, that the activity of explaining something to someone is quite different from the success of research and deliberation. The activity of explaining something to someone is analogous to certain activities of a teacher, and indeed, explaining something to someone may be most common in a pedagogical setting. The success of research and deliberation may well be useful to a person engaged in explaining something to someone, but it should not be confused with that activity.

(4') "Explanation" can also refer to the *discourse* used to state the results of research and deliberation. For example:

(a) "The meaning of 'tidal wave' among the world's leading geographers is . . ." (Entry in Smith's notebook.)
(b) "The project is a methodological disaster. I conclude that there are at least five assumptions that are . . ." (Entry in Marion's diary.)
(c) "Our data suggest that the decline of the large herbivorous dinosaurs, for example, the brontosaurus and brachiosaurus, were the result of . . ." (Sentence in research report.)

It should be noted that the discourse used to state the conclusions of research, e.g., what a scientist puts in his research report, may be quite different from the discourse used in explaining something to someone. Pragmatic factors enter into both cases in important ways that could well make the discourse diverge: for example, the discourse of the scientist explaining the decline of the dinosaurs to college freshmen may be different from the discourse he used in his research report. The former discourse may be free from technical terms and full of colorful metaphors and elaborations while the latter discourse may be technical, concise and abbreviated.

(5′) "Explanation" may also refer to linguistic expressions which stand in certain logical, semantic, and epistemological relations with the word, action, event, state, or law being explained.

Consider, for example, explanation as justification. Someone might argue that formally an action, A, is justified if and only if a sentence saying that A is permissible stands in relation R, a deductive relation, with a set of principles of action and factual premises, P, which meet certain epistemological standards, e.g., are themselves justified. For example, Marion's explanation (justification) for refusing to engage in a certain research project could be construed formally as follows. Let P be the following set of principles and premises:

(1) If a project, X, is based upon mistaken assumptions and these assumptions will probably adversely affect the results of the project, and if Y is expected but not required to engage in X and there are no overriding considerations; then it is permissible for Y to refrain from engaging in X.

(2) The project is based upon mistaken methodological assumptions.

(3) These assumptions will probably affect the outcome adversely.

(4) Marion is expected but not required to engage in the project.

(5) There are no overriding considerations.

Let S be:

(6) It is permissible for Marion to refrain from engaging in the project.

Now (6) is entailed by (1) through (5). Let us suppose that (1) through (5) are themselves justified. Then, given our assumptions about justification, the above argument provides a formal justification for Marion's refusal to engage in the project.

Whether this is an accurate account of a formal notion of the justification of an action we need not decide here. What is important for our purpose is to realize what this account does. It formalizes and makes explicit the notion of justification independently of the sort of pragmatic considerations that might enter into the activity of explaining (in the sense of justifying) something to someone. This does not mean that in actual practice justification conforms exactly to these criteria; pragmatic considerations may make exact fulfillment of them out of the question.

For example, Marion may find it much too tedious and time-consuming to state all the premises in P in his actual justifying activity. Some of these premises may indeed be tacitly assumed in the actual context of justification. Moreover, if Marion is justifying his action to his five-year-old-daughter, he may have to simplify the account somewhat, choosing words and concepts which she can understand, but which do not do full justice to his actual rationale. In short, Marion may have to sacrifice complete accuracy for other, practical considerations.

These modifications in actual practice do not mean that the formal notion of justification is without use. It may be used as a standard for evaluating the *formal and epistemological aspects* of the actual activity and discourse of explanation as justification. Pragmatic considerations would also have to be used in a complete evaluation of this activity and discourse.

A similar formal notion of explanation is needed for the other types of explanation we have been discussing. A formal notion of causal explanation, for instance, would specify the logical and epistemological relations between linguistic expressions, e.g., sentences, and the events, states, or processes being explained. Such a formal notion would be helpful in at least three respects. First, it would enable one to evaluate the discourse used in a causal explanation of something to someone else, such as Jones' discourse in explaining the decline of the dinosaurs to Smith, on purely logical and epistemological grounds independent of pragmatic considerations. Of course, pragmatic criteria would also be needed for a complete evaluation of Jones' discourse. It may be faultless logically and epistemologically, and yet be too technical for the age and background of Smith.

Secondly, the formal notion of causal explanation would set the logical and epistemological standards for the results of research. Put a different way, pragmatic considerations aside, the explanatory researcher should aim at producing a set of linguistic expressions meeting certain logical and epistemological criteria. Thirdly, the formal notion of explanation would provide logical and epistemological standards for evaluating the discourse of the researcher. It would answer the question: Pragmatic considerations aside, does the discourse of the researcher when he states his results provide a causal explanation, i.e., does it consist of sentences meeting certain logical and epistemological requirements?

So far we have distinguished various types of explanations. Some of these are more relevant than others for our purposes. In particular, the formal notion of causal explanation is quite relevant for recent discussions in the philosophy of science. In a moment we shall consider an attempt to formulate a formal notion of causal explanation. Secondly, in science teaching the notion of explaining something to someone is of crucial importance, and later in the chapter the role of explaining something to someone in science education will be considered. Thirdly, explaining the operation of an organ in an organism in terms of the organ's function in the organism—so called functional explanation—is important in biological science and this sort of explanation will be considered toward the end of the chapter.

The Deductive-Nomological Model of Explanation

One attempt to formulate a formal notion of causal explanation is the so-called *deductive-nomological* (D-N) model of explanation. This model has played an extremely important role in recent philosophical discussions of explanation in science. It has been expounded by many well-known philosophers of science, such as Popper,[2] Hempel,[3] and Nagel,[4] and discussion of this model by way of either criticism[5] or defense[6] has dominated recent philosophical literature on the topic of explanation in science.

Stated informally, the model is this: A causal explanation of some event is achieved when that event is subsumed under some causal law. Thus someone might ask why a particular substance conducts electricity. The answer might be that the substance in question is copper and that all copper conducts electricity. This subsumption constitutes the explanation of the phenomenon in question. Again, someone might ask why a rod lengthened. The answer might be that the rod is made of copper and that the rod was heated and copper expands when it is heated. Again the phenomenon to be explained is being brought under a causal law.

Put in the form of an argument, the two explanations would look like this:

(1) All copper conducts electricity.
This substance is copper.
∴ This substance conducts electricity.

(2) All copper expands when heated.
This rod is made of copper.
∴ This rod expands.

It should be noted that both of these explanatory arguments have the same general characteristics. At least one of the premises is a causal law; all the others are statements describing particular conditions that hold in a given situation. The conclusion which describes the event to be explained follows deductively from the premises.

Thus the general form of explanation, according to the D-N model, is this: Given a certain set of causal laws and statements of what have been called initial conditions, a statement describing the event to be explained follows. Put in a diagrammatic way, a D-N explanation would look like this:

$$\text{deduction} \begin{array}{ll} L_1 \,\&\, L_2 \ldots L_n & \text{causal laws} \\ C_1 \,\&\, C_2 \ldots C_n & \text{statement of initial conditions} \\ \hline E \end{array}$$

The laws and the sentences stating the initial conditions have to meet certain logical and epistemological requirements:

R_1 All the laws and initial conditions have to be essential for the deduction.

R_2 All the sentences have to be testable.

R_3 E must logically follow from the statement of initial conditions and laws.

There has been some disagreement over a fourth requirement. Some philosophers have argued:

R_4 All the sentences in the explanation must be true.

Others have argued:

R'_4 All the sentences in the explanation must be well confirmed relative to available evidence.

It should be clear that R_4 and R'_4 All the sentences in the explanation must be well confirmed relative to available evidence.

It should be clear that R_4 and R'_4 are logically independent requirements—neither requirement entails the other. Some sentences might be true without the available evidence confirming them. On the other hand, some sentences might be well confirmed by the available evidence and yet be false. In the first case, a scientist would have no justification for supposing he had a true explanation; in the second case the scientist would be justified in supposing that the explanation was true although the explanation was not true. In any case, it appears that there is no real disagreement here since two different formal notions of causal explanation are at issue. R_1, R_2, R_3, R_4 specify the requirements for a *true causal explanation; R_1, R_2, R_3, R'_4* specify the requirements for a *justified causal explanation*.

Let us consider one of the examples already given in the light of these requirements, namely, the explanation of why the rod lengthened as expressed in argument (2) above. The first requirement, R_1, is certainly fulfilled. The law and statements of initial conditions are essential for the deduction; none of these statements can be omitted if the conclusion is to follow. The second requirement, R_2, holds also since these sentences are testable. R_3 holds, for the conclusion "This rod expands" logically follows from the premises. Furthermore, R'_4 holds, for in the light of the available evidence the law and initial conditions are well confirmed. So argument (2) is a justified causal explanation of why the rod expanded. Moreover, according to confirmation theorists, R'_4 gives us good reason to suppose that R_4 holds. Hence, in their view we have good reason to suppose that this is a true causal explanation.

Again it should be stressed that pragmatic considerations may make it unnecessary or undesirable for the actual discourse of one who explains something causally to someone to conform exactly to the D-N model. For example, Jones may explain the lengthening of the rod to Smith by saying, "You see, the rod was heated." This may be all that is necessary or desirable to say to Smith. Nevertheless, Jones' discourse would be explanatory from a logical and epistemological point of view only because other things were tacitly assumed, namely, that the rod was made out of copper, that the law holds, and that the description of the event explained can be deduced from the law and the statement of initial conditions. The D-N model thus clarifies the tacit assumptions that must be made in an explanatory activity if its discourse is to be logically and epistemologically adequate.

The above point has often been misunderstood in criticism of the D-N model. Some philosophers of science have seemed to assume that, because the actual explanatory discourse of scientists does not conform to the requirement of the model, the model is incorrect. But the D-N model does not purport to reflect the actual explanatory discourse of the scientist, any more than the forms of arguments in logic books purport to reflect actual discourse. The D-N model purports to specify epistemological and logical requirements for explanatory discourse abstracted from practical considerations, just as the forms of arguments in logic books purport to formulate criteria for valid arguments abstracted from practical considerations.

To be sure, the requirements specified by the model might be wrong, and arguments might be offered which show that one or more of these requirements should be changed. However, merely showing that scientists do not put their explanatory discourse into D-N form, or that doing so would be inconvenient for scientists, is as irrelevant to showing that the D-N model is incorrect as showing that people do not put their arguments into syllogisms, and that it would be inconvenient for them to do so, is irrelevant to showing that the requirements in a logic textbook are incorrect.

In any case, one of the major advantages claimed by advocates of the D-N model is its ability to indicate the logical and epistemological problems in explanations. Consider, for example, the following piece of explanatory discourse:

> The causal factor responsible for the extinction of the large reptiles of antiquity—commonly known as dinosaurs—was the change in vegetation brought about by a change in climate. The plant-eating dinosaurs could not eat the tougher vegetation and died out. The flesh-eating dinosaurs who preyed on the plant-eating ones perished in turn.

What assumptions are being made by the speaker and what factual support is there for them? Perhaps these assumptions can be spelled out and their backing elaborated. If so, we might have a full-fledged D-N explanation. However, if they cannot be, this discourse will simply be an outline or a sketch of a causal explanation—what has been sometimes called an *explanation sketch*.[7] That the discourse as it stands needs to be filled in in accordance with the D-N model is made clear by the following:

> Putting the explanatory discourse into D-N form exposes the logical gaps and makes explicit what assumptions are being made and what others may have to be made. One can begin to see possible weak spots in the explanatory argument. For example, is C_3 true? If so, why weren't the plants too tough for other plant eaters to eat? It is clear that not all the plant-eating animals died out during this period. Is C_4' true? (This condition surely must be assumed, for unless it is there would seem to be

Sketch of D-N Explanation I

Laws assumed.   ?

Statement of initial conditions apparently assumed

C_1 Some dinosaurs are plant eaters.

C_2 During a certain period of time, t_1–t_2, plants in the dinosaurs' environment become tougher.

Other statements of initial conditions.   ?

∴ Plant-eating dinosaurs died off during period t_1–t_2.

Sketch of D-N Explanation II

Laws assumed.   ?

Statement of initial conditions apparently assumed.

C_1' Some dinosaurs were flesh eaters.

C_2' The flesh-eating dinosaurs preyed on the plant-eating dinosaurs.

C_3' Plant-eating dinosaurs died off during period t_1–t_2.

C_4'. Flesh-eating dinosaurs could find no other animals to prey on that would sustain them.

Other statements of initial conditions.   ?

∴ Flesh-eating dinosaurs died off during period t_1–t_2.

no reason why the flesh-eating dinosaurs could not have survived on nondinosaurs.) What is the supporting evidence? If there is none, this is a weak spot in the sketch. What laws are assumed by the explanation? What is the supporting evidence for these alleged laws?

Bringing questions like these to the fore has at least two values. First, it provides the scientific investigator with some guidelines for research in filling in the details of the sketch and producing a more complete explanatory argument. Secondly, it provides the science teacher or student of science with insight and understanding into the gaps in our scientific knowledge. We shall return to this point later when we consider explanation in the context of science education.

The Statistical-Probabilistic (S-P) Model of Explanation

So far we have assumed that the explanatory discourse should be evaluated in terms of the D-N model. Such a model assumes that general laws are necessary for a full-fledged explanation. Thus we have assumed that the laws presupposed in the explanation would have the form "All A and B." For example, perhaps a rough statement of a law presupposed in I above is:

L_1 All plant-eating land animals die when they no longer are able to eat the plants within a radius of two thousand miles from where they live.

However, this is not the only possible reconstruction of explanatory discourse. Perhaps instead of general laws being assumed, statistical laws are assumed. Such a reconstruction has certain advantages. Perhaps L_1 as it stands is false. Perhaps some land animals might be capable of traveling long distances to new environments where they can eat the vegetation. A more plausible assumption might be:

L_2 Most plant-eating land animals die when they no longer are able to eat the plants within a radius of two thousand miles from where they live.

Now such a statistical law could not explain—even when combined with appropriate initial conditions—why all dinosaurs died out; at most it would explain why most of them did. However, this incompleteness may suggest that more laws—either general or statistical—are needed for a complete explanation.

In any case, the consideration of statistical laws suggests a different formal model of explanation. Let us call this model the *statistical-probabilistic* (S-P) model.[8] This model is like the D-N model except for two things: (1) The laws in the premises of an explanatory argument are statistical laws rather than general laws. An example of such a law would be L_2 above. Such laws might be stated in a precise quantitative form, e.g., 90 percent of A's are B, or in a less precise way, e.g., Most A's are B, or Nearly all A's are B, or The proportion of A's that are B is close to 1, or

Any *A* has a good chance of being *B*. (2) The relation between the premises and the sentences describing the event, state, or process to be explained is probabilistic rather than deductive. Consider, for example, the following S-P explanation. We will assume that the premises of the argument are true.

Nearly all people having streptococcal infections who are treated with penicillin recover.
Jones had a streptococcal infection and was treated with penicillin.

∴ Jones recovered.

Now the conclusion cannot be logically deduced from the premises as in a D-N explanation. For the premises are true and yet the conclusion could be false. However, in a valid deductive argument if the premises are true, the conclusion must be true also. Nevertheless, the conclusion is probable relative to these premises. From this example we can abstract the general form of S-P explanations and diagram this form as follows:

probable inference
$$L_1 \,\&\, L_2 \ldots L_n$$ statistical laws
$$C_1 \,\&\, C_2 \ldots C_n$$ statements of initial conditions
$$E$$ statement describing event to be explained

Another example of an explanation with this form can be found in evolutionary theory.[9]

Suppose one is puzzled by the following phenomena: light-colored moths have not survived in a particular environment. Suppose that one learns that the environment is sooty and that moth-eating birds inhabit this environment. Now suppose the following sentences describe the event to be explained:

E_1 = Dark-colored moths have survived.
E_2 = Light-colored moths have not survived.

Now consider the following statistical laws derived from evolutionary theory:

L_3 In any environment, if any organisms possess advantageous characteristics lacked by other organisms of the environment, those organisms will have a good chance of surviving.

L_4 In any environment, if any organisms lack advantageous characteristics possessed by other organisms of the environment, those organisms will have very little chance of surviving.

Such laws combined with certain statements of initial conditions make E_1 and E_2 very probable relative to these laws and initial conditions. What sorts of initial conditions would these be? It seems clear that one would have to specify some property possessed by dark-colored moths that gives them an advantage. This presumably would be their dark color, which makes it more difficult for birds to find and eat them in this environment. Thus:

C_1 Dark-colored moths, because of their color, possess an advantageous characteristic in this environment which light-colored moths lack.

C_2 Light-colored moths, because of their color, lack an advantageous characteristic possessed by the dark-colored moths.

L_3 and L_4 plus C_1 and C_2 make E_1 and E_2 probable. Thus L_3 and L_4 and C_1 and C_2 provide a statistical-probabilistic explanation of the biological phenomena in question.

It should be noted that the phenomena described by E_1 and E_2 could have been predicted had we known the initial conditions prior to their occurrence. Thus it is not true, as has sometimes been alleged, that evolutionary theory allows for explanation but not for prediction. Predictions are possible if the initial conditions are known. Of course, it is often difficult to know the initial conditions, but this is a reflection on us rather than on evolutionary theory. (We will discuss the relation between prediction and explanation later in the chapter.)

It may be objected that the above explanation does not meet R_2, that L_3 and L_4 are in fact tautologies and thus cannot be tested. Thus it may be said that any organism which possesses advantageous characteristics would by definition have a good chance of surviving, since "advantageous" in this context only means that it aids survival. Hence L_3 and L_4 are true by definition.

However, this argument is mistaken. To say that an organism, Q_1, possesses advantageous characteristic *C* lacked by another organism, O_2. in environment *E* is to say:

(1) In *E* there is some condition *N* which must be satisfied by O_1 and O_2 or else O_1 and O_2 will die off and not reproduce themselves.
(2) *C* satisfies *N* or causes *N* to be satisfied.
(3) Either O_2 possesses no means of satisfying *A* or O_2 possesses less effective means of satisfying *N* in *E* than O_1.

N might be avoiding enemies, or seeing food, or getting water; and *C* might be running fast, or not being visible. Let us understand the phrases "have a good chance of surviving" and "have very little chance of surviving" to refer to a long-range frequency of survivals. Thus to say that O_1 has a better chance of survival than O_2 is just to say that in the long run the frequency of O_1's surviving is greater than the frequency of O_2's surviving.

Construed in this way—and this seems to be the way biologists actually construe L_3 and L_4—L_3 and L_4 are not tautologies. There would be nothing self-contradictory about an organism that had an advantageous characteristic yet did not survive, or about an organism that lacked such a characteristic yet did survive. Thus we see that L_1 and L_2 are not true by definition.

It is possible in branches of science in which statistical laws are used that these statistical laws will someday be replaced by general laws. Thus the statistical laws of evolutionary theory may someday be replaced by general laws. Such a replacement might involve, for example, discovering some additional property of organisms or of their environments which, when combined with the organisms' advantageous characteristics, would provide a nomologically sufficient condition for survival. The general form of a replacement would be this:

(1) Original statistical law:
   For every *x*, if *x* has *A*, then with frequency *F* *x* has *B*.
(2) Replaced by general law:
   For every *x*, if *x* has *A* and *P*, then *x* has *B*.

The replacement would turn on finding a suitable property *P*. Thus the use of statistical laws in science is logically compatible with the existence and eventual discovery of such a property *P*, and with the existence and eventual discovery of general laws. Whether such general laws do exist and whether, if they do, they will ever be discovered is another question.

Notes

1. This strand of the ambiguity is carefully analyzed by Jane R. Martin, *Explaining, Understanding, and Teaching* (New York: McGraw-Hill Book Co., 1970), ch. 2.
2. Kark Popper, *The Logic of Scientific Discovery* (London: Hutchinson, 1959).
3. Carl G. Hempel, *Aspects of Scientific Explanation* (New York: Free Press, 1965).
4. Ernest Nagel, *The Structure of Science* (New York: Harcourt Brace Javanovich, 1961).
5. For a typical criticism see Michael Scriven, "Explanations, Predictions and Laws," in *Minnesota Studies in the Philosophy of Science*, vol. 3, ed. H. Feigl and G. Maxwell (Minneapolis: University of Minnesota Press, 1962), pp. 170–230.
6. For a defense see May Brodbeck, "Explanation, Prediction, and 'Imperfect' Knowledge," in *Minnesota Studies in the Philosophy of Science,* vol. 3, ed. Feigl and Maxwell, pp. 231–272.
7. Hempel, *Aspects of Scientific Explanation*, pp. 423–25.
8. Ibid., pp. 381-403.
9. I am indebted here to the discussion of Hugh Lehman, "On the Form of Explanation in Evolutionary Theory," *Theoria* 32 (1966): 14–24.

CHAPTER 2

A Science of Behavior

B. F. Skinner

The immediate tangible results of science make it easier to appraise than philosophy, poetry, art, or theology. As George Sarton has pointed out, science is unique in showing a cumulative progress. Newton explained his tremendous achievements by saying that he stood on the shoulders of giants. All scientists, whether giants or not, enable those who follow them to begin a little further along. This is not necessarily true elsewhere. Our contemporary writers, artists, and philosophers are not appreciably more effective than those of the golden age of Greece, yet the average high-school student understands much more of nature than the greatest of Greek scientists. A comparison of the effectiveness of Greek and modern science is scarcely worth making.

It is clear, than, that science "has something." It is a unique intellectual process which yields remarkable results. The danger is that its astonishing accomplishments may conceal its true nature. This is especially important when we extend the methods of science to a new field. The basic characteristics of science are not restricted to any particular subject matter. When we study physics, chemistry, or biology, we study organized accumulations of information. These are not science itself but the products of science. We may not be able to use much of this material when we enter new territory. Nor should we allow ourselves to become enamored of instruments of research. We tend to think of the scientist in his observatory or laboratory, with his telescopes, microscopes, and cyclotrons. Instruments give us a dramatic picture of science in action. But although science could not have gone very far without the devices which improve our contact with the surrounding world, and although any advanced science would be helpless without them, they are not science itself. We should not be disturbed if familiar instruments are lacking in a new field. Nor is science to be identified with precise measurement or mathematical calculation. It is better to be exact than inexact, and much of modern science would be impossible without quantitative observations and without the mathematical tools needed to convert its reports into more general statements; but we may measure or be mathematical without being scientific at all, just as we may be scientific in an elementary way without these aids.

Some Important Characteristics of Science

Science is first of all a set of attitudes. It is a disposition to deal with the facts rather than with what someone has said about them. Rejection of authority was the theme of the revival of learning, when men dedicated themselves to the study of "nature, not books." Science rejects even its own authorities when they interfere with the observation of nature.

Science is a willingness to accept facts even when they are opposed to wishes. Thoughtful men have perhaps always known that we are likely to see things as we want to see them instead of as they are, but thanks to Sigmund Freud we are today much more clearly aware of "wishful thinking." The opposite of wishful thinking is intellectual honesty—an extremely important possession of the successful scientist. Scientists are by nature no more honest than other men but, as Bridgeman has pointed out [P. W. Bridgeman, *The Nature of Physical Theory* (Princeton, N.J.: Princeton University Press, 1936)], the practice of science puts an exceptionally high premium on honesty. It is characteristic of science that any lack of honesty quickly brings disaster. Consider, for example, a scientist who conducts research to test a theory for which he is already well known. The result may confirm his theory, contradict it, or leave it in doubt. In spite of any inclination to the contrary, he must report a contradiction just as readily as a confirmation. If he does not, someone else will—in a matter of weeks or months or at most a few years—and this will be more damaging to his prestige than if he himself had reported it. Where right and wrong are not so easily or so quickly established, there is no similar pressure. In the long run, the issue is not so much one of personal prestige as of effective procedure. Scientists have simply found that being honest—with oneself as much as with others—is essential to progress. Experiments do not always come out as one expects, but the facts must stand and the expectations fall. The subject matter, not the scientist, knows best. The same practical consequences have created the scientific atmosphere in which statements are constantly submitted to check, where nothing is put above a precise description of the facts, and where facts are accepted no matter how distasteful their momentary consequences.

Scientists have also discovered the value of remaining without an answer until a satisfactory one can be found. This is a difficult lesson. It takes considerable training to avoid premature conclusions, to refrain from making statements on insufficient evidence, and to avoid explanations which are pure invention. Yet the history of science has demonstrated again and again the advantage of these practices.

Science is, of course, more than a set of attitudes. It is a search for order, for uniformities, for lawful relations among the events in nature. It begins, as we all begin, by observing single episodes, but it quickly passes on to the general rule, to scientific law. Something very much like the order expressed in a scientific law appears in our behavior at an early age. We learn the rough geometry of the space in which we move. We learn the "laws of motion" as we move about, or push and pull objects, or throw and catch them. If we could not find some uniformity in the world, our conduct would remain haphazard and ineffective. Science sharpens and supplements this experience by demonstrating more and more relations among events and by demonstrating them more and more precisely. As Ernst Mach showed in tracing the history of the science of mechanics, the earliest laws of science were probably the rules used by craftsmen and artisans in training apprentices. The rules saved time because the experienced craftsman could teach an apprentice a variety of details in a single formula. By learning a rule the apprentice could deal with particular cases as they arose.

In a later stage science advances from the collection of rules or laws to larger systematic arrangements. Not only does it make statements about the world, it makes the statements about statements. It sets up a "model" of its subject matter, which helps to generate new rules very much as the rules themselves generate new practices in dealing with single cases. A science may not reach this stage for some time.

The scientific "system" like the law, is designed to enable us to handle a subject matter more efficiently. What we call the scientific conception of a thing is not passive knowledge. Science is not concerned with contemplation. When we have discovered the laws which govern a part of the world about us, and when we have organized these laws into a system, we are then ready to deal effectively with that part of the world. By predicting the occurrence of an event we are able to prepare for it. By arranging conditions in ways specified by the laws of a system, we not only predict, we control: we "cause" an event to occur or to assume certain characteristics.

Behavior as a Scientific Subject Matter

Behavior is not one of those subject matters which becomes accessible only with the invention of an instrument such as the telescope or microscope. We all know thousands of facts about behavior. Actually there is no subject matter with which we could be better acquainted, for we are always in the presence of at least one behaving organism. But this familiarity is something of a disadvantage, for it means that we have probably jumped to conclusions which will not be supported by the cautious methods of science. Even though we have observed behavior for many years, we are not necessarily able, without help, to express useful uniformities or lawful relations. We may show considerable skill in making plausible guesses about what our friends and acquaintances will do under various circumstances or what we ourselves will do. We may make plausible generalizations about the conduct of people in general. But very few of these will survive careful analysis. A great deal of unlearning generally take place in our early contact with a science of behavior.

Behavior is a difficult subject matter, not because it is inaccessible, but because it is extremely complex. Since it is a process, rather than a thing, it cannot easily be held still for observation. It is changing, fluid, and evanescent, and for this reason it makes great technical demands upon the ingenuity and energy of the scientist. But there is nothing essentially insoluble about the problems which arise from this fact.

Several kinds of statements about behavior are commonly made. When we tell an ancedote or pass along a bit of gossip, we report a *single event*—what someone did upon such and such an occasion: "She slammed the door and walked off without a word." Our report is a small bit of history. History itself is often nothing more than similar reporting on a broad scale. The biographer often confines himself to a series of episodes in the life of his subject. The case history, which occupies an important place in several fields of psychology, is a kind of biography which is also concerned mainly with what a particular person did at particular times and places: "When she was eleven, Mary went to live with her maiden aunt in Winchester." Novels and short stories may be thought of as veiled biography or history, since the ingredients of even a highly fanciful work of fiction are somehow or other taken from life. The narrative reporting of the behavior of people at particular times and places is also part of the sciences of archeology, ethnology, sociology, and anthropology.

These accounts have their uses. They broaden the experience of those who have not had firsthand access to similar data. But they are only the beginnings of a science. No matter how accurate or quantitative it may be, the report of the single case is only a preliminary step. The next step is the discovery of some sort of *uniformity*. When we tell an ancedote to support an argument, or report a case history to exemplify a principle, we imply a general rule, no matter how vaguely it may be expressed. The historian is seldom content with mere narration. He reports his facts to support a theory—of cycles, trends, or patterns of history. In doing so he passes from the single instance to the rule. When a biographer traces the influence of an early event upon a man's later life, he transcends simple reporting and asserts, no matter how hesitantly, that one thing has caused another. Fable and allegory are more than storytelling if they imply some kind of uniformity in human behavior, as they generally do. Our preference for "consistency of character" and our rejection of implausible coincidences in literature show that we expect lawfulness. The "manners" and "customs" of the sociologist and anthropologist report the *general* behavior of groups of people.

A vague sense of order emerges from any sustained observation of human behavior. Any plausible guess about what a friend will do or say in a given circumstance is a prediction based upon some such uniformity. If a reasonable order was not discoverable, we could scarcely be effective in dealing with human affairs. The methods of science are designed to clarify these uniformities and make them explicit. The techniques of field study of the anthropologist and social psychologist, the procedures of the psychological clinic, and the controlled experimental methods of the laboratory are all directed toward this end, as are also the mathematical and logical tools of science.

Many people interested in human behavior do not feel the need for the standards of proof characteristic of an exact science; the uniformities in behavior are "obvious" without them. At the same time, they are reluctant to accept the conclusions toward which such proof inescapably points if they do not "sense" the uniformity themselves. But these idiosyncrasies are a costly luxury. We need not defend the methods of science in their application to behavior. The experimental and mathematical techniques used in discovering and expressing uniformities are the common property of science in general. Almost every discipline has contributed to this pool of resources, and all disciplines borrow from it. The advantages are well established.

Some Objections to a Science of Behavior

The report of a single event raises no theoretical problems and comes into no conflict with philosophies of human behavior. The scientific laws or systems which express uniformities are likely to conflict with theory because they claim the same territory. When a science of behavior reaches the point of dealing with lawful relationships, it meets the resistance of those who give their allegiance to prescientific or extrascientific conceptions. The resistance does not always take the form of an overt rejection of science. It may be transmuted into claims of limitations, often expressed in highly scientific terms.

It has sometimes been pointed out, for example, that physical science has been unable to maintain its philosophy of determinism, particularly at the subatomic level. The Principle of Indeterminacy states that there are circumstances under which the physicist cannot put himeslf in possession of all relevant information: if he chooses to observe one event, he must relinquish the possibility of observing another. In our present state of knowledge, certain events therefore appear to be unpredictable. It does not follow that these events are free or capricious. Since human behavior is enormously complex and the human organism is of limited dimensions, many acts may involve processes to which the Principle of Indeterminacy applies. It does not follow that human behavior is free, but only that it may be beyond the range of a predictive or controlling science. Most students of behavior, however, would be willing to settle for the degree of prediction and control achieved by the physical sciences in spite of this limitation. A final answer to the problem of lawfulness to be sought, not in the limits of any hypothetical mechanism within the organism, but in our ability to demonstrate lawfulness in the behavior of the organism as a whole.

A similar objection has a logical flavor. It is contended that reason cannot comprehend itself or—in somewhat more substantial terms—that the behavior required in understanding one's own behavior must be something beyond the behavior which is understood. It is true that knowledge is limited by the limitations of the knowing organism. The number of things in the world which might be known certainly exceeds the number of possible different states in all possible knowers. But the laws and systems of science are designed to make a knowledge of particular events unimportant. It is by no means necessary that one man should understand all the facts in a given field, but only that he should understand all the *kinds* of facts. We have no reason to suppose that the human intellect is incapable of formulating or comprehending the basic principles of human behavior—certainly not until we have a clearer notion of what these principles are.

The assumption that behavior is a lawful scientific datum sometimes meets with another objection. Science is concerned with the general, but the behavior of the individual is necessarily unique. The "case history" has a richness and flavor which are in decided contrast with general principles. It is easy to convince oneself that there are two distinct worlds and that one is beyond the reach of science. This distinction is not peculiar to the study of behavior. It can always be made in the early stages of any science, when it is not clear what we may deduce from a general principle with respect to a particular case. What the science of physics has to say about the world is dull and colorless to the beginning student when compared with his daily experience, but he later dicovers that it is actually a more incisive account of even the single instance. When we wish to deal effectively with the single instance, we turn to science for help. The argument will lose cogency as a science of behavior progresses and as the implications of its general laws become clear. A comparable argument against the possibility of a science of medicine has already lost its significance. In *War and Peace*, Tolstoy wrote of the illness of a favorite character as follows:

> Doctors came to see Natasha, both separately and in consultation. They said a great deal in French, in German, and in Latin. They criticised one another, and prescribed the most diverse remedies for all the diseases they were familiar with. But it never occurred to one of them to make the simple reflection that they could not understand the disease from which Natasha was suffering, as no single disease can be fully understood in a living person: for every living person has his individual peculiarities and always has his own peculiar, new, complex compliants unknown to medicine—not a disease of the lungs, of the kidneys, of the skin, of the heart, and so on, as described in medical books, but a disease that consists of one out of the innumerable combinations of ailments of those organs.

Tolstoy was justified in calling every sickness a unique event. Every action of the individual is unique, as well as every event in physics and chemistry. But his objection to a science of medicine in terms of uniqueness was unwarranted. The argument was plausible enough at the time; no one could then contradict him by supplying the necessary general principles. But a great deal has happened in medical science since then, and today few people would care to argue that a disease cannot be described in general terms or that a single case cannot be discussed by referring to factors common to many cases. The intuitive wisdom of the old-style diagnostician has been largely replaced by the analytical procedures of the clinic, just as a scientific analysis of behavior will eventually replace the personal interpretation of unique instances.

A similar argument is leveled at the use of statistics in a science of behavior. A prediction of what the *average* individual will do is often of little or no value in dealing with a particular individual. The actuarial tables of life-insurance companies are of no value to a physician in predicting the death or survival of a particular patient. This issue is still alive in the physical sciences, where it is associated with the concepts of causality and probability. It is seldom that the science of physics deals with the behavior of individual molecules, atoms, or subatomic particles. When it is occasionally called upon to do so, all the problems of the particular event arise. In general a science is helpful in dealing with the individual only insofar as its laws refer to individuals. A science of behavior which concerns only the behavior of groups is not likely to be of help in our understanding of the particular case. But a science may also deal with the behavior of the individual, and its success in doing so must be evaluated in terms of its achievements rather than any a priori contentions.

The extraordinary complexity of behavior is sometimes held to be an added source of difficulty. Even though behavior may be lawful, it may be too complex to be dealt with in terms of law. Sir Oliver Lodge once asserted that "though an astronomer can calculate the orbit of a planet or comet or even a meteor, although a physicist can deal with the structure of atoms, and a chemist with their possible combinations, neither a biologist nor any scientific man can calculate the orbit of a common fly." This is a statement about the limitations of scientists or about their aspirations, not about the suitability of a subject matter. Even so, it is wrong. It may be said with some assurance that if no one has calculated the orbit of a fly, it is only because no one has been sufficiently interested in doing so. The tropistic movements of many insects are now fairly well understood, but the instrumentation needed to record the flight of a fly and to give an account of all the conditions affecting it would cost more than the importance of the subject justifies. There is, therefore, no reason to conclude, as the author does, that "an incalculable element of self-determination thus makes its appearance quite low down the animal scale." Self-determination does not follow from complexity. Difficulty in calculating the orbit of the fly does not prove capriciousness, though it may make it impossible to prove anything else. The problems imposed by the complexity of a subject matter must be dealt with as they arise.

Apparently hopeless cases often become manageable in time. It is only recently that any sort of lawful account of the weather has been possible. We often succeed in reducing complexity to a reasonable degree by simplifying conditions in the laboratory; but where this is impossible, a statistical analysis may be used to achieve an inferior, but in many ways acceptable, prediction. Certainly no one is prepared to say now what a science of behavior can or cannot accomplish eventually. Advance estimates of the limits of science have generally proved inaccurate. The issue is in the long run pragmatic: we cannot tell until we have tried.

Still another objection to the use of scientific method in the study of human behavior is that behavior is an anomalous subject matter because a prediction made about it may alter it. If we tell a friend that he is going to buy a particular kind of car, he may react to our prediction by buying a different kind. The same effect has been used to explain the failures of public opinion polls. In the presidential election of 1948 it was confidently predicted that a majority of the voters would vote for a candidate who, as it turned out, lost the election. It has been asserted that the electorate reacted to the prediction in a contrary way and that the published prediction therefore had an effect upon the predicted event. But it is by no means necessary that a prediction of behavior be permitted to affect the behaving individual. There may have been practical reasons why the results of the poll in question could not be withheld until after the election, but this would not be the case in a purely scientific endeavor.

There are other ways in which observer and observed interact. Study distorts the thing studied. But there is no special problem here peculiar to human behavior. It is now accepted as a general principle in scientific method that it is necessary to interfere in some degree with any phenomenon in the act of observing it. A scientist may have an effect upon behavior in the act of observing or analyzing it, and he must certainly take this effect into account. But behavior may also be observed with a minimum of interaction between subject and scientist, and this is the case with which one naturally tries to begin.

A final objection deals with the practical application of a scientific analysis. Even if we assume that behavior is lawful and that the methods of science will reveal the rules which govern it, we may be unable to make any technological use of these rules unless certain conditions can be brought under control. In the laboratory many conditions are simplified and irrelevant conditions often eliminated. But of what value are laboratory studies if we must predict and control behavior where a comparable simplification is impossible? It is true that we can gain control over behavior only insofar as we can control the factors responsible for it.

What a scientific study does is to enable us to make optimal use of the control we possess. The laboratory simplification reveals the relevance of factors which we might otherwise overlook.

We cannot avoid the problems raised by a science of behavior by simply denying that the necessary conditons can be controlled. In actual fact there is a considerable degree of control over many relevant conditions. In penal institutions and military organizations the control is extensive. We control the environment of the human organism in the nursery and in institutions which care for those to whom the conditions of the nursery remain necessary in later life. Fairly extensive control of conditions relevant to human behavior is maintained in industry in the form of wages and conditions of work, in schools in the form of grades and conditions of work, in commerce by anyone in possession of goods or money, by governmental agencies through the police and military, in the psychological clinic through the consent of the controllee, and so on. A degree of effective control, not so easily identified, rests in the hands of entertainers, writers, advertisers, and propagandists. These controls, which are often all too evident in their practical application, are more than sufficient to permit us to extend the results of a laboratory science to the interpretation of human behavior in daily affairs—for either theoretical or practical purposes. Since a science of behavior will continue to increase the effective use of this control, it is now more important than ever to understand the processes involved and to prepare ourselves for the problems which will certainly arise.

CHAPTER 3

The Relevance of Psychology to the Explanation of Social Phenomena

George C. Homans

Social phenomena will be taken here to mean all phenomena in which the action of at least one man affects directly or indirectly the action of another. Accordingly social phenomena provide by far the largest part of the subject-matter of psychology, history, political science, economics, anthropology, sociology, and probably linguistics.

In discussing the relevance of psychology to the explanation of social phenomena I must first say what I mean by explanation. It is, I think, the view of explanation taken by such philosophers as Braithwaite and Hempel, though I must state it here more briefly, and therefore more crudely, than they do.[1] It has been called, for short, the "covering law" view of explanation.

First, an explanation consists of a set of propositions, each proposition stating a relationship between properties of nature. To play its part in explanation, it is not enough for a proposition to say that there is *some* relationship between the properties. It must begin to state the nature of the relationship. It is, for instance, not enough to say, in the fashion of many propositions of social science, that a man's status *is related* to his power. One must go at least as far as saying that a man's status *increases* as his power increases, or that the two are *positively associated*. On the other hand, statements about probabilities may be legitimate propositions, and so may statements including theoretical terms, implicitly defined, such as the term *value* in the proposition: the greater the value of a

Reprinted from *Explanation in the Behavioral Sciences*, edited by Robert Borger and Frank Cioffi, by permission of Cambridge University Press. Copyright © 1970 by Cambridge University Press.

reward, the more likely a man is to perform an action that secures the reward. I shall say no more about the vexed problem of theoretical terms, but refer the reader to the discussion in Braithwaite.[2]

Second, the set of propositions forms a deductive system, such that the proposition to be explained, the *explicandum*, follows as a conclusion in logic from the others in the set. When the *explicandum* is shown so to follow from the others, it is said to be derived or deduced from them, and so to be explained by them. The reason why a proposition must state the nature of a relationship between properties of nature is that little in logic can be deduced from one that does not. But remember that in the social sciences a kind of sketchy logic is as much as we can ask and more than we usually get.

Third, the propositions from the the *explicandum* follows fall into two main classes: general propositions (sometimes called laws) and propositions introducing the given conditions within which the general propositions are to be applied. The former are general in that, unlike the *explicandum*, they cannot be deduced from others in the set, and often also in that they appear in many other explanations besides the one in question. It is the required presence of general propositions that leads the present view of explanation to be called the "covering law" view.

The given conditions may in turn be explainable, may in turn become the *explicanda* of new deductive systems, or, for lack of factual knowledge, they may not. And so may the general propositions, or, for lack of theoretical knowledge, they may not. That is, the still more general propositions from which they could in turn be deduced have yet to be discovered. This condition is unlikely to last for ever, but it may last for a long time, for example, the two hundred years between Newton and Einstein.

Finally, the propositions must be *contingent* in the sense that data, evidence, fact are relevant to their acceptance as true or false. This condition must be introduced because there are plenty of deductive systems which general propositions are non-contingent, accepted *a priori*. These are the deductive systems of pure mathematics. Scientific explanations may of course employ mathematics in making their deductions but they must not consist entirely on non-contingent propositions.

An explanation of a relationship is a theory of the relationship. But scholars often use the word *theory* in a broader sense than this—to refer to a cluster of explanations of related phenomena, when the explanations employ some of the same general propositions. Indeed when we speak of the power of a theory, we refer to the fact that a wide variety of *explicanda* (sometimes called empirical propositions) can be derived from a

54

single set of general propositions (the theory) under different given conditions.

There are those who argue that explanation in the social sciences must be essentially different from what it is in the physical sciences. I cannot agree with them. Explanations of social phenomena can certainly be put forward that have all the characteristics of explanation as described above. The process of explanation is the same for all the sciences, though the content of the propositions will naturally differ from science to science. Indeed the efforts to construct a sociological theory by simply translating, for instance, Newton's law into "social" terms in the forms of "social physics" have not been notably successful.

Let me now turn to the types of explanation that social scientists have put forward in the endeavour to account for social phenomena. They are well illustrated by the efforts made to explain social institutions. An institution is a rule or set of rules, which some members of a society say should be followed in particular circumstances, and which some actually do follow. Thus trial by jury is an institution of Anglo-Saxon societies and so, in some primitive societies, is a rule that a man ought to marry a woman belonging to some defined category of women. The explanations in question are explanations in the general sense that they are efforts to answer the question why institution X is one of the institutions of society A, and that they have obviously given some scholars some degree of intellectual satisfaction. Whether they are also explanations in the more specific senses I began by listing is a question I shall consider later. Four generic types can, I think be distinguished, through many actual explanations mix the genera.[3]

(1) Structural or "pattern" explanations. In these the social scientist points out that the institution in question, for example, a particular rule of marriage, occurs in association with other institutions of particular sorts, for instance, matrilineal descent, avunculocal residence, and the vesting of jural authority over a man in his mother's brothers. (To give the meaning of these technical terms is not necessary to my argument.) The social scientist feels that he has explained the institution by showing that it occurs as part of a structure, a pattern, of other institutions; and he may get great intellectual satisfaction out of doing so, especially if the pattern occurs in more than one society.

(2) Functional explanations. In these the social scientist argues that no society can survive unless it meets certain conditions, and that institutions of a particular sort enable a society to meet at least one of these conditions. Then if a particular society is surviving, it must possess an

institution of this sort, and if it does in fact possess one, the existence of the institution is explained. Sometimes the term "equilibrium" replaces the term "survival" in the argument. None of the types of explanation are confined to the social sciences, and this of course is the type of argument sometimes used in physiology to account, for instance, for the existence of a beating heart in a living human body. And just as the functional explanation of the beating heart presupposes a certain structure of the body: blood, organs to be nourished by blood, arteries for the blood to flow through, etc., so in social science functional explanations are often, though sketchily, associated with structural explanations.

(3) Historical explanations. In these the social scientist explains the existence in a particular society of the institution in question by tracing the historical process by which the institution, or its progenitor, came into being, developed, and was progressively modified up to the time when its presence among the institutions of the society is to be accounted for. Historical explanation obviously depends on the existence of historical records, and so is more apt to be used to explain the institutions of literate societies than those of non-literate ones, to explain trial by jury rather than cross-cousin marriage. Of course, if one goes back far enough, the historical records of even the literate societies run out, and the adequacy of the records for explanatory purposes runs out even sooner.

(4) Psychological explanations. In these the social scientist explains the institution by showing how its presence in a particular society follows from propositions about the behaviour of men, as men, under specified given conditions. A crude example might be an explanation of the punishment of criminals that pointed out how criminals, persons who violate the more strongly held rules of a society, present a threat to other members of the society, how men feel anger when threatened, and how they are likely, when angry, to take aggressive action against the source of the threat, provided they perceive they can do so with impunity. Punishment is aggressive action of this sort.

I call this type of explanation psychological because it employs propositions that are presumed to hold good of, to be general with respect to, the behavior of all men as individual human beings, as distinguished from what I shall call sociological propositions, propositions that are presumed to hold good of societies, groups, or other social aggregates rather than of the individuals who make them up. Functional explanations use sociological general propositions. The relevance of psychology to the explanation of social phenomena is a question of the use of psychological propositions in their explanation.

56

Now let me apply to each of these types the standards for explanation that I began by setting up. The structural type can usually be cast in a form that looks superfically like a deductive system. Thus institution X is positively associated with institution Y; institution Y with institution Z, and therefore institution X with institution Z. But it is possible to run the deductive system in the other direction and explain an original "premiss" using the original conclusion as a new "premiss." That is, the system contains no proposition more general than the other two. All the explanation does is assert that the institutions in question are positively associated. As such, it may represent a very considerable intellectual achievement, but it is not by the standards used here an explanation at all. It does nothing to answer the question why the institutions are related in the way they are. Though I have used an institutional example, structural explanation in the social sciences is by no means limited to explanations of the association of institutions.

The functional type of explanation cannot be ruled out for the same reason as the structural, for it characteristically contains a general proposition: If A is a surviving society (or a society in equilibrium), it will possess institutions (or other characteristics) of class Y. This purports to be a general proposition, general with respect to societies. That is, it is a sociological general proposition. The difficulties with functional explanation are of another kind. First, it is surprisingly difficult to specify what is meant by the survival of a society. It is even more difficult to define the term equilibrium. This does not mean that something we can recognize as social equilibrium never exists. Rather, no statement of the conditions of social equilibrium has yet been devised that is specific enough to allow difinite conclusions in logic to be drawn from it. Perhaps such a proposition will be invented in the future, and philosophy can certainly give no reason why it should not be invented, but it certainly has not been invented so far.

Second, survival is at least a clearer criterion that equilibrium, and the functional propositions purport to state the conditions for survival. It is possible to draw true conclusions from them: if A is a surviving society, it ought to possess institutions of class Y, and it often does. But it is also possible to draw false conclusions. For the propositions imply that if B is a non-surviving society, it ought not to have possessed characteristics of class Y. There are only a few societies that have clearly not survived, and fewer still whose social characteristics were recorded before their demise. But in all cases for which we have some evidence, the non-surviving societies possessed characteristics of class Y and indeed all the other suggested social requisites for survival, both jointly and severally. The biological requisites, such as resistance to alcohol, measles, or gunfire, are another matter. Functional explanation fails as explanation because its general propositions are not contingent: the social scientists who put them forward do not treat them as if data, fact, evidence were relevant to their acceptance or rejection.

The difficulty with historical explanations is different still. They appear to include, again and again, statements of the following sort. Smith (or the Smiths, persons sharing similar values) wanted a particular result and thought that a particular action was likely to get the result; therefore Smith took the action. Smith might well have been mistaken and might fail to get the result, if only because Jones (or the Joneses) wanted a contrary result and was able to thwart him. Or Robinson wanted still another, if not contrary result, and succeeded in modifying the effects of Smith's action. The final result might well be different from what anyone intended or expected. Intended or not, historical explanation took the form of showing that the final result, the *explicandum*, proceeded from combined actions, over time, of the Smiths, Joneses, Robinsons, etc.

Since propositions about particular persons like the Smiths are obviously not very general, it often appears that historical explanations do not meet the standards of explanation because they lack general propositions. But that is because they are characteristically *enthymemic*. That is, the historians leave their general propositions, the major premisses of their deductive systems, unstated. But what is missing can readily be supplied if necessary, and it is necessary if we are to understand what historical explanation involves. For the moment I shall consider only one, though the most prominent, of these propositions. It takes this form: not only Smith, but every man, in choosing between alternative actions, is likely to take that one for which, as perceived by him at the time, the value (v) of the result, multiplied by the probability (p) of getting the result, is the greater; and the larger the excess of $p \times v$ for the one action over the alternative, the more likely he is to take the former action. This has been called the *rationality proposition* or theory, even though actions taken under it may not seem rational in other senses, since a man's perceptions may be mistaken and the results may be "bad" for him. But, given his perceptions and evaluations, behavior taken in accordance with this proposition is held to be rational. Historical explanation often takes the form of applying this general proposition to the given conditions represented by the particular values, perceptions, and circumstances of the Smiths, Joneses, and Robinsons, and trying to show what the combined and cumulative effects will be of actions, each of which was taken in accordance with this general, though usually unstated, proposition.

One of the reasons why historical explanations leave their general propositions unstated is the following. The separate deductive systems by which the actions of particular persons or groups at particular times are explained are often uninteresting. Only when they are linked together in what have been called genetic chains do they begin to get interesting.[4] They become linked when the *explicandum* of one deductive system becomes one of the given conditions of another in the series, as when the action of Smith becomes a given condition for explaining the subsequent action of Jones and so forth. The separate deductive systems would be apt to contain some of the same general propositions, so that if the genetic chains were spelled out in full, the propositions would be repeated again and again. But that would be boring. Historians subconsciously realize this, and leave the general propositions implied but unstated.

Note now that the rationality proposition is what I have called a psychological general proposition: it is held to be general with respect to the behavior of men, rather than with respect to societies or social groups as such. Thus the historical type of explanation turns out upon examination to be the same type of explanation as the fourth type, the psychological. The differences between the two are differences of degree, not of kind. If strong and similar forces are at work in many societies and tend to produce similar results, if the societies, that is, are in some respect convergent, then the explanation of the results can afford to neglect the details of the historical chain of events producing the result in a particular society. This might be the case in explaining why in every society criminals are punished. But if these conditions do not obtain, the explanation cannot afford to neglect the details, the particular genetic chain. This would certainly be the case in explaining why trial by jury is an institution of the Anglo-Saxon societies. But in either case the explanations employ psychological general propositions.

Depending upon what is to be explained, they may of course contain general propositions of other sorts. For instance, some historical explanations, if spelled out in full, would have to contain the proposition: a man whose head is severed from his body is dead—which is surely a general proposition of human physiology. The explanations may include such propositions: they always include psychological ones.

Let me sum up the argument so far. Of the types of explanation used in the more "social" of the social sciences, those like anthropology and sociology that are specially interested in institutions, the structural type is not an explanation, and the functional type is non-contingent. There remain the historical and the psychological types. But the historical type turns out to be in fact psychological. By elimination, then, it looks so far as if the only type of explanation that stood a chance in social science were the psychological.

Though I have used it as an illustration, the rationality proposition is certainly not adequate for all psychological explanation. It can stand alone as a general proposition only if men's values and their perceptions can be taken as given, as known or obvious. It is true that they can often, for practical purposes, be so taken. One does not need to explain why a hungry man sets a high value on food or why most of us set some store by money. Nor does one always need to explain why a man perceives a certain action as likely to be successful. If a man is a trained carpenter, it requires physics, so to speak, and not psychology to explain why he takes certain actions in building a house and not others. More generally, what will be successful, or at least the probability of success (the risk), is given by the objective nature of things—and the man in question accurately knows the nature of things. But one does feel the need to explain— whether one can in fact do so or not—why a man finds self-punishment rewarding, or why a man who can have no objective knowledge what his chances of success may be—his situation is one of uncertainty and not of risk—nevertheless goes ahead and takes action. When values and perceptions cannot be taken for granted but themselves cry out for explanation, then the rationality proposition turns out not to be the only general proposition we need for our deductive system. We also need, as we shall see, propositions about the effects of past history, past experience, on present behavior. The rationality proposition deals only with the present.

In some ways economics has surely been the most successful of the social sciences. It has developed propositions of its own, which have shown considerable explanatory and predictive power. I speak especially of classical or microeconomics. One reason for the success of economics is that it deals with rather easily measured variables: the quantities of largely material goods and their prices. Another reason has been of a quite different sort. Economic explanation belongs to the psychological type, in the sense that economic propositions, such as the so-called laws of supply and demand, can readily be shown to follow from the rationality proposition.[5] Moreover, the latter is the only psychological assumption economics had felt the need to make, precisely because the values of men and their perceptions could largely be taken for granted in explaining the sorts of phenomena economics was interested in. The more obvious of the values of men are the material values, since they are shared by many people; and economics was specially concerned with the exchange of material goods for money. It was also interested in the gross effects, such as inflation, produced through the pursuit by many people of these widely shared values—effects to which the behaviors of individuals pursuing more idiosyncratic goals were irrelevant, or in which they tended to cancel themselves out. Classical economics also studied situations in which the success of action was not problematic: in the market it was assumed that a buyer could always find a willing seller, and the only question was whether the buyer was willing to pay the price. Above all, economics could afford to disregard the permanent or semi-permanent relationships between persons and groups that make up so much of the subject-matter of social sciences such as sociology and anthropology. Indeed, under the conditions assumed to exist in the classic market, no one buyer would have any reaon to trade regularly with one seller rather than another. And finally, economics could explain much behavior provided that certain institutions—the market itself, for instance—were taken as given. Though it was often difficult to explain their details, the institutions were at least the product of the other things economics took for granted: the relatively permanent relationships between people in groups. To put the matter another way: economic explanation was relatively unhistorical, for to explain relatively permanent relationships one needs to know how past behavior affects present behavior. For classical economics, a man's present behavior, his values given, was, or should be determined by his present options.

The rationality principle, as I have pointed out, is a psychological proposition in the sense that it refers to the behavior of men and not to the characteristics of social groups or aggregates as such. It is certainly not a psychological proposition in another possible sense: it is not the professional property of persons who call themselves psychologists. The wider set of general propositions, which needs to be added to the rationality proposition for the explanation of human behavior, is psychological not only in the first sense but also in the second: the propositions are usually stated and tested by professional psychologists. They are sometimes referred to as learning theory, but since they also apply to human behavior after it has in every usual sense of the word been learned, I prefer to speak of them as the propositions of behavioral psychology.

Obviously I do not have the space here to write a treatise on behavioral psychology. Not all psychologists would agree on which propositions should be included as the really fundamental ones, and even fewer on the terminology in which they should be stated, though I think in substance they would say much the same things. All I want to do is suggest their general nature.[5] One of the most important propositions would run as follows: if a man takes an action that is followed by a reward, the probability that he will repeat the action increases. This I call the success proposition: it has also been called the law of effect. It seems obvious enough. Why is it important, and what does it add to the rationality proposition? Let me take an example from history. Suppose we ask why William the Conqueror invaded England. We have independent evidence that he perceived that the conquest would be very rewarding to him, compared with his alternative of remaining as Duke of Normandy—provided the conquest were successful. That is, the value term in the rationality proposition is accounted for: the value of the result was high. But how about the success term? To a contemporary observer his chances of success may well have appeared low. In any event he had no way of assigning a definite probability to his chances: his situation was not one of risk but of uncertainty. Why then did he go ahead with the enterprise? The rationality proposition provides no answer. But at this point it is surely relevant to point out that William had a long record of success in his military enterprises in the past, and accordingly, by the success proposition of behavioral psychology, the probability that he would undertake military action again was apt to be high. In ordinary language, his past experience had given him confidence. To sum up: the rationality proposition would explain his behavior, provided his perception of success were given. Behavioral psychology explains his perception by relating it to his past experience. Or rather, the perception term, the intermediate term, drops out, and the present behavior is related directly to past experience. It is in this sense that behavioral psychology is an historical theory.

Another important proposition of behavioral psychology is the following: if in the past the occurrence of a particular stimulus-situation has been the occasion on which a person's action was rewarded, the recurrence of the stimuli in the present makes it more probable that the man will repeat the action. The stimulus-situation is, roughly speaking, the set of circumstances sourrounding the action. The stimuli may have this effect even if there was no rational connection between the presence of the stimuli and the success of the action in the past. Once again, present behavior is related to past experience.

The rational theory must take the values of men—what sorts of thing they find rewarding—as simply given. When, as a matter of common knowledge, we can assume the values to be shared by many men, the rational proposition does very well in explanation. When they are somehow queer values the rational theory is simply at a loss. But behavioral psychology, provided it has enough knowledge of a person's past experience, can sometimes account for the way values are acquired. New values, even queer ones, are acquired by being paired with older and more primordial values, just as money becomes, as we say, valuable in itself, when it is discovered to be a means of getting candy.

A behavioral psychology would also include a proposition about the effect of deprivation on increasing, and of satiation on decreasing, the value of a reward. It should include a proposition about the effect of punishment on behavior, pointing out that, just as reward includes both positive rewards and the removal of punishments, so punishments include both positive punishments and the removal of rewards. A behavioral psychology would include, finally, propositions about emotional behavior, such as the frustration-aggression proposition: when a man fails to receive an expected reward, or receives an unexpected punishment, the probability of his taking some form of aggressive action increases. But I have said enough to indicate that I mean by behavioral psychology.

Behavioral psychology leads on the one side towards the explanation of the phenomena of personality—that precariously integrated group of interrelated reponses that makes a man an individual. That is to say, modern students of personality, from Freud onwards, assume that the adult personality is a product of a long process of conditioning beginning with earliest childhood. Theorists disagree over the terms in which the gross features of this development and its results should be described: such terms, for instance, as id, ego, and superego. But there is nothing in modern personality theory incompatible with the view that the detailed steps in the conditioning process are those described by the propositions of behavioral psychology. Indeed a good case sould be made that Freud was the first great behavioral psychologist. Since this paper deals with the explanation of social phenomena, I shall have nothing further to say about individual personality—which does not mean in the least that the development of personality is not ? social process.

Behavioral psychology leads on the other side towards the explanation of the phenomena dealt with by social psychology, especially the phenomena created by the interaction of persons in small groups, phenomena such as co-operation, competition, conformity, deviance, status, power, leadership, and distributive justice.[7] These phenomena also occur, of course, in large organizations and societies, and there is no reason to believe that they are different there—no reason, indeed, to believe that any sharp line can be drawn between a micro- and a macrosociology. But the phenomena have been most intensively studied in small groups. It is this use of behavioral psychology in explanation that has attracted most criticism, and here I must move especially carefully.

The propositions of behavioral psychology are believed to hold good of all men, and they are stated in terms of the behavior of a single man: "If a man takes an action that is followed by a reward . . . etc." The propositions are particularly concerned with the effects of reward on behavior. There is nothing whatever in the propositions to suggest that the effect of reward is different when it comes from another man rather than from, for instance, the physical environment. But when two or more men are interacting, when the actions of each reward (or punish) the actions of the other, phenomena of course appear that are different from those that appear when an isolated person is being rewarded by the physical environment. New phenomena appear, which may be called social, but no new general propositions are required to explain them—only the new given condition that two or more men are interacting.

There is absolutely no general philosophical argument that will prove, or disprove, the contention that the propositions of behavioral psychology are adequate general propositions for the expansion of social behavior. All one can do is take particular phenomena and set up the deductive systems that will explain them. In this sense, behavioral psychology can in fact be used to explain a large number of the grosser social phenomena. But since the actual iteration of the explanations is the only possible argument, the argument can never be exhaustive and conclusive. It is obviously impossible to go through the work here, or for any large number of cases anywhere, and in any event behavioral psychology will never be able to explain everything. Even if one has confidence in one's general propositions, one may still not be able to use them in explanation, because one lacks information about the given conditions in which they are to be applied. For instance, much of the information needed for historical explanation has simply disappeared for ever.

But if the proponents of the position taken here can do no more in its support than provide examples of psychological explanation, they can at least require its opponents to do as much on their side. Again and again since the turn of the century scholars have been asserting that social phenomena can never be explained by the use of psychological propositions. The social whole, they say, is more than the sum of its parts; something new emerges over and above the behavior of individuals;

when many individuals act, they may produce results unintended by any one of them. All the actual facts that "wholeness," "emergence," and "unintended consequences" are supposed to refer to are conceded in advance. The question is how these facts are to be explained. The usual examples of such phenomena are readily explainable by the use of psychological propositions. More important, the persons who cite such phenomena in their favor never produce their own explanations of the phenomena. Let them begain to spell out their explanations. Then we should begin to see whether they in fact possess an alternative type of explanation, and especially whether they use an alternative type of general proposition, presumably what I have called sociological propositions. Until they are ready to explain emergent phenomena themselves, they had better stop throwing them up at us.

The issue considered here has been discussed by philosophers as methodological individualism versus methodological socialism (which has of course nothing to do with political socialism.[8] Methodological individualism holds that all social phenomena can be analyzed without residue into the actions of individuals, that such actions are what is really fundamental in the social sciences. If they are fundamental, then the general explanatory propositions of the social sciences are propositions about the actions of men: in my terms, they are psychological propositions. That is, methodological individualism entails psychologism. (But Sir Karl Popper says he believes in methodological individualism but not psychologism)[9] Finally, methodological individualism holds that sociological propositions, propositions about the characteristics of social groups or aggregates, can in principle be derived from, reduced to, propositions about the behavior of individuals. Methodological socialism on the other hand, would presumably hold that social phenomena could not be wholly resolved into individual actions, and that there are general sociological propositions not reducible to psychological propositions— sociological propositions, indeed, from which propositions about individual behavior could themselves be derived.

Again, there is no general philosophical argument that will resolve the issue. One can only appeal to current evidence. There are certainly sociological propositions of some generality, but many of them can be derived from psychological ones. On the other hand, there are, I believe, no general sociological propositions at present that meet the two following conditions: they cannot be derived from psychological ones, and from them many features of social behavior can themselves be derived. In this sense, it is my conviction that there is no current evidence in favour of methodological socialism. But a sociological proposition with the right properties may be discovered tomorrow, and if it is, mere argument will be at an end in face of the fact.

The only very general sociological propositions that have been put forward are those of the functional type. Usually the functionalists do not even begin to spell out their arguments, and so it is impossible to discover whether the arguments explain anything. But on at least one occasion functionalist have sketched out their line of reasoning. It may be instructive to look at a famous functionalist explanation of what is itself a general sociological proposition. It is the explanation offered by Professors Davis and Moore for the fact that all societies are stratified, that in all societies there are differences in status.[10]

Briefly, the explanation goes like this. In order to survive or remain in equilibrium, a society must motivate its members to carry out the activities necessary to its survival. The more important the activities— that is, the more crucial to its survival—the greater the society's need to motivate members to carry them out. But the supply of persons able and willing to carry them out is short. To ensure an adequate supply, the society must make the rewards for filling the more important positions greater than those for filling the less important ones. A stratification system does just this. Accordingly a society that survives or remains in equilibrium will have a stratification system. Q.E.D.

I shall not repeat here the general criticism of functional explanations that I offered earlier, but get down to the specifics of this one. It is not a purely sociological explanation, as it refers from the beginning to the motivation of members, that is, of individuals. Indeed it makes implicit use of a psychological proposition: that individuals will not act without rewards. Beyond that, the explanation raises more questions that it answers. How can one tell which activities are more crucial to the survival of a society than others? It is difficult to show that the peasants were less crucial to the survival of medieval societies than the knights, and yet individually they received lower rewards. Why should the supply of persons able and willing to provide the more crucial activities be short? And why should "society" have to give them greater rewards to do their jobs?

The functional argument puts matters the wrong way around. If in fact, and for whatever reasons, certain members of a society command capacities to reward others, capacities such as the putative control of magical power or the actual control of land, special skill, or physical force—physical force is a capacity to reward because the power to kill is also the power to spare—and if these rewards are valuable both in themselves and because they are in short supply relative to demand, then these members will be able to get from the other members, and not from "society" as such, disproportionately high rewards for themselves. The reason they will be able to do so lies ultimately in the psychological proposition: the higher the value of a reward, the more likely a person is to take action to get the reward. It follows from this proposition, that when two men (or groups) are exchanging rewards, the person for whom the reward the other is able to provide is the more valuable will do more to get it. He has, in fact, less power than the other.[11] And as, in this way, persons and groups tend to get rewards in proportion to their power, they create and maintain a stratification system.[12] Under this analysis the references in the functional argument to society, its survival, and the contributions different activities make to its survival simply disappear, and the explanation uses only psychological general propositions. I believe that this sort of fate awaits all sociological efforts at explanation. But no abstract argument will demonstrate that this is the case. Nothing but the analysis of examples will do, and they can be endless in number.

Perhaps I may end by suggesting some of the reasons why some scholars have found the psychological explanation of social phenomena difficult to accept. The first reason is powerful intuitively. Can those great institutional and organizational structures that, especially in the modern world, seem so strong as to dominate mere men and to lead a life of their own—can these great structures really be the product of what seems to be as weak as water: individual human choice? But if we remember that the choices of some men narrow the alternatives of others, and that the choices of men can jointly produce results none of the men, severally, would have envisaged, then it is clear that the structures are so produced and maintained.

The second reason lies in the sociology of knowledge. The scholars who have been most reluctant to accept the psychological explanation of social phenomena have been anthropologists and sociologists. Anthropology and sociology were the most "social" of the social sciences, peculiarly concerned with the larger institutional structures of society. They were also the latest of the social sciences to be recognized as academic disciplines. Insecure in their status, it was natural for them to insist that they had a unique type of contribution to make, and in view of their subject-matter, to insist that their uniqueness lay in a purely social explanation of social phenomena. Though sociology is now well established academically, some sociologists still fear that their subject will somehow lose its identity if it abandons its special claims.

The last reason is a queer one, but I sometimes think it is the most powerful of all. The propositions of behavioral psychology have been known for a very long time. Though the ordinary citizen may not phrase them as a psychologist would, and though he is often surprised by some of their further implications, in psychopathology for instance, still they do not in themselves strike him as unfamiliar. Indeed he, especially if he is a scholar, is apt to call them obvious or even trivial. And these facts get in the way of their acceptance as the most general propositions of social science. Our view of the nature of science is based on the history of physical science. A science is an enterprise in which the scientists make discoveries, and the later they make a discovery the more fundamental it is apt to be, like the structure of the atom. Now if the fundamental propositions of social science were never discovered by scientists but were for ages part of common knowledge, then (so this unconscious process of reasoning runs) either social science cannot be a science at all or, what is more important, its fundamental propositions must remain to be discovered and must accordingly be other than the propositions of behavioral psychology. Both horns of the dilemma get in the way of our recognizing the relevance of psychology to the explanation of social phenomena.

Notes

1. R. B. Braithwaite, *Scientific Explanation* (New York: Harper Torchbooks, 1953); C. G. Hempel, *Aspects of Scientific Explanation* (New York: Free Press, 1965), pp. 229–489.
2. Braithwaite, *Scientific Explanation*.
3. See G. C. Homans, "Contemporary Theory in Sociology," in *Handbook of Modern Sociology*, ed. R. E. L. Faris (Chicago, 1964), pp. 951–77.
4. On genetic explanations see Hempel, *Aspects of Scientific Explanation*, pp. 447–53.
5. G. C. Homans, *Social Behavior* (New York, 1961), pp. 68–70.
6. See especially B. F. Skinner, *Science and Human Behavior* (New York, 1953); Homans, *Social Behavior*, pp. 30–82.
7. See especially Homans, *Social Behavior*; A. W. Staats and C. K. Staats, *Complex Human Behavior* (New York, 1963).
8. See especially A. C. Danto, *Anatomical Philosophy of History* (Cambridge, Eng., 1965), pp. 257–84.
9. Karl R. Popper, *The Open Society and Its Enemies*, vol. 2 (New York, 1963), pp. 89–99.

10. K. Davis and W. E. Moore, "Some Principles of Stratification," *American Sociological Review* 10 (1945): 242–49.
11. See G. C. Homans, "A Theory of Social Interaction," *Transactions of the Fifth World Congress of Sociology* 4 (1964): 113–31.
12. G. Lenski, *Power and Privilege* (New York, 1966).

CHAPTER 4

Historical and Generalizing Approaches to Sociology

Joseph Berger, Morris Zelditch,
and Bo Anderson

Some sociologists want to know why Watts had a riot. Some want to understand the general process by which order and disorder are created: the nature of the process; its conditions, its consequences. Sometimes it is the same individual who asks both kinds of questions. Nevertheless, their character is different: The first is essentially *historical*: not so much in the sense that it deals with something in the past, but rather in the sense that it is particular in time and place; for what matters is a particular effect to be explained. The second is *generalizing*: What matters is the formulation of abstract and general laws to be used in an indefinitely large number of such explanations. The difference between the two questions is not a matter of their formal structure. From a formal point of view their logic is the same, for in both cases one or more statements of fact are inferred from other statements of fact by means of general laws. The difference is rather one of purpose. But differences in purpose are important, and in this case give rise to fundamental differences in strategy: In what is seen to be an important problem, in what facts are seen to be relevant to that problem, in what sorts of criteria are used to define a problem as solved. The difference between a historical and a generalizing strategy is greater, in our opinion, than the difference between quantitative and qualitative research, or micro- and macro-sociology, or formal and informal theory. . . .*

Reprinted with the permission of the authors from *Sociological Theories in Progress*, Volume 2, edited by Joseph Berger, Morris Zelditch, Jr., and Bo Anderson (Boston: Houghton Mifflin Co., 1972).
*Editors' deletion.

70

Character of Historical and Generalizing Strategies

An explanation is a deductive argument in which some effect is inferred from one or more initial conditions and one or more general laws.[1] The structure of such an argument is illustrated in the following example: In a 1925 paper on social distance, Bogardus reported that social distance was particularly emphasized in cities.[2] The increased emphasis on social distance in cities, he argued, was caused by the short physical distances in cities, which make geographical mobility easy; the absence of any laws or customs that prevented individuals of different social status from living in the same neighborhood; and the assumption in large urban areas that common residence implies common status. Given these conditions, he reasoned, it was often the case that individuals of different status lived in the same neighborhood; the effect of this was to increase the status of status inferiors but decrease the status of status superiors; decreasing status causes status anxiety; but increased emphasis on social distance reduces status anxiety. In this argument the emphasis on social distance in cities is the *effect* to be explained; geographical and social mobility and the fact that common urban residence implies common social status are *initial conditions*; that decreasing status causes anxiety and increased emphasis on social distance reduces it are *general laws*. We accept such an explanation if we agree that the initial conditions are true of cities; if we accept the general laws used in it; and can show that the effect is validly deduced from its premises.

We have already said that historical and generalizing strategies do not differ in formal structure. The logical structure just described is common to both. What makes them different is the way in which this logic of explanation is used in research. In a historical strategy of research the primary focus of interest is on the particular effect to be explained. Given that this is so, the investigator's problem is solved when he has identified the causes, the initial conditions, that produced the effect. That France had a revolution in May 1968 was due (let us suppose) to overcrowding of the Sorbonne, the high rate at which students failed their exams, the high degree of centralization of the educational bureaucracy, the slow rate at which urban wages increased during a period of great economic growth, and the rapid change in the French occupational structure. The list could be made longer; but the point is that explaining the particular event focuses primary attention on its identifiable initial conditions.

Not that general laws play no part in this search. But their role is secondary, not primary; of instrumental, rather than intrinsic, significance. Logically they are required in order to deduce the effect from the causes; and they may play an important role in justifying why one rather than another list of causes is accepted. One might claim that rapid change of the French occupational structure was indeed one of the causes of the May revolution by arguing that universities prepare students for careers; that the French university had become less useful in this respect; and, in general, individuals become alienated from institutions that require performance of tasks not instrumental to their goals. But formulating concepts, laws, or theories is not the purpose of the investigation: The relation between goals, tasks, and commitment is not in itself the point; the investigator is not trying to formulate this process more generally, nor understand its conditions or consequences. He is trying to explain some aspect of the May revolution. His interest in more general processes may be so slight that they are left implicit; implying that the general principles are of the sort everyone knows and no one needs to state. Or if stated, they may be either common sense propositions or empirical generalizations of a very low level of generality.

In historical investigations the explanation of a particular effect is the main purpose and laws are largely instrumental to this purpose. In generalizing investigations laws are the primary focus of interest. In explaining student unrest in the May revolution we may have used the law that individuals become alienated from institutions that require performance of tasks not instrumental to their goals. A generalizing investigation would have as its purpose the abstract, general formulation of this process; would be interested in a study of its nature, its conditions, its consequences; would make its subject commitment, not the May revolution.

Because the focus of interest is the law itself, and not any particular one of its concrete instances, a generalizing investigation has a considerable degree of latitude in choosing the setting for its investigation. For the attitude towards particular causes and effects is purely instrumental, in the same way and to the same degree that in historical investigations it is general laws that are purely instrumental. The purpose of a generalizing investigation is to test, reformulate, refine, or extend an abstract, general theory. A large number of concretely quite different settings serve equally well as instances of the process, for no particular one of them has any special importance for the investigation. Which initial conditions and which effects are chosen for investigation depend on purely pragmatic considerations: Which are most sensitive? Which offer the best prospect of control over the process? Which are least obscured by other processes of no immediate interest to the investigation? Pragmatic considerations of this sort, for example, would be more important than considerations of social significance, historical relevance, or common occurrence.

For most sociologists the distinction just made between historical and generalizing strategies of research will be too sharp. It will fly in the face, too, of a widely accepted solution to the problem of making research theoretically relevant and theory empirically testable: a solution according to which the "gap" between theory and research must be closed by having theory provide researchers with ideas to guide them, while researchers provide theorists with leads that emerge from their explanations of particular events.[3] We will argue that a sharper distinction is nevertheless necessary: a conclusion that follows if it is agreed that one of the goals of sociology is the accumulation of general knowledge of social behavior. For such knowledge accumulates only very slowly, if at all, from a purely historical strategy of research. Nor is it sufficient, in order to increase the rate at which it grows, to make the effects of a historical investigation also "theoretically relevant" if the aims, standards, and methods of such investigations remain in other respects historically oriented; for the aims, standards, and methods of such research can often be at cross-purposes with the objective of accumulating general knowledge. Hence, not closing the gap, but a clearer distinction between historical and generalizing strategies is required.

The Role of Laws in a Historical Strategy

Laws seldom emerge from a purely historical strategy: In the first place, laws are not the intrinsic interest of historical investigations; laws will therefore sometimes be left unstated; if stated, they will sometimes be either common sense propositions or empirical generalizations of a low degree of generality, sufficient to permit deduction of the effect to be explained but not much more; and even if they are general ideas, they will be suggested as leads for further investigation, but it will not be part of the purpose of the investigation to follow them up. In the second place, a particular effect is of intrinsic interest; it would therefore be irrelevant to follow up any theoretical leads it might suggest by choosing, on pragmatic grounds, some other effect, or some other set of initial conditions as the proper setting for an investigation; indeed, it would even be irrelevant to give the effect a highly abstract formulation. In the third place, a satisfactory explanation of a particular effect is defined as one that explains as much as possible of its variance; committing the investigation to criteria of "success" that assure complexity and holism rather than abstract, general formulation. In a sense, the pure historical investigation both demands less and insists on more than the formulation of abstract, general laws of behavior.

First: That laws are not of any intrinsic interest in a purely historical investigation makes it possible for the investigation to be content with a relatively unsystematic collection of relatively unformulated, relatively concrete, and relatively common sense propositions about social behavior. The difficulty is not so much in the fact that the purpose is atheorectical: For we will see that difficulties remain even if a socially important effect is also theoretically relevant. The difficulty is that it is an effect, not a law or set of laws, that is of central concern. For example: Sociologists have for a long time been interested in determinants of educational aspirations and in particular aspirations with respect to college. It is known that four variables determine these aspirations: father's education, father's occupation, parental pressures for college, and family size.[4] Partial correlation methods, furthermore, permit the conclusion that, although these variables are correlated with each other, each has an independent effect on college aspirations.[5] A causal model of this process may be formulated in which parental pressures are the most important determinant of the educational expectations of adolescent males. Parental pressures are determined by the father's education and occupation; the father's occupation is itself determined by the father's education. But the father's occupation and education have direct effects on the son's educational expectations over and above their effect on parental pressures; and family size reduces parental pressures on the son and independently of that, it also decreases the educational expectations of the son.[6] While such a model may require the guidance of a theory, it does not itself formulate any abstract theoretical principles: The statement that parental pressures account for 25 percent of the variance in the son's educational expectations is not a formulation of a principle of socialization. Furthermore, the independent effect of a father's education and occupation on a son's educational expectations is probably due to a process of role-modeling; but the analysis given here does not further our understanding of role-modeling as a general process. The effect of family size is presumably due both to a process of rational decision-making, having to do with allocation of resources, and to the part played by family size in decreasing the effectiveness of parental pressures on the son; but neither process is formulated by this model. The same argument can be multiplied, for several other processes are implied by the model; but the result of the argument is already sufficiently clear. What is important is the effect, educational aspirations. Educational aspirations might be explained by laws of role-modeling, decision-making, and other concepts, but the causal model of these aspirations does not formulate these laws, and could not, as a matter of fact, give a systematic and general analysis of them without being irrelevant to its main purpose. It would not make rational decision-making, role-modeling, or status maintenance processes the focus of the investigation; it would not make "status" or "resources" its principle concepts in place of "occupation" or "family size"; it would not even want to more abstractly formulate its narrowly limited scope: For the Rehberg-Westby model is a model of the aspirations of American male adolescents. It might be generalized, by more abstractly defining the kinds of occupational structures of which it is true. But for purposes of explaining the educational aspirations of American adolescent males there is no great need to do so.

Second: It does not serve the purpose of a historically oriented investigation to take a pragmatic attitude to an effect that is intrinsically important: It does not serve its purpose to (a) formulate that effect in terms of a more abstract, general process, and (b) investigate that process in a situation chosen on purely instrumental grounds. It is doubtful, for example, that educational aspirations are the best situation in which to study rational decision-making, or role-modeling, or status maintenance processes. We might possibly study rational allocation of resources by studying the effect of family size on aspirations; but the process is obviously confounded by another in which either sheer size, or else the addition of older siblings as competing agents of socialization, also determines the effect. Perhaps experimental bargaining games are a better situation in which to study rational decision-making: Such games are simpler; they are more readily controlled, so that confounding factors can be more easily ruled out; their effects are more direct operational definitions of the outcome associated with the process, so that the data are more readily interpreted, at the same time that they are more easily and precisely measured. But from a historically oriented point of view the simplicity of the situation makes it artificial; the manipulation of it, the fact that some of the conditions under which it is made to occur are uncommon, makes it unrealistic; and the effect, however revealing in other respects, is not educational aspirations and is therefore unrelated to the purposes of the original investigation. Not that experimental methods are the issue here: We are not arguing that a generalizing orientation requires experimentation. Comparative sociology has some equally abstract formulations, and its comparisons are sometimes made not for their intrinsic interest, but because they are most informative with respect to a general social process.[7] The argument, rather, is that whatever the choice of method one cannot formulate a process abstractly, and take towards any particular causes and effects of it an instrumental attitude, if the particular effect is itself intrinsically important.

Third: The degree to which a historical investigation is satisfactory is determined in part by the degree to which it takes every relevent factor into account. Hence, such investigations deal with quite complex processes. They are complex in at least two ways: They typically seek to explain quite a large number of different effects, and the effects themselves are often complex. For example, to understand the May revolution in France, it would be necessary to know not only why the students were so ready to riot, but also why their professors encouraged them to do so, why the riot police were so excessively brutal, why the government was at first so unsure of itself, why the workers broke out in wildcat strikes at approximately that time, why the Communist party was at first so reluctant to bring down the government, why in the end the party "joined" the revolution, why the provinces were so frightened by unrest in Paris, why Marseilles was violent but Tours peaceful, why Pompidou, after so fumbing a beginning, ended by being so masterful, and a good deal more.

The difficulty this creates is well known: The more of this one revolution we try to understand, the less general is our knowledge of revolutions. No other revolution is quite like the May revolution and as long as we maintain a holistic interest in it we bar ourselves from any general study of such phenomena as the radicalization of middle-class students, or the wage comparisons of workers in expanding economies, or the instability of many-party states, or the psychology of political understudies, or whatever other processes one supposes to be going on in this particular revolution.

But not all historically oriented investigations are holistic in this sense. Our notion of such an investigation encompasses not only the kind that explains many aspects of one situation, but also the kind that is concerned with one particular effect. It remains true that such an investigation is complex; complex in the sense that it is made up of more than one process. For example, suppose the effect that concerns us is the alienation of French middle-class students. One source of this alienation may be the difference between the goals or the student and the goals for which the university prepares the student, a difference made increasingly wide by changes in the French occupational structure. This is a factor we have already mentioned. But some students come to the university for exactly the sort of preparation it gives, which is, essentially, access to elite status in the society. One may never use the technical training that the École Polytechnique provides, or the training that the École Normale provides, or even the training that the Sorbonne provides, and yet by passing their examinations one is prepared for such later statuses as, say, membership in the Conseille d'État. Historically, the university has controlled access to such elite statuses, and students have gone to the university to acquire them. The university is still an elite gate-keeper, and is therefore very strict about its examinations. As the number of students entering the university keeps increasing, the number who do not pass the exams keeps increasing. This number may be as high as 50 to 70 percent of the total, depending on the faculty of the university in which the student is enrolled. One consequence is that French university education requires, among other things, a radical reconstruction of the self for large numbers of students. Already few students pass the Baccalaureate, which admits one to the university, and therefore admission to the university signifies that one is exceptional. But over half the students admitted must at some point come to terms with the fact that they are not good enough to complete a degree, which is no doubt a rather alienating experience. If this is true, the larger the number of students entering the university, the larger the pool of alienated intellectuals becomes. We do not insist that this explanation is true. But if it is true, the objectives of our investigation would require us to take it into account. For we would want to explain as high as possible a proportion of the variance in the effect.

Explaining more variance will usually mean complicating the process by which an effect is explained.[8] But complicating a process will lower its level of generality. This follows from the fact that invariance is a desirable property of any explanatory law. For complex processes are either nor general or else not invariant. For example, we have just argued that alienation is a complex process in the sense that it is produced by at least two distinct, independent processes. one a utility process, having to do with the instrument value of education for given goals; the other a self process, having to do with the radical reconstruction of the self required by failure.A law of alienation that does not distinguish the two is invariant if and only if they combine in other settings in the same way and to the same degree. Given a complex law of this sort, two strategies are possible; One is to confine its scope to those settings in which the utility and self-processes do combine in the same way. The other is to analyze the process into its distinct parts, studying each component process independently of the other. Either strategy will render a law invariant; but the former will render the law invariant at the expense of generality.[9] Explaining a greater proportion of the variance is a strategy of the first type: not that it is inappropriate to its purpose; it is precisely what is required by the explanation of a particular effect. But its purpose is not generalizing: generalizing requires a quite different strategy; and that alternative strategy, analysis, is discouraged by adding more sources of variation to the explanation of an effect.

It is important to observe that the difficulties of developing general explanatory propositions from historically oriented investigations lie neither in any technical inferiority nor in the fact that there are not yet enough of them. Rehberg and Westby's investigation of educational aspirations is in no sense technically inferior; path analysis, which is likely to become the model for their kind of investigation in the future, is unquestionably a rigorous method—though it aims are basically historical.[10] Furthermore, in the case of educational aspirations it cannot be argued that if only there were more replications we would be in a position to develop general explanatory propositions from them. There were already 200 replications of the sort of research on which Rehberg and Westby's model was based, and still no formulation has emerged of any of the general principles required to explain their results. The research is good research, and there is enough of it. The results have been stable, the findings consistent, but no laws emerge. The difficulty is not in its quality nor in its quanity, but in its objectives, and in the strategy implied by those objectives.

Is Theoretical Relevance Sufficient?

There is an obvious objection to the argument just made: The "pure" historically oriented investigation is pure fiction. There may once have been sociologists concerned only to explain particular effects, but more common today is the kind of strategy recommended by Rose in his presidential address to the American Sociological Association:

> What often starts out as a trivial question in market research or the evaluation of the success or failure of some agency program can become restated as an intriguing question at the heart of sociological theory. The ascertaining of why a given product or program is a "success" while another is a "failure," can lead to discoveries about basic aspects of human motivation and social structure—if such studies are carried on with sociological imagination.

In other words, a particular effect may also be seen as theoretically relevant: And if seen as theoretically relevant, the results of its investigation may suggest important questions for theorists to ask or even answers that have a more general significance.

This way of viewing the relevance of research to theory and of theory to research is in fact so widely accepted that good books on research method typically recognize theory as the mark of science's maturity: make accumulation of knowledge depend on the refinement, articulation, extension, or reformulation of theory rather than a linear increase in the number of sociology's discoveries of fact, and define problems as good to the degree that they are informative for some theory. All this is of course generalizing in orientation. It has as one of its consequences that pure historically oriented research may be inhibited in its development; that some people may come to regard urban poverty research, for example, as poor stuff because it is seen as having little theoretical relevance. But this view not only seeks to mnake empirical research theoretically relevant; it also seeks to make theory construction empirically relevant; Cross-fertilization of theory and research is its primary objective; and it accomplishes this objective by "closing the gap" between the two.

The image of the gap is a common image among sociologists, and it provides sociology with a rather definite idea of who is ranged on either side of the gap, what the gap itself consists, and what should be done to "close" it. On one side, is ranged those who "seek above all to general, to find their way as rapidly as possible to the formulation of sociological laws."[12] On the other is ranged "a hardy band who do not hunt too closely the implications of their research but who remain confident and assured that what they report is so."[13] On this account, our troubles are due to the fact that hasty generalizers are much too indifferent to tests; the hardy empiricists are much too indifferent to explaining what they find. And the solution, obviously, is to bring them closer together; Theory must guide research, research must correct theory.

Gamberg has called this way of regarding the mutual relevance of theory and research the "neo-empiricist" tradition; and has argued, correctly we think, that instead of increasing the rate at which general knowledge of social behavior accumulates, it becomes a "justification of ongoing research."[14] The neo-empiricist tradition tacitly assumes that it is sufficient to make a particular effect theoretically relevant for general knowledge to emerge from its investigation; but the research itself is essentially historical in strategy; there is no notion that the criteria by which such research is evaluated might defeat the purpose of generalization, or that a distinctive kind of research strategy might be necessary to effectively exploit the leads thus provided. Indeed, theorists in this view remain men who have great ideas; they think about the questions raised by historically oriented research, and they provide hypotheses for such research; but they do not have a distinctive research stratgegy which is their own. Consequently, it is in fact true that neo-empiricist research provides suggestions about more general social processes; but these suggestions remain provocative leads: They are not followed up; the general process is not abstractly formulated, independent of its particular effects, nor are general questions about the nature of process, its conditions, or its consequences investigated.

Something like this is seen particularly clearly in the history of research on status crystallization. Linski's first paper on status crystallization was an effort to explain political radicalism.[15] It was from our point of view therefore a historically oriented investigation. But his second was an effort to place these findings in the context of a process more general in its significance: a process essentially, of status ambiguity.[16] Situations in which two or more people interact need to be defined; inconsistency in statuses makes such definitions ambiguous; ambiguity produces tensions, embarrassments, conflicts; such tensions motivate individuals in ambiguous situations to in some way reduce the ambiguity or withdraw from them. [17] These "tests" were made of this formulation: First, Lenski in his 1956 paper sought to show that interaction was painful for inconsistents; second, I. Goffman, a student of Lenski's improved his measure of radicalism (which had been the size of the Democratic vote in Detroit) and made an effort to show that inconsistents prefer a change in the power structure:[18] third, Jackson, another Lenski student, made an effort to show that inconsistents have more psychosomatic symptoms than consistents, implying they have more tensions.[19] Nevertheless, only a small part of Lenski's 1956 paper is devoted to spelling out how the process he had in mind works; the question of the conditions under which it is found is not touched at all; its consequences remain very concrete in their formulation, and subsequent work has focused not on ambiguity as a general phenomenon, nor on its conditions and consequences, but rather on other particular effects that might be explained by such ambiguities. Of course, it is often argued that such investigations "test" theoretical formulations and can serve to suggest ways of reformulating them: But this is not so. Treiman, for example, has shown that inconsistency principles do not explain prejudice.[20] That inconsistency does not explain prejudice limits application of the theory: It does not suggest any reformulation of the way the process works, nor even of its conditons. It gives us no result that may be used in reformulating the general process by which statuses are defined. Even replications of Lenski's original work on radicalism, of which there have been several, do not do this. Kenkel has shown that Democratic voting in Columbus, Ohio, is not explained by the same principles as Democratic voting in Detroit.[21] we may from this fact safely conclude that politics in Detroit are different from politics in Columbus; even that political radicalism is a complex as opposed to a unitary phenomenon; but not that inconsistency does not produce status ambiguity, nor even that status ambiguity does not produce tension and conflict, nor even that tension and conflict do not lead to some kind of resolution behavior. Various efforts by sociologists to test, apply, and in some cases even to reformulate Lenski's original formulation have in fact done little either to dispose of it or to improve on it.[22]

Thus, a neo-empiricist strategy of research produces some theoretical ideas and asks some important theoretical questions: But these leads are exploited largely by investigations that continue to be historically oriented in objectives and standards, which therefore can neither test them, revise them, nor answer fundamental questions about the nature of the process. its conditions, or its consequences. The difficulty that stands in the way of increasing our knowledge of the general process, and of discovering its conditions and consequences, is that the strategy of this subsequent research is at cross-purposes with the objective of studying status ambiguity as an abstract, general process. For generalizing and historical strategies are not only different; they are in some respects contradictory. Neo-empiricist claims for the theoretical relevance of a particular explanation do not alter this fundamental difference. What is purely an instrumental decision in a generalizing strategy is in a historical strategy intrinsically important; what is intrinsically important in a generalizing strategy is in a historical strategy largely instrumental. It remains true of the neo-empiricist tradition that it uses standards of "reality," of social importance, of historical relevance in choosing particular settings for investigation of general processes; and by its standards, a simpler, more readily controlled, more operationally clear investigation of an abstract, general process is still artificial, manipulated, and trival. What is true with respect to choice of setting is true also with respect to criteria of solution: The explained variance criterion remains fundamental in neo-empiricist rsearch, even theoretically relevant research. Instead of pursuing an analytic investigation, therefore, one looks for more sources of variation. The effect is to make the investigation complex; and therefore to defeat the purpose of generalizing from the investigation. If, as is required by generality, the investigation should be analytic, should focus on a unitary process, it will appear overly simplified and incomplete. What remains, therefore, from "theoretically relevant" historical research are some interesting suggestions, which might become the basis of a generalizing investigation, but suggestions that are typically not followed up because the aims, methods, and standards of the investigation remain in other respects historical in orientation. That it is obligatory to provide such leads in the neo-empiricist tradition is not the same as carrying out generalizing research.

What Is to Be Done?

A historically oriented strategy alone does not create a body of generalized knowledge about social behavior: Its focus is on particular effects; it uses laws, but their significance is purely instrumental; it searches for multiple causes, not the nature, conditions, and consequences of an analytically formulated abstract process. Making a particular effect theoretically relevant does not alter the situation: The aims, methods, and standards of work remain in other respects historically oriented, and therefore in conflict with the purpose of generalizing from the research. Leads emerge; important questions are asked; but only very slowly, if at all, does general knowledge of social behavior accumulate.

If in fact sociology were a historically oriented discipline, there would be no reason to complain of the slow rate at which its generalized knowledge accumulates. And it would of course be possible to make the discipline historically oriented. No doubt there are some sociologists who view the discipline in this way, and if there are, there is no factual or logical rebuttal of their aims. The ultimate goals of a discipline are matters of value, not fact or logic. Our argument, however, is based on the belief that many sociologists view their discipline differently: They remain committed to the view that whatever else sociology is, it is also a generalizing science. Strategies of research in sociology may more often be historical than generalizing; but the ultimate goal is general knowledge of social behavior.

If sociology is a generalizing science; if historically oriented research alone will not create a body of general knowledge; if closing the gap between theory and research is insufficient remedy; it follows that sociologists require a distinctive research tradition the aims, methods, and standards of which are oriented to the accumulation of general knowledge. We emphasize that it is a tradition that is required; it is not enough simply to admire a few great men who have a few great ideas. Particular extraordinary men are not a tradition nor is having ideas enough. For some sociologists generalizing must be a customary, routine, ordinary way of work; individuals must be recruited, motivated, rewarded, trained for working in this way; and its practice must be seen as not the special province only of great men, but the distinctive strategy of those committed to explicitly developing general knowledge of social behavior.

This argument does not imply that less energy should be spent in historically oriented research. There are good reasons for historically oriented research, and this argument does not deny them. In fact, a clearer distinction between the two strategies, and a recognition of the cross-purposes at which they work, should free historically oriented research of some of the inhibitions implied in the obligation always to be theoretically relevant. There are good reasons for urban poverty research that have nothing to do with theoretical relevance; good reasons for explaining race riots that have nothing to do with testing theories about rising expectations. In any case, it is difficult to see what purpose a generalizing strategy would have if there were no historically oriented research. The purpose of a generalizing research orientation is to provide laws to be used in explanation, prediction, application. Of what point would the enterprise be if there were no explanation, prediction, or application? The two strategies are complementary; one could not supplant the other. All that we argue is that this complementary relation does not imply any similarity of aims, standards, or methods. The two strategies in fact work at cross-purposes: In our view, a clearer distinction between them contributes as much to the one as to the other. . . .*

Notes

1. This does not distinguish deductive-nomological from probabilistic explanation. Although there are important differences between the two, particularly concerning the nature of inference, from our point of view what they have in common is more important, and our argument is not affected by their differences. Hence, we will discuss the simpler case here. For general discussions of the problem of explanation, see C. G. Hempel, "The Functions of General Laws in History," *Journal of Philosophy* 39 (1942): 35–48; C. G. Hempel and P. Oppenheim, "Studies in the Logic of Explanation," *Philosophy of Science* 15 (1948): 135–75; C. G. Hempel, *Aspects of Scientific Explanation* (New York: Free Press, 1965), ch. 12; or E. Nagel, *The Structure of Science* (New York: Harcourt Brace and World, 1961).
2. E. S. Bogardus, "Social Distance in the City," *Papers and Proceedings of the American Sociological Society* 20 (1925): 40–46.
3. R. K. Merton, *Social Theory and Social Structure* (2nd ed.; Glencoe, Ill.: Free Press, 1957), chs. 2–3.
4. See R. A. Rehberg and D. L. Westby, "Parental Encouragement, Occupation, Education and Family Size: Artifactual or Independent Determinants of Adolescent Educational Expectations?" *Social Forces* 45 (1967): 362–74, for bibliography.
5. See ibid.

*Editors' deletion.

6. This model is taken from ibid.
7. For example, see Young's paper on the incest taboo (F. Young, "Incest Taboos and Social Solidarity," *American Journal of Sociology* 72 [1967]: 589–600). Young shows the incest taboo to be only a special case of a more general kind of solidarity norm, and proposes investigating it in other kinds of solidary groups. But so far as we know, no one has yet done so.
8. Not every use of this criterion complicates by adding more processes. For example, one could use it also to add more conditions to the scope of a simpler process.
9. It should be noted that whether or not a process is complex is an empirical issue; but given that it is complex, the argument that it is either not general or not invariant follows from the definition of the term *complex*.
10. O. D. Duncan, "Path Analysis: Sociological Examples," *American Journal of Sociology* 72 (1966): 1–16.
11. A. Rose, "Varieties of Sociological Imagination," *American Sociological Review* 34 (1969): 627.
12. Merton, *Social Theory and Social Structure*, p. 85.
13. Ibid.
14. H. Gamberg, "Science and Scientism: The State of Sociology," *American Sociologist* 4 (1969): 112.
15. G. Lenski, "Status Crystallization: A Non-Vertical Dimension of Social Status," *American Sociological Review* 19 (1954): 405–13.
16. G. Lenski, "Social Participation and Status Crystallization," *American Sociological Review* 21 (1956): 458–64.
17. Cf. E. C. Hughes, "Dilemmas and Contradictions of Status," *American Journal of Sociology* 50 (1945): 353–59.
18. I. W. Goffman, "Status Consistency and Preference for Change in Power Distribution," *American Sociological Review* 22 (1957): 275–81.
19. E. Jackson, "Status Consistency and Symptoms of Stress," *American Sociological Review* 27 (1962): 469–80; E. Jackson and P. Burke, "Status and Symptoms of Stress: Additive and Interaction Effects," *American Sociological Review* 30 (1965): 556–64.
20. D. J. Treiman, "Status Discrepancy and Prejudice," *American Journal of Sociology* 71 (1966): 651–664.
21. W. F. Kenkel, "The Relationship between Status Consistency and Politico-Economic Attitudes," *American Sociological Review* 21 (1956): 365–69.
22. Various methodological critiques have been made of this body of research, arguing that inconsistency effects cannot, for purely methodological reasons, be identified in survey data of the sort depended on by Lenski and his students, without additional *a priori* assumptions that would render the argument circular or beg the question. These arguments are sound, but they do not touch the central issue, for they tend to assume that historical investigations are the only source of empirical data relevant to the problem (R. E. Mitchell, "Methodological Notes on a Theory of Status Crystallization," *Public Opinion Quarterly* 28 [1964]: 315–25; M. D. Hyman, "Determining the Effects of Status Inconsistency," *Public Opinion Quarterly* 30 [1966]: 120–29; H. M. Blalock, "The Identification Problem and Theory Building: The Case of Status Inconsistency," *American Sociological Review* 31 [1966]: 52–61 H. M. Blalock, "Tests of Status Inconsistency Theory: A Note of Caution," *Pacific Sociological Review* 10 [1967]: 69–74.

CHAPTER 5

Inequalities in Educational Opportunities in the United States

Ernest Q. Campbell *and* James S. Coleman

The Civil Rights Act of 1964 required that a survey be conducted to determine the lack of availability of equal educational opportunities for individuals by reason of race and other factors at all levels of public instruction in the United States, its territories and possessions.[1] This paper is a summary of some of the findings of that survey, limited to a comparison of Negroes and whites, to the first twelve grades of school, and to the fifty states plus the District of Columbia.

Sample and Method

The sampling plan selected school systems (high school plus their feeder schools) in seven geographical regions divided into two strata representing the metropolitan and non-metropolitan areas in each region. The selection proceeded in such a way as to heavily magnify the chance that schools with a large non-white enrollment would be included and the final sample take includes approximately 35 percent non-white. In the first stage of the sample the nation was divided into metropolitan and other counties. The largest metropolitan areas were selected with certainty and the others by probabilities which depended on the proportion of non-white population. Counties outside metropolitan areas were selected with probabilities which increased with increasing proportion of non-white population.

In the second sample stage a list of high schools was made for each selected county and metropolitan area and then high schools were

Reprinted with the permission of the authors and the University of Illinois at Urbana-Champaign from a paper presented at the American Sociological Association meeting, Miami Beach, Florida, August 31, 1966.

selected by probabilities which increased with increasing proportion of non-white enrollment. Feeder schools which sent 90 percent or more of their graduates to a high school drawn in the sample were included with certainty and those that had fewer than 90 percent were selected by a probability equal to the proportion they fed to the high school. Then the sample schools, all superintendents, principals and teachers, were included in the survey as were pupils in the twelfth, ninth, sixth, and third grades, and in half of the first grades. Pupils in the first grade were given a very short simple test which their teachers helped them individually in completing; twelfth-grade students were given a forty-seven-page combination questionnaire and test booklet that required between four and five hours to complete. Around 70 percent of all schools drawn in the sample cooperated with the study and the final sample yield includes approximately 645,000 school children. Analysis of data concerning non-participating schools and systems suggests that their participation would not have materially altered the conclusions of the study.

Verbal and non-verbal reasoning tests were given in all five grades and in all except the first grade a reading comprehension and mathematics achievement test were given. In addition, ninth- and twelfth-grade students took a general information test that covered four broad areas—practical arts, natural sciences, social studies, and humanities—and was designed to give some measure of the depth of a school's training.

The Definitions of Inequality

Congress in requesting the survey did not define what it meant by educational inequalities, and it was necessary to consider a variety of possible definitions and to attempt to provide data appropriate to each. One common and traditional conception of inequality rests in the characteristics of the instructional staff and the physical facilities of the school: such things as the age, condition, and cost of the school plant; pupil-teacher ratios, the variety of instructional facilities and curricula; and such characteristics of the teachers as their salaries and experience. It would be argued that if Negroes attend older schools or less well-equipped ones or are taught by less well-trained teachers an inequality in educational opportunity exists.

A second definition of inequality is provided by the 1954 Supreme Court decision that segregated education is by definition unequal education. Thus data that reflect the probability that a white student will attend school with whites and the Negro student with Negroes might be said to index inequality of educational opportunity by this definition.

A third conception of inequality, perhaps implicit in the prior one, argues that the educationally relevant backgrounds from which students come invariably affect the quality and level of course work, conversation, and other interactions that occur in the classroom and hence that students who attend school with students from homes unlikely to support and reinforce the educational process are subject to inequality or opportunity.

A fourth and final view of educational inequality focuses not on the input of resources into the school but on the outcomes of the school's educational effort. This is, equality of educational opportunity would be said to exist if the public schools produced students who, as groups, are equally well prepared to compete for jobs and other rewards available in the society they will live in. Since the fundamental task of the schools is to prepare students for adult life, if the quality of that preparation varies systematically across groups such that some are competitively disadvantaged compared to others it would be argued that the nation's schools have failed to provide equal educational opportunity. This position argues that the allocation of resources should be determined so that quite apart from where children begin they have a real opportunity to end at the same point. If, on the other hand, the public schools fail to produce graduates to whom the labor market, the colleges and universities, and society at large can respond without regard to race insofar as educational performance is relevant to their judgment, then there has not been a true equality of educational opportunity.

This paper deals briefly with each of these measures of educational opportunity and will concentrate in two separate ways on the last named.

School Facilities

The survey determined the availability of a great variety of school facilities and it is impossible to represent the results in any simple summary form. Overall it can perhaps be said that a degree of educational inequality does exist in the United States such that whites are more likely than Negroes to have available a large variety of school facilities. However, it is rare on any given facility that the same direction of inequality holds across all regions considered in the survey. That is, if in any given region on any given factor there is an inequality that favors whites it is highly probable that in some other region there is an inequality that favors Negoes on the same factor. Also within any cluster of factors it is quite uncommon that the direction of inequality is consistent across the various components of the cluster. Our discussion will consider differences at the national level only. . . .*

School children differ relatively little in the physical school facilities available. In elementary schools they all have about the same number of pupils per instruction room and per teacher and the same number of makeshift instruction rooms. There is a difference that favors whites in the relative prevalence of science laboratories at the secondary school level. Centralized school libraries are available to almost all secondary school children in the country and to around three-quarters of the elementary school children. Very small differences by race of student are observed. However, when the average number of volumes in the library per student is computed, it is observed that the average white child attends a school that has more books per student in the library. Negro pupils in both elementary and secondary schools are more often found to attend schools within walking distance of the public library. Free textbooks are available almost equally to students of all races at the elementary level while at the secondary level the average Negro attends a school which has a higher percentage of free textbooks. On the other hand, textbooks are more often in short supply in schools attended by Negro pupils, especially in the elementary grades.

There are no important national differences in the recency of textbooks used by Negroes compared to whites. Negro pupils generally receive free lunches and free milk somewhat more often than do white pupils, and a higher percent of Negro pupils attend schools where there is a full- or part-time nurse. There are not noticeable differences in the nation in the service of school psychologists available to the different races. Free kindergartens are generally more available to Negro pupils, at least in the nation's metropolitan regions. A higher percentage of white pupils attend both regionally and state accredited schools, and white pupils tend to have more art and music teachers in their schools than do Negro pupils. There is no general tendency for Negro pupils to differ from whites on the length of school day or on the expected amount of daily homework. The average white is more likely to attend a secondary school that offers a college preparatory curriculum, and he is somewhat more likely to enroll in a school that offers a commercial curriculum. Negroes are slightly less likely than whites to be in a school classed by the principal as academic in its primary curricular emphasis. The average Negro pupil is much less likely to attend a school to which representatives

*Editors' deletion.

of predominantly white colleges are sent for recruitment purposes. Negroes are deficient relative to whites in the availability of remedial reading an arithmetic classes and in the availability of accelerated curriculums. According to the principal's report, achievement and intelligence tests are widely used in both elementary and secondary schools and there are no noteworthy differences by race in regard to achievement testing in the schools they attend. But Negroes are less often than whites attending scecondary schools which give interest inventories. In every region more Negro students are enrolled in schools which ability-group pupils at the elementary level; more pupils are in the lowest tracks in schools attended by Negroes than in schools attended by whites, whereas in most regions the average white pupil attends the schools which have a slightly larger proportion of pupils in the highest track. Negro students are less likely than whites to attend a school in which students who fail a course are required to repeat the entire grade, at least at the elementary level. When we look at extracurricular activities, the most important conclusion is that there is little difference between Negroes and whites in their availability overall.

Characteristics of Staff

Negro pupils are more likely to be taught by teachers who are locality-based in the sense that they are products of the area in which they teach and secured their public school training nearby. Negro pupils are more likely to have teachers who have lived in larger towns and cities than have the teachers of white pupils. Teachers of Negro students grew up in homes in which the educational attainments of parents were on the average somewhat less than is the case for the teachers of white students. Generally no race differences in the sex composition of faculties is observed nor are there gross differences in the average age of teachers, but there are sharp differences in the racial composition of the faculty. The average Negro elementary student attends a school in which 65 percent of the faculty are Negro and the average white elementary student attends a school in which 97 percent of the faculty are white. At secondary levels the corresponding figures are 59 percent and 97 percent. Sixty-one percent of Negro secondary students attend schools with Negro principals and 95 percent of white students attend schools with white principals. Negro principals are rare outside the southern states, but wherever they appear they are in charge of schools with a concentration of Negro students. Negro pupils are neither more nor less likely than whites to be taught by teachers with advanced degrees. The average Negro pupil is more likely, however, to be taught by teachers who score low on a short thirty-item verbal facility test that was administered to teachers on a voluntary basis. Negro pupils have teachers with slightly greater experience both in total years and in length of experience in the current school. Their teachers report reading more professional education journals and more time spent in class preparation. The general impression for the nation is that the average white and average Negro pupil do not differ in the type of college in which their teachers were trained, but the level of degree offered by the college does differ with teachers of Negro pupils more likely to be products of colleges that do not offer advanced degrees. Teachers of Negro pupils are much more likely to have been educated in colleges that had a large enrollment of Negro pupils and teachers of white pupils are likely to have had limited contact with Negroes as fellow students when they were in college. Teachers of the average Negro are somewhat less likely to be members of scholastic honorary societies such as Phi Beta Kappa or Kappa Delta Pi, more likely to have attended institutes that offer special training in professional upgrading, more likely to have participated in teachers' associations as officers or active workers, more likely to have attended institutes that offer special training in teaching or counseling the culturally disadvantaged. Race of student has no appreciable relation to the salary earned by either teacher or principal, nor to teacher absenteeism rates. A smaller proportion of the teachers of whites plan definitely to remain in teaching until retirement although more teachers of whites would re-enter teaching if they had the decision to make over again. Average class size tends to be one to two students larger for the teachers of Negroes than for the teachers of whites at the elementary school level, whereas it is two to three students larger for the teachers of Negroes at the secondary school level. Facilities are somewhat more stable in schools attended by Negroes and are more likely to fall under a tenure system. The National Teacher Examination or similar test is used more often in schools attended by the average Negro. The average white child is considerably more likely to be taught by teachers who express a special preference for teaching children of white-collar and professional workers, for teaching Anglo-Saxon children, and for teaching white pupils. They are also more likely to prefer to teach high ability students and to support the concept of the neighborhood elementary programs for the culturally disadvantaged, and to reject the idea that it is educationally sound to have white teachers for non-white pupils and non-white teachers for white pupils.

Characteristics of Fellow Students

An important part of a child's school environment consists not of the physical facilities of the school, the curriculum, and the teachers, but of his fellow students. These provide challenges to achievement or distractions from achievement; they provide the opportunities to learn outside the classroom through association and casual discussions. Indeed it seems likely that when the average citizen thinks of a good school in a community he most often measures it by the kind of student body it contains and implicitly recognizes that whatever the quality of the staff, curriculum, and facilities, the level of instruction must be geared to the composition of their student bodies, homogeneous as to race, socio-economic origins, or whatever may seem of relevance, it may be argued that the school holds the child in the environment of his origins and keeps out of his reach the environment of the larger society.

The average white elementary school child attends a school where 87 percent of his classmates are white and the average Negro attends a school where 16 percent of his classmates are white. The average Negro is more often in classes with pupils whose mothers are not high school graduates. Negro children are especially likely to be in classes with children who come from large families. The average Negro has fewer fellow students who come from homes that have such material possessions as telephones, vacuum cleaners, and automobiles. On the other hand, we do not observe a difference by race in the percent of fellow pupils who report their parents to be highly interested in their education, and, indeed, the average Negro child has more fellow students whose parents attend the PTA or other parent association meetings. Negro children attend classes with fellow students who report less reading matter in their homes. This applies to daily newspapers, encyclopedias, and the number of books.

Negro students attend schools in which a larger proportion of students drop out before finishing. If we assume that aspirations and performance can be dulled by association with those who will drop out of school, we must also assume that they can be raised by association with those who will go to college. The average Negro is less likely to attend a school in which the students have read a college catalog or talked with a college official about going to college, and fewer of his fellow classmates—at least in preceding grades—have in fact gone on to college. More of the classmates of whites than Negroes are in a college preparatory curriculum and more are taking courses ordinarily required for college. Negroes also attend schools in which fewer of their classmates report high overall grade averages. There is, however, some conflicting evidence. Negroes and whites are about equally exposed to classmates who report definite intentions to go to college and who have been encouraged to attend college by their teachers or counselors. Indeed the average Negro is more exposed to fellow students who report high interest in school and frequent reading activity, as he is more often exposed to fellow students who report strong aspirations to be among the best students in the school. Negro and white elementary children are about equally likely to attend school with pupils who report being one of the best students in my class and who agree with the statement that "I sometimes feel I just can't learn." At the secondary level the classmates of Negroes are somewhat less likely to agree that "I sometimes feel I just can't learn" or that "I would do better in school if teachers didn't go so fast."

Test Results and Their Predictions

The differences between whites and Negroes in test performances are great indeed. Negro averages tend to be about one standard deviation below those of the whites. The disadvantage appears to be about the same for all areas tested.[2] The regional variation is much greater for Negroes than for whites. The achievement disadvantage suffered by whites as a result of living in the rural South compared to the urban North is about fifteen percentile points in the distribution of white scores, whereas the disadvantage suffered by twelfth-grade Negroes as a result of living in the rural South compared to the urban North is about thirty percentile points in the distribution of Negro scores. Or, differently, the disadvantage suffered by Negroes in comparison to whites is about nine points in standard scores (mean of fifty and sigma of ten) in the metropolitan North but about twelve points in the rural South. In general, Negro scores differ little by region in the first grade but increasingly as school proceeds. In no region are there experiences that decrease the racial difference over the period of school. It is clear that the educational disadvantage with which a group begins remains the disadvantage with which it finishes school. In fact, in some areas of the country, notably the South and Southwest, the opportunities are not even enough for Negroes to maintain their position relative to that of whites, measured in standard deviation terms. Measured in grade-level terms, the gap widens at higher grades in all regions. Thus, the Negro child, since his school does not attempt or fails in the attempt to compensate for the cultural disadvantages with which he begins school, can expect to start his adult life with the handicap given him by the culture in which he resides compounded by the missed opportunities in schooling that this handicap has caused.

These test scores may be used in a very direct way as a measure of educational inequality. They describe what students know at different points in their schooling and when they finish school. And they are directly pertinent to the argument that educational inequality exists in proportion as the products of schools are unequally equipped to compete for college scholarships, the job market, or in other areas to which school-taught skills are relevant. In other words, to the extent that achievement tests measure the skills necessary for further education and for occupational achievement in our urban industrial society, any difference in achievement tests results may be interpreted as an educational disadvantage. But the test results may also be used to determine what things about schools make an educational difference, and thereby help us escape from the mire we are in when we look at a great variety of school facilities and other characteristics of schools and wonder whether the differences we observe do, in fact, make a difference. We can ask two related questions: first, whether given features of schools make any difference in what students achieve; second, what variation is there by race in access to those features of schools that do in fact make a difference in what students achieve?

Based on regression analysis, the most general statement we can make is that schools are very similar in the effect that they have on pupils' achievement when pupils' socio-economic background is taken into account.[3] In other words, differences between schools account for only a small part of the differences in individual pupil achievement (10 to 20 percent for whites and Negroes). Within the structure imposed by the fact that most of the total variance in pupil achievement, consists of differences of individual scores in a school about the school average—the within-school variance—we will note that schools do differ in the degree of their impact on various racial groups; specifically, the average white student's achievement is less affected by schools' curricula, facilities, and teachers than is the achievement of the average Negro. The implication is that improving the school of a Negro pupil will increase his achievement more than will improving the school of a white pupil increase his achievement.

Over 80 percent of the variation in achievement for each racial group is variation within the same student body. Furthermore, the existence of variations among schools does not itself indicate whether these differences are due to school factors, pupil background differences, or community differences in support of school achievement. A substantial part of school-to-school variation in achievement appears not to be a consequence of effects of school variations at all but of variations in family backgrounds of the entering student bodies. These two results taken together can be seen as a measure of the weakness of schools' influences. They simply have not found ways to break into the strong influences that family backgrounds and student body factors exert; schools do not develop an autonomous influence upon a child's achievement. Thus we see why minorities that begin with an educational disadvantage continue to exhibit this disadvantage throughout the twelve grades of school; the schools are unable to exert independent influences to make achievement levels less dependent on the child's background. Insofar as variations in school factors do make a difference in achievement they make most difference for children of minority groups. It is those children who come least prepared to school and whose achievement in school is generally low for when the characteristics of a school make the most difference. The data indicate that those least sensitive to the school's influences are, in general, those children from groups where achievement is highest when they begin school in the first grade, and the most sensitive are those with lowest initial levels of achievement.

We turn first to examine the effect of student background factors on achievement. By taking the school-to-school variations as given and examining the added variance accounted for by family background characteristics we show that portion of the within school variance can be accounted for by these factors. The amount of within-school variance accounted for by eight factors taken together is of the same order of magnitude as the variance associated with school-to-school factors.[4] It is well to remember here that many other aspects of the child's background are not measured and thus the variance accounted for in the present analysis is a kind of lower bound to the actual effects of background differences.

We turn now to examine the effects of various school characteristics on pupil achievement. We prefer to separate school characteristics into three groups: first, facilities, curriculum, and other characteristics of the school itself; second, characteristics of the teaching staff; and, third, characteristics of the student body. Having seen that school-to-school differences in achievement are a small part of the total variation, we are cautioned against attributing large effects fo any component.

The first step is to determine the relative effects of the three components. We observe that the attributes of other students account for far more variation in the achievement of minority group children than do any attributes of school facilities and slightly more than do attributes of staff. Of the five student body measures used, it appears particularly that as the educational aspirations and backgrounds of fellow students increase the achievement level increases even when the student's own background characteristics are controlled. . . .* School variables are allowed to

*Editors' deletion.

account for as much variance as they can and then characteristics of fellow students are added to see how much additional variance is explained. Even under this severe restriction, the explained variance is often more than doubled and always sharply increased. Comparisons of student body effects by race suggests that the environment provided by a student body is asymmetric in its effects in that it has its greatest effect on those from educationally deficient backgrounds. It is indeed those Negroes who are in the South whose achievement appears to vary most greatly with variations in the characteristics of their fellow students. The highest achieving groups show generally less dependence of achievement on characteristics of fellow students.

It is also found that as the proportion of whites in a school increases the achievement of students in both racial groups increases. This relationship increases as grade in school increases, being absent at grade three, stronger at grade nine, and strongest at grade twelve. This higher achievement of all racial and ethnic groups in schools with greater proportions of white students is largely perhaps wholly, accounted for by effects associated with the student body's educational background and aspirations. Thus the real influence comes not from racial composition per se, but from the better educational background and higher educational aspirations that are, on the average, found among white students.

Our next concern is with the effects of school facilities and curriculum. For school attended by Negroes in the South, but among no other groups, high per pupil instructional expenditure is associated with higher achievement at grades six, nine, and twelve after six background differences of students are controlled. (2.98 percent of variance explained.) Considering that the variance in per pupil expenditure among Negroes and whites in the South is only one-tenth to one-third as great as that for other parts of the nation, the contrast between this relationship for southern Negroes and its relative absence elsewhere is even more marked. It appears, however, that expenditure differences are really a surrogate for other differences in the community and this is evidenced by the fact that when student body characteristics are taken into account the unique contribution of per pupil expenditure for southern Negroes nearly vanishes. One variable that explains a relatively large amount of variance among Negroes at grades nine and twelve under the condition of controlling for student background and per pupil instructional expenditure but nothing else, is school size (2.55 percent grade twelve; 1.32 percent grade nine). Most of its apparent effect vanishes if various other facilities and curricular differences are controlled. That is, higher achievement in larger schools is largely accounted for by the additional facilities they

95

include. Tracking shows no relation to achievement and comprehensiveness of the curriculum shows very small and inconsistent relations. An accelerated program in the curriculum does show a consistent relation to achievement at grade twelve, both before and after other curriculum and facilities measures have been controlled. The number of volumes per student in the school library shows small and inconsistent relations to achievement. However, both the number of science laboratories (1.62 percent for Negroes, grade twelve) and the number of extracurricular activities (1.64 percent for Negroes, grade twelve) gave a consistent relation of moderate size to achievement.

Our effort to find effects, even small ones, of various facilities and curriculums, should not obscure the more central fact: School facilities and curriculum are the major variables by which attempts are made to improve schools; yet differences between them are so little related to achievement levels of students that with few exceptions their effects fail to appear even in a survey of this magnitude.

Next, the effects of teacher characteristics. Altogether, teachers' characteristics account for a higher proportion of student achievement than do other aspects of the school, excluding student body characteristics. Teacher variables selected for special examination were the average educational level of the teachers' families, average years of experience, localism, average level of education of the teachers themselves, average score on self-administered vocabulary test, teacher's preference for teaching middle class white-collar students, and proportion of teachers in the school who were white. The first important result is that the effect of teachers' characteristics shows a sharp increase over the years of school. Also the apparent effect of teacher characteristics for children is directly related to their need for good teachers. That is, good teachers matter more for children from groups with educationally deficient backgrounds. There is a strikingly stronger effect of teacher variables for Negroes than for whites. The variables which show most effect are the teachers' family educational level, the teachers' own education, and the score on the vocabulary test. The strongest result to derive from these tabulations is that teachers' verbal skills have a strong effect first showing at the sixth grade. The second and less strong effect for Negroes is that the teachers' educational level, or some variable for which this is a surrogate, begins to make a difference at grades nine and twelve.

Lastly, we turn to look at the effects of attitude on achievement. Three were examined: the students' interest in school and his reported casual reading; his self-concept specifically with regard to learning and success in school; and his sense of control of the environment.[5] Taken alone these attitudinal variables account for more of the variation in achievement than any other set of variables (all family background variables together or all school variables together). When added to any other set of variables they increase the accounted for variation more than does any other set of variables. Perhaps it is reasonable that self-concept should be so closely related to achievement since it represents the individual's own estimate of his learning ability. However, the other variables are not so logically related to achievement. One's interest in learning, it can be assumed, partly derived from family background and partly from his success in school; thus it is partly a cause of achievement, partly determined by past achievement. Of the three attitudinal variables, however, this is the weakest, especially among minority groups. For Negroes the child's sense of control of environment becomes the strongest predictor of achievement. (The questions on which this scale is based are a statement that "Good luck is more important than hard work for success," a statement that "Every time I try to get ahead something or someone stops me," and a statement that "People like me don't have much of a chance to be successful in life.") In both grades twelve and nine for both sexes Negroes who give "control" responses score higher on the test than do whites who give "no control" responses.

The implications of these findings are immense, for it may be that a causal chain runs by which experiencing an unrewarding environment leads to beliefs in the inefficacy of one's own behaviors which leads to behaviors not characterized by diligent, extended effort toward achievement and thus to low achievement levels in fact. We have seen that the larger task is less to secure an equitable input of resources into the nation's schools than to increase the effectiveness of this input measured by the responses Negro children make to and the benefits they derive from their schooling. It now appears that a critical step may be the development of an ordered set of increasingly more challenging, but rewarding activities by which the disadvantaged child gains an enlarging sense of the relevance of his efforts to affect the outcome he wishes to secure.

Notes

1. *Equality of Educational Opportunity*, Superintendent of Documents Catalog No. FS 5.238:38001 (Washington, D.C.: U.S. Government Printing Office, 1966).
2. Verbal ability and non-verbal ability in all five grades; reading comprehension and mathematics achievement in all except grade one; and five areas of general information at grades twelve and nine only.
3. Prediction is to the verbal ability score, based on these findings: (1) the

percent of variance that lies between schools is somewhat greater for this than for the "achievement" tests; (2) school-to-school variations as a percent of total variation decline less from lower to higher grades on this test that on the achievement tests; (3) holding family background constant, a higher proportion of variance in individual scores is explained to school characteristics on the verbal ability than on the achievement test scores; (4) the relation between family background factors and reading comprehension does not decline more over the years of school that does the relation between family background and verbal ability, though it should if schools affect reading comprehension more than they affect verbal ability.

4. Urbanism of background; parents' educational attainment; structural completeness of home; size of family; material items in the home; reading materials in the home; parents' interest in school; parents' desires for child.

5. Full measures available in grades twelve, nine, and six only.

CHAPTER 6

Self-Evaluation and
Performance Expectations

Murray Webster
and Barbara Sobieszek

Theoretical and empirical work in the social self tradition revolves about two major issues: first, the idea that the individual's conception of his various abilities is built on the perceived opinions of "significant others," and second, the suggestion that the self-evaluation produced in this way has some degree of permanence and directly affects the individual's subsequent behaviors in social situations. Therefore, it is reasonable to begin a theory of the social self by formulating precise concepts both of the characteristics of significant others and of the self-conception that significant others can produce.

The second task has been the object of sustained empirical and theoretical investigation initiated by and focused about Joseph Berger and his associates. These workers have been concerned with developing, testing, and extending a set of propositions to explain certain features of inequality among members of face-to-face problem-solving groups. By adopting this viewpoint for our interests in the social self, we gain a set of concepts and propositions that enable determinate empirical predictions for behavior as a function of ability conceptions. Since, in addition, there is a considerable body of empirical data in support of these propositions, we can focus our efforts on the first task: specifying clearly the characteristics that make an other significant in determining a given individual's ability self-conception. We begin by outlining Berger's way of analyzing interaction and by describing a standardized experimental setting to test the theory; then we indicate parallels between problems of interest in this tradition and problems of interest in the social self tradition.[1]

Expectation States Theory

Berger's tradition is oriented to explaining the following pervasive fact of social life: among members of a problem-solving group who are previously unacquainted with one another, the interaction process leads to unequal distribution of participation rates and unequal amounts of influence over the group decision and esteem received from other group members. This result is observable in an extremely wide variety of groups, including Bales-type discussion groups of college students, juries, children's play groups, and military teams.[2] Essentially, these phenomena are said to occur because during early phases of interaction members form differential ability conceptions, called *performance expectation states*, for one another. Once formed, these expectation states determine distribution of all observable components of power and prestige in the groups. To relate expectation theory to self-evaluation, we must specify precisely how expectation states form through interaction, precisely what an expectation state is, and precisely how expectation states determine future interaction. There are in fact several closely related theories, constructed for a variety of related phenomena. We describe those features most closely related to issues in the social self.

Expectation states theory applies to groups that meet two scope conditions: the members of the group must be *task oriented*, and they must be *collectively oriented*. Task orientation means that the members are engaged in a task that can be completed successfully or unsuccessfully; they are solving a problem or set of problems, and there exists a set of definite and recognizable correct outcomes for their efforts. For example, if members were assigned to solve a set of mathematical problems, the outcome of their work could be evaluated in terms of "correctness" by anyone who knew the standard rules for mathematics. For this reason, the evaluative standards of a task-oriented group can be called "extrasystemic." Members of a group whose purpose in meeting is to have a good time or to get to know one another better are engaged in a task for which success can be assessed only by the group members themselves. Such a task has intrasystemic standards, and groups with only intrasystemic standards usually are not task oriented. Individuals at a social gathering probably would constitute a *process-oriented* group, with intrasystemic standards of success.

The second scope condition, collective orientation, refers to types of interaction that are deemed proper by the group members, or to the manner in which the members try to solve the problems. In a collectively oriented group, it is not only appropriate, it is *required* that members take one anothers' opinions into account in solving the problem. By contrast, it is possible to speak of *individualistic orientation*, in which individuals work by themselves on a problem. A room full of students taking an examination (presumably) would not be collectively oriented.

For informally organized groups meeting these two scope conditions, it is possible to describe the interaction process quite abstractly. At this point we introduce some terminology of expectation states theory.

Imagine a collection of individuals coming together for the first time to meet as a problem-solving group, such as the Bales discussion groups. Their observable interaction will consist of orientation statements that attempt to marshal the group's knowledge and to organize members' efforts, suggestions about how to attack the problem, proposed solutions, criticisms of suggestions offered, laughter, and so on. Some proportion—perhaps 15 to 25 percent—of the interaction will consist of statements not directly relevant for solving the problem: joking, comments about the weather, concern for the psychological and emotional states of group members. This type of activity, since it is not directly relevant to task problems, constitutes a residual category of interaction for our purposes and is not included in the conceptualization.

Excluding irrelevant types of interaction, we view group interaction as composed of five components:

First, there are *action opportunities*, or socially distributed chances to perform. Asking a member's opinion about how best to solve the group problem constitutes giving an action opportunity to that member. For example, the question "What do you think about this, Bill?" is an action opportunity given to the actor Bill. In a discussion group it is also possible to give an action opportunity nonverbally by looking inquiringly at an actor, or simply by being silent when he looks as though he has something to say. In a more controlled setting, such as the clinical case problems used in some of Jones's research, . . .* action opportunities were distributed by the experimenter when he told each subject to give her best judgment of the probable response of the patient being discussed.

The second component of interaction is *performance outputs*, or problem-solving attempts. If an actor is given an action opportunity, he may accept it and make a performance output. Bill, for example, may say "I think the answer is. . . ." When the task is other than discussion, a performance output would be a different type of problem-solving attempt. For example, in the studies of Videbeck and Maehr, performance outputs were physical: running, jumping, throwing balls, and so on.

*Editors' deletion.

A performance output is any single unit attempt by an actor to do the activity required by the task; it is an attempt to achieve the group's goal.

A performance output is seldom made without an antecedent action opportunity. It is surprisingly unusual for an actor to try to solve the group problem without first having been "permitted" by other members to do so. In groups that are not strictly task oriented, members seem to make many suggestions without having their opinions solicited. A little consideration suggests a reason for this discrepant behavior. To the extent that members are strictly concerned with solving the group problem and are motivated to do the best possible job, they are not likely to want to hear any but the best suggestions. Not only will they overlook suggestions they feel are not helpful, they will take steps to suppress the individual who makes such suggestions. He will find that his opinions are not asked for, and when he ventures them unrequested he will meet silence, disapproving glances, and quite likely, open hostility. An individual perceived as making good suggestions will receive the opposite treatment: his opinion will be asked frequently, he will be listened to with interest and deference, he will be praised and otherwise encouraged to speak more. In process-oriented groups, irrelevant or low-quality performances are much less likely to be suppressed; they do not detract from any goal attainment.

If an actor accepts an action opportunity and makes a performance output, that performance may be evaluated, either by himself or by another member of the group. This is a *unit evaluation*, since it refers to a single unit act, and it is the third component of the observable interaction process. A unit evaluation may be either positive or negative; it may not be neutral. The actor who has made a suggestion toward solving the group problem may hear another member say, "I think that's right," or "I think he has a good idea." In the tasks used by Videbeck and Maehr, unit evaluations were distributed by the experimenter when he told subjects how well they had performed at each of the tasks. In less controlled situations, each group member is free to evaluate any member's performances, including his own. A unit evaluation is not made without an antecedent performance output, just as performance outputs usually follow action opportunities.

At some point we will want to distinguish public unit evaluations from private unit evaluations. We assume that private unit evaluations invariably are made of every performance output; everybody in the group who knows about the performance output is assumed to evaluate it. Sometimes the private unit evaluation is communicated to the individual making the performance output (e.g., by telling him he did well or poorly), but it need not be. In most cases, it is safe to assume that the private and the public unit evaluations are the same and are coextensive. That is, the individual making the unit evaluation will not disguise his true feelings as, for example, tact might require. This characteristic of public and private unit evaluations may also serve as a distinguishing feature of task-oriented groups. Members of process-oriented groups may seek to avoid offense or embarrassment by keeping certain evaluations private and may even state insincere evaluations publicly. For our purposes, when the term unit evaluation is not specified as either private or public, it is taken to mean that it is both.

The fourth observable component of interaction is *agreement or disagreement* with a given performance output. Many times in discussion groups it is difficult to distinguish positive unit evaluations from agreement, and negative unit evaluations from disagreement. In fact, speech customs frequently dictate that we equate the statements "I disagree with you" and "I think you are wrong." In principle, however, it is possible to distinguish between these two concepts, and in some instances it is useful to do so. In a discussion group, for example, we could be relatively certain that if two people make the same suggestion or guessed the same answer simultaneously, an instance of agreement had occurred. If the interaction were restricted so that no member could know any other person's performances until after he had made his own performances, it would be still easier to distinguish agreement from positive unit evaluations. And even in the open interaction of a discussion group, an observer frequently feels that he is witnessing an honest expression of agreement between members who have come to the same conclusion, without one of them relying solely on the other for the answer. The observer is likely to have greater confidence in his judgment that he is seeing an honest *dis*agreement when two members offer different and incompatible suggestions for ways to solve the group problem. For difficult tasks, the correct solutions are not at all clear or easy to discover, and it is likely that several members will make performance outputs that are in disagreement.

When disagreement does arise, we may observe *acceptance or rejection of influence*, the fifth component of interaction. If two members make different suggestions, or if two performance outputs imply incompatible courses of action, then one member must back down—that is, make a negative unit evaluation of his own performance output. In a discussion group, disagreement usually means that one of the disagreeing members must say, "I guess I was wrong and you were right." Before the group problem solving can proceed, the member who is to accept influence must accept the course of action proposed by the other. If the disagreement cannot be resolved, the group faces the very difficult problem of choosing between completely disregarding one member or finding a third alternative course of action.

Disagreements can be crucial to a problem-solving group for a reason that lies in the collective orientation condition. Recall that this condition stipulates that it is not only appropriate but *necessary* to take the opinions of every member into account. Thus when a disagreement arises, the group members who are working on a collective task are obliged to take action on it; they must decide which performance output was best. They may decide to ignore one of the suggestions and to follow the other by default, without explicitly announcing that they have thereby chosen to evaluate the first negatively and the second positively; but they may not ignore both suggestions.

All five of these interaction components have the property *scarcity*. If person *A* is given an action opportunity, person *B* is at the same time denied an action opportunity. Although there are no strict structural constraints that make agreement or positive unit evaluations scarce, it usually is the case that neither component is in endless supply. Thus such groups exhibit the results of forces producing a differentiation among the members according to the components of interaction. We now describe this differentiating process in more detail.

In the open interaction situation of a problem-solving discussion group, several regular features of the interaction have been reported repeatedly. As the first step toward developing a theory of interaction in problem-solving groups, these regularities are noted and stated in terms of the interaction components introduced previously.

First, after group members have had the opportunity to interact for a short period of time and to become familiar with one another and with the task, the components of interaction tend to be distributed *unequally* among the various group members. Some members come to receive more action opportunities than others, some receive relatively more positive unit evaluations, some make more performance outputs, and so on.

Second, not only is the distribution of the interaction components unequal; it is also *reciprocal*. The members who receive more action opportunities also make more performance outputs, are more likely to receive positive unit evaluations and agreements from others, and are less likely to accept influence in case of disagreement. Simply by counting the number of times a group member talks regardless of what he says, an observer will have a good idea of the ranking of members on likelihood of receiving positive unit evaluations and agreement, and of rejecting influence. Correlations above .80 of the rankings of group members on these components of interaction have been reported.

Third, the reciprocal inequality, once it emerges, tends to be *stable*. The members who talk most near the beginning of the group meeting are also very likely to be the ones who talk at the end of the session; moreover, they are very likely to talk most in subsequent sessions if the group meets more than once. Because of this stability, as well as the reciprocity of the inequality, it is possible to speak of the components of interaction as visible indicators of the *power and prestige structure of the group*.

It is reasonable, therefore, to infer that these inequalities indicate the existence of a hierarchy within the group and that if this hierarchy could be independently determined, it could be used to predict the distribution of the components of interaction. An explanation for these observations will rest on an explanation of the nature and the bases of the hierarchy and how it comes to exist.

At the outset of interaction, the interaction components are probably distributed randomly among the group members. That is, in the first few minutes of interaction, members make suggestions, receive positive and negative evaluations and agreement or disagreement, and accept or reject influence in ways that could not be predicted from any simple theory of group structure or process. We might expect, for example, that some individuals have learned to be more verbal than others, hence will make more performance outputs than others; or that some individuals characteristically are more likely than others to accept influence.

However, the evidence on the relation of action opportunities and performance outputs strongly suggests that individual differences are *not* the most important determinants of distribution of these interaction components after the earliest stages of group interaction. Furthermore, the highly regular relationship of all these components of interaction argues strongly against an interpretation that individual differences are the most important determinant of any single feature of the interaction, such as acceptance or rejection of influence. An explanation of the observed inequalities must reside elsewhere.

A differing type of explanation asserts that the important feature of the early stages of the interaction process is the individuals' formation of an idea of their relative abilities at the group task and of the relative likelihood that any given member will be able to make a useful contribution to the group effort. Once this determination has been made (and of course it can be made incorrectly if a member misperceives the usefulness or the quality of another's contributions), each group member will treat each other member unequally in terms of the components of interaction. He will distribute more action opportunities to those perceived to be likely to make useful suggestions, and he will be more likely to agree with them and to make positive unit evaluations of their performances.

The process may be explained, and also described more precisely, by introducing one final concept—that of a *performance expectation state*. At some point a series of negative or positive unit evaluations of performance outputs is believed to generalize into an overall ability evaluation for the individual making the performance outputs, or into an *expectation state* held for that individual. At some point the individual goes from saying "I think that's correct" to "I think he has high ability"; or he moves from saying "I think that's wrong" to "I think he has low ability at the task." This conception of overall ability *at the specific group task* is what is meant by an expectation state held for the performance of the individual. The statement "I think he has high ability" is significant because it carries with it the implication "I *expect* his future performances to be correct." Thus an expectation state is a cognitive state or belief about ability which is assumed to affect future responses of the individual holding the state.

Expectation states in this conceptualization function as theoretical constructs that are not directly observable but are theoretically linked to other concepts for which empirical indicators can be developed. In expectation states theory, the construct "expectation state" explains the observable features of interaction discussed earlier: once expectations exist and come to be held by the individual group members, all the theoretically important components of interaction will be distributed in accord with the expectations. The higher are the expectations held for the quality of an individual's performance (by both himself and others), the more action opportunities he will be given, the more likely he will be to accept a given action opportunity and to make a performance output, the more likely he will be to receive agreement and a positive unit evaluation for any given performance output, and the less likely he will be to accept influence in case of disagreement.

Expectations are spoken of as having both "self" and "other" components, and they are relative to any pair of individuals. Thus an individual can hold one of four possible combinations of self and other expectations: (1) (relatively) high expectations for his own performance and (relatively) low expectations for the performance of other; (2) low and high expectations for his own performance and that of the other, respectively; (3) high expectations both for himself and for other; or

(4) low expectations for both himself and other. The first two types of expectations are called *differentiated* expectations, since they are beliefs that differentiate individuals; the third and fourth types of expectations are *undifferentiated* expectations. For convenience, expectations are written with a plus or a minus sign representing the high and low states, and with expectations held by an individual for his own performance written first. Expectations of the four types thus are written: type 1, $(+ -)$; type 2, $(- +)$; type 3, $(+ +)$; type 4, $(- -)$.

Allowing expectations to take only two states, "relatively high" and "relatively low" means that to fully describe the structure of expectations in a group, it is necessary to follow the (admittedly laborious) procedure of taking all possible pairs of individuals. Even more significant, however, is the theory's emphasis on the *relativity* of expectations; it makes sense to speak of one individual's expectations for himself only *in relation to a specific other individual*. We refer to consequences of this relative conceptualization at several points in this work.

Experimental Tests

Expectation states theory has been developed in conjunction with a research program involving empirical tests in a social psychological laboratory. A task and an interaction situation are constructed and entered into by volunteer subjects whose behavior is predicted by the theory under consideration. Nearly all research in expectation states theory has employed a variant of one basic experiment and a single dependent variable—rejection of influence in case of disagreement—as the operational measure of expectation states. Using a standard experiment and the same measurement operation often means that the effects of new independent variables can be assessed by making direct comparisons of data across a large number of experiments, thus building cumulative information about the entire theory.

All expectation states theory experiments share the following features. In one or two preliminary phases, the attempt is made to produce a social situation described in the scope conditions of the theory: specifically, a problem-solving group composed of individuals possessing specific information about their task abilities. Either their abilities are unknown (which involves describing their task as requiring an entirely new ability just discovered and unrelated to other skills) or they are given specific expectations by performing the task and receiving public evaluations from the experimenter. The final phase of the experiment measures expectations held by subjects using the proportion of disagreements resolved in favor of self—a standard measure that is predicted to vary directly with the relative expectations held for self and other. . . .*

The first experiments were conducted to test the "basic expectation assumption": the claim that the pattern of relative expectation states held by subjects would determine important features of their subsequent interaction.[3] These experiments had two phases. In phase I, pairs of subjects judged a series of slides. After each trial, the experimenter told each subject publicly whether he was "correct." Scores assigned to subjects were either extremely high or extremely low, to produce all four patterns of relative self-other expectations. To produce (+ −) expectations, the subject was told that he was correct 17 times out of 20 and the other subject was correct 9 times out of 20. To produce (+ +) expectations, the subject was told that both he and the other subject were correct 17 times out of 20. For (− −) expectations, the subject was told that both he and the other subject got 9 right out of 20. To produce (− +) expectations, the subject was told that he got 9 out of 20 and the other subject got 17 out of 20.

After overall scores had been assigned to subjects and interpreted for them by reference to a table of "national standards," they began phase II, the data collection phase. Subjects were told they were to work together on a second set of slides. They would first make a private initial choice, next they would see their partner's initial choice, and then they would restudy the slide and make a final decision. Because communication was controlled, subjects could be told that their initial choices were in continual disagreement. Thus the experiment consisted of giving each subject an action opportunity, which he had to accept, and of the subject's making a performance output. The feedback of partner's choice constituted a disagreement, and the final choice constituted a disagreement resolution that had to include either acceptance or rejection of influence. Data were collected on the proportion of disagreements resolved in favor of self [called $P(s)$], which is predicted to vary directly with the *relative* self-other expectation states held. Thus the prediction for $P(s)$ from this experiment was: $(+ −) > (+ +) = (− −) > (− +)$. Table 7.1 shows that this prediction was confirmed.

Self-Expectation States and Self-Evaluations

The first crucial process in formation of expectation states is the distribution of unit evaluations for performance outputs. The greater the

*Editors' deletion.

Table 7.1   Rejection of Influence by Expectation States

Expectation State	P(s)
(+ −)	.76
(+ +)	.64
(− −)	.66
(− +)	.42

Adapted from S. F. Camilleri, J. Berger, and T. L. Conner, "A Formal Theory of Decision-Making," in *Sociological Theories in Progress*, ed. J. Berger, M. Zelditch Jr., and B. Anderson, vol. 2 (Boston: Houghton Mifflin, 1972), p. 34.

proportion of positive unit evaluations actor *A* makes of actor *B*'s performance, *if B* accepts these evaluations, the more likely *B* is to come to hold high expectations for his own performance. Therefore, the positive or negative unit evaluations that are distributed among members determine expectation states associated with members; hence they determine observable future interaction of the group.

Second, the agreement/disagreement process itself has an important effect on formation of expectation states: as we mentioned, only in cases of disagreement does the necessity arise for making differential evaluations of actors, thus for forming differentiated expectations. If undifferentiated expectations (either high or low) were formed for all actors in the group, there would be no unequal distribution of interaction components. But the unequal distribution does emerge regularly, and there have been both casual and systematic observations of considerable disagreement in problem-solving groups; therefore, it seems reasonable to attribute the differentiated expectations to the necessity of resolving disagreements between actors.

Of central interest here is the way in which individuals form expectations, both for their own performances and for those of others with whom they interact. Formation of performance expectations is in many ways equivalent to the processes referred to in other theoretical and research traditions as forming ability conceptions, the formation of self-expectations being analogous to the formation of a self-evaluation, and the formation of expectations for others being analogous to formation of opinions about others' abilities. . . .* [Elsewhere], we attempt to reformulate the ideas from the social self tradition into the concepts of expectation states theory, with the goal of extending expectation theory to explain many of the same kinds of situation that have been studied by

*Editors' deletion.

others in the social self tradition. Using this approach, it should be possible to extend the scope conditions and the determinacy of predictions that are possible from expectation states theory, and at the same time to provide precise answers to some of the major questions that have arisen in work conducted within the social self tradition.

It seems reasonable to suppose that if an actor in a problem-solving group is highly motivated to do the best possible job at the group's task, he will be actively "trying" to form performance expectations for himself and for the other members of the group. That is, if an individual is faced with a task that must be resolved through group effort, he will also decide, perhaps without ever making an explicit statement of the decision, that it is of central importance to determine whose suggestions and opinions are likely to be helpful and whose in all probability will not. In this sense, part of the "subtasks" an actor sets for himself is the deliberate assignment of expectation states to the various group members.

If an actor is concerned with forming useful expectations for himself and the others in the group, he has two basic sources of information available: he can evaluate his own and others' performances himself, or he can rely on the unit evaluations he sees others making. In open interaction in problem-solving groups, there are two types of condition that probably act to increase the reliance on others' unit evaluations. First, it seems reasonable to assume that it is more difficult to make an accurate evaluation of one's own performance outputs than it is of others' performances. Presumably, whenever an actor is willing to accept an action opportunity by making a performance output, he thinks he has a good idea. (Whether the idea sounds good when he says it is a different matter, but in any case, it seems safe to assume that in an open interaction situation, no actor would venture a performance output unless he thought it was a good one at the time.) Second, as the clarity of the evaluative standards diminishes, or as the difficulty of the task increases, it becomes more difficult for an actor to decide whether his own or others' performances are correct. By definition, a difficult task is one for which "right" or "good" performances are not clear, not easily recognizable; and this means that it is more difficult to have confidence either in a given performance output or in the accuracy of one's unit evaluation of a performance output. Also, there are tasks for which correct answers are not at all clear because many steps must be solved satisfactorily to reach the solution to the problem, and the evaluation of the unit steps to a solution is ambiguous. For such tasks, it is also difficult to be certain of one's own unit evaluations of performance outputs. In both these case types, we can suppose that if an actor feels unsure about the unit evaluations he would make of a given performance output, he will be more reliant on the unit evaluations he sees others making. In other words, both for determining an accurate self-expectation and for evaluating performance outputs made either by himself or by others when the task is very difficult or the evaluative standards are unclear, we would expect the opinions of others to become increasingly important determinants of the unit evaluations the actor makes of performances.

The idea of a self-expectation is more limited in several respects than the idea of a self-evaluation spoken of most frequently within the social self tradition. First, expectation states are situation specific: they are always discussed in terms of a single task and a single situation at a given time. By contrast, we sometimes speak of a self-evaluation in a manner suggesting that it is a transsituational phenomenon, possibly even an enduring idea that the individual carries around with him all his life. This difference between self-evaluation and expectation states is due largely to the more precise and explicit scope conditions of expectation theory. Although expectations may sometimes be transferred from one task situation to another, the conditions under which this is possible must be specified before such an assertion can be made.

The relationship between expectations a person holds for his own performance at a specific task and the idea of a self-evaluation may be either close or very distant, depending on the sense in which the latter term is intended. One simple relation may assert that an individual's overall level of self-evaluation is a weighted average of his task-specific performance expectations at various tasks in which he engages. Given such a relation, the relation of a specific task expectation to a self-evaluation would be analogous to the relation suggested earlier between self-evaluation and self-concept; the former is a part of, and consequently a partial determinant of, the latter. In both cases, the latter term is more general, but it usually is used with less precision than the former; people who speak of self-concept differ more widely in what they mean by that term than do people speaking of self-evaluation, and people speaking of self-evaluation have more dissimilar ideas in mind than do people speaking of self-expectations. This narrowing and refining process for terms that originally seemed to have a well-understood, shared meaning has clear precedents in fields characterized by cumulative foci of interest and theoretical development.

A second difference between self-evaluation and expectation states has already been noted: expectation states are relative to pairs of individuals, whereas self-evaluation seldom includes an explicit notion of relativity to a specific other. To specify the complete structure of expectations in a group, we would have to specify the relative expectation states existing for every possible pair of members. This would not be necessary for a nonrelative conception of self-evaluation. On close examination of the idea of a nonrelative self-evaluation, however, it becomes difficult to see how such an idea could have meaning or utility in a given social situation. To say that an individual has a high self-evaluation without specifying that the self-evaluation is high *relative* to the evaluation he holds of some other gives little useful information about his likely interaction patterns with others. Knowing that an individual possesses a high self-evaluation may tell something about his behavior when confronted with an other for whom he has no evaluative information, or about his behavior when confronted with an "average" other, *if* we are willing to make additional assumptions specifying how the individual of a high, medium, or low self-evaluation will treat an "average" other. Even then, however, it would not be possible to make predictions if we take a level of evaluation of the other as a given condition. This relative comparison is information that is used by individuals in governing their approach to others, and we therefore incorporate it in this version of expectation states theory.

We noted earlier that ideas in the social self tradition are not formulated as precisely as those in expectation states theory, nor do they enable such determinate predictions of behavior. On the other hand, questions addressed in the social self tradition have not previously been considered within the expectation theory point of view.[4] Basically, we need to know whose unit evaluations "matter" when an individual is forming performance expectations and whose evaluations are irrelevant. Put in terms of the social self tradition, this is a question of the characteristics that must be possessed by an effective source of performance expectations. The characteristics of a significant other have not been conceptualized clearly, explicitly, or concisely in the theory and research of the social self tradition; nor have the characteristics of an effective source of expectations been incorporated in expectation theory prior to this. . . .*

Notes

1. A more complete summary of this research program than the one given here is J. Berger, T. L. Conner, and M. H. Fisek, eds., *Expectation States Theory: A Theoretical Research Program* (Cambridge, Mass.: Winthrop, 1974).
2. See J. Berger, B. P. Cohen, and M. Zelditch Jr., "Status Characteristics and Social Interaction," *American Sociological Review* 37 (June 1972): 241–55.
3. These are reported in S. F. Camilleri, J. Berger, and T. L. Conner, "A

*Editors' deletion.

Formal Theory of Decision-Making," in *Sociological Theories in Progress*, ed. J. Berger, M. Zelditch Jr., and B. Anderson, vol. 2 (Boston: Houghton Mifflin, 1972), pp. 21–37.

4. An unpublished paper, "Status Conditions of Self-Evaluation," developed in the course of expectation states theory work in 1965. Although it was a definite stimulus to our ideas, the paper deals with issues different from those of interest to us here; primarily, it is concerned with social conditions making for a stable self-evaluation. Briefly, the theory presented argues that self-evaluation is produced originally by a *source*, an individual possessing both high status and socially defined right to confer honor or dishonor. However, self-evaluation is stable only if *peers* accept the conferred evaluation of the individual. (See J. Berger, M. Zelditch, B. Anderson, and B. P. Cohen, "Status Conditions of Self-Evaluation," Technical Report No. 27, Laboratory for Social Research, Stanford University, Stanford, Calif., for the most recent version of this paper.) We present our theory that status is not the major determinant of a potential source's effectiveness (except in the manner described in Chapter 6 [of *Sources of Self-Evaluation*]) and that social rights to evaluate are not crucial. In addition, we assert implicitly that an individual's level of self-evaluation tends to persist unless acted upon and that peer effects are negligible except when peers function as (theoretically defined) sources.

The Interpretive Approach to Social and Educational Research

Eric Bredo *and* Walter Feinberg

One of the fundamental assumptions of the positivistic approach is that observed facts, whether conceived of as "sense data" or as "observations of states of affairs" are independent of the law-like statement and theories that deductively explain them. This view has been subject to considerable criticism by those who question whether such an absolute distinction can be made between what we know and how we know it.[1] The problem is that the facts one arrives at are in part a function of the set of distinctions that one makes and the conventions governing the making of those distinctions. As Nelson Goodman puts it, "What you make of it depends upon how you take it."[2] This is not to suggest that facts are subjective or mere figments of the imagination, but it is to note that they are "theory laden." Facts are relative to the particular symbol scheme—the set of terms, concepts, labels—that is applied. As this set changes, so in general does what counts as an instance of a particular term. For example, what counts as "black" may vary depending upon whether we are contrasting it only with "white" or with an expanded set of terms including "dark grey," "light grey," and "white." The "facts" in this case are not entirely independent of the way of looking. A similar point applies at a higher level—namely, that what one observes depends upon the symbol system or set of symbol schemes being applied. By not acknowledging the way in which facts change with viewpoint or worldview, the positivist's assumption of the theory independence of facts implicitly takes one particular viewpoint or worldview as the only legitimate one.

A different way to make a similar point is by noting that a positivistic approach focuses only on the relationship between the individual scientist and the "external" reality and neglects the relationship between the scientist and the scientific community. However, it is the latter relation that creates and maintains authoritative standards as to what counts as an instance of a particular object or event. The standards adopted by the scientist for the correct usage or application of terms are a product of social interaction within the scientific community and typically involve competing conceptions, power struggles, and negotiations rather than unchanging consensus. As a result, the scientist's explanatory activities are not to be understood as merely the use of disembodied sets of conceptual distinctions, since learning to correctly use these distinctions involves learning how to become an interactionally competent member of the scientific community. When seen in this light, the rigid distinction between subject and object that the positivist accepts so easily becomes problematic. The way of looking at things—the scientist's subjectivity—is itself created as the scientist becomes socialized into the scientific community. The scientist is then no longer seen as totally detached from the "world" but as at least partially embedded within it.

The case of the social sciences and of educational research is even more complex, since here the scientist must be concerned with remaining true both to the standards of his or her discipline and its community and to those of the community that he or she studies. The social scientist's constructions are what Schutz terms "symbolizations of second degree"—that is, symbolizations of symbolizations. As Peter Winch observes in Chapter 8:

> The concepts and criteria according to which the sociologist judges that, in two situations, the same thing has happened, or the same action performed, must be understood *in relation to the rules governing sociological investigation*. But here we run against a difficulty; for whereas in the case of the natural scientist we have to deal with only one set of rules, namely those governing the scientist's investigation itself, here *what the sociologist is studying*, as well as his study of it, is a human activity and is therefore carried on according to rules. And it is these rules, rather than those which govern the sociologist's investigation, which specify what is to count as "doing the same kind of thing" in relation to that kind of activity.

For instance, what counts as "voting," "getting married," or even "committing suicide" depends upon social convention. It is possible to perform any of these things so wrongly that virtually all reasonably informed people would conclude that the claimed act did not "really" take place and that something else occurred. As Winch points out, it is precisely because it is possible to perform social practices wrongly that we can recognize them as rule-governed.

This is of considerable significance for the social scientist because if he or she is interested in studying such things as voting behavior, marriage, suicide, or any of a host of other social actions, the social conventions defining and making them what they are in the society being studied must be taken into account. Otherwise the social scientist will be in great danger of literally counting the wrong things. For example, in one culture a military charge in the face of obviously insuperable odds might be taken as a form of suicide, in another as merely a military charge. In one culture a person's relations to their mother's cousins might be conventionally defined very differently than their relations to their father's cousins, while in another they might be conceived of in equivalent terms. Or, in one culture the most significant indicator of one's political preferences might be whether one voted or not, not the candidate for whom one voted, while in another the selection from among a set of candidates would be the most significant act. In each of these cases the social scientist who imposes a set of conventions that does not take into account the conventions of those being studied is likely to count things as the "same" that are in fact "different" for those being studied. He or she will count "suicides" or "cousins" or "votes" in a way that makes no sense for those being studied. As a result people will behave differently in situations that the social scientist defines as the same and the generalizations that the social scientist attempts to establish will be systematically wrong.

The problem is that in counting or measuring behavior, the social scientist who imposes a conception of what he is studying that is insensitive to the conceptions of those being studied in effect rips the behavior from the social context which makes it what it is. Two apparently similar acts may have different meanings, depending on their contexts, just as two apparently different acts may have the same meanings. In other words, a social scientist who behaves in this way is like a person who, knowing a particular game well, insists on studying people playing every type of game as though they were playing the game the scientist knew. If the social scientist fails to recognize that his or her conventions of usage, like the rules of the game, may be different from those of the group being studied, then the very foundation of the study may be an initial and unrecognized breakdown in communication.

Levels of Meaning

Once it is recognized that social behavior is constituted by the social conventions adopted by those being studied, and hence that interpretation is often needed, it then becomes possible to distinguish different levels at which communication occurs among people and at which interpretive problems may arise. We will consider three such levels of communication and what is involved in understanding or misunderstanding at each level. Our discussion will begin with the more concrete and then move to the more abstract levels of communication.

When social behavior is considered in terms of a first level of communication, the problem consists of determining the institutional facts. For whom did a person vote? To whom did they get married? Did they submit an "A" or a "B" paper? Did they "speed" in the 35 mile per hour zone? As Searle suggests,[4]

> Such facts . . . I propose to call institutional facts. They are indeed facts; but their existence, unlike the existence of brute facts, presupposes the existence of certain human institutions. It is only given the institution of marriage that certain forms of behavior constitute Mr. Smith's marrying Miss Jones. Similarly, it is only given the institution of baseball that certain movements by certain men constitute the Dodgers' beating the Giants by 3 to 2 in eleven innings. And, at an even simpler level, it is only given the institution of money that I now have a five dollar bill in my hand. Take away the institution and all that I have is a piece of paper with various gray and green markings.

Much social science research consists of recording and interrelating facts of this type. One studies voting behavior, buying behavior, or teaching behavior and attempts to explain the pattern of relationships among the observed facts. These facts can often be rather routinely read off within an institutional context and thus appear unproblematic. However, it is well to remember that such facts simply would not exist without the institutions and practices which consitute them. There would be no "school achievement" without schools and no "voting behavior" without democratic institutions. As a result, these facts are not "brute" or natural facts, but rather are fundamentally dependent upon the conventions and distinctions of those being studied.

Taylor points out (in Chapter 9), that a tolerant brute data approach can study such facts, and indeed most social science research is tolerant in this way. What he means by this is that the social scientists tacitly accepts existing institutional definitions thereby implicitly recognizing that it is social rather than scientific convention that determines what counts as a given social act. However, the full implications of this tacit acceptance are often not recognized in social science research.

When misunderstanding occurs at this level it is a misunderstanding of what was literally done. It may be unclear whether someone voted "Republican" or "Democratic," whether they got an "A" or a "B," whether they were "speeding" or driving at a legal speed. The issue in each of these cases is which among some set of labels applies. In each case what makes the behavior a certain type of behavior depends upon the conventions of those being studied. Understanding what the behavior is, whether it is an "A" paper, or "speeding" involves interpretation, at least in questionable or novel cases, both by those classifying the behavior and by those who would understand the classification. Thus interpretation enters in to the determination of even the most literal social facts. Of course sometimes there are explicit rules as to what counts as a "vote," or as an "A" paper, or as "speeding," but these explicit rules depend upon operative social convention and are correct only when they do not violate those conventions. They are like various rules of thumb for spelling or grammar, such as "i before e except after c." Such rules are guidelines to help in spelling correctly, rather than being themselves definitive of correct spelling.

If social behavior is considered at a second level the issue is not so much what has literally been done, but rather how to take what has been done. Was it done playfully or seriously? Aggressively or passively? Affectionately or hostilely? The manner or style or way of doing something is one of the principal ways in which a social relationship is proposed between the actor and the person towards whom the behavior is directed. Depending on the implied relationship, different types of responses are suggested since different roles are implied for oneself. For instance, is the invitation to "Come up for a drink" a sexual invitation or merely a friendly one? What was said in such a case may be perfectly clear, even while the relational implications remain unclear.

Once one knows the role or capacity in which others are acting, and the counter-role in which they have placed you, then one knows the scheme in which to interpret their behavior. If you know that someone is acting as a "pitcher" to your "catcher" you have a framework in which to anticipate the kinds of things they are likely to do and the likely practical significance of their actions. If they are going through a wind up motion with their arm, you know that a ball is about to be thrown towards your glove. Of course you also know the scheme that they are likely to use in interpreting your behavior.

Misunderstandings at this level occur because one does not know where the other is "coming from," that is, one does not correctly recognize the role that is taken, or one interprets the role differently than they do. Taking the invitation for a drink the wrong way is an example. Misunderstandings of this type may occur even when the literal facts of what is done are clear to all parties. More commonly, however, a revision

119

in one's way of taking changes the "things" that are taken. Misunderstandings at this second level clearly involve a greater degree of uncertainty than misunderstandings that are limited to determining the correct "facts," since here it is not clear in what light the "facts" should be considered.

Understandings or misunderstandings at this level appear to be closely related to what Taylor refers to as "common meanings."

> By these I mean notions of what is significant that are not just shared in the sense that everyone has them, but are also common in the sense of being in the common reference world. . . . [T]he survival of a national identity as francophones is a common meaning of Quebeçois; for it is not just shared, and not just known to be shared, but its being a common aspiration is one of the common reference points of all debate, communication, and public life in the society.[5]

Other examples might include the usual stereotypes, that is, what is publicly thought of blacks and whites, men and women, or, at a lower level of analysis, the public conception of "C" stream or "EMH" pupils. As Taylor notes, such meanings form the basis for community, for a common indentify. On the other hand, disagreements over such meanings also form the basis for the most heated conflicts.

The important point, for our present purposes, is that such meanings are invisible using common brute data or empiricist approaches to social research. In the usual questionnaire study, for instance, one asks individuals about their beliefs, attitudes, or value and then finds out about collective facts by aggregating individual response. In this case social consensus is represented by the extent to which invididuals share the same beliefs, attitudes, or values. However, measures of "consensus" of this type do not get at common meanings. As Taylor puts it,[6]

> —[W]e cannot really understand this phenomenon (common meanings) through the usual definition of consensus as convergence of opinion and value. For what is meant here is something more than convergence. Convergence is what happens when our values are shared. But what is required for common meanings is that this shared value be part of the common world, that this sharing be shared.

To give another example, in meetings one often gets a "sense of the meeting," that is, a sense of the public positions of various people and the commitments that the group as a whole has made. These positions and commitments often do not correspond to the private beliefs of the individuals or to an average of the commitments that the individual members are willing to make. As a result, an individualistic approach simply fails to encompass these understandings at all.

To have either agreement or disagreement at the level of common meanings one must share a yet more fundamental set of assumptions. For instance, one cannot disagree over how first base should be played or over who should play it without first having a shared understanding of the rules of baseball. Nor can one have an argument without sharing the distinctions in terms of which the argument is couched. This brings to the third level of meaning or communication and to what Taylor terms "intersubjective" meanings.

Different cultures make different sorts of distinctions. They cut out different semantic spaces with their social vocabularies. The categorical distinctions in their language are constitutive of their institutions and practices, just as their institutions and practices are embodiments of their categorical distinctions. For instance, Taylor argues that much of our thinking in this culture starts from an image of an individualistic, bargaining, exchange society. For us, the individual with his or her preferences is primary, the elementary building block of all further social discussion. In contrast to this, an orthodox Marxist, for instance, would likely take the class structure as primary, and individual consciousness and preferences as derivative. What is "real" in this case is not the individual but the class structure. The two orientations are based on different ontological premises.

The types of semantic distinctions (or intersubjective meanings) that a people make are constitutive of their social institutions. Without our concepts of the individual, the market, and of social contracts, we could not have the kinds of institutions and social relationships that we have. On the other hand, these concepts are embodied in the concrete practices of buying and selling, hiring and firing. As people learn the institutional rules and intersubjective meanings they learn certain patterns of social relationship. For instance, the employer/employee relationship is a sort that would only be comprehensible in certain cultures or in certain historical periods. People are not born understanding how to take roles of this sort. The particular pattern that is learned then becomes constitutive of social reality for the individual. For instance, for some people or those from some cultures, what counts as "affection" or "distance," "friendship" or "hostility," will differ from what counts as these for others. As people show what counts for these various types of behavior for them, they communicate about their social reality to others.

In this discussion of intersubjective meanings, Taylor borrows the concept of a "constitutive" rule which Searle introduced and distinguished from a "regulative" rule. Constitutive rules are rules which create a new form of behavior, which make it what it is, rather than rules that tell one how to do existing forms of behavior. As Searle puts it,

> [W]e might say that regulative rules regulate antecedently or independently existing forms of behavior; for example, many rules of etiquette regulate inter-personal relationships which exist independently of the rules. But constitutive rules do not merely regulate, they create or define new forms of behavior. The rules of football or chess, for example, do not merely regulate playing football or chess, but as it were they create the very possibility of playing such games.[7]

Constitutive rules, like institutional rules, are rules that create certain classes of facts. They make certain types of behavior count as particular types of actions. The emphasis in an interpretive approach is on such constitutive rules rather than on regulative rules. In other words, the emphasis is on the rules or conventions that one must know to make sense of things, to understand what is going on, rather than merely on the rules that one must know to behave with propriety. To put this another way, the interpretive approach emphasizes a cognitive rather than a moral order. This distinction is useful for clarifying Winch's discussion of rules because Winch uses the term very broadly. The emphasis in his discussion should also be seen as on constitutive rather than regulative rules, although he does not make the distinction. Taylor attempts to broaden the notion of the constitutive by talking about constitutive distinctions, that is, linguistic distinctions which make certain types of institutions and practices what they are. This is what he means by "intersubjective meanings."

Intersubjective meanings and constitutive rules are not the property of individuals. They are not just assumptions or distinctions that happen to be held in the same way by many individuals. To quote Taylor again,

> It is not just that the people in our society all or mostly have a given set of ideas in their heads and subscribe to a given set of goals. The meanings and norms implicit in these practices are not just in the minds of the actors but are out there in the practices themselves, practices which cannot be conceived as a set of individual actions, but which are essentially modes of social relation, of mutual action. The actors may have all sorts of beliefs and attitudes which may be rightly thought of as their individual beliefs and attitudes, even if others share them. . . . They bring these with them into their negotiations and strive to satisfy them. But what they do not bring into the negotiations is the

set of ideas and norms constitutive of negotiations themselves. These must be the common property of the society before there can be any question of anyone entering into negotiation or not. Hence they are not subjective meanings, the property of one or some individuals, but rather intersubjective meanings, which are constitutive of the social matrix in which individuals find themselves and act.

When intersubjective meanings differ misunderstandings may be even more radical. For those coming from two quite different cultures the issue is not just disagreement over the attributes of one or another social identity, but rather a difference in the way in which the whole system of social identities is organized and conceptualized. There may be identities with analogous names, say "husband" and "wife" or "teacher" and "student" but if these take their place in a very different system of institutional rules they will mean very different things. It is like having two games, in both of which there are pieces labeled a "king" and a "queen", but imagine that the two games are chess and poker. In what sense do "king" and "queen" then mean the same thing? Yet people from different cultures are in the position of playing the analogous role in the wrong game. For instance, foreign students visiting here often adopt a student role in a way that differs from the way in which most American students adopt the role. Sometimes the teacher-student relation is handled in a very personalistic fashion, at other times in a quasi-feudal fashion. Both of these types of relationships differ from the American exchange view of the relation, and can create severe problems for the students when their behavior is misunderstood or fails to be efficacious.

When misunderstandings of this type occur, radical translation is necessary. One must understand the different form of life, the different pattern of social reality to which those of another culture have adapted in order to see how their behavior is rational or sensible. For instance, in some societies the best form of social security is to have many children so that they make take care of one in one's old age. Yet in our society, children are expensive to raise and often do not feel the same obligations to care for their elderly parents. Nonetheless, many immigrants continue to have large families because they are behaving in terms of the realities of the system from which they have come. Understanding these facts then makes their behavior comprehensible even though it may still not be adaptive in this context.

The most important point about intersubjective meanings, and constitutive rules, for the present discussion, however, is that both are a type of meaning that falls out of the grid of the usual empiricist approaches to

123

social research. Intersubjective meanings cannot be measured by aggregating data on individual beliefs or attitudes, or by standardized recording of individual behavior, just as the grammar of a language cannot be mapped by averaging individual usages.

Interpretation and Explanation

So far we have discussed three levels of meaning: factual, common, and intersubjective. We now need to look at how they are interrelated, how one develops an adequate interpretation using them, and how one explains social behavior in an interpretive mode.

The object of an interpretation is, as Taylor notes, to make something clear or coherent that was previously unclear or incoherent. In other words, in an interpretive approach one begins by assuming that communication is coherent, and then uses this assumption as a starting point for developing understanding. In a similar fashion, Quine suggests that one must begin by adopting the "principle of charity," which assumes that those one is attempting to understand are neither mad nor stupid but simply need to be considered more fully in their own terms.[9] Given this starting point the hermeneutic process is essentially circular, though not viciously so. The framework of the symbol scheme or system that is used helps generate a set of facts, and these facts are themselves used to test the adequacy of the framework. The process is much like that of a painter who, seeing an object in a certain way, attempts to paint what he sees. But what he paints on his canvas then modifies the way in which he sees the object, which leads him to correct his painting, and so on. As Taylor and Goodman suggest, there is no getting to the things themselves, independent of a symbol system, and if a person steadfastly refuses to enter into a system one cannot use that system to prove his or her view wrong. For example, one cannot prove to the steadfast paranoid that he or she is not really being victimized because all attempted proofs can be reinterpreted as elaborate attempts to harm, thereby confirming the initial presuppositions. Given appropriate conditions, however, the hermeneutic process may be continued until an adequately coherent interpretation is reached.

The relation between the three levels of meaning or communication just discussed is a metacommunicative one. That is, each higher level of communication comments on the preceeding level telling one how to take the prior level. It is all very well to know the literal "facts" of the case, but what if the telling of these facts was done in jest? One needs to know the style, form, or manner in which to construe these facts to know what to make of them. And this style or form may itself only make sense within a certain type of social system with a certain type of cultural pattern. Knowing the type of conceptual system being used tells one how to interpret the scheme being used, just as knowing the scheme helps one interpret the facts. When lower level meanings are ambiguous, they may be clarified by placing them in the contexts suggested by higher level messages. For instance, if you do not know what was literally done in some instance, you may be able to figure it out if you know the role that the person doing it was taking. On the other hand, lower level meanings are used to make higher level distinctions concrete, to suggest what they mean when applied to particular situations and contingencies. Thus communication at these various levels can be nicely supplementary.

When someone's behavior cannot be understood initially it can be explained or accounted for by placing it in the appropriate higher level context. If an ordinarily law-abiding person is suddenly seen going sixty-five miles per hour in a thirty-five mile per hour zone, this may be understood if one knows that she is rushing a seriously injured person to the hospital. She is behaving in a capacity of "friend," a role which is defined in terms of understood rules and motivations. On the other hand, the particular rules themselves might be incomprehensible. It might be unclear what it meant for someone to act out of "jealousy" for someone from a society in which mates were shared. In this case the particular rule would be explained by placing it in the context of a whole system of rules and form of life of a particular type. Needless to say, this conception of explanation, which works by placing the behavior in a broader context in which it makes sense, is quite different from the positivistic view of explanation as logical deducibility.

It is interesting that this view of the interpretive process suggested by Taylor differs, at least in emphasis, from the situation depicted by Winch. For Winch, coming to understand those one studies is primarily a matter of becoming resocialized. It involves learning an entirely new symbolic framework. For Taylor, however, understanding must always begin with one's initial symbol scheme or conceptual system and is always mediated by some such scheme or system. What is involved is a mediation or accommodation among frameworks. One must understand using some scheme but allow the scheme itself to be questioned or modified if it proves inadequate to understanding the range of meaningful behavior. Taylor's approach appears to be the more satisfactory because it is more consistent in its application of the principle that all perception and understanding uses a symbolic or conceptual scheme.

The criterion for a correct interpretation is not just logical consistency with any particular fact but rather overall "rightness."[10] Quine, for instance, suggests that knowledge may be thought of as like a spider web (or field) that must be anchored somewhere along some set of twigs (or boundary conditions) but whose overall configuration can vary. A successful web, like coherent knowledge, presumably has relatively low stresses—smaller inconsistencies—which are more or less evenly spread throughout. It is important to note here that while knowledge—like the web—is constructed, this does not mean that "anything goes." Rather, the knowledge is tested as vigorously as one may please. In fact, testing for logical truth may be *one* way of testing the rightness of an account. However, this conceptualization acknowledges the circular "chicken and egg" relationship between theories and facts (or between the overall configuration and the constraints of any particular strand). Acknowledging that any account must utilize some larger pattern and requires interpretation in terms of this pattern is thus not to suggest that an interpretive approach is less rigorous than a positivistic one, but rather that a positivistic one must also involve interpretation if it is ever to be applied to practical circumstances.

Criticisms of Interpretivism

Advocates of the interpretive approach have criticized positivism for, on the one hand, adopting an approach that is systematically blind to common and intersubjective meanings while, on the other, having an inadequate theory of knowledge that substitutes formal rationality for substantive rationality. Having given the interpretive approach its "inning," however, we should also consider some of the criticisms that have been launched against it. Two criticisms parallel those raised against positivism in Part Two: these concern, first, the interpretivist's assumptions about the relation between interpretive schemes and systems and that which is observed, and, second, the interpretive view of explanation. A third criticism concerns the relativism implicit in the interpretive position and the adequacy with which the interpretivist understands his or her own activity.

The core conviction with which the interpretivist approaches his or her "text" is that the text, or the subject, makes sense (e.g., Quine's principle of charity). This is rather like approaching a set of archaeological artifacts and assuming that they are all a product of the same era and hence of the same culture. Given this assumption, one then attempts to find a coherent pattern making sense of the disparate pieces. However, this approach would be wildly mistaken if applied to a set of artifacts that really came from different eras. In this case, the assumption of coherence would give one an erroneous interpretation by forcing one to fit together fragments that did not belong together. Those adopting a critical approach suggest that there may be systematic distortions in communication or in understanding such that seeing various levels of meaning as neatly supplementary levels of communication and metacommunication may be quite mistaken. Thus, before adopting an interpretive approach, one must determine, rather than assume, that the subject makes sense. By not taking this issue into account, the interpretive approach may be seen as incomplete and its adoption as, at least sometimes, producing incorrect interpretations.

A second objection concerns the interpretive approach to explanation. In general, those adopting an interpretive approach tend to avoid explaining the behavior of others, at least as positivists would understand such explanation. However, they do explain actions in the everyday sense of making others' reasons or motives comprehensible. In this sense people's actions are explained in terms of their reasons or motives, and in terms of the system of rules or conventions constituting these reasons or motives if not in terms of disembodied "forces" or "influences." The objection to this approach is that sometimes people act in a motivated way but are systematically unaware of their motives, and in fact think they are acting from other motives. The reasons that they give are not consistent with the motives that they are observed to have. In short, an interpretive approach to explaining action does not leave room for repression or false consciousness so at times results in incorrect explanation. To a certain extent, the interpretivist might respond that perhaps these are not real problems and need not be considered; they are the figments of some other theoretical approach. However, the interpretive criticism of positivism is itself very much along these lines—namely, that the positivistic version of social science is distorted because it mistakes the results of social interaction for the properties of individuals. As a result, if interpretivists want to retain their criticism of positivism it would seem that they must acknowledge the real possibility of systematically distorted understanding.

Both of these objections are then related to a third objection, which is to the relativism implicit in the interpretive approach. As Nelson Goodman[11] suggests, an approach that emphasizes the constituted nature of observation need not accept the notion that "anything goes" since accounts may be rigorously tested using prevailing standards of rationality. This does not really solve the problem, however, for if any intersubjective standards may be used to establish a domain of rigorous, rational discourse, we could have the absurdity of the inmates of a mental hospital establishing *their* standards of rationality and then proceeding to act in a rigorously rational (by this standard), if wildly maladaptive, fashion. Of course, as in the movie *King of Hearts*, in a crazy world it may be the inmates who are sane, but even this judgment relies on an understanding that some belief systems may be more adequate than others. The problem is that the interpretive approach does not allow for such judgments or for the existence of good reasons for switching from one set of conventions to another. Yet in personal and in institutional life we often find, even if only after the fact, that a change of approach dissolves old problems that seemed insoluble and allows for a freer range of adaptation. If this is true, then it suggests that there can be good reasons for preferring one approach over the other, and thus it argues for limitation on the interpretivist's relativistic position.

Notes

1. For example, W. V. Quine, *Word and Object* (Cambridge, Mass.: MIT Press, 1960).
2. Nelson Goodman, *Ways of Worldmaking* (Indianapolis: Hackett Press, 1978).
3. An important limitation of analogies such as this should be kept in mind, namely that the social rules we are discussing are in general not formal or explicit, unlike the rules of chess. These social rules are taught by example rather than by being explicitly stated.
4. John R. Searle, *Speech Acts: An Essay in the Philosophy of Language* (London, England: Cambridge University Press, 1969) p. 51.
5. Charles Taylor, "Interpretation and The Sciences of Man," *Review of Metaphysics* 25, 1971.
6. Ibid.
7. Searle, *Speech Acts*, p. 33.
8. Taylor, "Interpretation and The Sciences of Man."
9. Quine, *Word and Object*.
10. Goodman, *Ways of Worldmaking*, intro.
11. Ibid.

CHAPTER 7

The Way the World Is

Nelson Goodman

Introduction

Philosophers sometimes mistake features of discourse for features of the subject of discourse. We seldom conclude that the world consists of words just because a true description of it does, but we sometimes suppose that the structure of the world is the same as the structure of the description. This tendency may even reach the point of linguomorphism when we conceive the world as comprised of atomic objects corresponding to certain proper names, and of atomic facts corresponding to atomic sentences. A *reductio ad absurdum* blossoms when an occasional philosopher maintains that a simple description can be appropriate only if the world is simple; or asserts (and I have heard this said in all seriousness) that a coherent description will be a distortion unless the world happens to be coherent. According to this line of thinking, I suppose that before describing the world in English we ought to determine whether it is written in English, and that we ought to examine very carefully how the world is spelled.

Obviously enough the tongue, the spelling, the typography, the verbosity of a description reflect no parallel features in the world. Coherence is a characteristic of descriptions, not of the world: the significant question is not whether the world is coherent, but whether our account of it is. And what we call the simplicity of the world is merely the simplicity we are able to achieve in describing it.

But confusion of the sort I am speaking of is relatively transparent at the level of isolated sentences, and so relatively less dangerous than the error of supposing that the structure of a veridical systematic description mirrors forth the structure of the world. Since a system has basic or primitive terms or elements and a graded hierarchy built out of these, we easily come to suppose that the world must consist of corresponding atomic elements put together in similar fashion. No theory advocated in recent years by first-rate philosophers seems more obviously wrong than the picture theory of language. Yet we still find acute philosophers resorting under pressure to a notion of absolutely simple qualities or particles. And most of those who avoid thinking of the world as uniquely divisible into absolute elements still commonly suppose that *meanings* do resolve thus uniquely, and so accept the concealed absolutism involved in maintaining the distinction between analytic and synthetic propositions.

In this paper, however, I am not concerned with any of the more specific issues I have just touched upon, but with a more general question. I have been stressing the dangers of mistaking certain features of discourse for features of the world. This is a recurrent theme with me, but even this is not my main concern here. What I want to discuss is an uncomfortable feeling that comes upon me whenever I warn against the confusion in question. I can hear the anti-intellectualistic, the mystic— my arch enemy—saying something like this: "Yes, that's just what I've been telling you all along. All our descriptions are a sorry travesty. Science, language, perception, philosophy—none of these can ever be utterly faithful to the world as it is. All make abstractions or conventionalizations of one kind or another, all filter the world through the mind, through concepts, through the senses, through language; and all these filtering media in some way distort the world. It is not just that each gives only a partial truth, but that each introduces distortion of its own. We never achieve even in part a really faithful portrayal of the way the world is."

Here speaks the Bergsonian, the obscurantist, seemingly repeating my own words and asking, in effect, "What's the difference between us? Can't we be friends?" Before I am willing to admit that philosophy must make alliances that strange, I shall make a determined effort to formulate the difference between us. But I shall begin by discussing some preliminary, related questions.

The Way the World Is Given

Perhaps we can gain some light on the way the world is by examining the way it is given to us in experience. The question of the given has a slightly musty sound these days. Even hardened philosophers have become a little self-conscious about the futility of their debates over the given, and have the grace to rephrase the issue in terms of "ground-elements" or "protocol-sentences." But in one way or another we hear a good deal about getting down to the original, basic, bare elements from which all knowledge is manufactured. Knowing is tacitly conceived as a processing of raw material into a finished product; and an understanding of knowledge is thus supposed to require that we discover just what the raw material is.

Offhand, this seems easy enough. Carnap wanted the ground elements of his system in the *Aufbau* to be as nearly as possible epistemologically primary. In order to arrive at these, he says, we must leave out of ordinary experience all the results of any analysis to which we subject what we initially receive. This means leaving out all divisions along spatial or qualitative boundaries, so that our elements are big lumps, each containing everything in our experience at a given moment. But to say this is to make artificial temporal divisions; and the actual given, Carnap implies, consists not of these big lumps, but of one single stream.

But this way of arriving at the given assumes that the processes of knowing are all processes of analysis. Other philosophers have supposed rather that the processes are all processes of synthesis, and that the given therefore consists of minimal particles that have to be combined with one another in knowing. Still other thinkers hold that both these views are too extreme, and that the world is given in more familiar medium-size pieces, to which both analysis and synthesis are applied. Thus in views of the given we find duplicated the monism, atomism, and the intermediate pluralisms of metaphysics. But which view of the given is right?

Let's look at the question more closely. The several views do not differ about what is contained in the given, or what can be found there. A certain visual presentation, all agree, contains certain colors, places, designs, etc.; it contains the least perceptible particles and it is a whole. The question is not whether the given *is* a single undifferentiated lump or contains many tiny parts; it is a whole comprised of such parts. The issue is not *what* is given but *how* it is given. Is it *given* as a single whole or is it *given as* many small particles? This captures the precise issue—and at the same time discloses its emptiness. For I do not think any sense can be made of the phrase "*given as.*" That an experience is given as several parts surely does not mean that these parts are presented torn asunder; nor can it mean that these parts are partitioned off from one another by perceptible lines of demarcation. For if such lines of demarcation are there at all, they are there within the given, for any view of the given. The nearest we could come to finding any meaning to the question what the world is *given as* would be to say that this turns on whether the material in question is apprehended with a kind of feeling of wholeness or a feeling of broken-upness. To come that near to finding a meaning for "*given as*" is not to come near enough to count.

So I am afraid we can get no light on the way the world is by asking about the way it is given. For the question about the way it is given evaporates into thin air.

The Way the World Is to Be Seen

Perhaps we shall get further by asking how the world is best seen. If we can with some confidence grade ways of seeing or picturing the world according to their degrees of realism, of absence of distortion, of faithfulness in representing the way the world is, then surely by reading back from this we can learn a good deal about the way the world is.

We need consider our everyday ideas about pictures for only a moment to recognize this as an encouraging approach. For we rate pictures quite easily according to their approximate degree of realism. The most realistic picture is the one most like a color photograph; and pictures become progressively less realistic, and more conventionalized or abstract, as they depart from this standard. The way we see the world best, the nearest pictorial approach to the way the world is, is the way the camera sees it. This version of the whole matter is simple, straightforward, and quite generally held. But in philosophy as everywhere else, every silver lining has a big black cloud—and the view described has everything in its favor except that it is, I think, quite wrong.

If I take a photograph of a man with his feet towards me, the feet may come out as large as his torso. Is this the way I normally or properly see the man? If so, then why do we call such a photograph distorted? If not, then I can no longer claim to be taking the photographic view of the world as my standard of faithfulness.

The fact of the matter is that this "distorted" photograph calls our attention to something about seeing that we have ignored. Just in the way that it differs from an ordinary "realistic" picture, it reveals new facts and possibilities in visual experience. But the "distorted" photograph is a rather trivial example of something much more general and important. The "distortion" of the photograph is comparable to the distortion of new or unfamiliar styles of painting. Which is the more faithful portrait of a man—the one by Holbein or the one by Manet or the one by Sharaku or the one by Dürer or the one by Cézanne or the one by Picasso? Each different way of painting represents a different way of seeing; each makes its selection, its emphasis; each uses its own vocabulary of conventionalization. And we need only look hard at the pictures by any such artist to come to see the world in somewhat the same way. For seeing is an activity and the way we perform it depends in large part upon our training. I remember J. B. Neumann saying that once when he happened to see the faces of a movie audience in the reflected glare of the screen he first realized how an African sculptor saw faces. What we regard as the most realistic pictures are merely pictures of the sort that most of us, unfortunately, are brought up on. An African or a Japanese would make a quite different choice when asked to select the pictures that most closely depict what he sees. Indeed our resistance to new or exotic ways of painting stems from our normal lethargic resistance to retraining; and on the other hand the excitement lies in the acquisition of new skill. Thus the discovery of African art thrilled French painters and they learned from it new ways to see and paint. What is less often realized is that the discovery of European art is exciting to the African sculptor for the same reason; it shows him a new way of seeing, and he, too, modifies his work accordingly. Unfortunately, while European absorption of African style often results in an artistic advance, African adoption of European style almost always leads to artistic deterioration. But this is for incidental reasons. The first is that social deterioration of the African is usually simultaneous with the introduction of European art. The second reason is rather more intriguing: that while the French artist was influenced by the best of African art, the African was fed no doubt on calendar art and pin-up girls. Had he seen Greek and medieval sculpture instead, the results might have been radically different. But I am digressing.

The upshot of all this is that we cannot find out much about the way the world is by asking about the best or most faithful or most realistic way of seeing or picturing it. For the ways of seeing and picturing are many and various; some are strong, effective, useful, intriguing, or sensitive; others are weak, foolish, dull, banal, or blurred. But even if all the latter are excluded, still none of the rest can lay any good claim to be the way of seeing or picturing the world the way it is.

The Way the World Is to Be Described

We come now to a more familiar version of the question of the way the world is. How is the world to be described? Does what we call a true description faithfully depict the world?

Most of us have ringing in our ears Tarski's statement that "it is raining" is true if and only if it is raining, as well as his remark (I think erroneous, but that is beside the point here) that acceptance of this formula constitutes acceptance of a correspondence theory of truth. This way of putting the matter encourages a natural tendency to think of truth in terms of mirroring or faithful reproduction; and we have a slight shock whenever we happen to notice the obvious fact that the sentence "it is raining" is about as different as possible from the rainstorm. This disparity is of the same sort for a true as for a false description. Luckily, therefore, we need not here concern ourselves with the difficult technical matter of the nature of truth; we can confine our attention to admittedly true descriptions. What we must face is the fact that even the truest description comes nowhere near faithfully reproducing the way the world is.

A systematic description of the world, as I noted earlier, is even more vulnerable to this charge; for it has explicit primitives, routes of construction, etc., none of them features of the world described. Some philosophers contend, therefore, that if systematic descriptions introduce an arbitrary artificial order, then we should make our descriptions unsystematic to bring them more into accord with the world. Now the tacit assumption here is that the respects in which a description is unsatisfactory are *just those respects in which it falls short of being a faithful picture*; and the tacit *goal* is to achieve a description that as nearly as possible gives a living likeness. But the goal is a delusive one. For we have seen that even the most realistic way of picturing amounts merely to one kind of conventionalization. In painting, the selection, the emphasis, the conventions are different from but no less peculiar to the vehicle, and no less variable, than those of language. The idea of making verbal descriptions approximate pictorial depiction loses its point when we understand that to turn a description into the most faithful possible picture would amount to nothing more than exchanging some conventions for others.

Thus neither the way the world is given nor any way of seeing or picturing or describing it conveys to us the way the world is.

The Way the World Is

We come now to the question: what, then, is the way the world is? Am I still threatened with the friendship of my enemies? It looks very much that way, for I have just reached the mystic's conclusion that there is no representation of the way the world is. But if our accord seems on the surface to have been reinforced, a second look will show how it has been undermined, by what we have been saying.

The complaint that a given true description distorts or is unfaithful to the world has significance in terms of some grading of descriptions according to faithfulness, or in terms of a difference in degree of faithfulness between true descriptions and good pictures. But if we say that all true descriptions and good pictures are equally unfaithful, then in terms of what sample or standard of relative faithfulness are we speaking? We have no longer before us any clear notion of what faithfulness would be. Thus I reject the idea that there is some test of realism or faithfulness in addition to the tests of pictorial goodness and descriptive truth. There are very many different equally true descriptions of the world, and their truth is the only standard of their faithfulness. And when we say of them that they all involve conventionalizations, we are saying that no one of these different descriptions is *exclusively* true, since the others are also true. None of them tells us *the* way the world is, but each of them tells us *a* way the world is.

If I were asked what is *the food* for men, I should have to answer "none." For there are many foods. And if I am asked what is the way the world is, I must likewise answer, "none." For the world is many ways. The mystic holds that there is some way the world is and that this way is not captured by any description. For me, there is no way that is the way the world is; and so of course no description can capture it. But there are many ways the world is, and every true description captures one of them. The difference between my friend and me is, in sum, the enormous difference between absolutism and relativism.

Since the mystic is concerned with the way the world is and finds that the way cannot be expressed, his ultimate response to the question of the way the world is must be, as he recognizes, silence. Since I am concerned rather with the ways the world is, my response must be to construct one or many descriptions. The answer to the question "What is the way the world is? What are the ways the world is?" is not a shush, but a chatter.

Postscript

Near the beginning of this paper, I spoke of the obvious falsity of the picture theory of language. I declared rather smugly that a description does not picture what it describes, or even represent the structure of what it describes. The devastating charge against the picture theory of language was that a description cannot represent or mirror forth the world as it is. But we have since observed that a picture doesn't do this either. I began by dropping the picture theory of language and ended by adopting the language theory of pictures. I rejected the picture theory of language on the ground that the structure of a description does not conform to the structure of the world. But I then concluded that there is no such thing as the structure of the world for anything to conform or fail to conform to.

You might say that the picture theory of language is as false and as true as the picture theory of pictures; or in other words, that what is false is not the picture theory of language but a certain absolutistic notion concerning both pictures and language. Perhaps eventually I shall learn that what seems most obviously false sometimes isn't.

CHAPTER 8

The Idea of a Social Science

Peter Winch

The Investigation of Regularities

A follower of Mill might concede that explanations of human behavior must appeal not to casual generalizations about the individual's
reaction to his environment but to our knowledge of the institutions and
ways of life which give his acts that meaning. But he might argue that this
does not damage the fundamentals of Mill's thesis, since understanding
social institutions is still a matter of grasping empirical generalizations
which are logically on a footing with those of natural science. For an
institution is, after all, a certain kind of uniformity, and a uniformity can
only be grasped in a generalization. I shall now examine this argument.

A regularity or uniformity is the constant recurrence of the same kind
of event on the same kind of occasion; hence statements of uniformities
presuppose judgments of identity. But this takes us to an argument,
according to which criteria of identity are necessarily relative to some
rule: with the corollary that two events which count as qualitatively
similar from the point of view of one rule would count as different from
the point of view of another. So to investigate the type of regularity
studied in a given kind of enquiry is to examine the nature of the rule
according to which judgments of identity are made in that enquiry. Such
judgments are intelligible only relatively to a given mode of human
behavior, governed by its own rules.[1] In a physical science the relevant
rules are those governing the procedures of investigators in the science in
question. For instance, someone with no understanding of the problems
and procedures of nuclear physics would gain nothing from being present
at an experiment like the Cockcroft-Walton bombardment of lithium by

Reprinted in abridged form from pages 83–90, 111–116, and 123–136 of *The Idea of a
Social Science and Its Relation to Philosophy* by Peter Winch (London: Routledge and
Kegan Paul, 1958). Reprinted by permission of Humanities Press Inc., New Jersey 07716,
and of Routledge and Kegan Paul Ltd.

hydrogen; indeed even the description of what he saw in those terms would be unintelligible to him, since the term "bombardment" does not carry the sense in the context of the nuclear physicists' activities that it carries elsewhere. To understand what was going on in this experiment he would have to learn the nature of what nuclear physicists do; and this would include learning the criteria according to which they make judgments of identity.

Those rules, like all others, rest on a social context of common activity. So to understand the activities of an individual scientific investigator we must take account of two sets of relations: first, his relation to the phenomena which he investigates; second, his relation to his fellow-scientists. Both of these are essential to the sense of saying that he is "detecting regularities" or "discovering uniformities"; but writers on scientific "methodology" too often concentrate on the first and overlook the importance of the second. That they must belong to different types is evident from the following considerations.—The phenomena being investigated present themselves to the scientist as an *object* of study; he observes them and notices certain facts about them. But to say of a man that he does this presupposes that he already has a mode of communication in the use of which rules are already being observed. For to notice something is to identify relevant characteristics, which means that the noticer must have some *concept* of such characteristics; this is possible only if he is able to use some symbol according to a rule which makes it refer to those characteristics. So we come back to his relation to his fellow-scientists, in which context alone he can be spoken of as following such a rule. Hence the relation between N and his fellows, in virtue of which we say that N is folloing the same rule as they, cannot be simply a relation of observation: it cannot consist in the fact that N has noticed how his fellows behave and has decided to take that as a norm for his own behavior. For this would presuppose that we could give some account of the notion of "noticing how his fellows behave" *apart from* the relation between N and his fellows which we are trying to specify; and that, as has been shown, is untrue. To quote Rush Rhees: "We see that we understand one another, without noticing whether our reactions tally or not. *Because* we agree in our reactions, it is possible for me to tell you something, and it is possible for you to teach me something."[2]

In the course of his investigation the scientist applies and develops the concepts germane to his particular field of study. This application and modification are "influenced" both by the phenomena *to* which they are applied and also by the fellow-workers *in participation with* whom they are applied. But the two kinds of "influence" are different. Whereas it is on the basis of his observation of the phenomena (in the course of his experiments) that he develops his concepts as he does, he is able to do this only in virtue of his participation in an established form of activity with his fellow-scientists. When I speak of "participation" here I do not necessarily imply any direct physical conjunction or even any direct communication between fellow-participants. What is important is that they are all taking part in the same general kind of activity, which they have all *learned* in similar ways; that they are, therefore, *capable* of communicating with each other about what they are doing; that what any one of them is doing is in principle intelligible to the others.

Understanding Social Institutions

Mill's view is that understanding a social institution consists in observing regularities in the behavior of its participants and expressing these regularities in the form of generalizations. Now if the position of the sociological investigator (in a broad sense) can be regarded as comparable, in its main logical outlines, with that of the natural scientist, the following must be the case. The concepts and criteria according to which the sociologist judges that, in two situations, the same thing has happened, or same action performed, must be understood *in relation to the rules governing sociological investigation*. But here we run against a difficulty; for whereas in the case of the natural scientist we have to deal with only one set of rules, namely those governing the scientist's investigation itself, here *what the sociologist is studying*, as well as his study of it, is a human activity and is therefore carried on according to rules. And it is these rules, rather than those which govern the sociologist's investigation, which specify what is to count as "doing the same kind of thing" in relation to that kind of activity.

An example may make this clearer. Consider the parable of the Pharisee and the Publican (Luke, 18: 9). Was the Pharisee who said "God, I thank Thee that I am not as other men are" doing the same kind of thing as the Publican who prayed "God be merciful unto me a sinner"? To answer this one would have to start by considering what is involved in the idea of prayer; and that is a *religious* question. In other words, the appropriate criteria for deciding whether the actions of these two men were of the same kind or not belong to religion itself. Thus the sociologist of religion will be confronted with an answer to the question: Do these two acts belong to the same kind of activity? and this answer is given according to criteria which are not taken from sociology, but from religion itself.

But if the judgments of identity—and hence the generalizations—of the sociologist of religion rest on criteria taken from religion, then his relation to the performers of religious activity cannot be just that of observer to observed. It must rather be analogous to the participation of the natural scientist with his fellow-workers in the activities of scientific investigation. Putting the point generally, even if it is legitimate to speak of one's understanding of a mode of social activity as consisting in a knowledge of regularities, the nature of this knowledge must be very different from the nature of knowledge of physical regularities. So it is quite mistaken in principle to compare the activity of a student of a form of social behavior with that, of, say, an engineer studying the workings of a machine; and one does not advance matters by saying, with Mill, that the machine in question is of course immensely more complicated than any physical machine. If we are going to compare the social student to an engineer, we shall do better to compare him to an apprentice engineer who is studying what engineering—that is, the activity of engineering—is all about. His understanding of social phenomena is more like the engineer's understanding of his colleagues' activities than it is like the engineer's understanding of the mechanical systems which he studies.

This point is reflected in such common-sense considerations as the following: that a historian or sociologist of religion must himself have some religious feeling if he is to make sense of the religious movement he is studying and understand the considerations which govern the lives of its participants. A historian of art must have some aesthetic sense if he is to understand the problems confronting the artists of his period; and without this he will have left out of his account precisely what would have made it a history or *art*, as opposed to a rather puzzling external account of certain motions which certain people have been perceived to go through.

I do not wish to maintain that we must stop at the unreflective kind of understanding of which I gave as an instance the engineer's understanding of the activities of his colleagues. But I do want to say that any more reflective understanding must necessarily presuppose, if it is to count as genuine understanding at all, the participant's unreflective understanding. And this in itself makes it misleading to compare it with the natural scientist's understanding of his scientific data. Similarly, although the reflective student of society, or of a particular mode of social life, may find it necessary to use concepts which are not taken from the forms of activity which he is investigating, but which are taken rather from the context of his own investigation, still these technical concepts of his will imply a previous understanding of those other concepts which belong to the activities under investigation.

For example, liquidity preference is a technical concept of economics: it is not generally used by business men in the conduct of their affairs but by the economist who wishes to *explain* the nature and consequences of certain kinds of business behavior. But it is logically tied to concepts which do enter into business activity, for its use by the economist presupposes his understanding of what it is to conduct a business, which in turn involves an understanding of such business concepts as money, profit, cost, risk, etc. It is only the relation between his account and these concepts which makes it an account of economic activity as opposed, say, to a piece of theology.

Again, a psychoanalyst may explain a patient's neurotic behavior in terms of factors unknown to the patient and of concepts which would be unintelligible to him. Let us suppose that the psychoanalyst's explanation refers to events in the patient's early childhood. Well, the description of those events will presuppose an understanding of the concepts in terms of which family life, for example, is carried on in our society; for these will have entered, however rudimentarily, into the relations between the child and his family. A psychoanalyst who wished to give an account of the aetiology of neuroses amongst, say, the Trobriand Islanders, could not just apply without further reflection the concepts developed by Freud for situations arising in our own society. He would have first to investigate such things as the idea of fatherhood amongst the islanders and take into account any relevant aspects in which their idea differed from that current in his how society. And it is almost inevitable that such an investigation would lead to some modification in the psychological theory appropriate for explaining neurotic behavior in this new situaiton.

These considerations also provide some justification for the sort of historical skepticism which that underestimated philosopher, R. G. Collingwood, expresses in *The Idea of History*.[3] Although they need not be brought to the foregound where one is dealing with situations in one's own society or in societies with whose life one is reasonably familiar, the practical implications become pressing when the object of study is a society which is culturally remote from that of the investigator.

Max Weber: *Verstehen* and Causal Explanation

It is Max Weber who has said most about the peculiar sense which the world "understand" bears when applied to models of social life. The first issue on which I mean to concentrate is Weber's account of the relation between acquiring an "interpretative understanding" (*deutend verstehen*) of the meaning (*Sinn*) of a piece of behavior and providing a causal explanation (*Kausal erklären*) of what brought the behavior in question about and what its consequences are.

Now Weber never gives a clear account of the *logical* character of interpretative understanding. He speaks of it much of the time as if it were simply a psychological technique: a matter of putting oneself in the other fellow's position. This has led many writers to allege that Weber confuses what is simply a technique for framing hypotheses with the logical character of the evidence for such hypotheses. Thus Popper argues that although we may use our knowledge of our own mental processes in order to frame hypotheses about the similar processes of other people, "these hypotheses must be tested, they must be submitted to the method of selection by elimination. (By their intuition, some people are prevented from even imagining that anybody can possibly dislike chocolate.)"[4]

Nevertheless, however applicable such criticisms may be to Weber's vulgarizers, they cannot justly be used against his own views, for he is very insistent that mere "intuition" is not enough and must be tested by careful observation. However, what I think can be said against Weber is that he gives a wrong account of the process of checking the validity of suggested sociological interpretations. But the correction of Weber takes us farther away from, rather than closer to, the account which Popper, Ginsberg, and the many who think like them, would like to substitute.

Weber says:

> Every interpretation aims at self-evidence or immediate plausibility (*Evidenz*). But an interpretation which makes the meaning of a piece of behaviour as self-evidently obvious as you like cannot claim *just* on that account to be the causally *valid* interpretation as well. In itself it is nothing more than a particularly plausible hypothesis.[5]

He goes on to say that the appropriate way to verify such an hypothesis is to establish statistical laws based on observation of what happens. In this way he arrives at the conception of a sociological law as "a statistical regularity which corresponds to an intelligible intended meaning." Weber is clearly right in pointing out that the obvious interpretation need not be the right one. R. S. Lynd's interpretation of West Indian voodoo magic as "a system of imputedly true and reliable causal sequences" is a case in point;[6] and there is a plethora of similar examples in Frazer's *The*

Golden Bough. But I want to question Weber's implied suggestion that *Verstehen* is something which is logically incomplete and needs supplementing by a different method altogether, namely the collection of statistics. Against this, I want to insist that if a proffered interpretation is wrong, statistics, though they may suggest that that is so, are not the decisive and ultimate court of appeal for the validity of sociological interpretations in the way Weber suggests. What is then needed is a better interpretation, not something different in kind. The compatibility of an interpretation with the statistics does not prove its validity. Someone who interprets a tribe's magical rites as a form of misplaced scientific activity will not be corrected by statistics about what members of that tribe are likely to do on various kinds of occasion (though this might form *part* of the argument); what is ultimately required is a *philosophical* argument like, e.g., Collingwood's in *The Principles of Art*.[7] For a mistaken interpretation of a form of social activity is closely akin to the type of mistake dealt with in philosophy.

Wittgenstein says somewhere that when we get into philosophical difficulties over the use of some of the concepts of our language, we are like savages confronted with something from an alien culture. I am simply indicating a corollary of this: that sociologists who misinterpret an alien culture are like philosophers getting into difficulties over the use of their own concepts. There will be differences of course. The philosopher's difficulty is usually with something with which he is perfectly familiar but which he is for the moment failing to see in its proper perspective. The sociologist's difficulty will often be over something with which he is not at all familiar; he may have no suitable perspective to apply. This may sometimes make his task more difficult than the philosopher's, and it may also sometimes make it easier. But the analogy between their problems should be plain.

Some of Wittgenstein's procedures in his philosophical elucidations reinforce this point. He is prone to draw our attention to certain features of our own concepts by comparing them with those of an imaginary society, in which our own familiar ways of thinking are subtly distorted. For instance, he asks us to suppose that such a society sold wood in the following way: They "piled the timber in heaps of arbitrary, varying height and then sold it at a price proportionate to the area covered by the piles. And what if they even justified this with the words: 'Of course, if you buy more timber, you must pay more'?"[8] The important question for us is: in what circumstances could one say that one had *understood* this sort of behavior? As I have indicated, Weber often speaks as if the ultimate test were our ability to formulate statistical laws which would enable us to *predict* with fair accuracy what people would be likely to do in given circumstances. In line with this in his attempt to define a "social role" in terms of the probability (*Chance*) of actions of a certain sort being performed in given circumstances. But with Wittgenstein's example we might well be able to make predictions of great accuracy in this way and still not be able to claim any real understanding of what those people were doing. The difference is precisely analogous to that between being able to formulate statistical laws about the likely occurrences of words in a language and being able to understand what was being *said* by someone who spoke the language. The latter can never be reduced to the former; a man who understands Chinese is not a man who has a firm grasp of the statistical probabilities for the occurrence of the various words in the Chinese language. Indeed, he could have that without knowing that he was dealing with a language at all; and anyway, the knowledge that he was dealing with a language is not itself something that could be formulated statistically. "Understanding," in situations like this, is grasping the *point* or *meaning* of what is being done or said. This is a notion far removed from the world of statistics and causal laws: it is closer to the realm of discourse and to the internal relations that link the parts of a realm of discourse. The notion of meaning should be carefully distinguished from that of *function*, in its quasi-causal sense.

To give an account of the meaning of a word is to describe how it is used; and to describe how it is used is to describe the social intercourse into which it enters.

If social relations between men exist only in and through their ideas, then, since the relationships between ideas are internal relations, social relations must be a species of internal relation too. This brings me into conflict with a widely accepted principle of Hume's: "There is no object, which implies the existence of any other if we consider these objects in themselves, and never look beyond the ideas which we form of them." There is no doubt that Hume intended this to apply to human actions and social life as well as to the phenomena of nature. Now to start with, Hume's principle is not unqualifiedly true even of our knowledge of natural phenomena. If I hear a sound and recognize it as a clap of thunder, I already commit myself to believing in the occurrence of a number of other events—e.g., electrical discharges in the atmosphere—even in calling what I have heard "thunder." That is, from "the idea which I have formed" of what I heard I *can* legitimately infer "the existence of other objects." If I subsequently find that there was no electrical storm in the vicinity at the time I heard the sound I shall have to retract my claim that what I heard was thunder. To use a phrase of Gilbert

Ryle's, the word "thunder" is theory-impregnated; statements affirming the occurrence of thunder have logical connections with statements affirming the occurrence of other events. To say this, of course, is not to reintroduce any mysterious causal nexus *in rebus*, of a sort to which Hume could legitimately object. It is simply to point out that Hume overlooked the fact that "the idea we form of an object" does not just consist of elements drawn from our observation of that object in isolation, but includes the idea of connection between it and other objects. (And one could scarcely form a conception of a language in which this was not so.)

Consider now a very simple paradigm case of a relation between actions in a human society: that between an act of command and an act of obedience to that command. A sergeant calls, "Eyes right!" and his men all turn their eyes to the right. Now, in describing the men's act in terms of the notion of obedience to a command, one is of course commiting oneself to saying that a command has been issued. So far the situation looks precisely parallel to the relation between thunder and electrical storms. But now one needs to draw a distinction. An event's character as an act of obedience is *intrinsic* to it in a way which is not true of an event's character as a clap of thunder, and this is in general true of human acts as opposed to natural events. In the case of the latter, although human beings can think of the occurrences in question only in terms of the concepts they do in fact have of them, yet the events themselves have an existence independent of those concepts. There existed electrical storms and thunder long before there were human beings to form concepts of them or establish that there was any connection between them. But it does not make sense to suppose that human beings might have been issuing commands and obeying them before they came to form the concept of command and obedience. For their performance of such acts is itself the chief manifestation of their possession of those concepts. An act of obedience itself contains, as an essential element, a recognition of what went before as an order. But it would of course be senseless to suppose that a clap of thunder contained any recognition of what went before as an electrical storm; it is our recognition of the sound, rather than the sound itself, which contains that recognition of what went before.

Part of the opposition one feels to the idea that men can be related to each other through their actions in at all the same kind of way as propositions can be related to each other is probably due to an inadequate conception of what logical relations between propositions themselves are. One is inclined to think of the laws of logic as forming a *given* rigid structure to which men try, with greater or less (but never complete) success, to make what they say in their actual linguistic and social intercourse conform. One thinks of propositions as something ethereal, which just because of their ethereal, non-physical nature, can fit together more tightly than can be conceived in the case of anything so grossly material as flesh-and-blood men and their actions. In a sense one is right in this; for to treat of logical relations in a formal systematic way is to think at a very high level of abstraction, at which all the anomalies, imperfections, and crudities which characterize men's actual intercourse with each other in society have been removed. But, like any abstraction not recognized as such, this can be misleading. It may make one forget that it is only from their roots in this actual flesh-and-blood intercourse that those formal systems draw such life as they have; for the whole idea of a logical relation is only possible by virtue of the sort of agreement between men and their actions which is discussed by Wittgenstein in the *Philosophical Investigations*. Collingood's remark on formal grammar is apposite: "I likened the grammarian to a butcher; but if so, he is a butcher of a curious kind. Travellers say that certain African people will cut a steak from a living animal and cook it for dinner, the animal being not much the worse. This may serve to amend the original comparison."[9] It will seem less strange that social relations should be like logical relations between propositions once it is seen that logical relations between propositions themselves depend on social relations between men.

What I have been saying conflicts, of course, with Karl Popper's "postulate of methodological individualism" and appears to commit the sin of what he calls "methodological essentialism." Popper maintains that the theories of the social sciences apply to theoretical constructions or models which are formulated by the investigator in order to explain certain experiences, a method which he explicitly compares to the construction of theoretical models in the natural sciences.

> This use of models explains and at the same time destroys the claims of methodological essentialism. . . . It explains them, for the model is of an abstract or theoretical character, and we are liable to believe that we see it, either within or behind the changing observable events, as a kind of observable ghost or essence. And it destroys them because our task is to analyze our sociological models carefully in descriptive or nominalist terms, viz. *in terms of individuals*, their attitudes, expectations, relations, etc.—a postulate which may be called "methodological individualism."[10]

Popper's statement that social institutions are just explanatory models introduced by the social scientist for his own purposes is palpably untrue. The ways of thinking embodied in institutions govern the way the members of the societies studied by the social scientist behave. The idea of war, for instance, which is one of Popper's examples, was not simply invented by people who wanted to *explain* what happens when societies come into armed conflict. It is an idea which provides the criteria of what is appropriate in the behavior of members of the conflicting societies. Because my country is at war there are certain things which I must and certain things which I must not do. My behavior is governed, one could say, by my concept of myself as a member of a belligerent country. The concept of war belongs *essentially* to my behavior. But the concept of gravity does not belong essentially to the behavior of a falling apple in the same way: it belongs rather to the physicist's *explanation* of the apple's behavior. To recognize this has, *pace* Popper, nothing to do with a belief in ghosts behind the phenomena. Further, it is impossible to go far in specifying the attitudes, expectations, and relations of individuals without referring to concepts which enter into those attitudes, etc., and the meaning of which certainly cannot be explained in terms of the actions of any individual persons.[11]

Discursive and Non-Discursive "Ideas"

In the course of this argument I have linked the assertion that social relations are internal with the assertion that men's mutual interaction "embodies ideas," suggesting that social interaction can more profitably be compared to the exchange of ideas in a conversation than to the interaction of forces in a physical system. This may seem to put me in danger of over-intellectualizing social life, especially since the examples I have so far discussed have all been examples of behavior which expresses *discursive* ideas, that is, ideas which also have a straightforward linguistic expression. It is because the use of language is so intimately, so inseparably, bound up with the other, non-linguistic, activities which men perform, that it is possible to speak of their non-linguistic behavior also as expressing discursive ideas. Apart from the examples of this which I have already given in other connections, one needs only to recall the enormous extent to which the learning of any characteristically human activity normally involves talking as well: in connection, e.g., with discussions of alternative ways of doing things, the inculcation of standards of good work, the giving of reasons, and so on. But there is no sharp break between behavior which expresses discursive ideas and that which does not; and that which does not is sufficiently like that which does to make it necessary to regard it as analogous to the other. So, even where it would

147

be unnatural to say that a given kind of social relation expresses any ideas of a discursive nature, still it is closer to that general category than it is to that of the interaction of physical forces.

Consider the following scene from the film *Shane*. A lone horseman arrives at the isolated homestead of a small farmer on the American prairies who is suffering from the depredations of the rising class of big cattleowners. Although they hardly exchange a word, a bond of sympathy springs up between the stranger and the homesteader. The stranger silently joins the other in uprooting, with great effort, the stump of a tree in the yard; in pausing for breath, they happen to catch each other's eye and smile shyly at each other. Now any explicit account that one tried to give of the kind of understanding that had sprung up between these two, and which was expressed in that glance, would no doubt be very complicated and inadequate. We understand it, however, as we may understand the meaning of a pregnant pause (consider what it is that makes a pause *pregnant*), or as we may understand the meaning of a gesture that completes a statement. "There is a story that Buddha once, at the climax of a philosophical discussion . . . took a flower in his hand, and looked at it; one of his disciples smiled, and the master said to him, 'You have understood me.' "[12] And what I want to insist on is that, just as in a conversation the point of a remark (or of a pause) depends on its internal relation to what has gone before, so in the scene from the film the interchange of glances derives its full meaning from its internal relation to the situation in which it occurs: the loneliness, the threat of danger, the sharing of a common life in difficult circumstances, the satisfaction in physical effort, and so on.

It may be thought that there are certain kinds of social relation, particularly important for sociology and history, of which the foregoing considerations are not true: as for instance wars in which the issue between the combatants is not even remotely of an intellectual nature (as one might say, e.g., that the crusades were), but purely a struggle for physical survival as in a war between hunger migrants and the possessors of the land on which they are encroaching.[13] But even here, although the issue is in a sense a purely material one, the form which the struggle takes will still involve internal relations in a sense which will not apply to, say, a fight between two wild animals over a piece of meat. For the belligerents are *societies* in which much goes on besides eating, seeking shelter, and reproducing; in which life is carried on in terms of symbolic ideas which express certain attitudes as between man and man. These symbolic relationships, incidentally, will affect the character even of those basic "biological" activities: one does not throw much light on the particular form which the latter may take in a given society by speaking of them in Malinowski's neo-Marxist terminology as performing the "function" of providing for the satisfaction of the basic biological needs. Now of course, "out-group attitudes" between the members of my hypothetical warring societies will not be the same as "in-group attitudes." Nevertheless, the fact that the enemies are *men*, with their own ideas and institutions, and with whom it would be possible to communicate, will affect the attitudes of members of the other society to them—even if its only effect is to make them the more ferocious. Human war, like all other human activities, is governed by conventions; and where one is dealing with conventions, one is dealing with internal relations.

The Social Sciences and History

This view of the matter may make possible a new appreciation of Collingwood's conception of all human history as the history of thought. That is no doubt an exaggeration and the notion that the task of the historian is to re-think the thoughts of the historical participants is to some extent an intellectualistic distortion. But Collingwood is right if he is taken to mean that the way to understand events in human history, even those which cannot naturally be represented as conflicts between or developments of discursive ideas, is more closely analogous to the way in which we understand expressions of ideas than it is to the way we understand physical processes.

There is a certain respect, indeed, in which Collingwood pays insufficient attention to the manner in which a way of thinking and the historical situation to which it belongs form one indivisible whole. He says that the aim of the historian is to think the very same thoughts as were once thought, just as they were thought at the historical moment in question.[14] But though extinct ways of thinking may, in a sense, be recaptured by the historian, the way in which the historian thinks them will be colored by the fact that he has had to employ historiographical methods to recapture them. The medieval knight did not have to use those methods in order to view his lady in terms of the notions of courtly love: he just thought of her in those terms. Historical research may enable me to achieve some understanding of what was involved in this way of thinking, but that will not make it open to me to think of *my* lady in those terms. I should always be conscious that this was an anachronism, which means, of course, that I should not be thinking of her in just the same terms as did the knight of his lady. And naturally, it is even more impossible for me to think of *his* lady as he did.

Nevertheless, Collingwood's view is nearer the truth than is that most favored in empiricist methodologies of the social sciences, which runs somewhat as follows—on the one side we have human history which is a kind of repository of data. The historian unearths these data and presents them to his more theoretically minded colleagues who then produce scientific generalizations and theories establishing connections between one kind of social situation and another. These theories can then be applied to history itself in order to enhance our understanding of the ways in which its episodes are mutually connected. I have tried to show how this involves minimizing the importance of ideas in human history, since ideas and theories are constantly developing and changing, and since each system of ideas, its component elements being interrelated internally, has to be understood in and for itself, the combined result of which is to make systems of ideas a very unsuitable subject for broad generalizations. I have also tried to show that social relations really exist only in and through the ideas which are current in society, and, or, alternatively, that social relations fall into the same logical category as do relations between ideas. It follows that social relations must be an equally unsuitable subject for generalizations and theories of the scientific sort to be formulated about them. Historical explanation is not the application of generalizations and theories to particular instances: it is the tracing of internal relations. It is like applying one's knowledge of a language in order to understand a conversation rather than like applying one's knowledge of the laws of mechanics to understand the workings of a watch. Nonlinguistic behavior, for example, has an "idiom" in the same kind of way as has a language. In the same kind of way as it can be difficult to recapture the idiom of Greek thought in a translation into modern English of a Platonic dialogue, so it can be misleading to think of the behavior of people in remote societies in terms of the demeanor to which we are accustomed in our own society. Think of the uneasy feeling one often has about the authenticity of "racy" historical evocations like those in some of Robert Graves's novels: this has nothing to do with doubts about a writer's accuracy in matters of external detail.

The relation between sociological theories and historical narrative is less like the relation between scientific laws and the reports of experiments or observations than it is like that between theories of logic and arguments in particular languages. Consider for instance the explanation of a chemical reaction in terms of a theory about molecular structure and valency: here the theory *establishes* a connection between what happened at one moment when the two chemicals were brought together and what happened at a subsequent moment. It is only *in terms of the theory* that one can speak of the events being thus "connected" (as opposed to a simple spatio-temporal connection); the only way to grasp the connection is to learn the theory. But the application of a logical theory to a particular piece of reasoning is not like that. One does not have to know the theory in order to appreciate the connection between the steps of argument; on the contrary, it is only in so far as one can already grasp logical connections between particular statements in particular languages that one is even in a position to understand what the logical theory is all about. Whereas in natural science it is your theoretical knowledge which enables you to explain occurrences you have not previously met, a knowledge of logical theory on the other hand will not enable you to understand a piece of reasoning in an unknown language; you will have to learn that language, and that in itself *may* suffice to enable you to grasp the connections between the various parts of arguments in that language.

Consider now an example from sociology. Georg Simmel writes:

> The degeneration of a difference in convictions into hatred and fight occurs only when there were essential, original similarities between the parties. The (sociologically very significant) "respect for the enemy" is usually absent where the hostility has arisen on the basis of previous solidarity. And where enough similarities continue to make confusions and blurred outlines possible, points of difference need an emphasis not justified by the issue but only by that danger of confusion. This was involved, for instance, in the case of Catholicism in Berne. . . . Roman Catholicism does not have to fear any threat to its identity from external contact with a church so different as the Reformed Church, but quite from something as closely akin as Old-Catholicism.[15]

Here I want to say that it is not *through* Simmel's generalization that one understands the relationship he is pointing to between Roman and Old Catholicism: one understands that only to the extent that one understands the two religious systems themselves and their historical relations. The "sociological law" may be helpful in calling one's attention to features of historical situations which one might otherwise have overlooked and in suggesting useful analogies. Here for instance one may be led to compare Simmel's example with the relations between the Russian Communist Party and, on the one hand, the British Labour Party and, on the other, the British Conservatives. But no historical situation can be understood simply by "applying" such laws, as one applies laws to particular occurences in natural science. Indeed, it is only in so far as one has an *independent* historical grasp of situations like this one that one is able to understand what the law amounts to at all. That is not like having to know the kind of experiment on which a scientific theory is based before one can understand the theory, for there it makes no sense to speak of understanding the connections between the parts of the experiment except in terms of the scientific theory. But one could understand very well the nature of the relations between Roman Catholicism and Old Catholicism without ever having heard of Simmel's theory, or anything like it.

Notes

1. Cf. David Hume, *A Treatise of Human Nature*, (London, printed for J. Noon, 1739: rpt. ed., Oxford, Clarendon Press, 1888, 3 vols., intro.—"Tis evident, that all the sciences have a relation, greater or less, to human nature; and that however wide any of them may seem to run from it, they still return back by one passage or another."
2. Rush Rhees, "Can There Be a Private Language?" *Proceedings of the Aristotelian Society*, supp. vol. 28, 1954, pp. 77–94.
3. R. G. Collingwood, *The Idea of History* (London: Oxford University Press, 1946), passim.
4. Karl R. Popper, *The Poverty of Historicism* (London: Routledge and Kegan Paul, 1949), sec. 29.
5. Max Weber, *Wirtshaft und Gesellschaft* (Tübingen: Mohr, 1956), ch. 1.
6. R. S. Lynd, *Knowledge for What?* (Princeton, N.J.: Princeton University Press, 1948), p. 121.
7. R. G. Collingwood, *The Principles of Art* (London: Oxford University Press, 1938), bk, 1, ch. 4.
8. Ludwig Wittgenstein, *Remarks on the Foundations of Mathematics* (Oxford, Eng.: Blackwell, 1956), ch. 1, pp. 142–51.
9. Collingwood, *The Idea of History*, p. 259.
10. Popper, *The Poverty of Historicism*, sec. 29.
11. Maurice Mandelbaum, "Societal Facts," *British Journal of Sociology* 6, no. 4 (1955), pp. 305–17.
12. Collingwood, *The Principles of Art*, p. 243.
13. This example was suggested to me by a discussion with my colleague, Professor J. C. Rees, as indeed was the realization for the necessity for this whole section.
14. Collingwood, *The Idea of History*, pt. 5.
15. Georg Simmel, *Conflict* (Glencoe, Ill.: Free Press, 1955), ch. 1.

CHAPTER 9

Interpretation and
the Sciences of Man

Charles Taylor

I

i

Is there a sense in which interpretation is essential to explanation in the sciences of man? The view that it is, that there is an unavoidably "hermeneutical" component in the sciences of man, goes back to Dilthey. But recently the question has come again to the fore, for instance, in the work of Gadamer,[1] in Ricoeur's interpretation of Freud,[2] and in the writings of Habermas.[3]

Interpretation, in the sense relevant to hermeneutics, is an attempt to make clear, to make sense of an object of study. This object must, therefore, be a text, or a text-analogue, which in some way is confused, incomplete, cloudy, seemingly contradictory—in one way or another, unclear. The interpretation aims to bring to light an underlying coherence or sense.

This means that any science which can be called "hermeneutical," even in an extended sense, must be dealing with one or another of the confusingly interrelated forms of meaning. Let us try to see a little more clearly what this involves.

1. We need, first, an object or field of objects, about which we can speak in terms of coherence or its absence, of making sense or nonsense.

2. Second, we need to be able to make a distinction, even if only a relative one, between the sense or coherence made, and its embodiment in a particular field of carriers or signifiers. For otherwise, the task of making clear what is fragmentary or confused would be radically impossi-

Originally published in the *Review of Metaphysics*, Volume 25 (1971); reprinted by permission.

ble. No sense could be given to this idea. We have to be able to make for our interpretations claims of the order: the meaning confusedly present in this text or text-analogue is clearly expressed here. The meaning, in other words, is one which admits of more than one expression, and, in this sense, a distinction must be possible between meaning and expression.

The point of the above qualification, that this distinction may be only relative, is that there are cases where no clear, unambiguous, nonarbitrary line can be drawn between what is said and its expression. It can be plausibly argued (I think convincingly although there isn't space to go into it here) that this is the normal and fundamental condition of meaningful expression, that exact synonymy, or equivalence of meaning, is a rare and localized achievement of specialized languages or uses of civilization. But this, if true (and I think it is), doesn't do away with the distinction between meaning and expression. Even if there is an important sense in which a meaning re-expressed in a new medium can not be declared identical, this by no means entails that we can give no sense to the project of expressing a meaning in a new way. It does of course raise an interesting and difficult question about what can be meant by expressing it in a clearer way: what is the "it" which is clarified if equivalence is denied? I hope to return to this in examining interpretation in the sciences of man.

Hence the object of a science of interpretation must be describable in terms of sense and nonsense, coherence and its absence, and must admit of a distinction between meaning and its expression.

3. There is also a third condition it must meet. We can speak of sense or coherence, and of their different embodiments, in connection with such phenomena as gestalts, or patterns in rock formations, or snow crystals, where the notion of expression has no real warrant. What is lacking here is the notion of a subject for whom these meanings are. Without such a subject, the choice of criteria of sameness and difference, the choice among the different forms of coherence which can be identified in a given pattern, among the different conceptual fields in which it can be seen, is arbitrary.

In a text or text-analogue, on the other hand, we are trying to make explicit the meaning expressed, and this means expressed by or for a subject or subjects. The notion of expression refers us to that of a subject. The identification of the subject is by no means necessarily unproblematical, as we shall see further on; it may be one of the most difficult problems, an area in which prevailing epistemological prejudice may blind us to the nature of our object of study. I think this has been the case, as I will show below. And moreover, the identification of a subject does not assure us of a clear and absolute distinction between meaning and expression as we saw above. But any such distinction, even a relative one, is without any anchor at all, is totally arbitrary, without appeal to a subject.

The object of a science of interpretation must thus have: sense, distinguishable from its expression, which is for or by a subject.

ii

Before going on to see in what way, if any, these conditions are realized in the sciences of man, I think it would be useful to set out more clearly what rides on this question, why it matters whether or not we think of the sciences of man as hermeneutical, what issue is at stake here.

The issue here is at root an epistemological one. But it is inextricable from an ontological one, and, hence, cannot but be relevant to our notions of science and of the proper conduct of inquiry. We might say that it is an ontological issue which has been argued ever since the seventeenth century in terms of epistemological considerations which have appeared to some to be unanswerable.

The case could be put in these terms: what are the criteria of judgment in a hermeneutical science? A successful interpretation is one which makes clear the meaning originally present in a confused, fragmentary, cloudy form. But how does one know that this interpretation is correct? Presumably because it makes sense of the original text: what is strange, mystifying, puzzling, contradictory is no longer so, is accounted for. The interpretation appeals throughout to our understanding of the "language" of expression, which understanding allows us to see that this expression is puzzling, that it is in contradiction to that other, etc., and that these difficulties are cleared up when the meaning is expressed in a new way.

But this appeal to our understanding seems to be crucially inadequate. What if someone does not "see" the adequacy of our interpretation, does not accept our reading? We try to show him how it makes sense of the original non- or partial sense. But for him to follow us he must read the original language as we do, he must recognize these expressions as puzzling in a certain way, and hence be looking for a solution to our problem. If he does not, what can we do? The answer it would seem, can only be more of the same. We have to show him through the reading of other expressions why this expression must be read in the way we propose. But success here requires that he follow us in these other readings, and so on, it would seem, potentially forever. We cannot escape an ultimate appeal to a common understanding of the expressions, of the "language" involved. This is one way of trying to express what has been called the "hermeneutical circle." What we are trying to establish is a certain reading of text or expressions, and what we appeal to as our grounds for this reading can only be other readings. The circle can also be put in terms of part-whole relations: we are trying to establish a reading for the whole text, and for this we appeal to readings of its partial expressions; and yet because we are dealing with meaning, with making sense, where expressions only make sense or not in relation to others, the readings of partial expressions depend on those of others, and ultimately of the whole.

Put in forensic terms, as we started to do above, we can only convince an interlocutor if at some point he shares our understanding of the language concerned. If he does not, there is no further step to take in rational argument; we can try to awaken these intuitions in him, or we can simply give up; argument will advance us no further. But of course the forensic predicament can be transferred into my own judging: if I am this ill-equipped to convince a stubborn interlocutor, how can I convince myself? how can I be sure? Maybe my intuitions are wrong or distorted, maybe I am locked into a circle of illusion.

Now one, and perhaps the only sane response to this would be to say that such uncertainty is an ineradicable part of our epistemological pre-dicament. That even to characterize it as "uncertainty" is to adopt an absurdly severe criterion of "certainty," which deprives the concept of any sensible use. But this has not been the only or even the main response of our philosophical tradition. And it is another response which has had an important and far-reaching effect on the sciences of man. The demand has been for a level of certainty which can only be attained by breaking beyond the circle.

There are two ways in which this break-out has been envisaged. The first might be called the "rationalist" one and could be thought to reach a culmination in Hegel. It does not involve a negation of intuition, or of our understanding of meaning, but rather aspires to attainment of an under-standing of such clarity that it would carry with it the certainty of the undeniable. In Hegel's case, for instance, our full understanding of the whole in "thought" carries with it a grasp of its inner necessity, such that we see how it could not be otherwise. No higher grade of certainty is conceivable. For this aspiration the word "break-out" is badly chosen; the aim is rather to bring understanding to an inner clarity which is absolute.

The other way, which we can call "empiricist," is a genuine attempt to go beyond the circle of our own interpretations, to get beyond subjectivity. The attempt is to reconstruct knowledge in such a way that there is no need to make final appeal to readings or judgments which can not be checked further. That is why the basic building block of knowledge on this view is the impression, or sense-datum, a unit of information which is not the deliverance of a judgment, which has by definition no element in it of reading or interpretation, which is a brute datum. The highest ambition would be to build our knowledge from such building blocks by judgments which could be anchored in a certainty beyond subjective intuition. This is what underlies the attraction of the notion of the association of ideas, or if the same procedure is viewed as a method, induction. If the original acquisition of the units of information is not the fruit of judgment or interpretation, then the constatation that two such elements occur together need not either be the fruit of interpretation, of a reading or intuition which cannot be checked. For if the occurrence of a single element is a brute datum, then so is the co-occurrence of two such elements. The path to true knowledge would then repose crucially on the correct recording of such co-occurrences.

This is what lies behind an ideal of verification which is central to an important tradition in the philosophy of science, whose main contemporary protagonists are the logical empiricists. Verification must be grounded ultimately in the acquisition of brute data. By "brute data," I mean here and throughout data whose validity cannot be questioned by offering another interpretation or reading, data whose credibility cannot be confounded or undermined by further reasoning.[4] If such a difference of interpretation can arise over given data, then it must be possible to structure the argument so as to distinguish the basic, brute data from the inferences made on the basis of them.

The inferences themselves, of course, to be valid must similarly be beyond the challenge of a rival interpretation. Here the logical empiricists added to the armory of traditional empiricism, which set great store by the method of induction, the whole domain of logical and mathematical inference which had been central to the rationalist position (with Leibniz at least, although not with Hegel), and which offered another brand of unquestionable certainty.

Of course, mathematical inference and empirical verification were combined in such a way that two theories or more could be verified of the same domain of facts. But this was a consequence to which logical empiricism was willing to accommodate itself. As for the surplus meaning in a theory which could not be rigorously co-ordinated with brute data, it was considered to be quite outside the logic of verification.

157

As a theory of perception, this epistemology gave rise to all sorts of problems, not least of which was the perpetual threat of skepticism and solipsism inseparable from a conception of the basic data of knowledge as brute data, beyond investigation. As a theory of perception, however, it seems largely a thing of the past, in spite of a surprising recrudescence in the Anglo-Saxon world in the thirties and forties. But there is no doubt that it goes marching on, among other places, as a theory of how the human mind and human knowledge actually function.

In a sense, the contemporary period has seen a better, more rigorous statement of what this epistemology is about in the form of computer-influenced theories of intelligence. These try to model intelligence as consisting of operations on machine-recognizable input which could themselves be matched by programs which could be run on machines. The machine criterion provides us with our assurance against an appeal to intuition or interpretations which cannot be understood by fully explicit procedures operating on brute data—the input.[5]

The progress of natural science has lent great credibility to this epistemology, since it can be plausibly reconstructed on this model, as for instance has been done by the logical empiricists. And, of course, the temptation has been overwhelming to reconstruct the sciences of man on the same model; or rather to launch them in lines of inquiry that fit this paradigm, since they are constantly said to be in their "infancy." Psychology, where an earlier vogue of behaviorism is being replaced by a boom of computer-based models, is far from the only case.

The form this epistemological bias—one might say obsession—takes is different for different sciences. Later I would like to look at a particular case, the study of politics, where the issue can be followed out. But in general, the empiricist orientation must be hostile to a conduct of inquiry which is based on interpretation, and which encounters the hermeneutical circle as this was characterized above. This cannot meet the requirements of intersubjective, non-arbitrary verification which it considers essential to science. And along with the epistemological stance goes the ontological belief that reality must be susceptible to understanding and explanation by science so understood. From this follows a certain set of notions of what the sciences of man must be.

On the other hand, many, including myself, would like to argue that these notions about the sciences of man are sterile, that we cannot come to understand important dimensions of human life within the bounds set by this epistemological orientation. This dispute is of course familiar to all in at least some of its ramifications. What I want to claim is that the issue can be fruitfully posed in terms of the notion of interpretation as I began to outline it above.

I think this way of putting the question is useful because it allows us at once to bring to the surface the powerful epistemological beliefs which underlie the orthodox view of the sciences of man in our academy, and to make explicit the notion of our epistemological predicament implicit in the opposing thesis. This is in fact rather more way-out and shocking to the tradition of scientific thought than is often admitted or realized by the opponents of narrow scientism. It may not strengthen the case of the opposition to bring out fully what is involved in a hermeneutical science as far as convincing waverers is concerned, but a gain in clarity is surely worth a thinning of the ranks—at least in philosophy.

iii

Before going on to look at the case of political science, it might be worth asking another question: why should we even pose the question whether the sciences of man are hermeneutical? What gives us the idea in the first place that men and their actions constitute an object or a series of objects which meet the conditions outlined above?

The answer is that on the phenomenological level or that of ordinary speech (and the two converge for the purposes of this argument) a certain notion of meaning has an essential place in the characterization of human behavior. This is the sense in which we speak of a situation, an action, a demand, a prospect having a certain meaning for a person.

Now it is frequently thought that "meaning" is used here in a sense which is a kind of illegitimate extension from the notion of linguistic meaning. Whether it can be considered an extension or not is another matter; it certainly differs from linguistic meaning. But it would be very hard to argue that it is an illegitimate use of the term.

When we speak of the "meaning" of a given predicament, we are using a concept which has the following articulation. (*a*) Meaning is for a subject: it is not the meaning of the situation *in vacuo*, but its meaning for a subject, a specific subject, a group of subjects, or perhaps what its meaning is for the human subject as such (even though particular humans might be reproached with not admitting or realizing this). (*b*) Meaning is of something; that is, we can distinguish between a given element— situation, action, or whatever—and its meaning. But this is not to say that they are physically separable. Rather we are dealing with two descriptions of the element, in one of which it is characterized in terms of its meaning for the subject. But the relations between the two descriptions are not symmetrical. For, on the one hand, the description in terms of meaning cannot be unless descriptions of the other kind apply as well; or put differently, there can be no meaning without a substrate. But on the other hand, it may be that the same meaning may be borne by another substrate—e.g., a situation with the same meaning may be realized in different physical conditions. There is a necessary role for a potentially substitutable substrate; or all meanings are of something.

And thirdly, (c) things only have meaning in a field, that is, in relation to the meanings of other things. This means that there is no such thing as a single, unrelated meaningful element; and it means that changes in the other meanings in the field can involve changes in the given element. Meanings can't be identified except in relation to others, and in this way resemble words. The meaning of a word depends, for instance, on those words with which it contrasts, on those which define its place in the language (e.g., those defining "determinable" dimensions, like color, shape), on those which define the activity or "language game" it figures in (describing, invoking, establishing communion), and so on. The relations between meanings in this sense are like those between concepts in a semantic field.

Just as our color concepts are given their meanings by the field of contrast they set up together, so that the introduction of new concepts will alter the boundaries of others, so the various meanings that a subordinate's demeanor can have for us, as deferential, respectful, cringing, mildly mocking, ironical, insolent, provoking, downright rude, are established by a field of contrast; and as with finer discrimination on our part, or a more sophisticated culture, new possibilities are born, so other terms of this range are altered. And as the meaning of our terms "red," "blue," "green" is fixed by the definition of a field of contrast through the determinable term "color," so all these alternative demeanors are only available in a society which has, among other types, hierarchical relations of power and command. And corresponding to the underlying language game of designating colored objects is the set of social practices which sustain these hierarchical structures and are fulfilled in them.

Meaning in this sense—let us call it experiential meaning—thus is for a subject, of something, in a field. This distinguishes it from linguistic meaning which has a four- and not three-dimensional structure. Linguistic meaning is for subjects and in a field, but it is the meaning of signifiers and it is about a world of referents. Once we are clear about the likenesses and differences, there should be little doubt that the term "meaning" is not a misnomer, the product of an illegitimate extension into this context of experience and behavior.

There is thus a quite legitimate notion of meaning which we use when we speak of the meaning of a situation for an agent. And that this concept has a place is integral to our ordinary consciousness and hence speech about our actions. Our actions are ordinarily characterized by the purpose sought and explained by desires, feelings, emotions. But the language by which we describe our goals, feelings, desires is also a definition of the meaning things have for us. The vocabulary defining meaning—words like "terrifying," "attractive"—is linked with that describing feeling—"fear," "desire"—and that describing goals—"safety," "possession."

Moreover, our understanding of these terms moves inescapably in a hermeneutical circle. An emotion term like "shame," for instance, essentially refers us to a certain kind of situation, the "shameful," or "humiliating," and a certain mode of response, that of hiding oneself, of covering up, or else "wiping out" the blot. That is, it is essential to this feeling's being identified as shame that it be related to this situation and give rise to this type of disposition. But this situation in its turn can only be identified in relation to the feelings which it provokes; and the disposition is to a goal which can similarly not be understood without reference to the feelings experienced: the "hiding" in question is one which will cover up my shame; it is not the same as hiding from an armed pursuer; we can only understand what is meant by "hiding" here if we understand what kind of feeling and situation is being talked about. We have to be within the circle.

An emotion term like "shame" can only be explained by reference to other concepts which in turn cannot be understood without reference to shame. To understand these concepts we have to be in on a certain experience, we have to understand a certain language, not just of words, but also a certain language of mutual action and communication, by which we blame, exhort, admire, esteem each other. In the end we are in on this because we grow up in the ambit of certain common meanings. But we can often experience what it is like to be on the outside when we encounter the feeling, action, and experiential meaning language of another civilization. Here there is no translation, no way of explaining in other, more accessible concepts. We can only catch on by getting somehow into their way of life, if only in imagination. Thus if we look at human behavior as action done out of a background of desire, feeling, emotion, then we are looking at a reality which must be characterized in terms of meaning. But does this mean that it can be the object of a hermeneutical science as this was outlined above?

There are, to remind ourselves, three characteristics that the object of a science of interpretation has: it must have sense or coherence; this must be distinguishable from its expression, and this sense must be for a subject.

Now insofar as we are talking about behavior as action, hence in terms of meaning, the category of sense or coherence must apply to it. This is not to say that all behavior must "make sense," if we mean by this be rational, avoid contradiction, confusion of purpose, and the like. Plainly a great deal of our action falls short of this goal. But in another sense, even contradictory, irrational action is "made sense of," when we understand why it was engaged in. We make sense of action when there is a coherence between the actions of the agent and the meaning of his situation for him. We find his action puzzling until we find such a coherence. It may not be bad to repeat that this coherence in no way implies that the action is rational: the meaning of a situation for an agent may be full of confusion and contradiction; but the adequate depiction of this contradiction makes sense of it.

Making sense in this way through coherence of meaning and action, the meanings of action and situation cannot but move in a hermeneutical circle. Our conviction that the account makes sense is contingent on our reading of action and situation. But these readings cannot be explained or justified except by reference to other such readings, and their relation to the whole. If an interlocutor does not understand this kind of reading, or will not accept it as valid, there is nowhere else the argument can go. Ultimately, a good explanation is one which makes sense of the behavior; but then to appreciate a good explanation, one has to agree on what makes good sense; what makes good sense is a function of one's readings; and these in turn are based on the kind of sense one understands.

But how about the second characteristic, that sense should be distinguishable from its embodiment? This is necessary for a science of interpretation because interpretation lays a claim to make a confused meaning clearer; hence there must be some sense in which the "same" meaning is expressed, but differently.

This immediately raises a difficulty. In talking of experiential meaning above, I mentioned that we can distinguish between a given element and its meaning, between meaning and substrate. This carried the claim that a given meaning *may* be realized in another substrate. But does this mean that we can *always* embody the same meaning in another situation? Perhaps there are some situations, standing before death, for instance, which have a meaning which can't be embodied otherwise.

But fortunately this difficult question is irrelevant for our purposes. For here we have a case in which the analogy between text and behavior implicit in the notion of a hermeneutical science of man only applies with important modifications. The text is replaced in the interpretation by another text, one which is clearer. The text-analogue of behavior is not replaced by another such text-analogue. When this happens we have revolutionary theatre or terrorist acts designed to make propaganda of the deed, in which the hidden relations of a society are supposedly shown up in a dramatic confrontation. But this is not scientific understanding, even though it may perhaps be based on such understanding, or claim to be.

But in science the text-analogue is replaced by a text, an account. Which might prompt the question, how we can even begin to talk of interpretation here, of expressing the same meaning more clearly, when we have two such utterly different terms of comparison, a text and a tract of behavior? Is the whole thing not just a bad pun?

This question leads us to open up another aspect of experiential meaning which we abstracted from earlier. Experiential meanings are defined in fields of contrast, as words are in semantic fields.

But what was not mentioned above is that these two kinds of definition aren't independent of each other. The range of human desires, feelings, emotions, and hence meanings is bound up with the level and type of culture, which in turn is inseparable from the distinctions and categories marked by the language people speak. The field of meanings in which a given situation can find its place is bound up with the semantic field of the terms characterizing these meanings and the related feelings, desires, predicaments.

But the relationship involved here is not a simple one. There are two simple types of models of relation which could be offered here, but both are inadequate. We could think of the feeling vocabulary as simply describing preexisting feelings, as marking distinctions which would be there without them. But this is not adequate because we often experience in ourselves or others how achieving, say, a more sophisticated vocabulary of the emotions makes our emotional life more sophisticated and not just our descriptions of it. Reading a good, powerful novel may give me the picture of an emotion which I had not previously been aware of. But we can't draw a neat line between an increased ability to identify and an altered ability to feel emotions which this enables.

The other simple inadequate model of the relationship is to jump from the above to the conclusion that thinking makes it so. But this clearly won't do either, since not just any new definition can be forced on us, nor can we force it on ourselves; and some which we do gladly take up can be judged inauthentic, or in bad faith, or just wrong-headed by others. These judgments may be wrong, but they are not in principle illicit. Rather we make an effort to be lucid about ourselves and our feelings, and admire a man who achieves this.

Thus, neither the simple correspondence view is correct, nor the view that thinking makes it so. But both have *prima facie* warrant. There is such a thing as self-lucidity, which points us to a correspondence view; but the achievement of such lucidity means moral change, that is, it changes the object known. At the same time, error about oneself is not just an absence of correspondence; it is also in some form inauthenticity, bad faith, self-delusion, repression of one's human feelings, or something of the kind; it is a matter of the quality of what is felt just as much as what is known about this, just as self-knowledge is.

If this is so, then we have to think of man as a self-interpreting animal. He is necessarily so, for there is no such thing as the structure of meanings for him independently of his interpretation of them; for one is woven into the other. But then the text of our interpretation is not that heterogeneous from what is interpreted; for what is interpreted is itself an interpretation, a self-interpretation which is embedded in a stream of action. It is an interpretation of experiential meaning which contributes to the constitution of this meaning. Or to put it another way: that of which we are trying to find the coherence is itself partly constituted by self-interpretation.

Our aim is to replace this confused, incomplete, partly erroneous self-interpretation by a correct one. And in doing this we look not only to the self-interpretation but to the stream of behavior in which it is set, just as in interpreting a historical document we have to place it in the stream of events which it relates to. But of course the analogy is not exact, for here we are interpreting the interpretation and the stream of behavior in which it is set together, and not just one or the other.

There is thus no utter heterogeneity of interpretation to what it is about; rather there is a slide in the notion of interpretation. Already to be a living agent is to experience one's situation in terms of certain meanings; and this in a sense can be thought of as a sort of proto-"interpretation." This is in turn interpreted and shaped by the language in which the agent lives these meanings. This whole is then at a third level interpreted by the explanation we proffer of his actions.

In this way the second condition of a hermeneutical science is met. But this account poses in a new light the question mentioned at the beginning whether the interpretation can ever express the same meanings as the interpreted. And in this case, there is clearly a way in which the two will not be congruent. For if the explanation is really clearer than the lived interpretation then it will be such that it would alter in some way the behavior if it came to be internalized by the agent as his self-interpretation. In this way a hermeneutical science which achieves its goal, that is, attains greater clarity than the immediate understanding of agent or observer, must offer us an interpretation which is in this way crucially out of phase with the explicandum.

Thus, human behavior seen as action of agents who desire and are moved, who have goals and aspirations, necessarily offers a purchase for descriptions in terms of meaning—what I have called "experiential meaning." The norm of explanation which it posits is one which "makes sense" of the behavior, which shows a coherence of meaning. This "making sense of" is the proffering of an interpretation; and we have seen that what is interpreted meets the conditions of a science of interpretation: first, that we can speak of its sense or coherence; and second, that this sense can be expressed in another form, so that we can speak of the interpretation as giving clearer expression to what is only implicit in the explicandum. The third condition, that this sense be for a subject, is obviously met in this case, although who this subject is is by no means an unproblematical question as we shall see later on.

This should be enough to show that there is a good *prima facie* case to the effect that men and their actions are amenable to explanation of a hermeneutical kind. There is, therefore, some reason to raise the issue and challenge the epistemological orientation which would rule interpretation out of the sciences of man. A great deal more must be said to bring out what is involved in the hermeneutical sciences of man. But before getting on to this, it might help to clarify the issue with a couple of examples drawn from a specific field, that of politics.

II

i

In politics, too, the goal of a verifiable science has led to the concentration on features which can supposedly be identified in abstraction from our understanding or not understanding experiential meaning. These— let us call them brute data identifications—are what supposedly enable us to break out from the hermeneutical circle and found our science four square on a verification procedure which meets the requirements of the empiricist tradition.

But in politics the search for such brute data has not gone to the lengths which it has in psychology, where the object of science has been thought of by many as behavior qua "colorless movement," or as machine-recognizable properties. The tendency in politics has been to stop with something less basic, but—so it is thought—the identification of which cannot be challenged by the offering of another interpretation or reading of the data concerned. . . . This is what is referred to as "behavior" in the rhetoric of political scientists, but it has not the rock bottom quality of its psychological homonym.

Political behavior includes what we would ordinarily call actions, but ones that are supposedly brute data identifiable. How can this be so? Well, actions are usually described by the purpose or end-state realized. But the purposes of some actions can be specified in what might be thought to be brute data terms; some actions, for instance, have physical end-states, like getting the car in the garage or climbing the mountain. Others have end-states which are closely tied by institutional rules to some unmistakable physical movement; thus, when I raise my hand in the meeting at the appropriate time, I am voting for the motion. The only questions we can raise about the corresponding actions, given such movements or the realization of such end-states, are whether the agent was aware of what he was doing, was acting as against simply emitting reflex behavior, knew the institutional significance of his movement, etc. Any worries on this score generally turn out to be pretty artificial in the contexts political scientists are concerned with; and where they do arise they can be checked by relatively simple devices, e.g., asking the subject: did you mean to vote for the motion?

Hence, it would appear that there are actions which can be identified beyond fear of interpretative dispute; and this is what gives the foundation for the category of "political behavior." Thus, there are some acts of obvious political relevance which can be specified thus in physical terms, such as killing, sending tanks into the streets, seizing people and confining them to cells; and there is an immense range of others which can be specified from physical acts by institutional rules, such as voting, for instance. These can be the object of a science of politics which can hope to meet the stringent requirements of verification. The latter class particularly has provided matter for study in recent decades—most notably in the case of voting studies.

But of course a science of politics confined to such acts would be much too narrow. For on another level these actions also have meaning for the agents which is not exhausted in the brute data descriptions, and which is often crucial to understanding why they were done. Thus, in voting for the motion I am also saving the honor of my party, or defending the value of free speech, or vindicating public morality, or saving civilization from breakdown. It is in such terms that the agents talk about the motivation of much of their political action, and it is difficult to conceive a science of politics which doesn't come to grips with it.

Behavioral political science comes to grips with it by taking the meanings involved in action as facts about the agent, his beliefs, his affective reactions, his "values," as the term is frequently used. For it can be thought verifiable in the brute data sense that men will agree to subscribe or not to a certain form of words (expressing a belief, say); or express a positive or negative reaction to certain events, or symbols; or agree or not with the proposition that some act is right or wrong. We can thus get at meanings as just another form of brute data by the techniques of the opinion survey and content analysis.

An immediate objection springs to mind. If we are trying to deal with the meanings which inform political action, then surely interpretive acumen is unavoidable. Let us say we are trying to understand the goals and values of a certain group, or grasp their vision of the polity; we might try to probe this by a questionnaire asking them whether they assent or not to a number of propositions, which are meant to express different goals, evaluations, beliefs. But how did we design the questionnaire? How did we pick these propositions? Here we relied on our understanding of the goals, values, vision involved. But then this understanding can be challenged, and hence the significance of our results questioned. Perhaps the findings of our study, the compiling of proportions of assent and dissent to these propositions, is irrelevant, is without significance for understanding the agents or the polity concerned. This kind of attack is frequently made by critics of mainstream political science, or for that matter social science in general.

To this proponents of this mainstream reply with a standard move of logical empiricism: distinguishing the process of discovery from the logic of verification. Of course, it is our understanding of these meanings which enables us to draw up the questionnaire which will test people's attitudes in respect to them. And, of course, interpretive dispute about these meanings is potentially endless; there are no brute data at this level, every affirmation can be challenged by a rival interpretation. But this has nothing to do with verifiable science. What is firmly verified is the set of correlations between, say, the assent to certain propositions and certain behavior. We discover, for instance, that people who are active politically (defined by participation in a certain set of institutions) are more likely to consent to certain sets of propositions supposedly expressing the values underlying the system.[6] This finding is a firmly verified correlation no matter what one thinks of the reasoning, or simple hunches, that went into designing the research which established it. Political science as a

167

body of knowledge is made up of such correlations; it does not give a truth value to the background reasoning or hunch. A good interpretive nose may be useful in hitting on the right correlations to test, but science is never called on to arbitrate the disputes between interpretations.

Thus, in addition to those overt acts which can be defined physically or institutionally, the category of political behavior can include assent or dissent to verbal formulae, or the occurrence or not of verbal formulae in speech, or expressions of approval or rejection of certain events or measures as observed in institutionally defined behavior (for instance, turning out for a demonstration).

Now there are a number of objections which can be made to this notion of political behavior; one might question in all sorts of ways how interpretation-free it is in fact. But I would like to question it from another angle. One of the basic characteristics of this kind of social science is that it reconstructs reality in line with certain categorical principles. These allow for an intersubjective social reality which is made up of brute data, identifiable acts and structures, certain institutions, procedures, actions. It allows for beliefs, affective reactions, evaluations as the psychological properties of individuals. And it allows for correlations between these two orders or reality: e.g., that certain beliefs go along with certain acts, certain values with certain institutions, etc.

To put it another way, what is objectively (intersubjectively) real is brute data identifiable. This is what social reality *is*. Social reality described in terms of its meaning for the actors, such that disputes could arise about interpretation which couldn't be settled by brute data (e.g., are people rioting to get a hearing, or are they rioting to redress humiliation, out of blind anger, because they recover a sense of dignity in insurrection?), this is given subjective reality; that is, there are certain beliefs, affective reactions, evaluations which individuals make or have about or in relation to social reality. These beliefs or reactions can have an effect on this reality; and the fact that such a belief is held is a fact of objective social reality. But the social reality which is the object of these attitudes, beliefs, reactions can only be made up of brute data. Thus any description of reality in terms of meanings which is open to interpretive question is only allowed into this scientific discourse if it is placed, as it were, in quotes and attributed to individuals as their opinion, belief, attitude. That this opinion, belief, etc. is held is thought of as a brute datum, since it is redefined as the respondent's giving a certain answer to the questionnaire.

This aspect of social reality which concerns its meanings for the agents has been taken up in a number of ways, but recently it has been spoken of in terms of political culture. Now the way this is defined and studied illustrates clearly the categorial principles above. For instance, political cultural is referred to by Almond and Powell as the "psychological dimension of the political system."[7] Further on they state: "Political culture is the pattern of individual attitudes and orientations towards politics among the members of a political system. It is the subjective realm which underlies and gives meaning to political actions."[8] The authors then go on to distinguish three different kinds of orientations, cognitive (knowledge and beliefs), affective (feelings), and evaluative (judgments and opinions).

From the point of view of empiricist epistemology, this set of categorial principles leaves nothing out. Both reality and the meanings it has for actors are coped with. But what it in fact cannot allow for are intersubjective meanings; that is, it cannot allow for the validity of descriptions of social reality in terms of meanings, hence not as brute data, which are not in quotation marks and attributed as opinion, attitude, etc. to individual(s). Now it is this exclusion that I would like to challenge in the name of another set of categorial principles, inspired by a quite other epistemology.

ii

We spoke earlier about the brute data identification of acts by means of institutional rules. Thus, putting a cross beside someone's name on a slip of paper and putting this in a box counts in the right context as voting for that person; leaving the room, saying or writing a certain form of words, counts as breaking off the negotiations; writing one's name on a piece of paper counts as signing the petition, etc. But what is worth looking at is what underlies this set of identifications. These identifications are the application of a language of social life, a language which marks distinctions among different possible social acts, relations, structures. But what underlies this language?

Let us take the example of breaking off negotiations above. The language of our society recognizes states or actions like the following: entering into negotiation, breaking off negotiations, offering to negotiate, negotiating in good (bad) faith, concluding negotiations, making a new offer, etc. In other more jargon-infested language, the semantic "space" of this range of social activity is carved up in a certain way, by a certain set of distinctions which our vocabulary marks; and the shape and nature of these distinctions is the nature of our language in this area. These distinctions are applied in our society with more or less formalism in different contexts.

But of course this is not true of every society. Our whole notion of negotiation is bound up for instance with the distinct identity and autonomy of the parties, with the willed nature of their relations; it is a very contractual notion. But other societies have no such conception. It is reported about the traditional Japanese village that the foundation of its social life was a powerful form of consensus, which put a high premium on unanimous decision.[9] Such a consensus would be considered shattered if two clearly articulated parties were to separate out, pursuing opposed aims and attempting either to vote down the opposition or push it into a settlement on the most favorable possible terms for themselves. Discussion there must be, and some kind of adjustment of differences. But our idea of bargaining, with the assumption of distinct autonomous parties in willed relationship, has no place there; nor does a series of distinctions, like entering into and leaving negotiation, or bargaining in good faith (sc., with the genuine intention of seeking agreement).

Now the differences between our society and one of the kind just described could not be well expressed if we said we have a vocabulary to describe negotiation which they lack. We might say, for instance, that we have a vocabulary to describe the heavens that they lack, viz., that of Newtonian mechanics; for here we assume that they live under the same heavens as we do, only understand it differently. But it is not true that they have the same kind of bargaining as we do. The word, or whatever word of their language we translate as "bargaining," must have an entirely different gloss, which is marked by the distinctions their vocabulary allows in contrast to those marked by ours. But this different gloss is not just a difference of vocabulary, but also one of social reality.

But this still may be misleading as a way of putting the difference. For it might imply that there is a social reality which can be discovered in each society and which might exist quite independently of the vocabulary of that society, or indeed of any vocabulary, as the heavens would exist whether men theorized about them or not. And this is not the case; the realities here are practices; and these cannot be identified in abstraction from the language we use to describe them, or invoke them, or carry them out. That the practice of negotiation allows us to distinguish bargaining in good or bad faith, or entering into or breaking off negotiations, presupposes that our acts and situation have a certain description for us, e.g., that we are distinct parties entering into willed relations. But they cannot have these descriptions for us unless this is somehow expressed in our vocabulary of this practice, if not in our descriptions of the practices (for we may as yet be unconscious of some of the important distinctions) in the appropriate language for carrying them on. (Thus, the language marking a distinction between public and private acts or contexts may exist even where these terms or their equivalents are not part of this language; for the distinction will be marked by the different language which is appropriate in one context and the other, be it perhaps a difference of style, or dialect, even though the distinction is not designated by specific descriptive expressions.)

The situation we have here is one in which the vocabulary of a given social dimension is grounded in the shape of social practice in this dimension; that is, the vocabulary wouldn't make sense, couldn't be applied sensibly, where this range of practices didn't prevail. And yet this range of practices couldn't exist without the prevalence of this or some related vocabulary. There is no simple one-way dependence here. We can speak of mutual dependence if we like, but really what this points up is the artificiality of the distinction between social reality and the language of description of that social reality. The language is constitutive of the reality, is essential to its being the kind of reality it is. To separate the two and distinguish them as we quite rightly distinguish the heavens from our theories about them is forever to miss the point.

This type of relation has been recently explored, e.g., by John Searle, with his concept of a constitutive rule. As Searle points out, we are normally induced to think of rules as applying to behavior which could be available to us whether or not the rule existed.[10] Some rules are like this; they are regulative like commandments: don't take the goods of another. But there are other rules, e.g., that governing the Queen's move in chess, which are not so separable. If one suspends these rules, or imagines a state in which they have not yet been introduced, then the whole range of behavior in question, in this case, chess playing, would not be. There would still, of course, be the activity of pushing a wood piece around on a board made of squares 8 by 8; but this is not chess any longer. Rules of this kind are constitutive rules. By contrast again, there are other rules of chess, such as that one say "j'adoube" when one touches a piece without intending to play it, which are clearly regulative.[11]

I am suggesting that this notion of the constitutive be extended beyond the domain of rule-governed behavior. That is why I suggest the vaguer word "practice." Even in an area where there are no clearly defined rules, there are distinctions between different sorts of behavior such that one sort is considered the appropriate form for one action or context, the other for another action or context, e.g., doing or saying certain things amounts to breaking off negotiations, doing or saying other things amounts to making a new offer. But just as there are constitutive rules, i.e., rules such that the behavior they govern could not exist

171

without them, and which are in this sense inseparable from that behavior, so I am suggesting that there are constitutive distinctions, constitutive ranges of language which are similarly inseparable, in that certain practices are not without them.

We can reverse this relationship and say that all the institutions and practices by which we live are constituted by certain distinctions and hence a certain language which is thus essential to them. We can take voting, a practice which is central to large numbers of institutions in a democratic society. What is essential to the practice of voting is that some decision or verdict be delivered (a man elected, a measure passed), through some criterion of preponderance (simple majority, two-thirds majority, or whatever) out of a set of micro-choices (the votes of the citizens, MPs, delegates). If there is not some such significance attached to our behavior, no amount of marking and counting pieces of paper, raising hands, walking out into lobbies amounts to voting. From this it follows that the institution of voting must be such that certain distinctions have application: e.g., that between someone being elected, or a measure passed, and their failing of election, or passage; that between a valid vote and an invalid one which in turn requires a distinction between a real choice and one which is forced or counterfeited. For no matter how far we move from the Rousseauian notion that each man decide in full autonomy, the very institution of the vote requires that in some sense the enfranchised choose. For there to be voting in a sense recognizably like ours, there must be a distinction in men's self-interpretations between autonomy and forced choice.

This is to say that an activity of marking and counting papers has to bear intentional descriptions which fall within a certain range before we can agree to call it voting, just as the intercourse of two men or teams has to bear descriptions of a certain range before we will call it negotiation. Or in other words, that some practice is voting or negotiation has to do in part with the vocabulary established in a society as appropriate for engaging in it or describing it.

Hence implicit in these practices is a certain vision of the agent and his relation to others and to society. We saw in connection with negotiation in our society that it requires a picture of the parties as in some sense autonomous, and as entering into willed relations. And this picture carries with it certain implicit norms, such as that of good faith mentioned above, or a norm of rationality, that agreement correspond to one's goals as far as attainable, or the norm of continued freedom of action as far as attainable. These practices require that one's actions and relations be seen in the light of this picture and the accompanying norms, good faith, autonomy, and rationality. But men do not see themselves in this way in all societies, nor do they understand these norms in all societies. The experience of autonomy as we know it, the sense of rational action and the satisfactions thereof, are unavailable to them. The meaning of these terms is opaque to them because they have a different structure of experiential meaning open to them.

We can think of the difference between our society and the simplified version of the traditional Japanese village as consisting in this, that the range of meaning open to the members of the two societies is very different. But what we are dealing with here is not subjective meaning which can fit into the categorial grid of behavioral political science, but rather intersubjective meanings. It is not just that the people in our society all or mostly have a given set of ideas in their heads and subscribe to a given set of goals. The meanings and norms implicit in these practices are not just in the minds of the actors but are out there in the practices themselves, practices which cannot be conceived as a set of individual actions, but which are essentially modes of social relation, of mutual action.

The actors may have all sorts of beliefs and attitudes which may be rightly thought of as their individual beliefs and attitudes, even if others share them; they may subscribe to certain policy goals or certain forms of theory about the polity, or feel resentment at certain things, and so on. They bring these with them into their negotiations, and strive to satisfy them. But what they do not bring into the negotiations is the set of ideas and norms constitutive of negotiation themselves. These must be the common property of the society before there can be any question of anyone entering into negotiation or not. Hence they are not subjective meanings, the property of one or some individuals, but rather inter-subjective meanings, which are constitutive of the social matrix in which individuals find themselves and act.

The intersubjective meanings which are the background to social action are often treated by political scientists under the heading "consensus." By this is meant convergence of beliefs on certain basic matters, or of attitude. But the two are not the same. Whether there is consensus or not, the condition of there being either one or the other is a certain set of common terms of reference. A society in which this was lacking would not be a society in the normal sense of the term, but several. Perhaps some multi-racial or multi-tribal states approach this limit. Some multi-national states are bedevilled by consistent cross-purposes, e.g., my own country. But consensus as a convergence of beliefs or values is not the opposite of this kind of fundamental diversity. Rather the opposite of diversity is a high degree of intersubjective meanings. And this can go along with profound cleavage. Indeed, intersubjective meanings are a condition of a certain kind of very profound cleavage, such as was visible in the Reformation, or the American Civil War, or splits in left wing parties, where the dispute is at fever pitch just because both sides can fully understand the other.

In other words, convergence of belief or attitude or its absence presupposes a common language in which these beliefs can be formulated, and in which these foundations can be opposed. Much of this common language in any society is rooted in its institutions and practices: it is constitutive of these institutions and practices. It is part of the intersubjective meanings. To put the point another way, apart from the question of how much people's beliefs converge is the question of how much they have a common language of social and political reality in which these beliefs are expressed. This second question cannot be reduced to the first; intersubjective meaning is not a matter of converging beliefs or values. When we speak of consensus we speak of beliefs and values which could be the property of a single person, or many, or all; but intersubjective meanings could not be the property of a single person because they are rooted in social practice.

We can perhaps see this if we envisage the situation in which the ideas and norms underlying a practice are the property of single individuals. This is what happens when single individuals from one society interiorize the notions and values of another, e.g., children in missionary schools. Here we have a totally different situation. We *are* really talking now about subjective beliefs and attitudes. The ideas are abstract; they are mere social "ideals." Whereas in the original society, these ideas and norms are rooted in their social relations, and are that on the basis of which they can formulate opinions and ideals.

We can see this in connection with the example we have been using all along, that of negotiations. The vision of a society based on negotiation is coming in for heavy attack by a growing segment of modern youth, as are the attendant norms of rationality and the definition of autonomy. This is a dramatic failure of "consensus." But this cleavage takes place in the ambit of this intersubjective meaning, the social practice of negotiation as it is lived in our society. The rejection wouldn't have the bitter quality it has if what is rejected were not understood in common, because it is part of a social practice which we find it hard to avoid, so pervasive is it in our society. At the same time there is a reaching out for other forms which have still the "abstract" quality of ideals which are subjective in this sense, that is, not rooted in practice, which is what makes the rebellion look so "unreal" to outsiders, and so irrational.

iii

Intersubjective meanings, ways of experiencing action in society which are expressed in the language and descriptions constitutive of institutions and practices, do not fit into the categorial grid of mainstream political science. This allows only for an intersubjective reality which is brute data identifiable. But social practices and institutions which are partly constituted by certain ways of talking about them are not so identifiable. We have to understand the language, the underlying meanings, which constitute them.

We can allow, once we accept a certain set of institutions or practices as our starting point and not as objects of further questioning, that we can easily take as brute data that certain acts are judged to take place or certain states judged to hold within the semantic field of these practices—for instance, that someone has voted Liberal, or signed the petition. We can then go on to correlate certain subjective meanings—beliefs, attitudes, etc.—with this behavior or its lack. But this means that we give up trying to define further just what these practices and institutions are, what the meanings are which they require and hence sustain. For these meanings do not fit into the grid; they are not subjective beliefs or values, but are constitutive of social reality. In order to get at them we have to drop the basic premise that social reality is made up of brute data alone. For any characterization of the meanings underlying these practices is open to question by someone offering an alternative interpretation. The negation of this is what was meant as brute data. We have to admit that intersubjective social reality has to be partly defined in terms of meanings, that meanings as subjective are not just in causal interaction with a social reality made up of brute data, but that as intersubjective they are constitutive of this reality.

We have been talking here of intersubjective meanings. And earlier I was contrasting the question of intersubjective meaning with that of consensus as convergence of opinions. But there is another kind of nonsubjective meaning which is also often inadequately discussed under the head of "consensus." In a society with a strong web of intersubjective meanings, there can be a more or less powerful set of common meanings. By these I mean notions of what is significant which are not just shared in the sense that everyone has them, but are also common in the sense of being in the common reference world. Thus, almost everyone in our society may share a susceptibility to a certain kind of feminine beauty, but this may not be a common meaning. It may be known to no one, except perhaps market researchers, who play on it in their advertisements. But the survival of a national identity as francophones is a common meaning of *Québecois*; for it is not just shared, and not just known to be shared, but its being a common aspiration is one of the common reference points of all debate, communication, and all public life in the society.

We can speak of a shared belief, aspiration, etc. when there is convergence between the subjective beliefs, aspirations, of many individuals. But it is part of the meaning of a common aspiration, belief, celebration, etc. that it be not just shared but part of the common reference world. Or to put it another way, its being shared is a collective act, it is a consciousness which is communally sustained, whereas sharing is something we do each on his own, as it were, even if each of us is influenced by the others.

Common meanings are the basis of community. Intersubjective meaning gives a people a common language to talk about social reality and a common understanding of certain norms, but only with common meanings does this common reference world contain significant common actions, celebrations, and feelings. These are objects in the world that everybody shares. This is what makes community.

Once again, we cannot really understand this phenomenon through the usual definition of consensus as convergence of opinion and value. For what is meant here is something more than convergence. Convergence is what happens when our values are shared. But what is required for common meanings is that this shared value be part of the common world, that this sharing be shared. But we could also say that common meanings are quite other than consensus, for they can subsist with a high degree of cleavage; this is what happens when a common meaning comes to be lived and understood differently by different groups in a society. It remains a common meaning, because there is the reference point which is the common purpose, aspiration, celebration. Such is for example the American Way, or freedom as understood in the U.S.A. But this common meaning is differently articulated by different groups. This is the basis of the bitterest fights in a society, and this we are also seeing in the U.S. today. Perhaps one might say that a common meaning is very often the cause of the most bitter lack of consensus. It thus must not be confused with convergence of opinion, value, attitude.

Of course, common meanings and intersubjective meanings are closely interwoven. There must be a powerful net of intersubjective meanings for there to be common meanings; and the result of powerful common meanings is the development of a greater web of intersubjective meanings as people live in community.

On the other hand, when common meanings wither, which they can do through the kind of deep dissensus we described earlier, the groups tend to grow apart and develop different languages of social reality, hence to share less intersubjective meanings.

Hence, to take our above example again, there has been a powerful common meaning in our civilization around a certain vision of the free society in which bargaining has a central place. This has helped to entrench the social practice of negotiation which makes us participate in this intersubjective meaning. But there is a severe challenge to this common meaning today, as we have seen. Should those who object to it really succeed in building up an alternative society, there would develop a gap between those who remain in the present type of society and those who had founded the new one.

Common meanings, as well as intersubjective ones, fall through the net of mainstream social science. They can find no place in its categories. For they are not simply a converging set of subjective reactions, but part of the common world. What the ontology of mainstream social science lacks is the notion of meaning as not simply for an individual subject, of a subject who can be a "we" as well as an "I." The exclusion of this possibility, of the communal, comes once again from the baleful influence of the epistemological tradition for which all knowledge has to be reconstructed from the impressions imprinted on the individual subject. But if we free ourselves from the hold of these prejudices, this seems a wildly implausible view about the development of human consciousness; we are aware of the world through a "we" before we are through an "I." Hence we need the distinction between what is just shared in the sense that each of us has it in our individual worlds, and that which is in the common world. But the very idea of something which is in the common world in contradistinction to what is in all the individual worlds is totally opaque to empiricist epistemology. Hence it finds no place in mainstream social science. What this results in must now be seen.

III

Thus, to sum up the last pages: a social science which wishes to fulfill the requirements of the empiricist tradition naturally tries to reconstruct social reality as consisting of brute data alone. These data are the acts of people (behavior) as identified supposedly beyond interpretation either by physical descriptions or by descriptions clearly defined by institutions and practices; and secondly, they include all the subjective reality of individuals' beliefs, attitudes, values, as attested by their responses to certain forms of words, or in some cases their overt non-verbal behavior.

What this excludes is a consideration of social reality as characterized by intersubjective and common meanings. It excludes, for instance, an attempt to understand our civilization, in which negotiation plays such a central part both in fact and in justificatory theory, by probing the self-definitions of agent, other, and the social relatedness which it embodies. Such definitions which deal with the meaning for agents of their own and others' action, and of the social relations in which they stand, do not in any sense record brute data, in the sense that this term is being used in this argument; that is, they are in no sense beyond challenge by those who would quarrel with our interpretations of these meanings.

Thus, I tried to adumbrate above the vision implicit in the practice of negotiation by reference to certain notions of autonomy and rationality. But this reading will undoubtedly be challenged by those who have different fundamental conceptions of man, human motivation, the human condition; or even by those who judge other features of our present predicament to have greater importance. If we wish to avoid these disputes, and have a science grounded in verification as this is understood by the logical empiricists, then we have to avoid this level of study altogether and hope to make do with a correlation of behavior which is brute data identifiable.

A similar point goes for the distinction between common meanings and shared subjective meanings. We can hope to identify the subjective meanings of individuals if we take these in the sense in which there are adequate criteria for them in people's dissent or assent to verbal formulae or their brute data identifiable behavior. But once we allow the distinction between such subjective meanings which are widely shared and genuine common meanings, then we can no longer make do with brute data identification. We are in a domain where our definitions can be challenged by those with another reading.

The profound option of mainstream social scientists for the empiricist conception of knowledge and science makes it inevitable that they should accept the verification model of political science and the categorial principles that this entails. This means in turn that a study of our civilization in terms of its intersubjective and common meanings is ruled out. Rather this whole level of study is made invisible.

On the mainstream view, therefore, the different practices and institutions of different societies are not seen as related to different clusters of intersubjective or common meanings; rather, we should be able to differentiate them by different clusters of "behavior" and/or subjective meaning. The comparison between societies requires on this view that we elaborate a universal vocabulary of behavior which will allow us to present the different forms and practices of different societies in the same conceptual web.

Now present day political science is contemptuous of the older attempt at comparative politics via a comparison of institutions. An influential school of our day has therefore shifted comparison to certain practices, or very general classes of practices, and proposes to compare societies according to the different ways in which these practices are carried on. Such are the "functions" of the influential "developmental approach."[12] But it is epistemologically crucial that such functions be identified independently of those intersubjective meanings which are different in different societies; for otherwise, they will not be genuinely universal, or will be universal only in the loose and unilluminating sense that the function-name can be given application in every society but with varying, and often widely varying, meaning—the same term being "glossed" very differently by different sets of practices and intersubjective meanings. The danger that such universality might not hold is not even suspected by mainstream political scientists since they are unaware that there is such a level of description as that which defines intersubjective meanings and are convinced that functions and the various structures which perform them can be identified in terms of brute data behavior.

But the result of ignoring the difference in intersubjective meanings can be disastrous to a science of comparative politics, viz., that we interpret all other societies in the categories of our own. Ironically, this is what seems to have happened to American political science. Having strongly criticized the old institution-focussed comparative politics for its ethnocentricity (or Western bias), it proposes to understand the politics of all society in terms of such functions, for instance, as "interest articulation" and "interest aggregation," whose definition is strongly influenced by the bargaining culture of our civilization, but which is far from being guaranteed appropriateness elsewhere. The not surprising result is a theory of political development which places the Atlantic-type polity at the summit of human political achievement. . . .

IV

It can be argued, then, that mainstream social science is kept within certain limits by its categorial principles which are rooted in the traditional epistemology of empiricism; and secondly, that these restrictions are a severe handicap and prevent us from coming to grips with important problems of our day which should be the object of political science. We need to go beyond the bounds of a science based on verification to one which would study the intersubjective and common meanings embedded in social reality.

But this science would be hermeneutical in the sense that has been developed in this paper. It would not be founded on brute data; its most primitive data would be readings of meanings, and its object would have the three properties mentioned above: the meanings are for a subject in a field or fields; they are moreover meanings which are partially constituted by self-definitions, which are in this sense already interpretations, and which can thus be reexpressed or made explicit by a science of politics. In our case, the subject may be a society or community; but the intersubjective meanings, as we saw, embody a certain self-definition, a vision of the agent and his society, which is that of the society or community.

But then the difficulties which the proponents of the verification model foresee will arise. If we have a science which has no brute data, which relies on readings, then it cannot but move in a hermeneutical circle. A given reading of the intersubjective meanings of a society, or of given institutions or practices, may seem well founded, because it makes sense of these practices or the development of that society. But the conviction that it does make sense of this history itself is founded on further related readings. Thus, what I said above on the identity-crisis which is generated by our society makes sense and holds together only if one accepts this reading of the intersubjective meanings of our society, and if one accepts this reading of the rebellion against our society by many young people (sc., the reading in terms of identity-crisis). These two readings make sense together, so that in a sense the explanation as a whole presupposes on the readings, and the readings in their turn are strengthened by the explanation as a whole.

But if these readings seem implausible, or even more, if they are not understood by our interlocutor, there is no verification procedure which we can fall back on. We can only continue to offer interpretations; we are in an interpretive circle.

But the ideal of a science of verification is to find an appeal beyond differences of interpretation. Insight will always be useful in discovery, but should not have to play any part in establishing the truth of its findings. This ideal can be said to have been met by our natural sciences. But a hermeneutic science cannot but rely on insight. It requires that one have the sensibility and understanding necessary to be able to make and comprehend the readings by which we can explain the reality concerned.

180

In physics we might argue that if someone does not accept a true theory, then either he has not been shown enough (brute data) evidence (perhaps not enough is yet available), or he cannot understand and apply some formalized language. But in the sciences of man conceived as hermeneutical, the nonacceptance of a true or illuminating theory may come from neither of these, indeed is unlikely to be due to either of these, but rather from a failure to grasp the meaning field in question, an inability to make and understand readings of this field.

In other words, in a hermeneutical science, a certain measure of insight is indispensable, and this insight cannot be communicated by the gathering of brute data, or initiation in modes of formal reasoning or some combination of these. It is unformalizable. But this is a scandalous result according to the authoritative conception of science in our tradition, which is shared even by many of those who are highly critical of the approach of mainstream psychology, or sociology, or political science. For it means that this is not a study in which anyone can engage, regardless of their level of insight; that some claims of the form: "if you don't understand, then your intuitions are at fault, are blind or inadequate," some claims of this form will be justified; that some differences will be nonarbitrable by further evidence, but that each side can only make appeal to deeper insight on the part of the other. The superiority of one position over another will thus consist in this, that from the more adequate position one can understand one's own stand and that of one's opponent, but not the other way around. It goes without saying that this argument can only have weight for those in the superior position.

Thus, a hermeneutical science encounters a gap in intuitions, which is the other side, as it were, of the hermeneutical circle. But the situation is graver than this; for this gap is bound up with our divergent options in politics and life.

We speak of a gap when some cannot understand the kind of self-definition which others are proposing as underlying a certain society or set of institutions. Thus some positivistically minded thinkers will find the language of identity-theory quite opaque; and some thinkers will not recognize any theory which does not fit with the categorial presuppositions of empiricism. But self-definitions are not only important to us as scientists who are trying to understand some, perhaps distant, social reality. As men we are self-defining beings, and we are partly what we are in virtue of the self-definitions which we have accepted, however we have come by them. What self-definitions we understand and what ones we don't understand, is closely linked with the self-definitions which help to constitute what we are. If it is too simple to say that one only understands

181

an "ideology" which one subscribes to, it is nevertheless hard to deny that we have great difficulty grasping definitions whose terms structure the world in ways which are utterly different from, incompatible with, our own.

Hence the gap in intuitions doesn't just divide different theoretical positions, it also tends to divide different fundamental options in life. The practical and the theoretical are inextricably joined here. It may not just be that to understand a certain explanation one has to sharpen one's intuitions; it may be that one has to change one's orientation—if not in adopting another orientation, at least in living one's own in a way which allows for greater comprehension of others. Thus, in the sciences of man insofar as they are hermeneutical there can be a valid response to "I don't understand" which takes the form, not only "develop your intuitions," but more radically "change yourself." This puts an end to any aspiration to a value-free or "ideology-free" science of man. A study of the science of man is inseparable from an examination of the options between which men must choose.

This means that we can speak here not only of error, but of illusion. We speak of "illusion" when we are dealing with something of greater substance than error, error which in a sense builds a counterfeit reality of its own. But errors of interpretation of meaning, which are also self-definitions of those who interpret and hence inform their lives, are more than errors in this sense: they are sustained by certain practices of which they are constitutive. It is not implausible to single out as examples two rampant illusions in our present society. One is that of the proponents of the bargaining society who can recognize nothing but either bargaining gambits or madness in those who rebel against this society. Here the error is sustained by the practices of the bargaining culture, and given a semblance of reality by the refusal to treat any protests on other terms; it hence acquires the more substantive reality of illusion. The second example is provided by much "revolutionary" activity in our society which in desperate search for an alternative mode of life purports to see its situation in that of an Andean guerilla or Chinese peasants. Lived out, this passes from the stage of laughable error to tragic illusion. One illusion cannot recognize the possibility of human variation; the other cannot see any limits to man's ability to transform itself. Both make a valid science of man impossible.

In the face of all this, we might be so scandalized by the prospect of such a hermeneutical science that we will want to go back to the verification model. Why can we not take our understanding of meaning as part of the logic of discovery, as the logical empiricists suggest for our unformalizable insights, and still found our science on the exactness of our predictions? Our insightful understanding of the intersubjective meanings of our society will then serve to elaborate fruitful hypotheses, but the proof of these puddings will remain in the degree they enable us to predict.

The answer is that if the epistemological views underlying the science of interpretation are right, such exact prediction is radically impossible. This, for three reasons of ascending order of fundamentalness.

The first is the well-known "open system" predicament, one shared by human life and meteorology, that we cannot shield a certain domain of human events, the psychological, economic, political, from external interference; it is impossible to delineate a closed system.

The second, more fundamental, is that if we are to understand men by a science of interpretation, we cannot achieve the degree of fine exactitude of a science based on brute data. The data of natural science admit of measurement to virtually any degree of exactitude. But different interpretations cannot be judged in this way. At the same time different nuances of interpretation may lead to different predictions in some circumstances, and these different outcomes may eventually create widely varying futures. Hence it is more than easy to be wide of the mark.

But the third and most fundamental reason for the impossibility of hard prediction is that man is a self-defining animal. With changes in his self-definition go changes in what man is, such that he has to be understood in different terms. But the conceptual mutations in human history can and frequently do produce conceptual webs which are incommensurable, that is, where the terms can't be defined in relation to a common stratum of expressions. The entirely different notions of bargaining in our society and in some primitive ones provide an example. Each will be glossed in terms of practices, institutions, ideas in each society which have nothing corresponding to them in the other.

The success of prediction in the natural sciences is bound up with the fact that all states of the system, past and future, can be described in the same range of concepts, as values, say, of the same variables. Hence all future states of the solar system can be characterized, as past ones are, in the language of Newtonian mechanics. This is far from being a sufficient condition of exact prediction, but it is a necessary one in this sense, that only if past and future are brought under the same conceptual net can one understand the states of the latter as some function of the states of the former, and hence predict.

This conceptual unity is vitiated in the sciences of man by the fact of conceptual innovation which in turn alters human reality. The very terms in which the future will have to be characterized if we are to understand it properly are not all available to us at present. Hence we have such radically unpredictable events as the culture of youth today, the Puritan rebellion of the sixteenth and seventeenth centuries, the development of Soviet society, etc.

And thus, it is much easier to understand after the fact than it is to predict. Human science is largely *ex post* understanding. Or often one has the sense of impending change, of some big reorganization, but is powerless to make clear what it will consist in: one lacks the vocabulary. But there is a clear assymmetry here, which there is not (or not supposed to be) in natural science, where events are said to be predicted from the theory with exactly the same ease with which one explains past events and by exactly the same process. In human science this will never be the case.

Of course, we strive *ex post* to understand the changes, and to do this we try to develop a language in which we can situate the incommensurable webs of concepts. We see the rise of Puritanism, for instance, as a shift in man's stance to the sacred; and thus, we have a language in which we can express both stances—the earlier mediaeval Catholic one and the Puritan rebellion—as "glosses" on this fundamental term. We thus have a language in which to talk of the transition. But think how we acquired it. This general category of the sacred is acquired not only from our experience of the shift which came in the Reformation, but from the study of human religion in general, including primitive religion, and with the detachment which came with secularization. It would be conceivable, but unthinkable, that a mediaeval Catholic could have this conception—or for that matter a Puritan. These two protagonists only had a language of condemnation for each other: "heretic," "idolator." The place for such a concept was pre-empted by a certain way of living the sacred. After a big change has happened, and the trauma has been resorbed, it is possible to try to understand it, because one now has available the new language, the transformed meaning world. But hard prediction before just makes one a laughing stock. Really to be able to predict the future would be to have explicated so clearly the human condition that one would already have pre-empted all cultural innovation and transformation. This is hardly in the bounds of the possible.

Sometimes men show amazing prescience: the myth of Faust, for instance, which is treated several times at the beginning of the modern era. There is a kind of prophesy here, a premonition. But what characterizes these bursts of foresight is that they see through a glass darkly, for they see in terms of the old language: Faust sells his soul to the devil. They are in no sense hard predictions. Human science looks backward. It is inescapably historical.

There are thus good grounds both in epistemological arguments and in their greater fruitfulness for opting for hermeneutical sciences of man. But we cannot hide from ourselves how greatly this option breaks with certain commonly held notions about our scientific tradition. We cannot measure such sciences against the requirements of a science of verification: we cannot judge them by their predictive capacity. We have to accept that they are founded on intuitions which all do not share, and what is worse that these intuitions are closely bound up with our fundamental options. These sciences cannot be *"wertfrei"*; they are moral sciences in a more radical sense than the eighteenth century understood. Finally, their successful prosecution requires a high degree of self-knowledge, a freedom from illusion, in the sense of error which is rooted and expressed in one's way of life; for our incapacity to understand is rooted in our own self-definitions, hence in what we are. To say this is not to say anything new: Aristotle makes a similar point in Book I of the *Ethics*. But it is still radically shocking and unassimilable to the mainstream of modern science.

Notes

1. Cf., e.g., H. G. Gadamer, *Wahrheit und Methode* (Tübingen, 1960).
2. Cf. Paul Ricoeur, *De l'Interprétation* (Paris, 1965).
3. Cf., for instance, J. Habermas, *Erkenntnis und Interesse* (Frankfurt, 1968).
4. The notion of brute data here has some relation to, but is not at all the same as the "brute facts" discussed by Elizabeth Anscombe, "On Brute Facts," *Analysis* 18 (1957–1958): 69–72, and John Searle, *Speech Acts: An Essay in the Philosophy of Language* (Cambridge, Eng.: 1969), pp. 50–53. For Anscombe and Searle, brute facts are contrasted to what may be called "institutional facts," to use Searle's term, i.e., facts which presuppose the existence of certain institutions. Voting would be an example. But, as we shall see below in Part II, some institutional facts, such as X's having voted Liberal, can be verified as brute data in the sense used here, and thus find a place in the category of political behavior. What cannot as easily be described in terms of brute data are the institutions themselves. Cf. the discussion below in Part II.
5. Cf. discussion in M. Minsky, *Computation* (Englewood Cliffs, N.J., 1967), pp. 104–7, where Minsky explicitly argues that an effective procedure, which no longer requires intuition or interpretation, is one which can be realized by a machine.
6. Cf. H. McClosky, "Consensus and Ideology in American Politics," *American Political Science Review* 58 (1964): 361–82.
7. Gabriel A. Almond and G. Bingham Powell, *Comparative Politics: A Developmental Approach* (Boston and Toronto, 1966), p. 23.
8. Ibid, p. 50.
9. Cf. Thomas C. Smith, *The Agrarian Origins of Modern Japan* (Stanford,

1959), ch. 5. This type of consensus is also found in other traditional societies. Cf., for instance, the *desa* system of the Indonesian village.
10. Searle, *Speech Acts*, pp. 33–42.
11. Cf. the discussion in Stanley Cavell, *Must We Mean What We Say?* (New York, 1969), pp. 21–31.
12. Cf. Almond and Powell, *Comparative Politics*, p. 23.

CHAPTER 10

Phenomenology and Socialization: Some Comments on the Assumptions Underlying Socialization Theory

David M. Rafky

Introduction

This essay is addressed to one of the central problems in sociology, an area in which there is a concrete nexus between theory and empirical research: the process of socialization. This whole area is vague, somewhat muddled, and—according to some sociologists—suffers from an excess of "psychologizing." This essay presents neither new data nor original concepts. Our aims are to bring together some phenomenological strands of thinking on socialization and to make explicit the assumptions underlying much of the current thinking and research in this area. While a great deal of data has been collected on socialization into the professions, especially medicine, nursing, and dentistry, *little theoretical integration* has been attempted since the work of George Herbert Mead.[1] The reader may disagree and perhaps cite the Becker *et al.* study of medical students.[2] We believe, however, that sociologists have not attempted to reconcile traditional American socialization literature (mostly in the area of motivation) and the European perspectives of phenomenological reasoning (mostly in the areas of cognition and perception) together with Meadian symbolic interaction.[3] Perhaps this paper will suggest some basis for rapprochement. The following section presents a phenomenological framework for understanding the ends or aims of the socialization process. The concepts of the phenomenological philosophy codified by Edmund Husserl are not new to sociology: witness

Reprinted by permission of the author and publisher from *Sociological Analysis* 32, no. 1 (spring 1971).

their influence in the works of Litt, Vierkandt, Gurvitch, Monnerot, and Schütz.[4] Section two focuses on the assumptions underlying the Meadian analysis of socialization, many of which have been made explicit by phenomenologists. The third section examines selected differences between child and adult socialization. Socialization may entail enculturation, the introduction of a cultureless child into the adult culture of his society, or it may describe acculturation, the transition of an adult from one culture into another. Again, the focus is on underlying assumptions.

The Contents of the "World"

A model of socialization ultimately rests on an analysis of the contents of the "world" into which the newborn child is socialized.[5] The infant is born into a world of real objects or artifacts which exist independent of his self and delimit his immediate and pretended behavior. For example, a child cannot walk through a tree: he *must* go around it. The nature of this veridical world is not wholly independent of the particular society which inhabits it. If the material substratum is conceived as simply primary or subatomic particles in motion, then there is no ontological reason for one particular object or congeries of particles to be perceived rather than another, for "the relationship between the particles in one object and in another object are just as real and just as important as the relationships found between the particles within any single object itself."[6] There are, therefore, an infinite variety of "real" objects which may be carved out of the continuum of the material substratum.

This does not deny that some objects which impose themselves on consciousness are the result of certain particle relations that exist in the very structure of matter; these are ontological necessities. Other objects are carved out of the material substratum by structures and processes in the nervous system.[7] Gestalt psychologists and phenomenologists (e.g., Köhler) have investigated these physiologically necessary perceptions.[8] Merleau-Ponty, the phenomenological psychologist, suggests that the human nervous system contains inborn structures which organize selected stimuli into the objects of ego and other:

> For a child, language which is understood, or simply sketched, the appearance of a face or that of a use-object, must from the beginning be the sonorous, motor or visual envelope of a significant intention coming from another. The organization and the sense of understood language can be very minimal at first; it will be the inflection of the voice, the intonation which will be understood, rather than the verbal material. But from the beginning the sonorous phenomena—whether I speak or another speaks—will be inte-

grated into the structure: expression-expressed; the face—whether I touch my own or I see that of another—will be integrated into the structure: alter-ego.[9]

Finally, one category of objects obtains its reality or being from social necessity; each culture carves out objects or isolates patterns of particle relations from the panorama of potential objects in accordance with its needs, inclinations, and language structure.[10] The so-called real world of objects which surrounds the infant is, therefore, partly socially defined and structured, and comprises the primary constituent of the world he enters at birth.

The newborn also enters a world of social institutions, the conventionally defined and shared values and norms—symbols—toward which members of his society orient their conduct. Social institutions have a reality identical to that of veridical objects. They exist outside the child in what Emile Durkheim calls the collective conscience and delimit present and anticipated behavior—they coerce the child in the same manner as a tree.[11]

Social institutions derive their objectivity from the fact that they have real or behavioral consequences.[12] For example, the institution of the family consists of rules of descent, inheritance, and conduct which exist or are real only insofar as they are obeyed. They are perceived by the infant as having a prior, external, objective—and thus coercive—existence in relation to himself; that is, social institutions are perceived as veridical objects. Social institutions are the second constituent of the world into which the child is born. In contrast to material objects, institutions are socially defined in their totality.[13]

These two elements, objects and institutions, comprise the world of everyday life. It is this reality into which the child is socialized. The phenomenological analysis of Alfred Schütz reveals the contents of this world in modern western society.[14] The world of everyday life is characterized by a particular tension of consciousness or level of awareness: this is the wide-awake attitude with which the individual gives his full attention and interest to life. The wide-awake self belongs to a person who is working in the real world, whose actions gear or mesh with those of other egos, who strives to change his environment and become modified by it. Working is subjectively meaningful or intentional because the individual is conscious of a projected state of affairs which he attempts to realize.

The world of everyday life is also characterized by a particular time perspective: the vivid present. The vivid present may be understood as the intersection between one's subjective sense of inner time (*durée*) and cosmic time. *Durée* is the imminent ordering and structuring of one's experiences whereby they "are connected within the past by recollections and retentions and with the future by protentions and anticipations."[15] Cosmic time is the ordering of events in the outer or non-subjective sphere. While participating in the world of everyday life we experience our working actions as a series of events which partake both of outer and inner time: that is, we experience them as a single flux which has an internal or subjective structure which corresponds to an external or cosmic ordering. In this sense, the vivid present may be understood as the standard time of modern western society.

The world of everyday life has a specific *epoché* of the natural attitude. *Epoché* implies suspension, and as used by Schütz refers to the individual suspending or giving up any doubt he might have about the existence of the world of everyday life in which he lives.[16] That is, to live in a cultural world and remain sane, one cannot doubt that it is, indeed, real; one cannot seriously entertain the idea that other worlds or modes of reality may be just as real, for this implies that one's own world is unreal. The motive for this is the fundamental anxiety from which all other fears, motives, etc., are derived.[17] Finally, the world of everyday life is characterized by a specific form of sociality. The world is inter-subjective: it is made up of other people (selves or subjectivities), and is shared by them. This state of affairs, brought about by communication of symbols and meanings, makes possible social action.

Thus, *our* world of everyday life is characterized by a specific tension of consciousness (wide-awakeness), a prevalent form of spontaneity (work), a particular time perspective (the vivid present), a specific *epoché*, and a unique form of sociality (a common intersubjective world).[18] There is more than one real world: the world of everyday life differs from culture to culture in its contents and cognitive structure (i.e., in the attributes listed above). For example, the level of awareness differs from society to society, just as their forms of spontaneity may not be identical. These life-worlds (*Lebenswelten*) not only change from one society to another, but vary to some extent within a particular society. In western industrialized society, for example, there exists side by side the world of dreams and the world of occupations. Various authors discuss life-worlds: William James calls them sub-universes; Alfred Schütz speaks of them as finite provinces of meaning; and Peter Berger and Thomas Luckmann coin the term "symbolic universe."[19]

Berger and Luckmann describe the content of symbolic universes or life-worlds as the legitimations (justifications or explanations) of the social institutions that comprise them.[20] In one sense, legitimations integrate the total institutional order of the society so that it "makes sense" to

Phenomenology and Socialization

the many people who participate in the various social institutions. On the other hand, legitimations make subjectively meaningful to a single individual the various stages of his own progress through the institutional order of his society. The first level or analysis is pre-theoretical. This level is first in the sense of logical priority, not temporal priority. The brute fact that an institution exists and is named legitimates it. For example, the very fact that a child learns to call an adult "father" legitimates the child's differential conduct towards him. The acquisition of a role is usually coupled with the learning of appropriate labels. "To this first level of incipient legitimation belong all the simple traditional affirmations."[21] For example, when a child asks the proverbial question, "Why?" the adult's evasive answer, "Because this is how things are done," constitutes the first order of legitimation.

The second level of legitimation is theoretical in a rudimentary sense. This level is characterized by wise sayings, saws, legends, and folktales. A child may be told not to masturbate because doing so will make him a dullard. The third level of legitimation is theoretical. Thus, in the realm of sexual behavior, a body of psychological theory may be employed as an explanation or justification for punishing a child's masturbatory behavior. On the fourth and final analytical level of legitimation, whole clusters of theories are synthesized and crystalized into a total world view. This world view or ideology legitimates the totality of institutionalized behavior patterns in a given society.

Thus, the life-world the newborn enters contains more than objects and social institutions. It is also characterized by a complex of legitimations which explain and integrate the various action patterns of the group, a "matrix of all socially objectivated and subjectively real meanings; the entire historic society and the entire biography of the individual are seen as events taking place within this universe."[22] In short, the individual has acquired a set or mode for interpreting the world meaningfully; he perceives it in an ordered and subjectively understandable frame of reference. Becker *et al.* arrive at the same idea by combining the Meadian explication of socialization with Thomas' concept of the definition of the situation. Becker *et al.* thus speak of "perspective," which results from a group's collective adaptation to common problems.[23]

Mechanisms of Socialization and Their Underlying Assumptions

Socialization is the process whereby the objective, i.e., external and coercive world of social objects, norms, values, institutions, and legitimations, become subjectively real to the individual. His consciousness is structured in accordance with the world view of his contemporaries and thus the symbolic universe acquires for the individual what William James calls the "accent of reality."[24] The goal of the socialization process is an individual who identifies with other people or situations. This is a result of the child's introjecting or "absorbing the environment or person-ality of others into . . . [his] own psyche to the extent of reacting to external events as though they were internal ones."[25] This process is not based on conscious imitation: introjection is an unconscious act.[26] The specific mechanisms mediating these processes are examined below and the assumptions that a Meadian analysis of socialization takes for granted are made explicit.

Explanations of socialization ultimately rest on the assumed exis-tence of the unique individual consciousness. The Cartesian statement *cogito ergo sum* cannot be accepted as proof of self-existence; it is merely a *post hoc, ergo propter hoc* statement of faith. The existence of self as a discrete entity is a function of the *ego cogito cogitatum* certitude.[27] According to this scheme, the self exists by virtue of its ability to indicate or "point to" things which transcend it (i.e., which exist as objects in relation to the self). In this way, the self is differentiated from other objects as it takes on a subject-object relationship with them.

The next assumption posits ego's knowledge of the existence of other selves or subjectivities. This constitutes the problem of intersubjectivity which has occupied such scholars as Scheler, Sartre, Husserl, and Schütz;[28] each attempts to explain the origin of the individual's subjective understanding (cognition) of other selves. W. I. Thomas' famous dictum, "If men define situations as real, they are real in their consequences," lies at the heart of any consideration of intersubjectivity.[29] According to Thomas, the actor's "definition of the situation" is only one element in the "total situation" which guides his behavior. Social behavior can only be understood (i.e., is only possible) when it is placed within the total situation which includes other subjectivities. Since individual behavior is necessarily situational, and varies widely from one situation to another, the self, if it enters into behavior, must have some situational aspect. Since social behavior is in conception interactive, what others do in response to an action or self presentation will make a difference to the actor; it will influence his behavior. He must, therefore, have some knowledge of other selves.

In a recent autobiographical essay, Talcott Parsons tackles the issue of intersubjectivity and comes to a position similar to our own, namely, that no satisfactory explanation of this phenomenon has yet been offered.[30] In his discussion of the rational complex and social order, Parsons asks: How is it possible to gain rational understanding of the non-rational? In an intriguing footnote he traces the origins of his position:

It may be of interest to note that I took a Kantian approach to the problem of order. Very broadly, with respect to the epistomology of empirical knowledge, Hume asked "is valid knowledge of the external world possible?" and came out with, by and large, a negative answer. Kant, on the other hand, posed the question in a more complex way. He first asserted that "we in fact *have* valid knowledge of the external world" then proceeded to ask "how is it possible?", that is, under what assumptions? Similarly some social theorists have wondered whether social order was possible at all, and often denied its possibility. I, on the other hand, have always assumed that social order in fact existed, however imperfectly, and proceeded to ask under what conditions this fact of its existence could be explained.[31]

The existence of other selves may, therefore, have to be accepted as a brute fact—a given with no explanation. It is fruitful, we believe, to first postulate the existence of other selves and then to ask, "How do we acquire knowledge of other subjectivities?" or "How do other selves become real to us?" Thus, we return full circle to Thomas' theorem. Perhaps an adequate approach to the problem of intersubjectivity must await a clarification of the concept of empathy and an elaboration of the Wundtian analysis of body gestures.[32]

The self is assumed to be a process; it flows between subject and object forms—that is, the self is reflexive.[33] The self as subject perceives, feels and acts on or towards other objects. The self bends around and perceives, feels, and literally observes itself as if it were an external object. Because the individual can, in this manner, make himself the object of his own actions, he is able to indicate or "designate things to himself—his wants, his pains, his goals, objects around him, the presence of others, their actions, their expected actions, or whatnot."[34] The individual acts towards himself as he acts towards others. His own gestures elicit in him the same meanings that they elicit in others. His actions are the result of meanings he bestows on vocal and other significant gestures which then become symbols.[35]

It is the reflexivity of the self which enables the child to "take on the attitude"[36] or role of significant or important others. He does this in two ways. In the first, he simply imitates the behavior of another person in his play activity. For example, children often play mother. Part of their selves (self as subject) imitates the role behavior of mother. The child (self as subject) addresses his self (self as object) with mother's words: "Be a good boy and wash your hands." The child then obeys the command. This mechanism of social control leads to the youngster's development of the child role. In the second case, the child's behavior, which has a particular meaning for his mother, elicits the same meaning in himself. His dirty hands, which typically cause mother to request him to wash, are perceived by the child. He (self as subject) takes on the role of mother and commands himself (self as object) to wash. In either case, the child learns to act in the manner expected by significant others. In taking on the role of the child, the child has also internalized the roles of his significant others; it is this which allows him to interact or relate to these significant others. The internalized roles of significant others are synthesized within the child and make up the role of the generalized other: this enables the child to relate to people in general, to those who are not his significant others, and even to people he has not encountered. The self is, therefore, a conglomeration of roles that the child has introjected. The question, "Who are you?" typically elicits from a child a list of roles or characteristics which represent a synthesis of introjected roles. This is the meaning of the concept of identity. "When an individual becomes involved in the maintenance of a rule [role], he tends also to become committed to a particular image of self."[37]

Mead causes some confusion by his use of the phrases "attitude-taking," "role-taking," and "identity" interchangeably.[38] The meanings and interpretations of these concepts *vis-à-vis* the individual and his *Lebenswelt* are clarified in this rather lengthy passage from Berger:

> Socialization not only ensures that the individual is "real" to himself in a certain way, but that he will ongoingly respond to his experience of the world with the cognitive and emotive patterns appropriate to this "reality." For example, successful socialization shapes a self that apprehends itself exclusively and in a taken-for-granted way in terms of one or the other of two socially defined sexes, that knows this self-apprehension to be the only "real" one, and rejects as "unreal" any contrary modes of apprehension or emotionality. . . . Every society contains a repertoire of identities that is part of the "objective knowledge" of its members. It is "known" as a matter "of course" that there are men and women, that they have such-and-such psychological traits and that they will have such-and-such psychological reactions in typical circumstances. As the individual is socialized, these identities are "internalized." They are then not only taken for granted as constituents of an objective reality "out there" but as inevitable structures of the individual's own consciousness. The objective reality, as defined by

society, is subjectively appropriated. In other words, socialization brings about symmetry between objective and subjective reality, objective and subjective identity. The degree of this symmetry provides the criterion of the successfulness of socialization. The psychological reality of the successfully socialized individual thus verifies subjectively what his society has objectively defined as real. He is then no longer required to turn outside himself for "knowledge " concerning the nature proper of men and women. He can obtain that result by simple introspection. He "knows who he is." He feels accordingly. He can conduct himself "spontaneously," because the firmly internalized cognitive and emotive structures make it unnecessary or even impossible for him to reflect upon alternative possibilities of conduct. . . . Socialization is only possible if, as Mead put it, the individual "takes the attitude" [role, identity] of others, that is, relates to himself as others have first related to him. . . . The combined significance of these root perspectives of social psychology and the sociology of knowledge for the sociological understanding of identity, one may answer in a rather simple statement: *Identity, with its appropriate attachments of psychological reality, is always identity within a specific, socially constructed world.* Or, as seen from the viewpoint of the individual: *One identifies oneself, as one is identified by others, by being located in a common world.*[39]

Several corollaries follow from the above analysis. First, socialization requires other people—significant others—with whom the child interacts. Second, the child's identity is a system, either additive or integrative, of the roles, attitudes, identities or "whatnot" (to use an expression of Blumer) which significant others display *vis-à-vis* him when relating to him.[40] Third, and most important, socialization is continuous. It is not useful to conceive of socialization as a process that ends at some point in the biography of an individual. Thus, a change in significant others leads to a corresponding change in identity: a child interacts with new significant others and, therefore, makes additions to the sediment of his self-system or identity. For an individual to maintain a stable identity, the presence of significant others must be continuous.[41] A fourth corollary is supplied by Goffman, who elaborates the function of context in the development and presentation of self.[42] The self is situational in that other people and objects (social and physical) are necessary for its expression. For example, a person who presents a self defined as important and elevated may do so only to the extent that others act deferentially towards him. Thus, the self as it is presented and interpreted is a product of the interaction of ego, other subjectivities, physical objects (props, make-up, etc.), social institutions, and the symbolic universe.[43]

Some Differences Between Child and Adult Socialization

The following discussion is not intended to be exhaustive; we do not discuss what to some readers may be crucial differences between child and adult socialization, such as setting, the nature of process, the multiplicity of roles involved, the active contributions of child and adult, etc. We merely point out some selected differences between child and adult socialization which we feel deserve greater attention by researchers and theoreticians. The child, initially a *tabula rasa*, is enculturated: cultureless, he is introduced into the symbolic universe of his parent society. On the other hand, the adult, possessing a world-view, is acculturated: he moves from one symbolic universe into another. A more accurate description of adult socialization is, therefore, re-socialization. The archetype of adult re-socialization is the immigrant who assimilates the world-view of a society very different from the society of his birth. The child is socialized involuntarily whereas the adult may or may not be a willing subject. Adults who enter a new symbolic universe by religious or political conversion, or through psychoanalysis, are willing and often active participants in their re-socialization. Inmates of mental hospitals, political refugees, and prisoners in indoctrination camps typically are involuntary and passive participants.

The infant introjects the external world passively and unconsciously. The world-changing adult is more conscious of the socialization process itself; he imitates (consciously) more and identifies (unconsciously) less than the child. The adult also has more mechanisms than the child to facilitate acquisition of a new world-view. Whereas the infant uses only introjection, the adult introjects, displaces or substitutes, and projects in order to include new people and objects in the structure of his consciousness, i.e., in order to produce a state of internal identification with the external world.[44]

Many discussions of identification stress the importance of an emotional bond between the self and significant others.[45] There is some evidence that an emotional tie between subject and object is more prevalent and decisive during child socialization than in adult re-socialization.[46] Perhaps this is explained by the observation that the child, in his domestication, is in greater conflict with his trainers than is the adult.[47] The child, lacking a mature reality principle, is driven by primordial lust and rebellion. The adult has already been domesticated (i.e., socialized); therefore, additional socialization is not a new experience—it is the content of the socialization process which is unique. Thus, an emotional link is necessary to overcome the child's initial resistance to a new process, but is not required to overcome the adult's lesser resistance to the familiar process of world-view acquisition.[48]

Physiologists point out another important difference between adult re-socialization and enculturation. The full-term infant is premature. It is not simply that he has not grown to his adult body size; rather, certain physiological processes and structures are not mature at the time of birth. The myelin sheaths have not formed around the pyramidal (nerve fiber) tract by birth, but are completed later; ceratin endocrine products are lacking in the newborn; and, electroencephalographic recordings are "not mature."[49] The infant is, while undergoing socialization, developing both morphologically and physiologically. The implications of the interaction of biological and socializing processes have been largely ignored.[50] To speculate that there are biological consequences of social phenomena and social repercussions of biological changes is not to specify the results of this interaction. Needless to say, the adult undergoing re-socialization is fully matured biologically.[51]

The acquisition of language, concomitant with the child's biological development and initial socialization, is completed by adulthood. As the child's ability to symbolize increases, so does his rate of role acquisition. In contrast, the adult's symbolizing capacity is more or less fixed; therefore, the socialization of the adult progresses at a more constant rate than the socialization of the child.[52]

Finally, we would like to see additional research on negative and anticipatory socialization, two processes which are quite important in adult re-socialization. A great deal of professional education is not prescriptive, but is proscriptive and focuses on behavior which is defined as inappropriate. Furthermore, many adult socializng institutions screen out recruits who have not already acquired components of the world-view to be pursued in the institution.[53]

Conclusion

Rather than attempting a critique of the massive literature on socialization, we have presented some threads of thinking from phenomenology that bear on socialization. Our aim was to categorize the assumptions implicit in current thinking in the area and to stimulate further questions by theoreticians and researchers. Although many sociologists tend to share our feeling of how things are subjectively, they are uneasy about an analysis of socialization which they believe consciously turns away from what we know empirically about the process through which the behavior of human infants comes to be socialized and turns toward appeals to "the structure of consciousness," "the uniqueness of consciousness," and "introjection" as grounds for the development of an argument. Perhaps they are correct and the position developed in this paper can be equally or better supported by appeals to the knowledge we have about the organization of behavior—better supported because we do not have to totter over the cliff of phenomenological introspection, where every man's introspective report is the ultimate datum.

These doubts can best be resolved by additional synthesis and research which is theoretically grounded. The task, as we see it, is to identify and codify the assumptions common to traditional American socialization literature, current European phenomenological perspectives, and Meadian symbolic interaction. Once these assumptions are identified, they could be discussed in the concrete terms of, for example, the medical profession. Such an analysis might begin with a demonstration that traditional socialization literature in the area of child and adult socialization (perhaps best represented by Brim and Wheeler) is inadequate and then point out what phenomenological perspectives can offer by way of improvement.[54] Perhaps a close acquaintance with Alex Inkeles' formulations of the content of personality may help in such a task.[55]

1. What is the veridical or real world of physicians? This is partly socially defined and structured. It could be argued that physicians perceive objects (fine gradations in muscle tonus, for example) that are invisible to the layman. Psychoanalysts may live in a different veridical world than laymen, in that psychoanalytic theories, inclinations, and language structure enable the physician to carve patterns out of the world that are unknown to others. The veridical world consists of:
   a. ontological necessities.
   b. physiological necessary objects and relations.
   c. patterns and relations determined by needs and inclinations.
2. What is the content of the socially constructed world of physicians? This includes social institutions, conventionally defined and shared values and norms—symbols—toward which members of the medical profession orient their conduct. These permit the physician to interpret the world meaningfully in an ordered and subjectively understandable frame of reference. In short, what are the values, norms, and ideology of physicians which differentiate them from other members of society: norms about patient care, sickness, and so on. Specific elements in the life-world of physicians which may or may not differentiate them from non-physicians are:
   a. level of awareness (in the hospital, office, etc.).
   b. time perspective.

c. strength of belief in the objective reality of his life-world (cynicism, psychosis in the extreme).

d. predominant form of sociality.

e. legitimations or world view (in order of increasing complexity).

    i. names and labels

    ii. wise sayings, saws, about medicine and the profession

    iii. theory (germ theory of disease)

    iv. synthetic world-view (ideology of rationality and orderliness in all human endeavors).

3. How does the objective world (all of the above) become subjectively real to the physician? How does his identity become objectified? This process is based on the following assumptions and contingencies:

a. the self is reflexive and takes both subject and object forms.

b. other selves (physicians and non-physicians) exist.

c. the physician "takes on the attitude" of others. That is, he constructs his identity *vis-à-vis* the reactions of others to him, and the reactions of his self as subject to his self as object.

d. analysis of the procession of other selves (significant others) in the physician's career.

e. study of the context in which the presentation of self takes place (bedside, hospital, etc.).

f. to what extent this process is

    i. imitative

    ii. conscious

    iii. characterized by an emotional bond

    iv. anticipatory, and

    v. proscriptive.

We anxiously await a reevaluation of existing theories with a specificity of the kind suggested above.

Notes

Acknowledgments. I would like to thank Professor Peter Berger of the Graduate Faculty at the New School for Social Research for introducing me to the current trends in European social thought. Also, I would like to express appreciation to several anonymous reviewers whose suggestions are incorporated into this final draft.

1. G. H. Mead, *Mind, Self and Society* (Chicago: University of Chicago Press, 1934).

2. H. S. Becker, B. Geer, E. C. Hughes, and A. L. Strauss, *Boys in White: Student Culture in Medical School* (Chicago: University of Chicago Press, 1961).

3. Two noteworthy exceptions are Tiryakian's essay (E. A. Tiryakian, "Existential Phenomenology and the Sociological Tradition," *American Sociolo-*

Part Two: The Interpretive Approach

gical Review 30 [1965]: 674–88) and Berger and Luckmann's treatise on the sociology of knowledge (P. L. Berger and T. Luckmann, *The Social Construction of Reality: A Treatise in the Sociology of Knowledge* [New York: Doubleday and Co., 1966]), which spell out many of the connections between phenomenological philosophy and sociology. In addition, Mead's model, in *Mind, Self and Society*, has been used to guide studies of socialization into the professions; see, for example, Davis and Olesen's paper on student nurses (F. Davis and V. Olesen, "Initiation into a Women's Profession: Identity Problems in the Status Transition of Co-ed to Student Nurse," *Sociometry* 26 [1963]: 89–101) and the Becker *et al.* study of student physicians, *Boys in White*.

4. E. Husserl, *Cartesianische Meditationen*, ed. S. Strasser (The Hague: Martinus Nijhoff, 1950); T. Litt, *Individuum und Gemeinschaft* (Leipzig: B. G. Teubner, 1919; A. Vierkandt, *Naturvölker und Kulturvölker* (Leipzig: Duncker and Humbolt, 1896); G. Gurvitch, *La Vocation actuelle de la sociologie* (2nd ed.; Paris: Presses Universitaires de France, 1957); J. Monnerot, *Les Faits sociaux ne sont pas des choses* (Paris: Gallimard, 1946); A. Schütz, *Collected Papers: The Problems of Social Reality*, vol. 1 (The Hague: Martinus Nijhoff, 1962).

5. The use of the word "child" in this context is questionable. Child implies human-ness: one may legitimately question whether newborn, unsocialized *Homo sapiens* are, indeed, human. It is only after the process of socialization or domestication has taken place, that the infant may be said to be a human or a social animal. Thus, the human-ness is an acquired characteristic and feral men are not human in this sense.

6. G. H. Mead, "Evolution Becomes a General Idea," *George Herbert Mead on Social Psychology*, ed. A. Strauss (Chicago: University of Chicago Press, 1934), p. 5.

7. Kant called this structure the "faculty of understanding." This concept is useful in epitemology, and may be helpful in understanding the origins of purportedly *a priori* cognitions.

8. For example, W. Kohler, *Gestalt Psychology* (New York: Horace Liveright, 1929).

9. M. Merleau-Ponty, *The Structure of Behavior*, trans. A. L. Fisher (Boston: Beacon Press, 1963), pp. 170–71.

10. B. L. Whorf, *Language, Thought, and Reality* (New York: John Wiley and Sons, 1956).

11. E. Durkheim, *The Rules of Sociological Method* (Chicago: University of Chicago Press, 1938).

12. W. I. Thomas, "The Definition of the Situation," *Sociological Theory: A Book of Readings*, ed. L. A. Coser and B. Rosenberg (New York: MacMillan, 1957), pp. 233–35.

13. In the words of Durkheim (*The Rules of Sociological Method*, pp. 1–2): "When I perform my obligations as brother, husband, or citizen, when I execute my contracts, I perform duties which are defined, externally to myself and my acts, in law and in custom. Even if they conform to my own sentiments and I feel their reality subjectively, such reality is still objective, for I did not create them. . . . Here, then, are ways of acting, thinking, and feeling that present the noteworthy property of existing outside the indi-

vidual consciousness. These types of conduct or thought are not only external to the individual but are, moreover, endowed with coercive power, by virtue of which they impose themselves upon him, independent of his individual will."

14. Schütz, *Collected Papers*, vol. 1.

15. Ibid., pp. 215–216.

16. Here Schütz (ibid.) turns Husserl "on his head." For Husserl, *epoché* is the suspension of any *belief* relating to the existence or nonexistence of the external world, as a necessary procedure in the transcendental phenomenological reduction (Q. Lauer, *Phenomenology: Its Genesis and Prospect* [New York: Harper and Row, 1958]). Schütz (*Collected Papers*) uses *epoché* to indicate the suspension of *doubt*: that is, the veridicality of the external world is accepted without doubt.

17. Schütz defines the fundamental anxiety as follows: "I know that I shall die and I fear to die" (*Collected Papers*, p. 228).

18. At this point it may be helpful to make a rather fine—but nevertheless crucial—distinction. *Lebenswelt*, the lived-in-world, is also the taken-for-granted world, the world of how-to-do-it. These concepts are at different levels of understanding and should not be used interchangeably. See H. Garfinkel, *Studies in Ethnomethodology* (Englewood Cliffs, N.J.: Prentice-Hall, 1967), for a discussion of the how-to-do-it world.

19. Because "it is the meaning of our experiences and not the ontological structure of the objects which constitutes reality" (Schütz, *Collected Papers*, p. 230.

20. Berger and Luckmann, *The Social Construction of Reality*, point out that the concept of symbolic universe is similar to Durkheim's "idea of religion" (*The Rules of Sociological Method*) and Sartre's notion of "totalization" (J.-P. Sartre, (*L'Etre et le néant* [Paris: Gallimard, 1943]).

21. Berger and Luckmann, *The Social Construction of Reality*, p. 87.

22. Ibid., p. 89.

23. Becker *et al.*, *Boys in White*; Mead, *Mind, Self and Society*; Thomas, "The Definition of the Situation."

24. W. James, *Principles of Psychology*, vol. 2 (New York: Holt, 1890).

25. H. C. Warren, ed., *Dictionary of Psychology* (Boston: Houghton Mifflin, 1934), p. 143.

26. G. S. Blum, *Psychoanalytical Theories of Personality* (New York: McGraw-Hill, 1953).

27. Lauer, *Phenomenology*.

28. M. Scheler, *Die Wissensformen und die Gesellschaft: Probleme einer Soziologie des Wissens* (Bern: Frauke, 1966); Sartre, *L'Etre at le néant*; Husserl, *Cartesianische Meditationen*; Schütz, *Collected Papers*.

29. N. Timasheff. *Sociological Theory: Its Nature and Growth* (New York: Random House, 1957).

30. T. Parsons, "On Building Social System Theory: A Personal History," *Daedalus* 99 (1970): 826–881.

31. Ibid., p. 881.

32. Some progress has been made along these lines. See M. Henle, ed., *Documents of Gestalt Psychology* (Berkeley and Los Angeles: University of California Press, 1961), for an interesting analysis of empathy, and Mills's—

dated, yet still theoretically definitive—discussion of verbal gestures or symbols in the development and expression of motives in C. W. Mills, "Situated Actions and Vocabularies of Motive," *American Sociological Review* 4 no. 5 (1940): 904–913.

33. Mead, "Evolution Becomes a General Idea."

34. H. Blumer, "Sociological Implications of the Thought of George Herbert Mead," *American Journal of Sociology* 71 (1966): 535.

35. H. Blumer, "Society as Symbolic Interaction," *Human Behavior and Social Processes: An Interactionist Approach*, ed. A. M. Rose (Boston: Houghton Mifflin, 1962), pp. 179–93.

36. Mead, *Mind, Self and Society*.

37. E. Goffman, "The Nature of Deference and Demeanor," *American Anthropologist* 58 (1956): 474.

38. Mead, *Mind, Self and Society*.

39. P. Berger, "Identity as a Problem in the Sociology of Knowledge," *European Journal of Sociology* 7 (1966): 106–7, 111.

40. Blumer, "Sociological Implications." To most social psychologists it seems clear that the idea of socialization entails the notion of acting persons who know enough about what they are doing to constitute a society. Perhaps it is not so clear that "the child's identity is a system. . . ." They are correct in the sense that we already know something about processes and products of self-dissociation, and about failures to organize behavior in ways that support inferences to a self (in autistic children, for example) or behavioral disorganization which makes inference to a self difficult or impossible (in so-called "psychotic states," for example).

41. O. G. Brim, "Socialization through the Life Cycle," in Brim and S. Wheeler, *Socialization after Childhood: Two Essays* (New York: John Wiley and Sons, 1966), points out that as an individual becomes older, society's expectations of him change, and as a consequence, the need for adult socialization arises. He fails to recognize, however, that adult socialization is necessary even if new behavior is not required of an individual: socialization and world maintaining mechanisms are necessary to maintain and support *current* behavior. People who "share a common culture are continually supporting one another's perspectives, by each responding to the other in expected ways" (T. Shibutani, "Reference Groups and Social Control," *Human Behavior and Social Processes*, ed. Rose, p. 143). Interaction with significant others in any context is sufficient to maintain one's identity. In fact, interaction with patients is probably sufficient for this purpose (J. Tomich, "Home Care: A Technique for Generating Professional Identity," *Journal of Medical Education* 41 [1966]: 202–7). The presence of significant others for the maintenance or change of identity must not be taken only to mean *physical* presence. Mead (*Mind, Self and Society*) has probably been misinterpreted on this point; his discussions of memory and historical biography clearly indicate that the physical presence of significant others is not required. Consider, for example, the religious ascetic or hermit who lives in social isolation. They do communicate, however, if only with God or retentions of significant others.

42. Goffman, "The Nature of Deference and Demeanor."

43. E. Goffman, *The Presentation of Self in Everyday Life* (Garden City, N.Y.: Doubleday Anchor, 1959).

44. R. P. Knight, "Introjection, Projection and Identfication," *Psychoanalytic Quarterly* 9 (1940): 334–41. Knight (p. 335) states that the introjection "always involves previous projections onto the object of the subject's own unacceptable tendencies."

45. For example, Warren, ed., *Dictionary of Psychology.*

46. Brim ("Socialization through the Life Cycle") believes that the emotional tie between significant others and the child is intense, due to the strength and frequency of physical rewards and punishments administered by them to the child. This is not to say, however, that there are no emotional ties evident during adult identification. For example, during psychoanalysis, positive transference—the warm feeling which passes between analyst and patient—is a classic observation. One must determine whether this emotional bond is necessary for the adult to change world-views, or simply a concomitant of this change.

47. J. Dollard, "Culture, Society, Impulse, and Socialization," *American Journal of Sociology* 45 (1939): 50–64.

48. This resistance is described almost poetically by Dollard (ibid., p. 53): "It seems clear from the present data that socialization is a process full of conflict between the child and its trainers. Growing up is not a smooth automatic process of assimilating the folkways and mores; on the contrary, society has to deal with a rebellious animal full of animal lust and anger. The domestication of this animal is without exception a process attended by conflict and strain."

49. C. G. Thompson, *Child Psychology: Growth Trends in Psychological Adjustment* (Boston: Houghton Mifflin, 1952).

50. Studies of institutionalized infants (ibid.) indicate that their future development is, indeed, affected by early lack of interaction with parent surrogates. While language and social responsiveness are most likely to be permanently retarded, there is some evidence that the child's perceptual and motor skills may also be affected (although not necessarily permanently). These children exhibit apathy and less then normal affect. Brim ("Socialization through the Life Cycle") concludes that primary socialization is more durable and lasting because it takes place early in the biological history of the organism.

51. Adult socialization must also take the biological status of the individual into account. E. C. Hughes, in *Men and Their Work* (Glencoe, Ill.: Free Press, 1958), discusses the biological requirements of certain roles, such as strength and vitality. People accommodate to certain biological concomitants of their roles and may thus find themselves unable or unwilling to adjust to the more "primitive" conditions of new roles (Brim, "Socialization through the Life Cycle").

52. Brim, "Socialization through the Life Cycle."

53. Becker *et al.*, *Boys in White*; H. S. Becker, "The Nature of a Profession," *Sixty-first Yearbook of the National Society for the Study of Education*, pt. 2 (Chicago: University of Chicago Press, 1962), pp. 27–46; Brim, "Socialization through the Life Cycle"; E. C. Hughes, "Education for a Profession," *Library Quarterly* 31 (1961): 336–43; N. Rogoff, "The Decision to Study Medicine," *The Student-Physician*, ed. R. K. Merton *et al.* (Cambridge, Mass.: Harvard University Press, 1957), pp. 109–31; D. B. Stuit, S. D. Gwendolen, T. F. Jordan, and L. Schloreb, *Predicting Success in Profes-*

sional Schools (Washington, D.C.: American Council on Education, 1949); and W. Thielens, "Some Comparisons of Entrants to Medical and Law School," *The Student-Physician*, ed. Merton *et al.*, pp. 131–53.
54. Brim and Wheeler, *Socialization after Childhood*.
55. A. Inkeles, "Society, Social Structure, and Child Socialization," *Socialization and Society*, ed. John A. Clausen (Boston: Little, Brown, 1968), pp. 73–129.

CHAPTER 11

A Theory of Play and Fantasy

Gregory Bateson

This research was planned and started with an hypothesis to guide our investigations, the task of the investigators being to collect relevant observational data and, in the process, to amplify and modify the hypothesis.

The hypothesis will here be described as it has grown in our thinking.

Earlier fundamental work of Whitehead, Russell,[1] Wittgenstein,[2] Carnap,[3] Whorf,[4] etc., as well as my own attempts[5] to use this earlier thinking as an epistemological base for psychiatric theory, led to a series of generalizations:

1. That human verbal communication can operate and always does operate at many contrasting levels of abstraction. These range in two directions from the seemingly simple denotative level ("The cat is on the mat"). One range or set of these more abstract levels includes those explicit or implicit messages where the subject of discourse is the language. We will call these metalinguistic (for example, "The verbal sound 'cat' stands for any member of such and such class of objects," or "The word, 'cat,' has no fur and cannot scratch"). The other set of levels of abstraction we will call metacommunicative (e.g., "My telling you where to find the cat was friendly," or "This is play"). In these, the subject of discourse is the relationship between the speakers.

It will be noted that the vast majority of both metalinguistic and metacommunicative messages remain implicit; and also that, especially in the psychiatric interview, there occurs a further class of implicit messages about how metacommunicative messages of friendship and hostility are to be interpreted.

This essay was read (by Jay Haley) at the A.P.A. Regional Research Conference in Mexico City, March 11, 1954. It is here reprinted from *Psychiatric Research Reports*, II (Washington, D.C.: American Psychiatric Association, 1955), by permission of the publisher.

2. If we speculate about the evolution of communication, it is evident that a very important stage in this evolution occurs when the organism gradually ceases to respond quite "automatically" to the mood-signs of another and becomes able to recognize the sign as a signal: that is, to recognize that the other individual's and its own signals are only signals, which can be trusted, distrusted, falsified, denied, amplified, corrected, and so forth.

Clearly this realization that signals are signals is by no means complete even among the human species. We all too often respond automatically to newspaper headlines as though these stimuli were direct object-indications of events in our environment instead of signals concocted and transmitted by creatures as complexly motivated as ourselves. The nonhuman mammal is automatically excited by the sexual odor of another; and rightly so, inasmuch as the secretion of that sign is an "involuntary" mood-sign; i.e., an outwardly perceptible event which is a part of the physiological process which we have called a mood. In the human species a more complex state of affairs begins to be the rule. Deodorants mask the involuntary olfactory signs, and in their place the cosmetic industry provides the individual with perfumes which are not involuntary signs but voluntary signals, recognizable as such. Many a man has been thrown off balance by a whiff of perfume, and if we are to believe the advertisers, it seems that these signals, voluntarily worn, have sometimes an automatic and autosuggestive effect even upon the voluntary wearer.

Be that as it may, this brief digression will serve to illustrate a stage of evolution—the drama precipitated when organisms, having eaten of the fruit of the Tree of Knowledge, discover that their signals are signals. Not only the characteristically human invention of language can then follow, but also all the complexities of empathy, identification, projection, and so on. And with these comes the possibility of communicating at the multiplicity of levels of abstraction mentioned above.

3. The first definite step in the formulation of the hypothesis guiding this research occurred in January 1952, when I went to the Fleishhacker Zoo in San Francisco to look for behavioral criteria which would indicate whether any given organism is or is not able to recognize that the signs emitted by itself and other members of the species are signals. In theory, I had thought out what such criteria might look like—that the occurrence of metacommunicative signs (or signals) in the stream of interaction between the animals would indicate that the animals have at least some awareness (conscious or unconscious) that the signs about which they metacommunicate are signals.

I knew, of course, that there was no likelihood of finding denotative messages among nonhuman mammals, but I was still not aware that the animal data would require an almost total revision of my thinking. What I encountered at the zoo was a phenomenon well known to everybody: I saw two young monkeys *playing*, i.e., engaged in an interactive sequence of which the unit actions or signals were similar to but not the same as those of combat. It was evident, even to the human observer, that the sequence as a whole was not combat, and evident to the human observer that to the participant monkeys this was "not combat."

Now, this phenomenon, play, could only occur if the participant organisms were capable of some degree of metacommunication, i.e., of exchanging signals which would carry the message "this is play."

4. The next step was the examination of the message "This is play," and the realization that this message contains those elements which necessarily generate a paradox of the Russellian or Epimenides type—a negative statement containing an implicit negative metastatement. Expanded, the statement "This is play" looks something like this: "These actions in which we now engage do not denote what those actions *for which they stand* would denote."

We now ask about the italicized words, "*for which they stand.*" We say the word "cat" stands for any member of a certain class. That is, the phrase "stands for" is a near-synonym of "denotes." If we now substitute "which they denote" for the words "for which they stand" in the expanded definition of play, the result is: "These actions, in which we now engage, do not denote what would be denoted by those actions which these actions denote." The playful nip denotes the bite, but it does not denote what would be denoted by the bite.

According to the Theory of Logical Types such a message is of course inadmissable, because the word "denote" is being used in two degrees of abstraction, and these two uses are treated as synonymous. But all that we learn from such a criticism is that it would be bad natural history to expect the mental processes and communicative habits of mammals to conform to the logician's ideal. Indeed, if human thought and communication always conformed to the ideal, Russell would not—in fact could not—have formulated the ideal.

5. A related problem in the evolution of communication concerns the origin of what Korzybski has called the map-territory relation: the fact that a message, of whatever kind, does not consist of those objects which it denotes ("The word 'cat' cannot scratch us").[6] Rather, language bears to the objects which it denotes a relationship comparable to that which a map bears to a territory. Denotative communication as it occurs

at the human level is only possible *after* the evolution of a complex set of metalinguistic (but not verbalized) rules which govern how words and sentences shall be related to objects and events.[7] It is therefore appropriate to look for the evolution of such metalinguistic and/or metacommunicative rules at a prehuman and preverbal level.

It appears from what is said above that play is a phenomenon in which the actions of "play" are related to, or denote, other actions of "not play." We therefore meet in play with an instance of signals standing for other events, and it appears, therefore, that the evolution of play may have been an important step in the evolution of communication.

6. *Threat* is another phenomenon which resembles play in that actions denote, but are different from, other actions. The clenched fist of threat is different from the punch, but it refers to a possible future (but at present nonexistent) punch. And threat also is commonly recognizable among nonhuman mammals. Indeed it has lately been argued that a great part of what appears to be combat among members of a single species is rather to be regarded as threat.[8]

7. Histrionic behavior and deceit are other examples of the primitive occurrence of map-territory differentiation. And there is evidence that dramatization occurs among birds: a jackdaw may imitate her own mood-signs,[9] and deceit has been observed among howler monkeys.[10]

8. We might expect threat, play, and histrionics to be three independent phenomena all contributing to the evolution of the discrimination between map and territory. But it seems that this would be wrong, at least so far as mammalian communication is concerned. Very brief analysis of childhood behavior shows that such combinations as histrionic play, bluff, physical threat, teasing play in response to threat, histrionic threat, and so on form together a single total complex of phenomena. And such adult phenomena as gambling and playing with risk have their roots in the combination of threat and play. It is evident also that not only threat but the reciprocal of threat—the behavior of the threatened individual—are a part of this complex. It is probable that not only histrionics but also spectatorship should be included within this field. It is also appropriate to mention self-pity.

9. A further extension of this thinking leads us to include ritual within this general field in which the discrimination is drawn, but not completely, between denotative action and that which is to be denoted. Anthropological studies of peace-making ceremonies, to cite only one example, support this conclusion.

In the Andaman Islands, peace is concluded after each side has been given ceremonial freedom to strike the other. This example, however, also illustrates the labile nature of the frame "This is play," or "This is ritual." The discrimination between map and territory is always liable to break down, and the ritual blows of peace-making are always liable to be mistaken for the "real" blows of combat. In this event, the peace-making ceremony becomes a battle.[11]

10. But this leads us to recognition of a more complex form of play; the game which is constructed not upon the premise "This is play" but rather around the question "Is this play?" And this type of interaction also has its ritual forms, e.g., in the hazing of initiation.

11. Paradox is doubly present in the signals which are exchanged within the context of play, fantasy, threat, etc. Not only does the playful nip not denote what would be denoted by the bite for which it stands, but, in addition, the bite itself is fictional. Not only do the playing animals not quite mean what they are saying but, also, they are usually communicating about something which does not exist. At the human level, this leads to a vast variety of complications and inversions in the fields of play, fantasy, and art. Conjurers and painters of the *trompe l'oeil* school concentrate upon acquiring a virtuosity whose only reward is reached after the viewer detects that he has been deceived and is forced to smile or marvel at the skill of the deceiver. Hollywood film-makers spend millions of dollars to increase the realism of a shadow. Other artists, perhaps more realistically, insist that art be nonrepresentational; and poker players achieve a strange addictive realism by equating the chips for which they play with dollars. They still insist, however, that the loser accept his loss as part of the game.

Finally, in the dim region where art, magic, and religion meet and overlap, human beings have evolved the "metaphor that is meant," the flag which men will die to save, and the sacrament that is felt to be more than "an outward and visible sign, given unto us." Here we can recognize an attempt to deny the difference between map and territory, and to get back to the absolute innocence of communication by means of pure mood-signs.

12. We face then two peculiarities of play: (*a*) that the messages or signals exchanged in play are in a certain sense untrue or not meant; and (*b*) that that which is denoted by these signals is nonexistent. These two peculiarities sometimes combine strangely to reverse a conclusion reached above. It was stated (4) that the playful nip denotes the bite, but does not denote that which would be denoted by the bite. But there are other instances where an opposite phenomenon occurs. A man experiences the full intensity of subjective terror when a spear is flung at him out of the 3D screen or when he falls headlong from some peak created in his

own mind in the intensity of nightmare. At the moment of terror there was no questioning of "reality," but still there was no spear in the movie house and no cliff in the bedroom. The images did not denote that which they seemed to denote, but these same images did really evoke that terror which would have been evoked by a real spear or a real precipice. By a similar trick of self-contradiction, the film-makers of Hollywood are free to offer to a puritanical public a vast range of pseudosexual fantasy which otherwise would not be tolerated. In *David and Bathsheba*, Bathsheba can be a Troilistic link between David and Uriah. And in *Hans Christian Andersen*, the hero starts out accompanied by a boy. He tries to get a woman, but when he is defeated in this attempt, he returns to the boy. In all of this, there is, of course, no homosexuality, but the choice of these symbolisms is associated in these fantasies with certain characteristic ideas, e.g., about the hopelessness of the heterosexual masculine position when faced with certain sorts of women or with certain sorts of male authority. In sum, the pseudohomosexuality of the fantasy does not stand for any real homosexuality, but does stand for and express attitudes which might accompany a real homosexuality or feed its etiological roots. The symbols do not denote homosexuality, but do denote ideas for which homosexuality is an appropriate symbol. Evidently it is necessary to re-examine the precise semantic validity of the interpretations which the psychiatrist offers to a patient, and, as preliminary to this analysis, it will be necessary to examine the nature of the frame in which these interpretations are offered.

13. What has previously been said about play can be used as an introductory example for the discussion of frames and contexts. In sum, it is our hypothesis that the message "This is play" establishes a paradoxical frame comparable to Epimenides' paradox. This frame may be diagrammed thus:

> All statements within this frame are untrue.
>
> I love you.
>
> I hate you.

The first statement within this frame is a self-contradictory proposition about itself. If this first statement is true, then it must be false. If it be false, then it must be true. But this first statement carries with it all the other statements in the frame. So, if the first statement be true, then all the others must be false; and vice versa, if the first statement be untrue then all the others must be true.

14. The logically minded will notice a non sequitur. It could be urged that even if the first statement is false, there remains a logical possibility that some of the other statements in the frame are untrue. It is, however, a characteristic of unconscious or "primary-process" thinking that the thinker is unable to discriminate between "some" and "all," and unable to discriminate between "not all" and "none." It seems that the achievement of these discriminations is performed by higher or more conscious mental processes which serve in the nonpsychotic individual to correct the black-and-white thinking of the lower levels. We assume, and this seems to be an orthodox assumption, that primary process is continually operating, and that the psychological validity of the paradoxical play frame depends upon this part of the mind.

15. But, conversely, while it is necessary to invoke the primary process as an explanatory principle in order to delete the notion of "some" from between "all" and "none," this does not mean that play is simply a primary-process phenomenon. The discrimination between "play" and "nonplay," like the discrimination between fantasy and non-fantasy, is certainly a function of secondary process, or "ego." Within the dream the dreamer is usually unaware that he is dreaming, and within "play" he must often be reminded that "This is play."

Similarly, within dream or fantasy the dreamer does not operate with the concept "untrue." He operates with all sorts of statements but with a curious inability to achieve metastatements. He cannot, unless close to waking, dream a statement referring to (i.e., framing) his dream.

It therefore follows that the play frame as here used as an explanatory principle implies a special combination of primary and secondary processes. This, however, is related to what was said earlier, when it was argued that play marks a step forward in the evolution of communication—the crucial step in the discovery of map-territory relations. In primary process, map and territory are equated; in secondary process, they can be discriminated. In play, they are both equated and discriminated.

16. Another logical anomaly in this system must be mentioned: that the relationship between two propositions which is commonly described by the word "premise" has become intransitive. In general, all asymmetrical relationships are transitive. The relationship "greater than" is typical in this respect; it is conventional to argue that if A is greater than B, and B is greater than C, then A is greater than C. But in psychological processes the transivity of asymmetrical relations is not observed. The

proposition P may be a premise for Q; Q may be a premise for R; and R may be a premise for P. Specifically, in the system which we are considering, the circle is still more contracted. The message, "All statements within this frame are untrue" is itself to be taken as a premise in evaluating its own truth or untruth. (Cf. the intransivity of psychological preference discussed by McCulloch.[12] The paradigm for all paradoxes of this general type is Russell's[13] "class of classes which are not members of themselves." Here Russell demonstrates that paradox is generated by treating the relationship, "is a member of," as an intransitive.) With this caveat, that the "premise" relation in psychology is likely to be intransitive, we shall use the word "premise" to denote a dependency of one idea or message upon another comparable to the dependency of one proposition upon another which is referred to in logic by saying that the proposition P is a premise for Q.

17. All this, however, leaves unclear what is meant by "frame" and the related notion of "context." To clarify these, it is necessary to insist first that these are psychological concepts. We use two sorts of analogy to discuss these notions: the physical analogy of the picture frame and the more abstract, but still not psychological, analogy of the mathematical set. In set theory the mathematicians have developed axioms and theorems to discuss with rigor the logical implications of membership in overlapping categories or "sets." The relationships between sets are commonly illustrated by diagrams in which the items or members of a larger universe are represented by dots, and the smaller sets are delimited by imaginary lines enclosing the members of each set. Such diagrams then illustrate a topological approach to the logic of classification. The first step in defining a psychological frame might be to say that it is (or delimits) a class or set of messages (or meaningful actions). The play of two individuals on a certain occasion would then be defined as the set of all messages exchanged by them within a limited period of time and modified by the paradoxical premise system which we have described. In a set-theoretical diagram these messages might be represented by dots, and the "set" enclosed by a line which would separate these from other dots representing nonplay messages. The mathematical analogy breaks down, however, because the psychological frame is not satisfactorily represented by an imaginary line. We assume that the psychological frame has some degree of real existence. In many instances, the frame is consciously recognized and even represented in vocabulary ("play," "movie," "interview," "job," "language," etc.). In other cases, there may be no explicit verbal reference to the frame, and the subject may have no consciousness of it. The analyst, however, finds that his own

thinking is simplified if he uses the notion of an unconscious frame as an explanatory principle; usually he goes further than this and infers its existence in the subject's unconscious.

But while the analogy of the mathematical set is perhaps over abstract, the analogy of the picture frame is excessively concrete. The psychological concept which we are trying to define is neither physical nor logical. Rather, the actual physical frame is, we believe, added by human beings to physical pictures because these human beings operate more easily in a universe in which some of their psychological characteristics are externalized. It is these characteristics which we are trying to discuss, using the externalization as an illustrative device.

18. The common functions and uses of psychological frames may now be listed and illustrated by reference to the analogies whose limitations have been indicated in the previous paragraph:

a. Psychological frames are exclusive, i.e., by including certain messages (or meaningful actions) within a frame, certain other messages are excluded.

b. Psychological frames are inclusive, i.e., by excluding certain messages certain others are included. From the point of view of set theory these two functions are synonymous, but from the point of view of psychology it is necessary to list them separately. The frame around a picture, if we consider this frame as a message intended to order or organize the perception of the viewer, says, "Attend to what is within and do not attend to what is outside." Figure and ground, as these terms are used by gestalt psychologists, are not symmetrically related as are the set and nonset of set theory. Perception of the ground must be positively inhibited and perception of the figure (in this case the picture) must be positively enhanced.

c. Psychological frames are related to what we have called "premises." The picture frame tells the viewer that he is not to use the same sort of thinking in interpreting the picture that he might use in interpreting the wallpaper outside the frame. Or, in terms of the analogy from set theory, the messages enclosed within the imaginary line are defined as members of a class by virtue of their sharing common premises or mutual relevance. The frame itself thus becomes a part of the premise system. Either, as in the case of the play frame, the frame is involved in the evaluation of the messages which it contains, or the frame merely assists the mind in understanding the contained messages by reminding the thinker that these messages are mutually relevant and the message outside the frame may be ignored.

d. In the sense of the previous paragraph, a frame is metacommunicative. Any message, which either explicitly or implicitly defines a frame, ipso facto gives the receiver instructions or aids in his attempt to understand the messages included within the frame.

e. The converse of (*d*) is also true. Every metacommunicative or metalinguistic message defines, either explicitly or implicitly, the set of messages about which it communicates, i.e., every metacommunicative message is or defines a psychological frame. This, for example, is very evident in regard to such small metacommunicative signals as punctuation marks in a printed message, but applies equally to such complex metacommunicative messages as the psychiatrist's definition of his own curative role in terms of which his contributions to the whole mass of messages in psychotherapy are to be understood.

f. The relation between psychological frame and perceptual gestalt needs to be considered, and here the analogy of the picture frame is useful. In a painting by Rouault or Blake, the human figures and other objects represented are outlined. "Wise men see outlines and therefore they draw them." But outside these lines, which delimit the perceptual gestalt or "figure," there is a background or "ground" which in turn is limited by the picture frame. Similarly, in set-theoretical diagrams, the larger universe within which the smaller sets are drawn is itself enclosed in a frame. This double framing is, we believe, not merely a matter of "frames within frames" but an indication that mental processes resemble logic in *needing* an outer frame to delimit the ground against which the figures are to be perceived. This need is often unsatisfied, as when we see a piece of sculpture in a junk shop window, but this is uncomfortable. We suggest that the need for this outer limit to the ground is related to a preference for avoiding the paradoxes of abstraction. When a logical class or set of items is defined—for example, the class of matchboxes—it is necessary to delimit the set of items which are to be excluded, in this case, all those things which are not matchboxes. But the items to be included in the background set must be of the same degree of abstraction, i.e., of the same "logical type" as those within the set itself. Specifically, if paradox is to be avoided, the "class of matchboxes" and the "class of nonmatchboxes" (even though both these items are clearly not matchboxes) must not be regarded as members of the class of nonmatchboxes. No class can be a member of itself. The picture frame then, because it delimits a background, is here regarded as an external representation of a very special and important type of psychological frame—namely a frame whose function is to delimit a logical type. This, in fact, is what was indicated above when it was said that the picture frame is an instruction to the viewer that he should not extend the premises which obtain between the figures within the picture to the wallpaper behind it.

But, it is precisely this sort of frame that precipitates paradox. The rule for avoiding paradoxes insists that the items outside any enclosing line be of the same logical type as those within, but the picture frame, as analyzed above, is a line dividing items of one logical type from those of another. In passing, it is interesting to note that Russell's rule cannot be stated without breaking the rule. Russell insists that all items of inappropriate logical type be excluded (i.e., by an imaginary line) from the background of any class, i.e., he insists upon the drawing of an imaginary line of precisely the sort which he prohibits.

19. This whole matter of frames and paradoxes may be illustrated in terms of animal behavior, where three types of message may be recognized or deduced: (*a*) Messages of the sort which we here call mood-signs; (*b*) messages which simulate mood-signs (in play, threat, histrionics, etc.); and (*c*) messages which enable the receiver to discriminate between mood-signs and those other signs which resemble them. The message "This is play" is of this third type. It tells the receiver that certain nips and other meaningful actions are not messages of the first type.

The message "This is play" thus sets a frame of the sort which is likely to precipitate paradox: it is an attempt to discriminate between, or to draw a line between, categories of different logical types.

20. This discussion of play and psychological frames establishes a type of triadic constellation (or system of relationships) between messages. One instance of this constellation is analyzed in paragraph 19, but it is evident that constellations of this sort occur not only at the nonhuman level but also in the much more complex communication of human beings. A fantasy or myth may simulate a denotative narrative, and, to discriminate between these types of discourse, people use messages of the frame-setting type, and so on.

21. In conclusion, we arrive at the complex task of applying this theoretical approach to the particular phenomena of psychotherapy. Here the lines of our thinking may most briefly be summarized by presenting and partially answering these questions:

a. Is there any indication that certain forms of psychopathology are specifically characterized by abnormalities in the patient's handling of frames and paradoxes?

b. Is there any indication that the techniques of psychotherapy necessarily depend upon the manipulation of frames and paradoxes?

c. Is it possible to describe the process of a given psychotherapy in terms of the interaction between the patient's abnormal use of frames and the therapist's manipulation of them?

22. In reply to the first question, it seems that the "word salad" of schizophrenia can be described in terms of the patient's failure to recognize the metaphoric nature of his fantasies. In what should be triadic constellations of messages, the frame-setting message (e.g., the phrase "as if") is omitted, and the metaphor or fantasy is narrated and acted upon in a manner which would be appropriate if the fantasy were a message of the more direct kind. The absence of metacommunicative framing which was noted in the case of dreams (15) is characteristic of the waking communications of the schizophrenic. With the loss of the ability to set metacommunicative frames, there is also a loss of ability to achieve the more primary or primitive message. The metaphor is treated directly as a message of the more primary type. (This matter is discussed at greater length in the paper given by Jay Haley at this Conference.)

23. The dependence of psychotherapy upon the manipulation of frames follows from the fact that therapy is an attempt to change the patient's metacommunicative habits. Before therapy, the patient thinks and operates in terms of a certain set of rules for the making and understanding of messages. After successful therapy, he operates in terms of a different set of such rules. (Rules of this sort are in general, unverbalized, and unconscious both before and after.) It follows that, in the process of therapy, there must have been communication at a level *meta* to these rules. There must have been communication about a *change* in rules.

But such a communication about change could not conceivably occur in messages of the type permitted by the patient's metacommunicative rules as they existed either before or after therapy.

It was suggested above that the paradoxes of play are characteristic of an evolutionary step. Here we suggest that similar paradoxes are a necessary ingredient in that process of change which we call psychotherapy.

The resemblance between the process of therapy and the phenomenon of play is, in fact, profound. Both occur within a delimited psychological frame, a spatial and temporal bounding of a set of interactive messages. In both play and therapy, the messages have a spatial and peculiar relationship to a more concrete or basic reality. Just as the pseudocombat of play is not real combat, so also the pseudolove and pseudohate of therapy are not real love and hate. The "transfer" is discriminated from real love and hate by signals invoking the psychological frame; and indeed it is this frame which permits the transfer to reach its full intensity and to be discussed between patient and therapist.

The formal characteristics of the therapeutic process may be illustrated by building up a model in stages. Imagine first two players who engage in a game of canasta according to a standard set of rules. So long as these rules govern and are unquestioned by both players, the game is unchanging, i.e., no therapeutic change will occur. (Indeed many attempts at psychotherapy fail for this reason.) We may imagine, however, that at a certain moment the two canasta players cease to play canasta and start a discussion of the rules. Their discourse is now of a different logical type from that of their play. At the end of this discussion, we can imagine that they return to playing but with modified rules.

This sequence of events is, however, still an imperfect model of therapeutic interaction, though it illustrates our contention that therapy necessarily involves a combination of discrepant logical types of discourse. Our imaginary players avoided paradox by separating their discussion of the rules from their play, and it is precisely this separation that is impossible in psychotherapy. As we see it, the process of psychotherapy is framed interaction between two persons, in which the rules are implicit but subject to change. Such change can only be proposed by experimental action, but every such experimental action, in which a proposal to change the rules is implicit, is itself a part of the ongoing game. It is this combination of logical types within the single meaningful act that gives to therapy the character not of a rigid game like canasta but, instead, that of an evolving system of interaction. The play of kittens or otters has this character.

24. In regard to the specific relationship between the way in which the patient handles frames and the way in which the therapist manipulates them, very little can at present be said. It is, however, suggestive to observe that the psychological frame of therapy is an analogue of the frame-setting message which the schizophrenic is unable to achieve. To talk in "word salad" within the psychological frame of therapy is, in a sense, not pathological. Indeed the neurotic is specifically encouraged to do precisely this, narrating his dreams and free associations so that patient and therapist may achieve an understanding of this material. By the process of interpretation, the neurotic is driven to insert an "as if" clause into the productions of his primary process thinking, which productions he had previously deprecated or repressed. He must learn that fantasy contains truth.

For the schizophrenic the problem is somewhat different. His error is in treating the metaphors of primary process with the full intensity of literal truth. Through the discovery of what these metaphors stand for he must discover that they are only metaphors.

25. From the point of view of the project, however, psychotherapy constitutes only one of the many fields which we are attempting to investigate. Our central thesis may be summed up as a statement of the necessity of the paradoxes of abstraction. It is not merely bad natural history to suggest that people might or should obey the Theory of Logical Types in their communications; their failure to do this is not due to mere carelessness or ignorance. Rather, we believe that the paradoxes of abstraction must make their appearance in all communication more complex than that of mood-signals, and that without these paradoxes the evolution of communication would be at an end. Life would then be an endless interchange of stylized messages, a game with rigid rules, unrelieved by change or humor.

Notes

1. A. N. Whitehead and B. Russell, *Principia Mathematica* (3 vols., 2nd ed.; Cambridge, Eng.: Cambridge University Press, 1910–1913).
2. L. Wittgenstein, *Tractatus Logico-Philosophicus* (London: Harcourt Brace, 1922).
3. R. Carnap, *The Logical Syntax of Language* (New York: Harcourt Brace, 1937).
4. B. L. Whorf, "Science and Linguistics," *Technology Review* 44 (1940): 229–48.
5. J. Ruesch and G. Bateson, *Communication: The Social Matrix of Psychiatry* (New York: Norton, 1951).
6. A. Korzybski, *Science and Sanity* (New York: Science Press, 1941).
7. The verbalization of these metalinguistic rules is a much later achievement which can only occur after the evolution of a nonverbalized meta-metalinguistics.
8. N. Tinbergen, *Social Behavior in Animals with Special Reference to Vertebrates* (London: Methuen, 1953); K. Z. Lorenz, *King Solomon's Ring* (New York: Crowell, 1952).
9. Lorenz, *King Solomon's Ring*.
10. C. R. Carpenter, "A Field Study of the Behavior and Social Relations of Howling Monkeys," *Comparative Psychology Monographs* 10 (1934): 1–168.
11. A. R. Radcliffe-Brown, *The Andaman Islanders* (Cambridge, Eng.: Cambridge University Press, 1922).
12. W. S. McCulloch, "A Heterarchy of Values, etc.," *Bulletin of Mathematical Biophysics* 7 (1945): 89–93.
13. Whitehead and Russell, *Principia Mathematica*.

CHAPTER 12

Classroom Knowledge

Nell Keddie

One consequence of the particular normative orientation of much
sociology of education has been its definition of educational failure:
explanations of educational failure are most often given in terms of
pupils' ethnic and social class antecedents[1] and rely on a concept of social
pathology rather than one of cultural diversity.[2] It is only recently that
attention has been given to the defining processes occurring within the
school itself[3] and to the social organization of curriculum knowledge.[4]
The studies suggest that the processes by which pupils are categorized are
not self-evident and point to an overlooked consequence of a differentiated curriculum: that it is part of the process by which educational
deviants are created and their deviant identities maintained.[5] Here I hope
to raise questions about these processes by considering two aspects of
classroom knowledge: what knowledge teachers have of pupils, and what
counts as knowledge to be made available and evaluated in the classroom. This involves casting as problematic what are held to be knowledge
and ability in schools rather than taking either as given.

The empirical data on which this account is based[6] were collected by
observation, tape recording, and questionnaire in a large mixed comprehensive school with a fairly heterogeneous social class intake, although in
the school, as in its catchment area, social class III is over-represented.
Pupils from social classes I and II tend to be placed in A streams and those
from social classes IV and V in C streams.[7] The study is focused on the
humanities department which in 1969/70 introduced an examination
course based on history, geography, and social science to fourth-year
pupils. The course was constructed to be taught as an undifferentiated
program across the ability range, and to be examined by mode 3 at

Reprinted from *Knowledge and Control: New Directions for the Sociology of Education*
edited by Michael F. D. Young (London: Collier-Macmillan, 1971) by permission of the
Macmillan Publishing Co. Inc., *for* Cassell.

ordinary level and C.S.E. at the end of the fifth year.[8] The course is described as "enquiry based" and is taught by "key lessons" to introduce a topic, and a workcard system to allow children to work individually and at their own speed. In the fifth year the work is often organized around topics; in the fourth year it is generally organized in "blocks" of different subjects. This study is concerned with the first social science block which has socialization as its theme and follows directly after a geographical study of regions of Britain. Both were taught from material prepared by the department's teachers (in this case sociologists, a psychologist, an economist, and geographers), so that each class keeps the same teacher for both geographical and social science studies.

The school is probably atypical of secondary schools in this country in its high degree of institutionalized innovation (every subject is now examined by mode 3 at C.S.E.) and therefore if the data has any claim to generality it must be because the school stands as a critical case and illustrates the fate of innovatory ideals in practice. Throughout this account references to teachers and pupils are specifically references to teachers and pupils of this one school.

A central issue for teachers in the school is whether or not the school should unstream. Bourdieu[9] points out that conflict indicates consensus about which issues are deemed worthy of conflict. In this debate consensus that is not articulated is the most interesting because it is not questioned and includes, as I shall show, evaluations of what constitutes knowledge and ability and thus evaluations of what pupils are and ought to be like in critical respects. In the fourth year pupils are divided into three broad ability bands, A, B, and C, and some departments stream rigidly within these bands. The humanities department divides pupils into parallel groups within each band and looks forward to teaching completely mixed ability groups.

In casting as problematic what counts as knowledge and ability, I begin with what teachers themselves find problematic: the teaching of C stream pupils. C stream pupils present teachers with problems both of social control and in the preparation and presentation of teaching material. By their characterization of C stream pupils as "that type of child" and "these children," teachers tell that they feel that C stream pupils are unlike themselves. By inference, teachers feel that A stream pupils are more like themselves, at least in ways that count in school. Teaching A stream pupils seems to be relatively unproblematic for teachers: they take the activities in these classrooms for granted, they rarely make explicit the criteria which guide the preparation and presentation of teaching material for these pupils, and what counts as knowledge is left implicit, and, apparently, consensual. The "question" to which C. Wright Mills[10] refers rarely arises: the empirical problem is the phenomenon which Garfinkel calls the "unavailability" of the "formal structures of practical actions."[11] The assumption underlying my interpretation of data is that C stream pupils disrupt teachers' expectations and violate their norms of appropriate social, moral, and intellectual pupil behavior. In so far as C stream pupils' behavior is explicitly seen by teachers as inappropriate or inadequate, it makes more visible or available what is held to be appropriate pupil behavior because it provokes questions about the norms which govern teachers' expectations about appropriate pupil behavior.

The Ideal Pupil

Becker[12] developed the concept of the *ideal pupil* to refer to that set of teacher expectations which constitute a taken for granted notion of appropriate pupil behavior. In examining discrepancies between what I shall call *educationist* and *teacher* contexts I shall argue that it is in the likeness of the images of the ideal pupil from one context to the other that the relation and the disjunction between the views expressed by teachers in these contexts is explained.

The fundamental discrepancy between the views of teachers as they emerge in these contexts can be expressed as that between theory and practice, or what Selznick calls doctrine and commitment:

> Doctrine, being abstract, is judiciously selective and may be qualified at will in discourse, subject only to restrictions of sense and logic. But action is concrete, generating consequences which define a sphere of interest and responsibility together with a corresponding chain of commitments. Fundamentally, the discrepancy between doctrine and commitment arises from the essential distinction between the interrelation of ideas and the interrelation of phenomena.[13]

This is a distinction between "words" and "deeds"[14] and it is necessary to remember that words like deeds are situated in the ongoing interaction in which they arise. "Doctrine" as the ideology and theory of the humanities department is enunciated in the educationist context, which may also be called the context of *discussion* of school politics, in particular discussion which evokes interdepartmental conflicts, especially those about streaming. (The actual context of school politics, for example, heads of departments' meetings, may provoke something else again.) The other aspect of the educationist context is the discussion of educational theory, and here talk of the department's policy often evokes statements about its alignment with or opposition to other humanities programs[15] constructed by other course makers. The educationist context may be called into b ing by the presence of an outsider to whom explanations of the department's activities must be given or by a forthcoming school meeting which necessitates discussion of policy of how things *ought* to be in school.

By contrast, the teacher context is that in which teachers move most of the time. It is the world of *is* in which teachers anticipate interaction with pupils in planning lessons, in which they act in the classroom and in which when the lesson is over they usually recount or explain what has happened. I shall elaborate on the characteristics of both contexts to suggest their relation to each other and the implications for the possible fate of educational innovation in schools.

The Educationist Context

The educational policy of the course and of the department draws selectively and consciously on educational theory and research, and is seen by at least some of the department as an informed and expert view of education, as opposed to the lay and commonsense views advanced by other departments. The "pure" educational policy of the department seems to contain the following as its components:

1. Intelligence is not primarily determined by heredity. Differential educational performance may be accounted for by differential motivation rather than differential intelligence. Ability is to be accounted for as much by motivation as by intelligence and is largely determined by the child's social class antecedents.
2. Streaming by ability weights the school environment against those whose family background has already lessened their chances of educational achievement, because it "fixes" the expectations that both teachers and pupil have of a pupil's performance and is thereby likely to lower the motivation of pupils with low achievement-orientation who have been assigned to low streams.
3. The criteria by which pupils are allocated to streams or sets when they enter the school (the mathematics department, for example, are said to use verbal IQ scores) have been discredited by both psychologists and sociologists; but their lack of reliability is not understood by those who use them.
4. Streaming perpetuates the distinction between grammar and secondary modern school under one roof, and creates or maintains social divisiveness, since like the grammar school it favors middle-class children.
5. A differentiated curriculum divides pupils. The school should try to unite them.

222

Those in the school who favor streaming oppose the views given above on the grounds that the individual child is best helped by being placed in a stream with those like himself so that he can receive teaching appropriate to his pace and level.

I have sufficient data about the extent to which teachers in the humanities department hold this educational policy in its "pure" form. Probably most select out of it aspects of it that are most relevant to them. Outwardly at least, all members of the department are in favor of the mixed ability teaching which the department has introduced into the first and second years. The department is committed eventually to teaching mixed ability groups in the higher forms, but sees the matter as sufficiently problematic to delay until a new teaching block is ready in a couple of years' time. The main point, however, is that those teachers who will advance the educationist view in the discussion of school and educational policy will speak and act in ways that are discrepant with this view when the context is that of the *teacher*. While, therefore, some educational aims may be formulated by teachers as *educationists*, it will not be surprising if "doctrine" is contradicted by "commitments" which arise in the situation in which they must act as *teachers*.

The way in which the course is set up reveals how teachers can hold discrepant views without normally having to take cognizance of the contradictions which may arise. For example, a resolution is partially effected by shifting the meaning of motivation from an assertion of the desirable in the educationist context to an explanation of the desirable in the teacher context. Thus the educationist assumes that in the ideal environment of the unstreamed school with an undifferentiated curriculum, the differential motivation which now leads to under-achievement will be greatly reduced. In the teacher context, in which teachers move in their everyday activities as teachers, motivation becomes an explanation of pupils' behavior. In this exchange, two teachers who also hold the educationist's view in part are talking about the A stream class of the teacher who speaks first:

TEACHER J: [Some of the class] have written to Oldham Town Council for material for the New Town project.
TEACHER C: They're really bright, are they?
TEACHER J: Mostly from middle-class families, well motivated.

Here the relationship between initiative, intelligence, social class, and motivation is the assumption taken for granted that makes the exchange of comments possible, and also illustrates well the portrayal of social skills as cognitive ones.

In the educationist's view, motivation is subsumed in a notion of rationality as leading to autonomy for the individual. The ideal pupil in the educationist context is the one who can perceive and rationally evaluate alternatives. He will become the ideal man of a society which embraces consensus politics and a convergence thesis of social class. In an interview the head of department spoke of the "qualities of mind" that the course will attempt to develop:

> I think mainly rationality—this is the essence of what we're trying to teach. Not, I hope, a belief that rationality will always . . . produce good moral answers because it won't, clearly; but a person who is prepared to weigh evidence. . . . This is the last opportunity many of them get for a structured view of society. This is political education . . . a participating society does not mean to my mind a population that is attending lots of planning meetings. It's a population that's aware of what's involved in planning. . . . It's educating people to be aware of what's involved in making political decisions. . . .[16]

Whether or not all the department's teachers share these educational aims and subscribe to this image of society, the course is set up with intentions of developing in pupils modes of work and thought which will help them to become more autonomous and rational beings. That is, it is set up in the hope that the conception of enquiry-based work will help to create the ideal pupil. I select three main aspects of the course to show how it also in fact caters for a pupil who already exists: the A stream academic and usually middle-class pupil. Thus the course embodies not only an image of what the ideal pupil ought to be, but also what he already is. These three aspects are:

1. "Working at your own speed"—this notion is very firmly embedded in the ideology of the course and it is significant that a teacher I heard "selling" the course to pupils described it as "self-regulating work which allows you to get ahead." The corollary of this is that others fall behind, at least in relation to the pace of the course. Teachers were constantly urging pupils: "You must finish that this week because next week we're going on to a new topic." Teachers frequently remarked how much more quickly A pupils work than C pupils, and A pupils generally expressed approval of the notion of "working at your own speed"—it is *their* speed. It would seem inevitable that the principle of individual speeds should be incompatible with a course that moves in a structured way from topic to topic. The only leeway is for some pupils to work through more workcards than others.

2. All the studies on achievement orientation stress the middle-class

child's tendency to thrive on an individualistic and competitive approach to learning. It follows that a workcard system which puts a premium on the individual working by himself rather than in a group is probably set up in advance for the success of some pupils rather than others because they already value that kind of autonomy. Observation suggested that the result of this was that while pupils worked or rested from working, they talked in the peer group about matters like football and boy friends. Talk about work tended to be of the order: "Do you know the answer to question 2?" Thus the content of the work rarely becomes the content of peer-group interaction but becomes separate from it. An analogy might be drawn with the doing of repetitive industrial tasks, where satisfaction derives from group interaction rather than from the work which brings in the money (or grades). The possibility for pupils of continuous interaction with friends may, however, be an important element in reducing social control problems for teachers.

3. Teachers express regret that a problem in motivating C stream pupils is their tendency to see education in vocational terms. It was never made explicit (if realized at all by some teachers) that the educational aims of a course like this one also fulfill the vocational purposes of the more successful pupils. A stream pupils have been told, and they told me, that learning to work independently (of teacher and textbook) will help them "in the sixth form and at university." I also heard a teacher telling a B group that "any worker who can think for himself is worth his weight in gold to his employer." It is likely that lower stream pupils know this to be a highly questionable statement and do not look forward to this kind of satisfaction from their work. Thus while teachers do not, on the whole, perceive higher education as vocational, C stream pupils do not find the vocational rationale of the course commensurate with their expectations of what work will be like.

Both (1) and (2) suggest that the short-term aims of the course, where it impinges immediately on the pupils' work situation, are weighted in favor of A stream pupils, giving priority to skills and attitudes they are most likely to possess. In its long-term aims the same pattern emerges. It seems likely that an undifferentiated course will be set up with an image of the pupil in mind. Because in the educationist context the perspective is one of how things *ought* to be, it is not so obvious to teachers that they are drawing, albeit selectively, on what already *is*. As I shall show, in the teacher context teachers organize their activities around values which as educationists they may deny. These values arise from the conjunction of social class and ability in the judgments teachers make on pupils. It is by exploring what is judged to be appropriate behavior that it becomes clear how ability and social class which are held separate in the educationist context are confounded in the teacher context.

The Teacher Context

1. *Normal Pupils*

In this context what a teacher "knows" about pupils derives from the organizational device of banding or streaming, which in turn derives from the dominant organizing category of what counts as ability. The "normal" characteristics (the term is taken from Sudnow)[17] of a pupil are those which are imputed to his band or stream as a whole. A pupil who is perceived as atypical is perceived in relation to the norm for the stream: "She's bright for a B" (teacher H); or in relation to the norm for another group: "They're as good as Bs" (teacher J of three hardworking pupils in his C stream group). This knowledge of what pupils are like is often at odds with the image of pupils the same teachers may hold as educationists, since it derives from streaming whose validity the educationist denies.

Although teachers in the humanities department might express disagreement with other teachers over teaching methods, evaluations of pupils, and so on, there seems, in the teacher context, to be almost complete consensus about what normal pupils are like. It is probable, given the basis of categorization, that members of the department are, in terms of "what everyone knows" about pupils, much closer to other teachers in the school than they themselves commonly imply. As house tutors, most of their negotiations with teachers outside the department must be carried on in terms of shared meanings. Because these meanings are taken for granted both within and outside the department they are not made explicit as a set of assumptions because they continue to refer to an unquestionable reality "out there." It is possible to disagree about an individual pupil and to couch the disagreement in terms of his typical or atypical "B-ness," but in the teacher context it would be disruptive of interaction and of action-to-be-taken to question that "B-ness" exists. Like the concept of ability from which it derives it is unexamined in the teacher context since it belongs to the shared understandings that make interaction possible. In the educationist context, where other interests are at stake, "ability" and "streaming" shift into new categories of meaning. Although the teacher may be the same person in both contexts, what he "knows" as educationist about pupils may not be that which he as teacher "knows" about them. The frame of reference shifts from a concern with "things as they *are*" to "things as they *ought* to be,"[18] and in this context both ability and streaming may become problematic as they cannot be for the practical ongoing purpose of the teacher.

The imputation of normal attributes to pupils by teachers does not tell us objectively about pupils. Rather it is the case that in certain areas of school life teachers and different groups of pupils maintain conflicting definitions of the situation. For the teacher, social control may depend on his being able in the classroom to maintain publicly his definition of the situation. He may do this by attempting to render pupil definitions invalid. Thus he may treat pupils' complaints about the course with skepticism and subsume them under normal categories like: "he's trying to get out of work," "it's just a bit of 'agro,' " "they'll try anything on." These explanations may or may not coincide with pupils' explanations of their motives. The general effect of teachers' explanations is to recognize the situation as conflictual, but to render invalid the particular point the pupil is making and thus to delineate the extent of pupils' rights. Equal rights are not granted to all pupils since the "same" behavior may have different meanings attributed to it, depending on the normal status of the pupil. In one C stream lesson a pupil asked the teacher:

PUPIL: This is geography, isn't it? Why don't we learn about where countries are and that?
TEACHER: This is socialization.
PUPIL: What's that? I'd rather do geography. . . . Netsilik Eskimo—I don't know where that is.
TEACHER: [ironically]: After the lesson we'll go and get the atlas and I'll show you. (Teacher D)

A few days earlier I had asked this teacher whether any pupil had asked in class (as they had in some other classes): "Why should we do social science?" and had had the reply:

TEACHER: No, but if I were asked by Cs I would try to sidestep it because it would be the same question as "Why do anything? Why work?"
OBSERVER: What if you were asked by an A group?
TEACHER: Then I'd probably try to answer.

For me, as observer, learning how to recognize normal pupils was an important aspect of my socialization as observer from the teachers' point of view. Teachers took some care that I should understand what pupils were like, especially C pupils. In my first days in the school they frequently prepared me for what I should expect when I attended their lesson, and they afterwards explained to me why the lesson had gone as it

227

had. These explanations tended to take the form: "C stream pupils are . . ." or "low ability pupils are . . ." This aspect of "learning the ropes"[19] is presumably an important element in the socialization of student and probationary teachers.

The "normalization" of pupils tends to produce a polarity between A and C pupils in which they reflect reversed images of each other. The B stream pupil is left in the middle and tends to shift around in the typology. Generally when special workcards are prepared it is for C groups and it is assumed that Bs will follow the same work as A pupils. On the other hand, teachers often see B pupils as posing the same social control problems as C streams. One teacher saw this as the *result* of their undefined status and characterized B stream pupils as suffering from identity problems. His characterization could as well refer to teachers' problems in being unable to define clearly the normal B pupil, as to the perspective of the pupils themselves, who may have quite clear notions of their own position and status, though they are liable to be defined out by the teachers. Similarly A pupils who present discipline problems to teachers are likely to be described as pupils who "are really Bs." This characterization is not necessarily applied to those A pupils who will probably be entered for C.S.E. and not "O" level in the humanities examinations and might therefore be seen as right for a B stream. This is in keeping with the tendency not only for normative judgments to predominate—teachers speak more about the "moral" and "social" qualities of pupils than of their cognitive skills—but for the former qualities to be presented as though they were cognitive skills:

TEACHER K: If you want, you can go on to the Depression later in the term. There's also material on America in the twenties.
TEACHER B: Isn't it true to say that although it's C material in a sense, the level of response depends on the level of intelligence. For example, some of the moral problems you pose—it would take an A child really to see the implications. Some of the girls would find it interesting.
TEACHER K: Yes, it could be used at all levels.   (At a staff meeting)

2. Ability and Social Class

Most children enter secondary schools with their educational identities partially established in the records, and by the fourth year the question is rather how these identities are maintained than how they were established. Teachers appear to have two principal organizing categories: ability and social class. Social class, however, tends to be a latent and implicit category for sorting pupil behavior. On occasion though, some teachers appear to use social class as an explanation of educational performance:

Teacher B of a group of boys he described as "working class who belong to a B group":

> they don't work but they came up high in a test which tested their grasp of concepts.

On another occasion he spoke of the same boys as:

> really from a higher stream—able but they don't work.

Teacher H distinguished between the performance of two "bright" girls in his A stream class:

> one is the daughter of a primary school headmaster; a home with books and lots of encouragement . . . [the other one] comes from quite a different kind of home which doesn't encourage homework. . . .

He felt that the latter had potential ability she was not using to the full.

Another teacher (L) characterized a girl whom he thought "works only for grades" as a "trade unionist."

Teacher J had a threefold typology of his C stream class (which he told me before I observed his class for the first time) in which he linked certain kinds of psychological disturbance with a working-class culture. It is possible to identify two types of pupil in what follows: the remedial child and the pathologically disturbed child:

> TEACHER: The difficulties with the least able child are those of remedial children: children who don't work in normally accepted ways in school—with these children I'm not succeeding, humanities aren't succeeding. The Cs who fail can't meet [the head of department's] criteria [of autonomous work]. They need to be in a group with only a few teachers. . . . Many have working-class parents—Jane's got problems. Her father's a not-very-bright milkman and her mother ran away. Lots of difficult children have disturbed backgrounds and this is often more important than innate abilities.
> OBSERVER: What do you mean by disturbed?
> TEACHER: Fathers who beat mothers, nervous breakdowns in the family, that sort of thing.

He speaks of "that kind of child" and says they "fluctuate in behavior". . . "Jane has little idea of how to behave generally . . . [but Susan] is a big mouthing fishwife who can, on occasion, work solidly and be pleasant."

The third type of child was identified only after the lesson: the quiet child who works fairly hard through most lessons. In terms of social control this pupil is not a problem and this is why the casual listener-in to teachers' talk might get the impression that all C stream pupils are constant problems for teachers.

After the lesson this teacher, like others, wondered if he were too lenient with the problem pupils; he said of Jane "Perhaps she gets away with too much . . . [but] she can't concentrate and needs the teacher all the time." The key phrase in his general description is probably the reference to "children who don't work in normally accepted ways in school." These pupils' behavior can be seen as generally inappropriate. Like the concept of the disadvantaged child the reference contains a notion of "under-socialization" and instability originating in the social disorganization[20] of the "background" of the pupil. The dominant notion here seems akin to some social psychological accounts of delinquency[21] which specify a multiplicity of factors like a "bad" home as a cause of deviance without making it clear what a bad home is, how it causes deviance, or why other homes, which should on the same criteria be "bad," do not produce delinquents. Because the social pathology approach allows explanations of pupil behavior to be made in terms of discrete factors, teachers tend not to perceive the collective social class basis of pupils' experience but to fragment that experience into the problems of individual (and "disadvantaged") pupils. This makes it likely that the pupils' collective definition of the educational situation will be rendered invisible to teachers,[22] and failure individualized.

This teacher's (J) normal C pupil is probably cast in a more explicit model of psychological disturbance than many, but this does not affect the essential outline of the image, in which instability plays a large part and is frequently linked with aggression. In terms of social control instability means unpredictability and the social control problems as perceived by the teacher are demonstrated in the remark of this teacher who said that many C stream pupils are "awkward customers" and are allowed to get away with too much: "it's important if you're to get anywhere not to antagonize these children." This teacher, like most of the teachers in the department, expects his C pupils to behave differently in class from his A pupils: for example, he expects and allows them to make more noise and to achieve a great deal less work than A pupils. It is not possible to estimate the degree to which his expectations are instrumental in creating the situation as he defines it.

Frequently C, and occasionally, B pupils become "characters"; for example: "Clare will envelop Dick one of these days. The girls think Dick is very sexy." A stream pupils are not spoken of in this way. This is linked with another normal characteristic of C pupils—their immaturity.[23] Thus after showing a film called *The First Fifteen Minutes of Life* to groups of pupils, the noise made by B and C groups was described as "covering up embarrassment" and as "the back row of the cinema," indicating the pupils' response had been characterized as contextually inappropriate. A pupils who were much more silent (but were also hushed quite systematically) were characterized as more "mature" in their response, although the comments of a girl to her friends: "they shouldn't show films like that to fifteen year olds," suggested that some of these pupils, at least, found the film difficult to accept. It may have been relevant to the C pupils' response that they were quite unable to see a rationale for the showing of the film since the label "socialization" had no explanatory significance for them. Many defined the film as "biology" and said "we've done it before."

Clearly, A stream pupils' definition of appropriate behavior in the situation was taken over from or coincided with that of the teachers. It is already clear that teachers are most concerned with what they perceive as the negative characteristics of C pupils' behavior and that this is to some extent linked with expectations of appropriate behavior that have a social class basis and differentiation. C stream pupils are often seen to lack those qualities which are deemed by teachers desirable in themselves and appropriate to school,[24] whereas A stream pupils appear to possess these qualities. The negative aspects of the normal C pupil emerge whenever a teacher compares C and A pupils:

It's amazing how much quicker As are than Cs. The As have almost caught Cs now. (Teacher D)

I did it slightly differently with the As because they're rushed for time. With the As I used the pink card more, but I still put diagrams on the board. But it was still quicker. (Teacher J)

I meant to find out [what "ulu," an Eskimo word, meant] but I knew the Cs wouldn't ask. It's remarkable how they can read through and not notice words they don't understand. (Teacher D)

I didn't know any more than was on the workcard—this was all right with Cs, but it wouldn't be with As. (Teacher G)

These comments indicate that teachers have notions about the organization of time and material (and the degree of preparation necessary) in the classroom which depend on the normal characteristics of the ability group they are teaching. Thus what teachers "know" about pupils as social, moral, and psychological persons is extended to what they know about them as intellectual persons, which as I shall show leads to the differentiation of an undifferentiated curriculum.

3. *Ability and Knowledge*

One of the remarkable features of the tendency to attribute to pupils the normal characteristics of their ability band is that what is held to constitute ability is rarely made explicit. When teachers discuss whether material is suitable for teaching to A, B, or C streams, the criteria on which they make judgments remain largely implicit and consensual. Throughout it is difficult to separate out references to cognitive skills from imputed social and moral characteristics on the one hand and from characterization of teaching material on the other. This comment on teaching material about the Depression is typical:

> Some of the economic implications are difficult—it's O level type of material . . . but some of the human elements may be C material. (Teacher at staff meeting)

Material is categorized in terms of its suitability for a given ability band and, by implication, ability is categorized in terms of whether or not these pupils can manage that material. Like the pupils who are categorized in terms of levels of ability, knowledge in school is categorized in terms of its supposed hierarchical nature with reference to criteria of age and ability. I shall be concerned with how teachers organize knowledge in relation to the normal attributes of the pupils they are teaching, according to criteria used to establish the hierarchies of ability and knowledge. This approach involves starting from the assumption that not only is ability not a given factor but also that we do not know what the knowledge to be got or the subject to be mastered properly is. We can only learn what they are by learning what teachers and pupils who are involved in defining that knowledge claim to be doing: subjects are what practitioners do with them.

Within the course itself, the enquiry-based mode is intended to change the emphasis from mastery of given contents of a subject to mastery of the method of enquiry itself. The workcards are to some extent structured around the "concepts" it is desirable for pupils to acquire through working through the material. Thus the teacher who speaks of the "working-class" boys in his B group who are "able but don't work, but come up high in a test which tested their grasp of concepts," is using the term concept partly in the in-language of the course. The term derives from Bloom,[25] who uses it in his taxonomy of the hierarchical organization of knowledge where each level subsumes, under more general categories, the categories of the level below. The head of the humanities department here shows how the notion of concept, which appears to be glossed as "idea" or "structure," is embedded in the organization of the teaching material:

> When you begin to think in terms of drawing things together, although, as I say, there are certain contents more important than other contents, and that's why we do the British economy rather than endless regional studies of Britain or endless historical studies of the treaties of the nineteenth century, the most important element in the work is teaching the children how to work. Teaching them a mode of enquiry is, I think, fundamental to the whole thing. Because this is the common ingredient of the historian's work, the geographer's work, the social scientist's work, and this is the lasting influence on the child, not the memory of a particular date, and I regard as part of the teaching of that mode of enquiry the development of concepts and ideas which obviously increases the degree of sophistication in their mode of enquiry. The more ideas they've got, the more ideas of structures they've got, the better equipped they are to think in an orderly mode of enquiry.[26]

It appears from this that what he is describing is not so much a change from an emphasis on contents to an emphasis on method, but a change in content in terms of how that content is organized. It may not be intrinsic to the way the course is set up that teachers treat the teaching material as a body of knowledge or "facts" to be got across to pupils, rather than as ways of organizing facts or contents in relation to each other. In the classroom it often seems that pupils are more enquiry-minded than teachers, whose presentation of material does not allow concepts to be distinguished from content because the concept is presented in terms of its content. This relationship is also clearly illustrated in the end-of-topic test where many questions ask the pupil to match a content to a term or "concept," for example:

> In some experiments hungry animals are given a food pellet each time they produce a particular response, such as pressing a bar or pecking at a disc. This is called: *stimulus, extinction, motivation, reinforcement.*

Thus although the course was deliberately set up by teachers as educationists to counteract what they saw as an inappropriate exercise of authority by the teacher in the traditional talk-and-chalk presentation of material, in the teacher context enquiry for the pupil is still heavily teacher directed.

In the following extract from a C stream lesson, the teacher (E)—who is not a sociologist and has to rely on prepared material on a pink card[27] which includes a description of the joint family, but not of the extended family as it is defined in Britain today—rejects alternative definitions to the nuclear family suggested by pupils because his reading of the material leads him to see common residence as a critical criterion:

TEACHER: Now who'd like to tell me what we mean by the family? [Pause] It's not as obvious as you might think. What is a family? Derek?

DEREK: A mother, a daddy.

TEACHER: Yeah.

DEREK: A couple of kids if they got them.

TEACHER: Yes.

DEREK: A granddaddy, a grandmummy.

TEACHER: Yes.

DEREK: An aunt, an uncle.

TEACHER: You'd include that in the family.

BOY: Yes, you would.

GIRL: [untranscribable]

TEACHER: Anybody disagree with that—that in a family you'd include grandparents?

DEREK: Well they are 'cos they're your mother's and father's mothers and fathers.

TEACHER: And it's all part of one family?

BOY: Yeah.

TEACHER: Anybody disagree or like to add to it at all? What we mean by the family?

GIRL [she has probably been reading the pink card]: It's also a group of people living under one roof.

GIRL: No, it's not. [Other pupils agree and disagree].

TEACHER: Ah, a group of people living under one roof—aah—that differs from what Derek said, isn't it? Because the group—ssh, Derek. . . .

DEREK [his voice emerges above the teacher's voice]: . . . would still be the same as your mum, wouldn't it? It'd still be your family.

TEACHER: Yeah, the group that Derek mentioned doesn't live under one roof. Now we can limit the family to say its a group of people related by blood, er, who live under one roof; or we can extend its meaning to include what Derek said: grandparents, aunts, and uncles and so on, who may in individual cases live under the same roof, but it's not normal. The British family, I say the

British family because the idea of families differs, as we shall see, over the world. Peter and Derek, you're not listening.

PETER: I am.

TEACHER: . . . British family is parents and children, that is what you might call the, er, nuclear family; in other words, the core of the family. They tend to live together until the children have developed, matured, if you like, into adults. . . .

The way the exchange goes is not entirely a matter of "how much" sociology this teacher knows; it is also a question of the relation between the categories he is using to structure this knowledge in the classroom and those used by the boy which derive from his everyday knowledge of "what everyone knows" about families. The teacher moves outside this everyday knowledge since there must be occasions when he refers to his own relations as "family" even if his ties with them are less close than those of Derek with his extended kin. The teacher cues the class that he wants them to move into another reality[28] with the words: "It's not as obvious as you might think." The C girls who said to me "why should we learn about families? I mean we know about families, we live in them," have not made this shift to seeing that the family might be viewed as problematic. It appears at this point, and I discuss the matter further below, that the ability to "grasp a concept" in the context of the course and probably in its wider sense refers to a pupil's willingness or ability to take over or accept the teacher's categories. This may mean, as it would have done for Derek, having to make a choice between apparently contradictory sets of statements unless he can see a reason for shifting his perspective to another set of categories. I shall suggest that Derek's stance is common among C pupils and differs from that of A stream pupils, who assume that the knowledge the teacher will purvey to them has a structure in which what they are asked to do has some place. This does not mean that the A pupil expects that knowledge to be relevant to his everyday experience. The argument is that A and C pupils tend to approach classroom knowledge from different positions and with different expectations. This argument makes no assumptions about the hierarchical status of the knowledge they are being asked to "grasp" or about the degree of generalization or "abstraction" involved. The concept of intelligence as a differential ability to deal with abstractions is implicit in the teachers' frequent reference to the "levels" of difficulty in the material and the "levels" of pupils' response.

I turn now to teachers' discussion of teaching material before and after use in the classroom, and follow this with a consideration of the data provided by pupils' responses to a questionnaire and to the teaching material in the classroom.

4. The Teaching Material: "Subjects" and Pupils

When teachers talk about how they have or will teach material they speak nearly always about the problems of teaching C stream pupils. Teaching the material to the A stream pupils for whom it is primarily prepared and who stand in some sense as ideal pupils appears relatively unproblematic; although, as I shall argue, there are reasons why it might be regarded as highly problematic. I have already quoted comments from staff meetings which showed the difficulty of "economic implications" as opposed to "human elements" (p. 232). Similarly the comments showed a link between the level of response to "moral problems" and the "level of intelligence" (p. 228). The following extracts from teachers' comments bring out these points more clearly:

Yes, worth bringing out with the more able group. (Teacher B)

I envisage problems with 4Cs in understanding unusual relationships. The meaning of relationships, it's going to be very difficult to get this over to them. (Teacher J)

Yes, um, when we did it with the 4Cs before they, er, didn't seem particularly interested that, er, other people had family groups of their own. Because it wasn't real to them, it was so far removed, it didn't seem of complete . . . of any relevance to them. (Teacher L)

I think if you're dealing with it purely in terms of kinship diagrams and white sheets,[29] again you're actually reducing the interest again, if you make it too intellectual. What illustrative material is there on this? . . . I think I've said this before . . . that sociology has its validity in its abstractions and in its intellectual [untranscribable] . . . to what extent the 4Cs will take that or to what extent it will remain a series of stories about families. . . . (Teacher J—not himself a sociologist)

The picture that emerges from these comments which are highly representative, is one of oppositions that describe material and pupils: "intellectual" is opposed to "real," and "abstractions" to "stories." One teacher implies that so long as the material is accessible only in terms of kinship diagrams and buff cards it will be too "intellectual." To make it "real," illustrative material is needed. The points they make are not ones simply of method, but are about methods relating to C stream pupils, and so questions arise not only about why C pupils are believed to need non-intellectual material, but also why A pupils are believed not to need illustrative material and not to have problems in understanding "the meaning of relationships." The suggestion in these comments is that there is something in the material which "it might be possible to bring out with the As." The phrases "bring it out," "make explicit," the "implications of moral problems," "economic implications," seem to point to a range of understanding that is not available to C pupils who can engage only marginally with the material. Teacher J provides a further gloss[30] on this when he says after a lesson with a C group:

> This stuff [on language] is much too difficult for them. . . . On the other hand they could cope with the family stuff. They could say something in their own words about different kinds of family, because they already knew something about them even if they did not know the correct term.

"The correct term" implies something about how status may be attributed to knowledge. The pupils' ignorance of the "correct term" suggests their deficiency. In the following discussion it is further suggested that the range of understanding that is available to C stream pupils must be rooted in their "experience," and that this is linked with another phrase teachers often use about adapting teaching material for C pupils: "putting it in language they can understand":

> TEACHER J: How about the family for the Cs? It may have more in it for them because it's nearer home.
> TEACHER B: There'll be a lot of visual stimulus for discussion. . . . The Cs should be able to get somewhere with discussion . . . we won't do the history of the family with them, it's too difficult, probably too difficult for anyone.

What seems to emerge overall from the way teachers discuss teaching material in relation to pupils' abilities is an assumption that C pupils cannot master subjects: both the "abstractions of sociology" and the "economic implications" are inaccessible to them. The problem then in teaching C pupils is that you cannot teach them subjects. When A pupils do subjects it can be assumed by teachers that they do what, in terms of the *subject*, is held to be appropriate, and material is prepared with regard to what is seen as the demands of the *subject*. In teaching C pupils modifications must be made with regard to the *pupil*, and it is as though the subject is scanned for or reduced to residual "human elements" or a "series of stories."

The clearest statement of the differential emphasis on subject and pupils is that made by Teacher K. He is describing how he is able to "gear" his study of the British economy for a C pupil at "quite a different level" from the level at which he teaches it to his A group. He says:

I can streamline it so it's got various grades of content and I can, I hope, do things which are very useful and valuable to the C child which I don't feel are as necessary for the A child. But they're all doing economics, they're all doing certain vital basic studies in how the economy works. . . .

He describes how the study is dealing with "land, labor, and capital . . . in answer to what we call the 'for whom' question in economics":

Well, that leads on to a special study of labor for the Cs. Rewards for labor—wages. Wages can then be considered for girls in terms of why they're paid often lower than men's pay and what sorts of factors determine the different wages rates for different sorts of employment—something that's very immediate for these children.

Later he says:

Looking at a mixed economy he can angle that study much more towards taxation and the practical elements of how to fill in tax forms and what you get relief for, whereas . . . I'd be much more concerned with how the different types of taxation work, with the higher ability child: the difference between direct and indirect taxation and S.E.T. and so on. And also the effects that different forms of taxation have on the rates of economic growth—the more sophisticated elements which the lower ability child, it may not be possible for him to grasp the ideas that are part of that type of study but he's still able to study taxation and at a simpler level; but he's not being discriminated against.

Here it is clear that one consequence of a differential treatment of the economy is the way in which categories of analysis are made available to or withheld from pupils. This teacher held the educationist view in almost its pure form, and the political implications of his teaching of economics should probably be seen as an unintentional and unrecognized manifestation of consensus politics arising from an image of society as consensus. The teaching cannot be said to be intentionally prescriptive: it is presented as an objective account of the economic system rather than one of a number of possible accounts. He is not deliberately restricting the categories that are available to A pupils, since his teaching reflects his own thinking. When he further restricts C stream pupils to a study of labor and that in terms of differential wages, he sees this as "valuable" for the C pupils in terms of their ascribed status as workers. He does not intentionally withhold the framework which would allow the pupil to raise questions about the taxation policy as a whole, but he does effectively prevent, by a process of fragmentation, the question of how such knowledge becomes available.[31]

5. *The Pupils' Response*

I shall now attempt some account of the relation between teachers' and pupils' definitions of the classroom situation. The main contention is that the differences attributed to A and C pupils by teachers are substantive, but they may be open to interpretations other than those habitually made by teachers. In presenting the data I look at the ways in which teachers and pupils scan each others' activities in the classroom and attribute meaning to them.

The first indication of a differentiated response of A and C pupils comes from the responses to a questionnaire administered to the whole fourth year which sought information on the degree to which pupils have access to or have taken over the teachers' definitions of the humanities course.

A pupils all knew the terminology of the course and did not have to ask what "key lesson" or pink card meant. Question 2 is quite open-ended: "Do you think key lessons are a good idea or not, and why?" The majority of A pupils chose to answer it in terms of the structure of the course as teachers defined it, with answers that indicate that they saw the key lesson as an introduction to a new topic suggesting the nature of the work to follow:

It introduces you to the topic.
It helps you to understand the topic better.
You see what a subject is about.
You're not dropped into a mass of facts.

The table (p. 240) shows the pattern of responses to questions 2 and 3 of the questionnaire. Question 3 asked pupils to explain what a pink card, a buff card, and a yellow workcard are respectively. A pupils show a much higher tendency to distinguish the "blue sheet" from the "white sheet" as a "summary," "an introduction to a topic," or "a key lesson on paper," and not to describe both simply as "information sheets."

239

Percentages of those accepting the teachers' definition of:

Stream	(a) The course	(b) Pink cards	(c) Yellow workcards
A	68	68	40*
B	50†	44	23
C	8‡	19	3

Total number of respondents: A—111; B—102; C—112.

*It is likely that A pupils are more often encouraged to think of the yellow workcards as a "guide" to using other workcards rather than as just "questions on the white sheet."

†Nearly half of these responses, 23 from a class of 29, came from one class, which suggests that the teacher is in some way acting differently with this B group.

‡C pupils' answers are very diverse and no distinct trend emerges, although they tend to be more concerned with how the lesson is organized for learning, and the showing of films is contrasted favorably with "just talking" and workcards as teaching methods.

A pupils were also more likely to pick up and use the terms "social science" or "sociology" as an overall label for their studies and were more likely to characterize the film, *The First Fifteen Minutes of Life*, which introduced the study of socialization, as about "learning" rather than as "biology" or as well as "biology"; although they were generally unable, when asked, to gloss[32] the term "learning" despite the fact that they had written up notes on it.

A pupils are generally more sensitive to what they have been told *about* the course. Thus when I asked them what they thought of the course, typical responses were:

It's very good; you can disagree with the teacher.
You can link up subjects.
You can think out things for yourself.
It's good for learning how to work at university.

It seems likely they had accepted definitions received from teachers, because when I asked these pupils to tell me about a time they had disagreed with the teacher or about a time when they had been able to link up between subjects, they could recall no instances of either. There appears to be a discrepancy between their definition and their experience of the course of which they were not aware.

It seems probable that the pupils who come to be perceived by teachers as the most able, and who in a streamed school reach the top streams, are those who have access to or are willing to take over the teachers' definition of the situation. As A pupils' behavior is generally seen by the teachers as appropriate, so also is their handling of what is presented as knowledge. Appropriate pupil behavior here seems to be defined by the pupil's ability to do a subject. This is not necessarily a question of the ability to move to higher levels of generalization and abstraction so much as an ability to move into an alternative system of thought from that of his everyday knowledge. In practical terms this means being able to work within the framework which the teacher constructs and by which the teacher is then himself constrained, as the position of the teacher (E) teaching the family (already quoted on pages 234–235) suggests. In teacher E's lesson pupils' definitions of the family which stemmed from their everyday knowledge of families conflicted with the teacher's "expert" definition. The following extracts are from a lesson on the same material with A pupils and teacher D:

TEACHER: Ninety per cent of British families are nuclear families.
BOY: What are the other ten per cent?
TEACHER: We're going on to those. . . .

BOY: What are joint families?
TEACHER: Where you have two or more related families living in the same house. There may be three generations.
GIRL: If you have your granny and grandad living with you is that a joint family?
TEACHER: Yes. . . .

PUPIL: What about single people?
TEACHER: They're not really a family unless they have children. . . .
TEACHER: Another group that's rare throughout the world but is found among the Netsilik Eskimo is the polyandrous group. . . .
PUPIL: What country is that found in? . . .

Here the questions from the pupils take the framework the teacher presents for granted, and the pupils show a willingness to accept the terminology (the "correct term") as part of that framework. The skepticism of many C pupils, which leads them to question the teachers' mode of organizing their material, means that they do not learn what may be taken for granted within a subject, which is part of the process of learning what questions may be asked within a particular subject perspective.[33] It would appear that the willingness to take over the teacher's definition of what is to constitute the problem and what is to count as knowledge may require pupils to regard as irrelevant or inappropriate what they might see as problems in a context of everyday meaning. (In this they resemble the teacher who made irrelevant the everyday use of the term "family.") This means that those pupils who are willing to take over the teachers' definitions must often be less rather than more autonomous (autonomy being a quality or characteristic the enquiry mode is intended to foster) and accept the teacher's presentation on trust. One unit of the socialization theme was work on isolated children, intended to show the necessity of socialization by presenting a negative case. In one account of an isolated child, Patrick, the description did not make clear that he was isolated in a henhouse because he was illegitimate and that the woman who put him there was his mother. In doing this workcard, A pupils generally did not raise problems about why the boy's mother treated him as she did, but got on with the workcard, although it emerged when they were questioned that they had not realized that the child was illegitimate. Some C pupils who wanted first to know why the woman had treated the child like this were told by their teacher: "Well, we're not too interested in that but in the actual influence on the development of the child." Here not only is there a clear resemblance between the way that A pupils and the teacher had each shifted categories of meaning so that enquiry into the question "Why would anyone treat a child like that?" becomes inappropriate, but also that the material is already in some sense "real" and "immediate" to C pupils, but that the teacher took no cognizance of this. It is often assumed by teachers that the comprehension of everyday meaning of material will be obvious to A pupils. Here it is suggested that this cannot be taken for granted. It may be clear to C pupils, whose first concern is likely to be with this kind of meaning.

It may be that the important thing for A pupils is the belief that the knowledge is structured and that the material they are asked to work with has sufficient closure to make "finding the answer" possible. They are usually willing to work within the framework outlined by the teacher and within his terms. Thus a new term like "social science" is at first a label with little meaning but is self-legitimating, and A pupils seem content to wait and let the content emerge so long as they can undertake the immediate task of completing a workcard. This means they frequently do not understand the generalizations teachers make to explain the theme which links several units of work, but this is not apparent to teachers or pupils so long as the work is structured in more or less self-contained units.

Because A pupils are prepared to take over teachers' definitions on trust, they were much quicker to accept social science as a new "subject" within the course, while C pupils continued to refer to the material on socialization in terms of subjects they already knew, like geography or biology, and to question the validity of what they saw as an unjustifiable change of content. A pupils were not generally able to explain the rationale of the socialization theme as teachers had explained it to them[34] but they accpeted that the study could be legitimated and were prepared to operate within the "finite reality" of the subject as the teacher established it. This enabled them to move more quickly into what Blum[35] calls the "common culture" of the subject and to use its terminology. A striking example of this mastery of the language of the subject comes from an A class taught by a psychologist where pupils have acquired a set of terms they can use without gloss.[36] This is from a discussion of Patrick, the child shut in the henhouse:

TEACHER: So we should, when he was found at the age of eight and a half, have been able to teach him to speak?
GIRL: Yes.
BOY: Yes, it was like he'd, um, he'd, um, been sort of lost for ages and had difficulties in speaking.
TEACHER: It's not quite the same. Yes, er . . .
BOY: He's just regressed in er er er in understanding things like.
TEACHER: Mm, but he has been using his vocal chords in some way, as Graham pointed out. He's been imitating chickens. Do you think this could retard his development at all?
BOY: Yes, associating—if you asso—if we associate foreign language words with one of those, it does mean the same thing in his language———
TEACHER: Do you th———
BOY: —he'd be able to speak but he wouldn't think in that language.

The following extract from a C lesson makes an interesting contrast since it may be that the mastery of terms like "regression" represents closure in the questions likely to be asked. In the following, the boy is able to pose the "commonsense" question about "unlearning" because the material has suddenly enabled him to see something taken for granted as problematic:

BOY: Who knew he was in there, then?
TEACHER: Only his mother.
BOY: Where was his father, then?
TEACHER: His mother had separated from his father—she pretended to be a respectable widow. . . . The interesting thing is that the boy was fostered out. He was illegitimate, you see. If you think about it he must have learnt to walk and probably had the beginnings of speech—so what do you think happened?
BOY: The woman who put him in the chicken coop had made him go backwards.
TEACHER: Very good . . .
BOY 2: Well done . . .

BOY: How do you unlearn?
TEACHER: Well you simply forget—in school—tests show that.
BOY: [makes some objection—untranscribable].
TEACHER: You need to keep practicing skills.

A noticeable feature of this sequence is that the teacher's response renders the question unproblematic: "Well you simply forget." Here is another extract where the same process can be seen. The group is a C group, the teacher has been through the pink cards with the class as a whole and the pupils are now working with workcards. Most pupils are having difficulty with a question which runs: "Is it biologically absolutely necessary that this division of labor (between the sexes) should be as rigid as it is?"

TEACHER: Yeah, in other words is it bio-um-physically impossible for the women to do the men's tasks. . . . Well, supposing you said is it biologically necessary for that division. . . . It is *not* biologically necessary. It's um er social reasons.
BOY: Will you come and tell us that, sir, please.
TEACHER: Well it's obviously not biologically necessary. I mean there's no physical reason why the women can't do the men's jobs; they wouldn't be able to do it as well because they're not as strong.
BOY: Aren't women the stronger sex?
TEACHER: Not in the [. . .] sense. The [. . .] says that they have more resistance to pain usually, and so on, and tend to live longer—they're stronger in that sense.
BOY: [untranscribable] . . . feel it.
TEACHER: No, they feel the same pain but they have a greater resistance to it.
BOY: What they always crying for?
TEACHER: Well, that's temperament, isn't it? Anyway we're getting away from the point about the Eskimos, aren't we?

In each of the last two sequences the material had led the pupil to pose as problematic an event he had probably previously taken for granted, and in each case the teacher closes the question in such a way as to render it (for himself if not for the pupil) unproblematic again, apparently because he is not able to accommodate it within the structure he is using. In the first instance the pupil's question could have opened up major issues about learning, in the second about the relative strength of heredity and environment. In neither instance was the pupil's enquiry integrated into the unfolding of the lesson although very germane to its theme.

The matter is complicated here by the teacher's unfamiliarity with the material, but it seems that what counts is whether the pupil's comment or question may be seen as having meaning within the relevance structure[37] the teacher is using, which derives from his notion of what counts as knowledge within a given subject. This relevance structure may, however, shift with respect to the knowledge the teacher has about the pupil, so that the pupil's questions and comments are seen by the teacher as deriving from different relevance structures depending on the status of the pupil with respect to his imputed ability. Thus both the "knowledge" the teacher has of his subject and the "knowledge" he has of the pupil must be seen as variables in the organization and evaluation of what counts as knowledge in the classroom. This may mean that when similar questions are asked by A and C pupils they are categorized differently by the teacher. This is a consequence of the implied notion that A pupils can master subjects while C pupils cannot. The A pupils' questions will be seen as relevant if they can be seen as helping to make explicit the implications of the subject. C pupils' questions are seen as ends in themselves: they arise out of "experience" or everyday reality, beyond which these pupils supposedly cannot go, and are therefore scanned for different kinds of meaning. It seems likely that it is here that teachers' expectations of pupils most effectively operate to set levels of pupil achievement: C pupils are not expected to progress in terms of mastering the nature of a subject, and so their questions are less likely to be seen as making a leap into the reality of the subject. These expectations seem to be implied in the remarks of teachers who said they could get away with not preparing work for C pupils but would not risk that with A pupils. The questions of the latter will require the knowledge of the teacher as "expert."

It seems that in considering what might be involved in the pupil's educational career it would be necessary to specify possible interactional sequences between teacher and pupil in which the pupil's educational identity is established in terms of the expectations the teacher has of him. It is likely that one of the crucial differences in the "latent cultures"[38] from which pupils come is in providing children with modes of acquiring knowledge that leads to differential access to the ways in which teachers structure knowledge: not so much to the particular structures as to the notion that it will be structured in ways that may make it remote from everyday experience. It may be that it is this remoteness from everyday life that is an important element in legitimating academic knowledge in schools. Pupils who have easy access to this knowledge need an ability to sustain uncertainty about the nature of the learning activity in the belief that some pattern will emerge. This requires a willingness to rely on the teacher's authority in delineating what the salient areas of a problem are to be. This will often mean a pupil putting aside what he "knows" to be the case in an everyday context. Children who demonstrate this facility are likely to be regarded as more educable, and to find their way into high-ability groups or to be defined as of high ability, since these are pupils with whom teachers can feel they are making progress. It is likely, as C pupils' questions demonstrate, that all pupils can move between "common sense" and "finite provinces of meaning," but that the particular shifts that the school requires and legitimates are based on a social organization of knowledge that is most likely to be achieved by the predominantly middle-class pupils in A streams.

Once pupils are placed in high-ability groups the wish to achieve at school in the school's terms is confirmed and situated in school activities, and is reinforced by their long-term vocational expectations. These are the pupils in the study who when asked about the humanities course in general terms show they tend to see it in the terms in which teachers define it. These pupils are more likely to move towards using the language of the subject as the teacher presents it, and, equally important, their behavioral style is more likely to seem to the teacher appropriate to the occasion, than the style of C pupils.[39] Once pupils are accredited by streaming or some other device as of high ability, their questions are likely to be scanned by teachers for a different kind of meaning and to be used to a different end from those of C pupils. Teachers will also tend to assume for A pupils that the ability to move into the structure of a subject presupposes that understanding at a "lower," "concrete," "experiential" level which they attribute to C pupils as the limits of their ability. However, it can be argued that A pupils do not necessarily have this understanding, which may involve a different mode of thought and not a simple hierarchical progression from low- to high-order generalizations as teachers seem often to suppose, at least implicitly. It was assumed, for example, that A pupils had a commonsense understanding of why Patrick had been isolated, which in many cases they did not. They had, like the teacher of the C stream group who asked why he had been isolated, apparently defined it out of what it was relevant to inquire into, because neither teacher nor workcard referred to it.

Teachers also tend to assume that A pupils grasp the rationale of the subject in terms of the way teachers indicate progression of linkage from one piece of work to the next. In view of the fact that A pupils generally did not seem to have grasped what the linkage was except in the most general terms, it appears that teachers make assumptions about A pupils' ability to master subjects that are not justified; but because they present and evaluate material in discrete units, this assumption is not often tested.

Conclusions

In the presentation and discussion of data an attempt has been made to examine what teachers "know" about their pupils and how that knowledge is related to the organization of curriculum knowledge in the classroom. Ability is an organizing and unexamined concept for teachers whose categorization of pupils on the grounds of ability derives largely from social class judgments of pupils' social, moral, and intellectual behavior. These judgments are frequently confounded with what are held to be rational values of a general nature. There is between teachers and A pupils a reciprocity of perspective which allows teachers to define, unchallenged by A pupils, as they may be challenged by C pupils, the nature and boundaries of what is to count as knowledge. It would seem to be the failure of high-ability pupils to question what they are taught in schools that contributes in large measure to their educational achievement.

It seems that one use to which the school puts knowledge is to establish that subjects represent the way about which the world is normally known in an "expert" as opposed to a "commonsense" mode of knowing. This establishes and maintains normative order[40] in and within subjects, and accredits as successful to the world outside school those who can master subjects. The school may be seen as maintaining the social order through the taken for granted categories of its superordinates who process pupils and knowledge in mutually confirming ways. The ability to maintain these categories as consensual, when there are among the clients in school conflicting definitions of the situation, resides in the unequal distribution of power. There is a need to see how this enters into and shapes the interactional situation in the classroom. Clearly there is also a need to examine the linkages between schools and other institutions, and attempt to understand the nature of the relationship between what counts as knowledge in schools and what counts as knowledge in other relevant societal areas. In particular, there is a need to understand the relationship between the social distribution of power and the distribution of knowledge, in order to understand the generation of categorizations of pupil, and categories of organization of curriculum knowledge in the school situation. (Because these linkages are unspecified here, the comments I have made about teachers may at times appear to be critical of the "failures" of individuals.)

In the wider context of educational discussion, two panaceas currently put forward to reform the educational system are unstreaming and an undifferentiated curriculum. It seems likely that these prescriptions overlook the fact that streaming is itself a response to an organizing notion of differential ability. It seems likely that the hierarchical categories of ability and knowledge may well persist[41] in unstreamed classrooms and lead to the differentiation of undifferentiated curricula, because teachers differentiate in selection of content and in pedagogy between pupils perceived as of high and low ability. The origins of these categories are likely to lie outside the school and within the structure of the society itself in its wider distribution of power. It seems likely, therefore, that innovation in schools will not be of a very radical kind unless the categories teachers use to organize what they know about pupils and to determine what counts as knowledge undergo a fundamental change.

Notes

Acknowledgments. My thanks are first and foremost to the teachers and pupils of the school of the study. The teachers in the humanities department were, throughout the time I was at the school, unfailingly helpful in giving me their time and allowing me into their lessons with a tape recorder. I am indebted to Gillian Frost, who was also carrying out research at the school, both for the discussions we had, and for the data she made available to me.

The London Borough of Bromley made it possible for me to study for the Master's Degree of the University of London, by seconding me for a year, giving me the time to carry out the study on which this paper is based. I should like to thank Professor Basil Bernstein for his encouragement and for his assistance in getting the tape recordings transcribed. My thanks are also due to John Hayes and Michael Young, with whom I discussed the material at various stages and to whom I owe very many insights that helped me to organize the data. I owe similar thanks to my fellow graduate students, in particular to John Bartholomew, and also to John Beck. My thanks are also to Michael Young for reading this paper in an earlier draft and making many detailed and constructive comments which helped me to clarify confusions and inconsistencies.

1. The direction of mainstream sociology of education in this respect can be seen in the very comprehensive account of available studies in chapters 3, 4, and 5 of Olive Banks's *The Sociology of Education* (London: Batesford, 1968).

2. S. Baratz and J. Baratz, "Early Childhood Intervention: The Social Science Basis of Institutionalized Racism," *Harvard Education Review* 40 (Feb. 1970).

3. A. V. Cicourel and J. I. Kitsuse, *The Educational Decision Makers* (Indian-

apolis: Bobbs-Merrill, 1963); R. V. Dumont and M. L. Wax, "Cherokee School Society and the Intercultural Classroom," *Human Organization* 28, no. 3 (fall 1969); M. L. Wax and R. H. Wax, "Formal Education in an American Indian Community," *Social Problems Monographs* 2 (spring 1964).

4. B. B. Bernstein, "On the Classification and Framing of Educational Knowledge," *Knowledge and Control: New Directions for the Sociology of Education*, ed. M. F. D. Young (London: Collier-Macmillan, 1971), ch. 2; M. F. D. Young, "An Approach to the Study of Curricula as Socially Organized Knowledge," *Knowledge and Control*, ed. Young, ch. 1.

5. Cicourel and Kitsuse (*The Educational Decision Makers*) show the importance in this context of the processes by which students are allocated to college or non-college courses. The Schools Council's acceptance of a differentiated curriculum, like the Newsome Report, maintains a distinction between the "academic" and the "non-academic" child.

6. N. G. Keddie, "The Social Basis of Classroom Knowledge: A Case Study," M.A. thesis, University of London, 1970.

7. I have to thank Gillian Frost for making this information available to me.

8. This mode of examination allows teachers to construct and examine their own courses with moderation from an external examiner.

9. P. Bourdieu, "Systems of Education and Systems of Thought," *International Social Science Journal* 19, no. 3 (1967), reprinted in *Knowledge and Control*, ed. Young, ch. 7.

10. C. W. Mills, "Situated Actions and Vocabularies of Motive," *American Sociological Review* 4, no. 5 (1940).

11. H. Garfinkel and H. Sacks, "On Formal Structures of Practical Actions," *Theoretical Sociology: Perspectives and Development*, ed. J. McKinney and E. Tiryakian (New York: Appleton-Century-Crofts, 1970).

12. H. S. Becker and B. Geer, "Latent Culture: A Note on the Theory of Latent Social Roles," *Administrative Science Quarterly* 5, no. 2 (1960).

13. P. Selznick, *T.V.A. and the Grass Roots: A Study in the Sociology of Formal Organizations* (Berkeley and Los Angeles: University of California Press, 1949). I have to thank John Bartholomew for bringing this to my notice.

14. I. Deutscher, "Words and Deeds: Social Science and Social Policy," *Social Problems* 13 (winter 1966).

15. For example, the Humanities Curriculum Project of the Schools Council directed by Lawrence Stenhouse.

16. An interview with Gillian Frost, whom I thank for making it available to me.

17. D. Sudnow, "Normal Crimes: Sociological Features of the Penal Code in a Public Defender Office," *Social Problems* 15 (winter 1968).

18. "Is" and "ought" are not necessarily discrepant. There is no reason why there should not be a fit between them.

19. B. Geer, J. Haas, C. Vivona, S. J. Miller, C. Miller, and H. S. Becker, "Learning the Ropes: Situational Learning in Four Occupational Training Programmes," *Among the People: Encounters with the Poor*, ed. I. Deutscher and E. J. Thompson (New York: Basic Books, 1968).

20. A. K. Cohen, "The Study of Social Disorganization and Deviant Behavior," *Sociology Today: Problems and Prospects*, ed. R. K. Merton, L. Broom, and L. S. Cottrell (New York: Basic Books, 1959).

21. M. Deutsch, "The Disadvantaged Child and the Learning Process," *Education in Depressed Areas*, ed. H. Passow (New York: Teachers College Press, 1963).

22. Dumont and Wax ("Cherokee School Society") make a similar point about the culture of the Cherokee Indian. There is clearly a relationship between individualization of failure and the psychologistic notion of a curriculum based on pupils' "needs." See also N. L. Friedman, "Cultural Deprivation: A Commentary in the Sociology of Knowledge," *Journal of Educational Thought* 1 (Aug. 1967).

23. This relationship is also apparent in the data of Hargreaves: "On one occasion a teacher left the room to investigate some noise in the corridor. 'Who are you lot?' he cried. '3B, sir,' came the reply. 'You sound more like 1E than 3B.' was the master's crushing retort" (D. Hargreaves, *Social Relations in a Secondary School* [London: Routledge and Kegan Paul, 1967], p. 95).

24. Wax and Wax ("Formal Education in an American Indian Community") find the same situation in what they call a "vacuum ideology" which is attributed to the Cherokee Indian by white teachers.

25. B. S. Bloom, *Taxonomy of Educational Objectives* (New York: David McKay, 1956).

26. Interview with Gillian Frost.

27. Workcards for pupils are of three kinds: pink cards written by a member of staff which give an overview of the topic to be studied ("concepts" are generally printed in capital letters to point the organization of material to the pupils); buff cards which are also referred to as "documents" because they often reproduce original sources and deal with areas of the topic in more detail; yellow workcards which have questions intended to guide pupils in the use of the other workcards. Many pupils treated these straightforwardly as question sheets.

28. The concept here is that of "multiple realities" developed by Schütz (A. Schütz, *Collected Papers*, vol. 1 *The Problem of Social Reality*; The Hague: Martinus Nijhoff, 1967). In organizing the data I have also been greatly influenced by the distinction between "commonsense" and "expert" knowledge made by Horton (R. Horton, "African Traditional Thought and Western Science," *Africa* 67 [1967]; reprinted in *Knowledge and Control*, ed. Young, ch. 8). I have also used this article in attempting to conceptualize A and C pupils' approaches to knowledge as the outcome of alternative thought systems, as opposed to seeing the differences in terms of a hierarchical relationship.

29. See note 27, above.

30. Garfinkel and Sacks, "On Formal Structures of Practical Actions," pp. 342–45 and 362–66.

31. There is a need for studies of the models of society inherent in subjects as they are taught in schools and in textbooks. T. S. Kuhn, *The Structure of Scientific Revolutions* (2nd ed.; Chicago: University of Chicago Press, 1970), suggests how an authoritarian model of science is built into science subjects as they are taught and the textbooks as they are used. Other studies might cast light on how a normative order is transmitted through the contents of subjects in schools and, in relation to this, what counts as "objectivity" in that subject and how it operates to maintain that normative order.

32. Garfinkel and Sacks, "On Formal Structures of Practical Actions," pp. 342–45 and 362–66.

33. One exposition of a subject from this point of view is made by R. K. Merton ("Notes on Problem-Finding," *Sociology Today*, ed. Merton *et al.*).

34. For example, most teachers explained to pupils that the film showed how early the human child begins to learn, and that the study of isolated children showed how necessary it is for a child to be brought up among human beings if his learning is to proceed and he is to become human. Nevertheless most pupils were unable to point to any link between the units of study. At the most they were able to say that both were "about learning."

35. A. Blum, "The Corpus of Knowledge as a Normative Order: Intellectual Critiques of the Social Order of Knowledge and Commonsense Features of Bodies of Knowledge" (1970), reprinted in *Knowledge and Control*, ed. Young, ch. 4.

36. Garfinkel and Sacks, "On Formal Structures of Practical Actions," pp. 342–45 and 362–66.

37. Schütz, *Collected Papers*, vol. 1, p. 5ff.

38. The concept here is that the school represents the *manifest* culture. See H. S. Becker, "Social Class Variations in the Teacher-Pupil Relationship," *Journal of Educational Sociology* 25 (April 1952); also in R. Bell and H. Stubb, eds., *The Sociology of Education: A Sourcebook* (Homewood, Ill.: Dorsey Press, 1968).

39. It seems likely that teachers frequently pay more attention to the style than to the content of pupils' comments. Clearly this is linked to problems of social control. C pupils in particular tend to call out in class. There is probably also a problem for teachers in how C pupils actually phrase their comments or questions. When I reported to the humanities department on the research, I gave as examples of pupils asking questions from the point of view of their own commonsense views of the world, one question already quoted: "What are they [women] always crying for then?" and another from the key lesson in which pupils were shown slides of the foetus in the womb, when a C boy asked about the foetus: "How does it go to the toilet then?" This latter question, which seems to be an intelligent one, probably could not be asked more precisely without a concept of the body's "functions." When I gave these two questions as examples one teacher said the boys "must have been joking." At the least he implies that these questions are not appropriate to the business of learning and it is likely that his response is to the pupil's language and has a social class basis. Probably this teacher made explicit what many teachers feel: that the C pupil's attitudes and manners are inappropriate to the classroom; similar attitudes of teachers are to be found in: Hargreaves, *Social Relations in a Secondary School*, and C. Werthman, "Delinquency in Schools: A Test for the Legitimacy of Authority," *Berkeley Journal of Sociology* 8 (1963).

40. Blum, "The Corpus of Knowledge as a Normative Order."

41. J. C. Barker Lunn, *Streaming in the Primary School* (Slough: National Foundation for Educational Research, 1970), suggests that teachers often carry attitudes appropriate to streaming into unstreamed classes and that this is particularly damaging for the "low-ability" working-class child.

CHAPTER 13

Social Relations as Contexts
for Learning in School

R. P. McDermott

Accounts of what is wrong with our schools are legion. But what is it that works in classrooms? Rather than suggesting certain teaching techniques, this paper will examine the importance of the social relations between teachers and children in the development of learning environments in classrooms. Successful learning environments provide children with the possibility of discovering clearly defined tasks, and the time to work on them until mastery is achieved.[1] Unsuccessful learning environments are marked by children spending years struggling to get organized and to pay attention rather than learning.

Although the data are anecdotal and the generalizations not powerfully warranted, this article will perform a dual service by reporting some methods for studying the relational foundations of successful pedagogy and by citing some important cases which can alter our sense of "problem" children and the kinds of theories we need to understand such children.

The claim of this paper is that the relations between children and teachers underlie the organizational work necessary for learning tasks to be presented and worked on by children. By the relations between teachers and children, I mean "working agreements" or "consensuses" about who they are and what is going on between them, agreements which they formulate, act upon, and use together to make sense of each other.[2] In particular, I am interested in what I call "trusting relations," a crucial subset of the working agreements people use to make sense of each other. In the classroom, these issues translate into how the teacher

Reprinted with the permission of the publisher from *Harvard Educational Review* 47, no. 2 (May 1977): 198–213. Copyright © 1977 by President and Fellows of Harvard College.

and children can understand each other's behavior as directed to the best interests of what they are trying to do together and how they can hold each other accountable for any breach of the formulated consensus.

It is important that the reader not take "trusting relations" in the ordinary sense, which implies that trust is a property of a person's personality. The developmental literature is filled with references to a child's acquisition of "basic trust" as if it becomes a property of the child to be used in all situations. However, I am talking about trust as a quality of the relations among people, as a product of the work they do to achieve a shared focus. Trust is achieved and managed through interaction.[3] It takes constant effort for two or more people to achieve trusting relations, and the slightest lag in that work can demand extensive remedial efforts.

Although I am claiming a central role for trusting relations in the organization of a successful classroom, I am not suggesting that some children or teachers are more trusting than others and thus they learn better in school. Trust is not a property of persons but a product of the work people do to achieve trusting relations, given particular institutional contexts. What I am suggesting is that in contexts that offer teachers and children enough resources to work together to establish a trusting environment, children will have sufficient time and energy to devote themselves to the intellectual tasks set before them. In other words, trusting relations are framed by the contexts in which people are asked to relate, and where trusting relations occur, learning is a possibility. Where trusting relations are not possible, learning can only result from solitary effort.

Behavior modifiers who work in the classroom can point to some excellent short-term results. They can construct environments in which children and their teachers know what to expect of each other. For the duration of the specially prepared environments, both trusting relations and learning can evolve.[4] Their results can seldom be generalized, however, because the larger community does not usually supply the same kind of consistent environment. Still, in the world beyond the reach of most behavior therapists, many communities naturally produce successful learning environments. These positive examples are marked by trusting relational environments which allow the children time on learning tasks. We are just beginning to discover how cultural and institutional resources are crucial to understanding of the differences between successful and unsuccessful classrooms.

Observers have noted that in the average elementary school about 50 percent of class time is spent in getting organized.[5] Success in getting organized for learning depends on how well the participants communicate to each other the importance of the learning tasks. Moreover, the problem of organization operates at all levels of school activity. Even the organizationally efficient teacher who divides a class into small tracked groups will have groups that differ in the amount of time spent on learning tasks even while the teacher is with them. In order to understand why some children spend more time on learning tasks than others do, it is necessary to examine both how children establish relations with their teachers and the contexts in which they are asked to do so.

The first section of this paper will claim that there is an order or logic in the ways people relate to each other. They use this order to organize their behavior with each other, demonstrating the particulars of this in their activities. Sensitive approaches to describing the work people do to organize and maintain the order of their relations have been developed in several branches of social science. Their thrust will be summarized in a discussion of *ethnography* as a tool for the study of relations between people. Generally, this term is used by anthropologists to describe their efforts to record the cultures of different peoples around the world. I will use "ethnography" more specifically to refer to any rigorous attempt to account for people's behavior in terms of their relations with those around them in differing situations.

In the second section, I will examine how an ethnography of class-room relations can offer us a different vision of what children and teachers do there and what might be successful or unsuccessful classroom talk. In particular, I will consider two ways of attempting to gain children's attention in classrooms: an authoritarian method in which a child's every moment in the classroom is organized by the teacher's directives; and a guidance-based method in which the child is encouraged to explore an environment for what is most interesting and most useful for the life of the group. Both methods are forms of coercion that are successful depending upon the relational foundations for communicating in the classroom.

In the last section of this paper, I will apply some of the principles developed in the first two sections to an analysis of how children become organized for learning to read. Although almost no ethnographic research has been done on how children learn to read in schools, we have information indicating that relational contexts are crucial.

The Ethnography of Relations

At its best, an ethnography should account for the behavior of people by describing what enables them to behave sensibly with others in their community.[6] All people, especially those from different cultures, appear to behave differently, and we all attempt haphazard ethnographies when we struggle to decipher the logic of the behavior of different peoples. We acknowledge this in everyday talk by saying that successful social relations depend on knowing "where a person is coming from" or "where a person's head is at." Successful psychiatry certainly demands this level of understanding, and so does successful teaching.[7] The first principle of good pedagogy, namely, beginning at a student's present skill level, calls for good ethnography. Too often, however, teachers, psychiatrists, and the rest of us proceed intuitively. Professional ethnographers differ from us only in that they are more disciplined and self-conscious in gathering information about how people relate to the world around them. Rather than assuming "where a person's head is at," they struggle to define rigorously the practices a person displays in interpreting and generating behavior in particular situations.

Consider the following illustrations of what an ethnography attempts to describe. When a scientist publishes a report, the scientific community has procedures for holding her or him accountable for the findings. Was the experiment performed under the proper conditions? Were the proper statistical analyses performed? Were the interpretations of the data consistent with methods previously used for interpreting similar data? These and other questions act as legitimate ways to hold a scientist accountable. This is called a methodology, and it constitutes a canon in terms of which scientists make sense of each other. Such a canon is explicit; ideally scientists should be aware of the assumptions underlying their methodology and its implications. The point of this illustration is that people in everyday life also have methods for holding each other accountable.[8] An ethnography is an attempt to describe a group's methodology, that is, an attempt to describe the procedures group members use to relate to each other in culturally sensible ways.[9] Unfortunately, the procedures used in everyday life are never very explicit. For example, how many of us can list in detail the procedures we use in greeting another person or walking down a street? Greetings involve a head toss, a presentation of the palm of the hand, a brief motion of the eyebrows, and a flash of the teeth in a smile.[10] Walking down a street involves computing complex trajectories for people moving in different directions and discerning who is with whom in order to avoid collisions.[11] We all greet people and navigate the streets, but few of us can be explicit about how we do it.

In science and in everyday life, methodologies and procedures differ and lead to varied consequences. A behaviorist studies different problems and reaches quite different conclusions than a psychologist following a psychoanalytic canon. Similarly, the procedures we use in our daily activities have consequences for us and for all those around us. A successful ethnography should help us to become aware of our actions and their consequences. If we all walked down the street or greeted each other in the same way without regard for the circumstances, then an ethnogrpahy of our street behavior would be uninteresting. We are, however, quite selective in our interaction with others. Some people attract us and others do not, most often for reasons which we ourselves do not understand. Much of what happens to us in everyday life results from the limited and unarticulated methods we use to handle the world and to hold each other accountable. How many of us are aware, for example, that when passing through the neighborhood of a different ethnic group we generally display "the posture of territorial behavior"? We lower our heads, curl our shoulders so that our chests do not protrude, bring our hands close to or in front of our bodies, and keep our eyes down.[12] Such behavior may make us a little less noticeable, but it also curtails our communication with people in that neighborhood. In other words, such behavior helps to maintain the very boundaries which prevent interethnic communication.

People develop elaborate procedures for relating to each other in different situations. These procedures are rarely obvious to the participants but offer them a quick and easy way of achieving working agreements. We are all embedded in our own procedures, which make us both very smart in one situation and blind and stupid in the next. Any change in these procedures, either cultural or personal, can reveal unimagined consequences of the ways we choose to relate to each other. This is illustrated by the clinical account of a family disrupted by the husband's extreme dependence upon his wife.[13] According to all involved, the problem was that the man was illiterate and showed little promise of upward mobility. After extensive therapy and instruction, the man acquired enough reading competence to become more independent. Soon after, the wife filed for divorce. Prior to the husband's treatment, the couple apparently had developed a rather special way of dealing with each other which unfortunately left the man dependent upon his wife. When the husband became literate, however, the dependent nature of their relationship was undermined and the marriage dissolved. Apparently neither partner knew what they were each contributing to and gaining from the dependency relationships. Is it possible that the logic of many of our relationshipe is equally well hidden?

Turning now to education, we hope that the ethnographic study of classrooms will allow us to look carefully at how we as teachers make sense and hold students accountable to our way of making sense. The problem with common sense, of course, is that sense must be made in common with other people within institutional contexts, which place different demands on each of the participants. Accordingly, sustained common sense is a rare achievement, and teachers and children often work out mutually regressive relations in their classrooms for reasons generally unrecognized by both groups. All teachers lose some students in every class. Talented teachers and intelligent children sometimes find themselves on opposite sides of the fence. Pain and failure often result for all involved, and no one quite knows why. In the early years some students do not even learn to read, and in later years many suffer from alienation and crippling anxieties. Some analysts blame the children, their genes, their families, or television, while others blame the teachers for being lazy, insensitive, prejudiced, or badly trained. In most cases, neither the children nor their teachers are to be blamed; communication breakdowns always have two sides. The question is not Who is at fault? but rather What is it about the way teachers and children relate that enables them to make sense of each other as coparticipants in the educational process, on the one hand, or as enemies, on the other?

Consider the case of Rosa, a failing student in a first-grade classroom that I have been analyzing. She is in the bottom of one of three reading-skill groups in the class where she constantly struggles to get a turn to read. Yet, day after day, she is passed by. Why is Rosa so consistently ignored? How will she ever learn to read if she spends all her time in the classroom trying to get a turn? After analyzing a film I made of the reading group, I began to understand the teacher's position. Rosa is one of the least skilled readers in the group. Although her English is adequate for everyday affairs, her native tongue is Spanish, and she apparently had little training in learning how to read either language before coming to school. There is no reason to think that Rosa's handicap is permanent; not learning how to read by age six says little about what a child can do by age seven or eight if given the proper learning environment.[14] Bilingualism should offer no serious handicap to a child learning to read, again provided a proper learning environment is available.[15] The teacher's behavior in this particular classroom is sensible; she is simply giving Rosa time to develop enough competence to read without embarrassing her in front of her peers.

Will Rosa ever get the opportunity to master reading in school? I will only outline the answer to the question in order to point to how an ethnographer might proceed and to the interesting results to be had from an ethnographic approach. I proceed by examining repeatedly the film of the reading group in order to isolate the working agreements which Rosa and the teacher use to make sense of each other. Only those agreements which the participants themselves identify in their behavior are accepted as adequately described relational contexts.[16]

What are the relations between Rosa and the teacher? The teacher says of Rosa, "I just can't reach her," and Rosa offers only a blushing silence when asked about her relationship to the teacher. On the surface, their relationship does not sound workable, but an underlying logic can be seen in their interactions. A careful look at Rosa's behavior reveals that she in fact conspires with the teacher in not getting a turn to read. Although she often requests a turn to read, she does so in unusual ways: she checks to see what page the other children are reading, turns to a different page, and then calls for a turn; she waits for the teacher to start to call on another child and then quickly calls for a turn; or she calls for a turn while looking away from the teacher. The teacher often attends to these signals before calling on another child. The teacher organizes the turn taking in the group randomly, so that Rosa never has to be asked to read as she would if the teacher called on children in order around the reading table. Accordingly, too much of the group's time at the table is spent in organizing who is to read next. During these times, outsiders enter the group to ask the teacher questions and group members complain that everyone is not being treated fairly. The result is that the bottom reading group spends only a third as much time on reading tasks as the top group, although they spend an equal amount of time at the reading table. Rosa spends her time avoiding a turn to read.

Rosa's actions make sense when one considers her beginning reading skills, the competitive pressures of the classroom, and the teacher's organizational methods. The teacher's behavior makes sense given her task—teaching a child to read while keeping a whole roomful of children busy at other tasks. Together, they behave sensibly in relation to each other and appear to be doing their best. But together they do not achieve trusting relations. Rosa and the teacher do not understand each other's behavior as directed to the best interest of what they are trying to do together, namely, to get Rosa organized for learning how to read. Their failure to achieve trusting relations has its consequences. Rosa spends little time trying to read in the classoom; she either will learn to read at home or suffer school failure. In fact, at the end of the second grade, Rosa was sent to a special school for slow learners.

Such relational problems run deep in our compe⌐itive culture, where school systems are designed to sort out the capable from the incapable.[17] Solutions will require more than simple changes in pedagogical style.[18] To illustrate this point, I will consider two ways of organizing classrooms, the success of both of which depends on the relational work of teachers and children in getting organized for learning tasks. Why some communities have the resources for doing this work while others do not remains an unanwered question.

Teacher-Student Relations

Teaching is invariably a form of coercion. While some teachers handle coercion directly, others are less direct and more guidance-oriented. In the contemporary idiom, the difference is referred to in terms of closed and open classrooms. Although the constraints can be framed differently and with quite different consequences for the organization of the social structure, coercion is always present in classrooms.[19] All teachers, regardless of their orientation, are faced with the task of getting and directing the children's attention, directing it to a problem, and leading them to some way of handling it.[20]

Generally, teachers use speech to direct children to learning tasks. The specific verbal strategies teachers use are not so important as whether or not the strategies make good sense to the children. A teacher must establish working agreements wherein the children can trust the teacher's coercion to be in their best interests.

Successful Authoritarian Classroom Communication

The Old Order Amish schools of Pennsylvania provide an example of a pedagogically successful, authoritarian strategy for handling classroom activities.[21] Amish children did not do well academically when forced by local authorities into public schools, and there was little reason to think that they would perform better in their own schools. Amish teachers seldom have more than eight years of academic training; they must teach children raised speaking a Germanic language to read English; and their classrooms prohibit competition, which many consider to be a key element of group learning in our culture. Finally, the Amish teachers' communicative style, on the surface at least, is contrary to much of the educational ideology in America. The teachers dominate their classrooms, and an analysis of classroom interactions has shown a heavy use of commands and a high degree of direct instruction.[22] Nevertheless, Amish community schools are quite successful, not only by Amish standards, but by those of other American schools as well. Amish children score above the norms in standardized reading and arithmetic tests.[23] What then is the relation between teaching style and these pupils' successes in academic subjects?

259

To answer this question, we must look to the kinds of social relations which make sense to children raised in the Amish culture. Socialization patterns among the Amish are quite different from those found elsewhere in America. Indeed, many aspects of Amish identity in America have been forged in opposition to and in defense against other ways of being human in a modern technological society. Such a defensive strategy, common among minority cultures, is marked by the merging of individual identities into a group life that is organized around unifying symbols transmitted by a small number of authoritarian leaders.[24] The Amish educational system fits this model nicely. Its symbols are religious and are used to establish trusting relations. The teacher is in total control of the children's development, telling them what to do and when and how to do it. In terms of learning to read and enhancing an Amish identity, this system is highly successful. Children and their teachers live in a closed community with highly specific routines, where everyone is accountable to everyone else. Amish community members use a specific code to achieve common sense and mutual trust. In this context, instructions are not blind commands but, rather, sensible suggestions about what to do next to further common goals. There is a warm relational fabric that underlies the instructions and transforms them from orders into sensible ways of organizing everyday life. What appears to many to be an author-itarian and oppressive system for organizing a classroom may in fact make great sense to the children. Outsiders simply miss the cues which ground teacher-student activities in trust and accountability.

Unsuccessful Authoritarian Classroom Communication

No matter how successful authoritarian speech behavior is within small communities, there is much evidence that the authoritarian teacher is encountering difficulties in contemporary America. Apparently the trust which makes direct commands possible in the Amish classroom is not present in more open communities. Even in less conservative Amish communities, in fact, teachers use much less direct forms of control.[25]

The failure of attempts to teach with direct methods in the absence of a foundation of trusting relations is well documented. In such situations, children simply "don't listen," and the teacher expends most of the class time controlling "behavior problems" or, to borrow a phrase from a past principal of mine, "keeping the lid on." Too often teachers fall back on a formal definition of their role as teachers and expect children to conduct themselves as if this role placed an exact set of rules on the children's behavior. In such situations, the teacher relies on institutional rewards and punishments, saying "Do this, because, if you don't, the principal will deal with you," rather than "Do this, because it's a sensible thing to do."

Teachers' efforts to define roles in the classrooms create some strange forms of behavior. For example, a teacher who fails to motivate a class may camouflage this failure with a lesson directed to a nonexistence audience. Examples of this phenomenon are unfortunately common in ethnographic studies of urban schools.[26] Rist offers an example of what he calls a "phantom performance":

> She asks the children to repeat the poem, and no child makes a sound. She asks the children to repeat the poem line by line after her, first with the words and then a second time through simply saying "lu, lu, lu" in place of the words. The children are completely baffled and say nothing. At the end of the second competition she comments, "Okay, that was good. We will have to do that again next week."[27]

The relational ground underlying a phantom performance is not fertile soil for building trusting relations. The children's definition of the teacher's role comes to include not attending to the class, and they begin to dismiss teaching as an essentially insensitive task; the teacher is expected to be "mean."

In addition to intensive role definition, direct control over a class can be built on insult and status degradation. Interpersonal warfare, rather than trust and accountability, is the result. Much of what were described to me as teaching and classroom-control techniques by a teacher trainer in the New York City schools amounted to insults that could bind a child into silence. Even when the authoritarian approach to classroom management keeps children under control, if it is not founded on a mutual understanding extending beyond threats of detention or suspension, little learning will take place. Defensive blackboard boredom is no more academically productive than the overt misbehavior of the less controlled blackboard jungle.[28] It is in the context of an authoritarian classroom without a grounding in trust and accountability that it is possible to talk of children achieving school failure.[29] In response to the teacher's authority, children develop their own classroom organization, in which not working and disrupting the teacher's procedures become goals.

Unsuccessful Guidance Classroom Communication

Less direct forms of coercing children into attending to classroom tasks are not uniformly better or worse than the authoritarian approach.[30] If there is no proper relational foundation, a child is no more likely to follow a gentle suggestion than a direct order.

Guidance approaches to teaching make much use of question-commands rather than direct orders. A teacher can say, "Close the door" or "Why don't you close the door?" In either case the door must be closed by the student. The child is neither expected nor permitted to answer with a statement such as "I am not closing the door because I don't feel like it." The question is not meant to be a question but rather a command. Linguists have recently been studying such phenomena and have given them the delightful name of "whimperatives."[31] A whimperative stands for a command stated in a question form with a "wh——" word. But if "whim" or "whimper" is taken as the root, a whimperative can mean something quite different. So it is with "wh——" commands in everyday conversation; they can be interpreted in many ways, depending on the context in which they are used.[32]

The kind of response elicited by a whimperative depends upon how it is understood, which in turn depends on how the conversationalists define their relations at a particular time. Imagine the difficulty of telling a child what to do when there is no working consensus that the child should do what he or she is told. Now imagine trying to hide from the child that he or she is in fact being told what to do. In this way, a command framed as a question becomes a whimper. In question form, the command to close a door only suggests an expectation that the door be closed and hides the fact that there is likely to be a system of constraints behind the teacher's request. This problem does not arise when a trusting relation underlies the teacher's command; the child interprets the teacher as acting in the best interest of what they are trying to do together in the classroom and simply does what the teacher suggests. Without this relationship, the whimpering nature of the command is more apparent to the child. In such a context, learning tasks seldom receive the attention required for the child to make progress.

Successful Guidance Classroom Communication

Guidance approaches to communication in the classroom need not result in such relational disasters between teachers and children. In a trusting environment, such approaches can be most powerful, particularly when attention is directed to the individual needs of the children. Indeed, in many of our urban schools, where children come from diverse communities, a guidance approach may be the best alternative. Without the possibility of drawing on shared images and life experiences, many teachers face the task of creating a system of trusting relations with only the resources of the classroom at hand.[33] In such cases, a guidance approach affords the children an opportunity to explore their environments and to discover learning tasks for themselves. This may be the only way for the teacher to hold the interest of the children long enough to establish a working consensus. Once such working relationships are established, the teacher will have to use them wisely in order to sustain their effectiveness.

Teacher-Student Relations and Learning to Read

I have tried to show that teachers and children use a system of relations to make sense of each other and that this system underlies the sustained attention of children to learning tasks. To understand these relational systems adequately, better ethnographic accounts of life in the classroom are necessary. Even in the absence of such accounts, however, anecdotal reports of children learning to read suggest that the successful acquisition of literacy, like the successful use of a pedagogical style, depends on the achievement of trusting relations. If this hypothesis is correct, we may gain a new perspective on why some children do not learn to read in our schools. Rather than pointing to inadequacies in either the children or their teachers, perhaps we should examine the rational adaptations made by teachers and children within the institutional contexts we offer them.

Consider how the Hanunoo learn to read. The Hanunoo, a small group of farmers isolated in the rugged mountains of the island of Mindoro in the Philippines, achieve a 60 percent literacy rate with a rare Indic-derived script imported centuries ago and virtually unknown to surrounding groups. The Hanunoo receive no formal training in reading and writing and, in fact, are not concerned about literacy until early puberty. They appear, however, to have the ultimate organizational device for learning to read. Literacy is used almost exclusively in courtship among the Hanunoo, and at the time of puberty the children work diligently at learning the script until they can carve songs onto bamboo cylinders in order to support an active love life. They achieve literacy within only months.[34]

There are numerous examples of similar achievements of people having to master very rapidly an orthography for social and religious purposes in a nonschool environment.[35] Although none of these accounts specifies the relational contexts which guide the people to learn and become literate, they all raise an important question. If it is the case that people can learn to read quickly and under such diverse conditions, why do so many of our children fail to learn how to read despite so many years in school?

I suspect that many of our children spend most of their time in relational battles rather than on learning tasks. This is especially the case for minority children who enter the schools with an uncertain status in the eyes of teachers. Some have held that minority-group members do badly in schools because they have a different language, dialect, and rules for taking turns in conversation. When minority students and their teachers are unable to understand each other, however, I believe they have a choice of turning their misunderstanding into a social barrier or of working with each other until they can repair their misunderstanding.[36] The alternatives chosen depend on the relational contexts in which the misunderstanding arises.

Although equivalent examples of other kinds of communicative-code interference in the classroom are available, the following example from the study of dialect interference in learning how to read seems particularly relevant. Most of the children in the first-grade classrooms studied by Piestrup in Oakland, California, schools spoke a Black English vernacular.[37] To the extent that their teachers tried to stop them from using dialect in the classroom, the children were unable to get to the task of learning to read. These children's use of dialect either remained the same or increased depending on how often the teachers corrected their speech. For children whose use of dialect was often corrected, reading scores tended to be low. In classrooms where the children were allowed to talk and read in dialect, vernacular use did not increase and reading scores were higher, with many children scoring above national norms. When the dialect was not treated as a barrier to communication, the children and the teacher were able to spend time on reading tasks. However, when dialect was treated as a problem in the relations between the teacher and children, it interfered with their formulating trusting agreements about what they were trying to do with each other. Thus, they spent more time doing relational work and less time learning to read. In this way, the use of dialect and the children's participation in learning tasks become politicized. The logical result is seen in older Black children for whom there are significant correlations among dialect use, school failure, and participation in peer-group gangs.[38]

The problem for many minority-group children in mainstream schools is in establishing trusting relations with the teacher. Even if many of these children come to school different from their peers—lagging behind in the development of certain school skills (phonics, for example) with divergent communicative skills, or with completely different expectations about what a classroom is—they can still learn to read. If, however, these children become engaged in an endless battle to relate to the teacher, they will never have the time to catch up with their peers. Our school system is harsh to those who fall behind; it sorts these children out, labels them, and finally pushes them aside. Certain minorities have bypassed this system by teaching their children how to read outside the public schools, either in private schools or at home. But most minority groups that have relied on the public schools have paid a price, identity struggles replace learning tasks, and children often leave school knowing little more about reading than when they entered.

These examples suggest the primacy of social relations in determining children's success or failure in school. If social relations are, in fact, important, then we may have to reconsider our notions of who are "problem children" and how to best understand and help them. In particular, we may have to question our own role in the failures of these children and examine how we help create such destructive environments.

Conclusion

An awareness of the primacy of trusting relations in the organization of successful classrooms and of the usefulness of ethnography as a tool with which to study the nature of classroom relations leads to questions that may help us to reformulate our theory and practice in teaching children who do not learn in school. Evidence indicates that the efficacy of varying pedagogical styles and ways of learning to read depends on the social relations established with different children in different classrooms.

Since the relations between teachers and children are central to the organization of time in the classroom, we teachers must ask how our ways of relating result in some children spending more time getting organized than being on task. There appears to be an order or logic to our ways of relating, even when they are not successful. We must ask just what our contribution is to this order. The specifics of these difficult questions are probably different across classrooms and children. Two facts, however, may help us understand what we may be doing wrong. First, we often do not see the underlying order in the children's behavior when they engage us in relational struggles. Second, we blame them for their regressive behavior, although they could not act regressively without us.

These facts raise the most crucial question of all: *how do we create environments which allow children to act sensibly, but which also allow us to remain blind to the good sense of their behavior?* In the future, ethnographic studies of the classroom might be addressed to answering this question in empirical terms. In the meantime, simply knowing that the question is important is a major step forward. By asking this question, we alter our perspective on problem children by acknowledging that they are acting sensibly within the environments we have afforded them: any labeling of children as inadequate without a corresponding account of how their behavior makes sense is necessarily unfair. By asking this question, we also require that our theories of problem children account for the uneven distribution of resources available to different children and their teachers for making sense of each other and achieving trusting relations in institutional contexts; any description of problem children is necessarily political. Finally, until we can gain more control over the institutional contexts we share with children, we can reduce our expectation that schools can function as a mechanism for massive social change; until we can control the particulars of our own institutional lives, it is foolish to think that we can easily direct the institutional lives of our children.

Once we start asking this type of question, we will not be able to lay the blame for school failure solely at the children's feet. They simply act much too sensibly for that, and their ways of relating are as much a function of our expectations as theirs. Unidirectional solutions cannot cure relational problems. To reorder our relations with problem children, we must first deal with the relations that have already been established. Efforts to build trusting relations and develop successful learning environments must start with an adequate ethnographic sense of what we are really trying to do with children and of the nature of institutional contexts within which we are making these attempts.

Notes

Note. A few pages in the sections of this article on the ethnography of relations and teacher student relations were adapted from "Ethnography of Speaking and Reading," by R. P. McDermott, published in Roger Shuy, ed., *Linguistic Theory: What Can It Say about Reading?* (Newark, Del.: International Reading Association, 1977). Permission to publish these pages has been granted by the author and the publisher. Writing time for the most recent version of this article was supported by grants from the Carnegie Corporation to Michael Cole and the Laboratory of Comparative Human Cognition at The Rockefeller University. Cole and some diligent companions at the Laboratory, John Dore, Ken Gospodinoff, Lois Hood, and Kenneth Traupmann, found the time to criticize the paper and to help it into its current shape. The problems which remain are of my own hand.

1. B. Bloom, "Time and Learning," *American Psychologist* 29 (1974): 682–688.
2. E. Goffman, *The Presentation of Self in Everyday Life* (New York: Anchor, 1959); E. Goffman, "Replies and Responses," *Language in Society* 5 (1976): 257–313; A. Kendon, *Studies in the Behavior of Face-to-Face Interaction* (New York: Humanities Press, in press).
3. H. Garfinkel, "A Conception of and Experiments with 'Trust' as a Condition of Stable Concerted Actions," *Motivation and Social Interaction*, ed. O. J. Harvey (New York: Roland Press, 1963); R. P. McDermott and J. Church, "Making Sense and Feeling Good: The Ethnography of Communication and Identity Work," *Communication* 2 (1976): 121–142.
4. K. D. O'Leary, "Token Reinforcement in the Classroom," *The Analysis of Behavior*, ed. T. Brigham and C. Catania (New York: Wiley, in press).
5. P. Gump, "Education as an Environmental Enterprise," *Observation of Pupils and Teachers in Mainstream and Special Education*, ed. R. Weinberg and F. Wood (Reston, Va.: Council for Exceptional Children, 1975).
6. This use of the term ethnography is consistent with its use in mainstream anthropology. Although rooted in cognitive anthropology (H. Conklin, "Ethnogeneological Method," *Explorations in Cultural Anthropology*, ed. W. Goodenough, New York: McGraw-Hill, 1964; C. Frake, "A Structural Description of Subanum 'Religious Behavior,'" *Explorations in Cultural Anthropology*, ed. Goodenough; C. Frake, "Plying Frames Can Be Dangerous: An Assessment of Methodology in Cognitive Anthropology," paper presented at the Conference on Methods in Cognitive Anthropology, Durham, N.C., April 1974) and ethnomethodology (A. Cicourel, *Cognitive Sociology* New York: Free Press, 1974; H. Garfinkel, *Studies in Ethnomethodology* Englewood Cliffs, N.J.: Prentice-Hall, 1967; H. Mehan and H. Wood, *The Reality of Ethnomethodology* New York: Wiley Interscience, 1975), the kind of ethnography called for here is consistent with the goals of such diverse schools of social science as the ethological (H. Beck, "Attentional Struggles and Silencing Strategies in a Human Political Conflict: The Case of the Vietnam Moratoria," *The Social Structure of Attention*, ed. M. Chance and R. Larson, New York: Wiley, 1976; H. Beck, "Neuropsychological Servosystems, Consciousness, and the Problem of Embodiment," *Behavioral Science* 21 1976: 139–160), the interactionist (C. Arensberg and S. Kimball, *Family and Community in Ireland* Cambridge, Mass.: Harvard University Press, 1940), the linguistic (D. Hymes, *Foundations in Sociolinguistics: An Ethnographic Approach* Philadelphia: University of Pennsylvania Press, 1974), and the communicative (R. Birdwhistell, *Kinesics and Context* Philadelphia: University of Pennsylvania Press, 1970; Kendon, *Studies in the Behavior of Face-to-Face Interaction*; A. Scheflen, *Communicational Structure* Bloomington, Ind.: Indiana University Press, 1973). Newcomers to the field may want to start with a delightful introduction by Spradley and McCurdy (J. Spradley and J. McCurdy, eds., *The Cultural Experience: Ethnography in Complex Society* Palo Alto, Calif.: Science Research Associates, 1972).
7. E. Sapir, "Cultural Anthropology and Psychiatry," *Selected Writings of Edward Sapir*, ed. D. Mandelbaum (Berkeley: University of California Press, 1949; orig. pub. 1932).
8. H. Garfinkel, "Comments," *Proceedings of the Purdue Symposium on*

Ethnomethodology, ed. R. Hill and K. Crittenden (Purdue, Ind.: Purdue Research Foundation, 1968).

9. Cicourel, *Cognitive Sociology*; Frake, "Plying Frames Can Be Dangerous"; Garfinkel, *Studies in Ethnomethodology*.

10. A. Kendon and A. Ferber, "A Description of Some Human Greetings," *Comparative Ecology and Behavior of Primates*, ed. R. Michael and J. Crook (New York: Academic Press, 1973).

11. E. Goffman, *Relations in Public* (New York: Harper Colophon, 1971); M. Wolf, "Notes on the Behavior of Pedestrians," *People in Places*, ed. A. Birenbaum and E. Sagaren (New York: Praeger, 1973).

12. A. Scheflen, *Human Territories* (Englewood Cliffs, N.J.: Prentice-Hall, 1976).

13. P. Watzlawick, J. Beavin, and D. Jackson, *Pragmatics of Human Communication* (New York: Mouton, 1967).

14. J. Downing, *Comparative Reading* (New York: Macmillan, 1973); W. Rohwer, "Prime Time for Education," *Harvard Educational Review* 41 (1971): 316–341; H. Singer, "IQ Is and Is Not Related to Reading," *Testing Reading Proficiency*, ed. S. Wanat (Arlington, Va.: Center for Applied Linguistics, in press); S. Wanat, "Reading Readiness," *Visible Language* 10 (1976): 101–127.

15. A. R. Diebold, "The Consequences of Early Bilingualism in Cognitive Development and Personality Formation," *The Study of Personality*, ed. E. Norbeck, D. Price-Williams, and W. McCord (New York: Holt, Rinehart and Winston, 1968); M. Modiano, *Indian Education in the Chiapas Highlands* (New York: Holt, Rinehart and Winston, 1973).

16. The procedures and criteria for producing an ethnographically adequate account of activities and their contexts are elaborated in R. P. McDermott, "Kids Make Sense: An Ethnographic Account of the Interactional Management of Success and Failure in One First-Grade Classroom," Ph.D. diss., Stanford University, 1976. For similar procedures and results, see Scheflen, *Communicational Structure*; an extensive report by H. Mehan, C. Cazden, L. Coles, S. Fisher, and N. Maroules, *Social Organization of Classroom Lessons* (Report no. 67–68; San Diego: University of California, Center for Human Information Processing, 1976); and a summary statement by F. Erickson and J. Schultz, "When Is a Context? Some Issues and Methods in the Analysis of Social Competence," *Quarterly Newsletter of the Institute for Comparative Human Development* 1, no. 2 (1977): 5–10.

17. J. Henry, *Culture against Man* (New York: Vintage, 1963); G. D. Spindler, *The Transmission of American Culture* (Cambridge, Mass.: Harvard University Press, 1969).

18. C. Cazden, "How Knowledge about Language Helps the Classroom Teacher—or Does It?" paper presented at the American Educational Research Association meetings, San Francisco, April 1976; J. Church, "Psychology and the Social Order," *Annals of the New York Academy of Sciences* 270 (1976): 141–151.

19. B. Bernstein, "Class and Pedagogies: Visible and Invisible," *Educational Studies* 1 (1975): 23–41.

20. E. Mishler, "Implications of Teacher Strategies for Language and Cogni-

tion," *Functions of Language in the Classroom*, ed. C. Cazden, V. John, and D. Hymes (New York: Teachers College Press, 1972).

21. J. Hostetler, "Education in Communitarian Societies," *Education and Cultural Process*, ed. G. Spindler (New York: Holt, Rinehart and Winston, 1974); J. Hostetler, "The Cultural Context of the Wisconsin Case," *Compulsory Education and the Amish*, ed. A. Keim (Boston: Beacon Press, 1975); J. Hostetler and G. Huntington, *Children in Amish Society* (New York: Holt, Rinehart and Winston, 1971).

22. J. Payne, "Analysis of Teacher-Student Classroom Interaction in Amish and Non-Amish Schools," *Social Problems* 19 (1971): 79–90.

23. Hostetler, "The Cultural Context of the Wisconsin Case"; Hostetler and Huntington, *Children in Amish Society*.

24. B. Siegel, "Defensive Structuring and Environmental Stress," *American Journal of Sociology* 76 (1970): 11–32.

25. Payne, "Analysis of Teacher-Student Classroom Interaction."

26. J. Robert, *Scene of the Battle: Group Behavior in the Classrooms* (New York: Doubleday, 1970); G. Rosenfeld, *"Shut Those Thick Lips": A Study in Slum School Failure* (New York: Holt, Rinehart and Winston, 1971).

27. R. Rist, *The Urban School* (Cambridge, Mass.: MIT Press, 1973), p. 107.

28. Robert, *Scene of the Battle*; Rosenfeld, *"Shut Those Thick Lips."*

29. R. P. McDermott, "Achieving School Failure," *Education and Cultural Process*, ed. Spindler.

30. By claiming that guidance approaches to classroom organization are uniformly no better or worse than authoritarian approaches, I am not trying to deny that a particular style of pedagogy has systematic ties to the social structure and value networks in which it is immersed (Bernstein, "Class and Pedagogies"; J. McDermott, *The Culture of Experience* New York: New York University Press, 1976). In fact, my point is quite the opposite. No one pedagogical style is inherently better than any other. If children and teachers can understand the style well enough to construct working agreements and trusting relations, then it will work.

31. G. Green, "How to Get People to Do Things with Words," *Some New Directions in Linguistics*, ed. R. Shuy (Washington, D.C.: Georgetown University Press, 1973); J. Sadock, "Whimperatives," *Studies Presented to Robert B. Lees by His Students*, ed. J. Sadock and A. Vanek (Edmonton: Linguistic Research, 1969).

32. For the most part, linguists are concerned with whimperatives because they represent interesting uses of syntactic form for conveying a variety of linguistic functions. Their concern stems from an effort to account for all the allowable sentences in our language with a finite set of grammatical rules. There is serious question, however, whether this is the most useful goal for linguistic description (Hymes, *Foundations in Sociolinguistics*, particularly ch. 9; V. N. Volosinov, *Marxism and the Philosophy of Language* New York: Seminar Press, 1973). More interesting approaches to requestive systems in actual speech, of which whimperatives are but a subgrouping, and the ways they interface with the social world of people doing relational work with each other are now available in J. Dore, "The Structure of Nursery School Conversation," *Children's Language*, ed. K. Nelson (New York: Garden

City Press, in press), and S. Ervin-Tripp, "Wait for Me, Roller-Skate!" *Child Discourse*, ed. C. Mitchell-Kernan and S. Ervin-Tripp (New York: Academic Press, in press).

33. G. D. Spindler, "Schooling in Schonhausen," *Education and Cultural Process*, ed. Spindler.

34. H. Conklin, "Bamboo Literacy on Mindoro," *Pacific Discovery* 2 (1949): 4–11; H. Conklin, "Maling, a Hununoo Girl from the Philippines," *In the Company of Man*, ed. J. Casagrande (New York: Harper, 1960).

35. K. Basso and N. Anderson, "The Western Apache Writing System," *Science* 180 (1973): 1013–1021; C. Ferguson, "Contrasting Patterns of Literacy Acquisition in a Multilingual Nation," *Language Use and Social Change*, ed. W. Whitely (London: International African Institute, 1972); J. Goody, M. Cole, and S. Scribner, "Writing and Formal Operations: A Case Study among the Vai," *Africa* (in press); M. Meggitt, "Uses of Literacy in New Guinea and Melanesia," *Bijdragen Tot de Taal, Landren Volkenkinde* 73 (1967): 71–82; W. Walker, "Notes on Native Systems and the Design of Native Literacy Programs," *Anthropological Linguistics* 11 (1972): 148–166.

36. F. Erickson, "Gatekeeping and the Melting Pot," *Harvard Educational Review* 45 (1975): 44–70; R. P. McDermott and K. Gospodinoff, "Social Contexts for Ethnic Borders and School Failure," paper presented at the International Conference on Nonverbal Behavior, Ontario Institute for Studies in Education, Toronto, 1976.

37. A. Piestrup, *Black Dialect Interference and Accommodation of Reading Instruction in First Grade* (*Monographs of the Language-Behavior Research Laboratory*, vol. 4; Berkeley: University of California, 1973).

38. W. Labov and C. Robins, "A Note on the Relation of Reading Failure to Peer-Group Status in Urban Ghettos," *Florida Fl. Reporter* 7 (1969): 54–57, 167.

PART THREE

The Critical Approach to
Social and Educational Research

Eric Bredo *and* Walter Feinberg

Critical theory is not as well known in the United States as either the positivistic or interpretive traditions. Moreover, its influence on educational and social scientific scholarship, while growing, lags significantly behind that of the other traditions. If positivism is the dominant orientation in social and educational research, and if interpretivism has the status of the loyal opposition, critical theory is a minor party whose platform and insights have yet to penetrate the thinking of most researchers. Nevertheless, its insights are important and deserve wider hearing than they have received until now.

   The roots of critical theory are to be found in German philosophy, especially in the writings of Hegel and Marx. The movement had its beginning in the early 1920s with the formation of the Frankfurt Institute of Social Research, many of whose members were concerned with understanding why the revolution predicted by Marx had not come to pass, given what they saw to be the appropriate social and economic conditions. In order to answer this question many of the early scholars who were associated with the Institute, both in Germany and later in its period of exile in the United States, began to turn to Freudian theory to shed light on possible inhibiting factors in the consciousness of the putative vanguard of the revolution, the working class. In addition, they began to examine the effects of different forms of family life and the influence of popular culture on the development of consciousness. Hence their studies marked a significant shift in Marxist studies away from the economic and political features of social life and towards the cultural and ideological ones.[1] This shift in theoretical emphasis had particular significance because it was responsive to one of the most important social changes that began to take place at that time—namely, the growth of the

271

mass media. The communications media opened up new possibilities for rational social decision-making. However, they also created new means for manipulation and social control on a mass scale. The shift to an emphasis on cultural and ideological phenomena allowed critical theorists to address these developments.

More recently, Jürgen Habermas, the foremost contemporary representative of critical theory, has elaborated many of the earlier concerns of the Frankfurt school in a way that relates the German philosophical tradition more closely to work in the Anglo-American tradition.[2] In particular, his work, a sample of which is included in Chapter 15, seeks to incorporate into critical theory many of the advances that have been made in linguistic philosophy and in the pragmatics of human communication. The earlier critical theorists saw themselves as offering an alternative to positivism; their discussions with positivists were often polemical and left room for little real communication. Habermas has been considerably more forthcoming in relating to other traditions, including the positivistic one. The result of his work has been the development of an approach to social and educational research that is quite different from either the interpretive or positivistic traditions but that attempts to incorporate many of the concerns and insights of both.

Critical theory attempts to evaluate the contributions made to social knowledge by positivistic researchers, on the one hand, and by interpretive researchers, on the other, and to find a way of synthesizing them. It attempts to do this by viewing both of these approaches in a broader and more enduring context, so as to assess their limitations and possibilities. Just as the interpretivist tries to transcend the categorical distinctions implicit in positivism by appealing to the wider context provided by a shared culture and form of life, so the critical theorist attempts to transcend the dichotomies implicit in an interpretive approach by appealing to an even broader context. But within what context can these dichotomies, such as the distinction between action and behavior, between understanding and explanation, or between reasons and causes, be transcended? This is attempted in critical theory by viewing knowledge in the context of human social evolution. For the critical theorist, knowledge must be seen in the context of its constitution in and potential contribution to social evolution, where social evolution is conceived of in terms of the possibility for progressive material and symbolic emancipation. This view places knowledge in a societal and historical-developmental perspective that highlights its repressive or emancipatory potentials.

Viewing knowledge from a long-run social evolutionary perspective contrasts with both the individualistic approach of positivism, with the priority it gives to the individual's observations or sense data, and with the collective approach of interpretivism, with its emphasis on inter-subjective meanings within a given (rather than evolving) form of life. It also contrasts with these other approaches in suggesting that social knowledge must be seen in terms of its implications for progressive social change. By placing knowledge in this broad, social evolutionary perspective, the critical theorist in effect creates a hierarchy of contexts and of types of knowledge, running from the narrowest individual context to the collective context to the social evolutionary context. Understanding the nature of social knowledge involves understanding these contexts and their interrelationships.

In Habermas' view, social evolution depends upon two principal ways in which men act to shape the world and themselves, through labor or instrumental action and through symbolic or communicative action.[3] Through instrumental action people attempt to satisfy their material wants by acting upon and shaping the material world; through communicative action they attempt to maintain social integration—that is, to reach agreement on norms and to hold others responsible for complying with these norms. The institutional rules that result from communicative action provide the context within which instrumental action takes place. Social evolution occurs through a dialectical interplay between these two categorically distinct though practically interrelated forms of action. Technical advance can result in movement towards new forms of instrumental activity and lessened dependence on physical nature, but its adoption and implementation may be limited by existing forms of social relationship. On the other hand, progress towards less repressive forms of social relationship is also possible, but the practical possibility of these new forms may be limited by the state of technical progress. The dialectical interplay of these two forms of action, which allows for the (contingent) possibility of movement towards greater autonomy in both of these dimensions, then helps create the third, social evolutionary, context.[4]

Knowledge and Human Interests

In critical theory these types of action are seen as closely related to three types of knowledge that are also hierarchically interrelated. The need for instrumental adaptation is related to an interest in that kind of knowledge that allows for the prediction and control of events. Habermas terms this a "technical" cognitive interest. Second, the need for social integration creates a related interest in knowledge that facilitates the understanding and the reaching of understandings with others. This is termed a "practical" cognitive interest. Finally, the need to resolve contradictions between the first two types of action, in the direction of greater autonomy, creates an interest in knowledge that facilitates this resolution. This third interest is termed an "emancipatory" cognitive interest.

Each of these three cognitive interests is seen as constituting a different type of knowledge or a different object domain and set of methodological standards. Keat and Urry offer the following helpful example of the way in which knowledge is constituted by interest. Using the technical interest as an illustration they write:

> Habermas argues that the technical interest constitutes knowledge at two related levels. First, it provides a criterion as to what counts as an 'object', about which the propositions of empirical-analytic science give us knowledge. What is real, in relation to the technical interest, is what can be detected, measured and manipulated in the situation of controlled experiments, in which information is received through our perceptual mechanisms. Second, the technical interest determines the general character of the standards employed in assessing the truth or falsity of statements made about these objects. An example of such a standard is that of falsification, which requires us to reject those statements whose predictive consequences are unsuccessful.[5]

Presumably the very nature of instrumental action creates its own experiences from which instrumental learnings can be derived. Furthermore, by implication, the instrumental learning that is possible at any one point in history depends upon the available technology that can be used in creating such experiences.

The second, practical, cognitive interest also serves to define an object domain and set of procedural standards. In this case the object realm is the realm of intersubjective meanings rather than of technically constituted "things," and the procedural standards that are defined are the procedures required for correct or valid interpretations—that is, hermeneutic methods. This object domain and set of procedures is presumably implicit in the very activity of symbolic interaction and the experiences it creates. Again, the practical knowledge that one can gain will depend upon the historical state of social development at the time.

Finally, in the case of the third, emancipatory, cognitive interest the object realm consists of the systematic distortions in learning and in communication that result from contradictions between the first two types of learning. Since this cognitive interest deals with the interrelation between the other two interests it is considered by Habermas to be derivative. At the same time, it can be considered more fundamental in that it is an interest in the correct usage of the other two modes of learning that focuses on the adequacy of knowledge itself.

By each constituting a different object domain and set of methodological standards, the three knowledge-constitutive cognitive interests lay the basis for different types of sciences. In Habermas' view the empirical-analytic sciences, which include the natural sciences and the systematic social sciences, are constituted by the technical interest; the historical-hermeneutic sciences, such as much of history and anthropology, are constituted by the practical interest; and the critical sciences, such as psychoanalysis and ideology critique, are constituted by the emancipatory interest. The effect of this conception of the different sciences is to legitimize not only the historical-hermeneutic but also the critical sciences as valid types of sciences in addition to the empirical-analytic sciences. It clearly also serves to create categorical distinctions between these different types of sciences.

The conceptualization of different cognitive interests and of their related sciences described here is closely related to the three theories of knowledge considered in this volume. Simply stated, the relationship is as follows: Positivism is a *theory* of knowledge that implicitly takes the technical interest as constitutive of all knowledge. It implicitly claims that the technical cognitive interest is the only, or the only legitimate, cognitive interest. Similarly, interpretivism is a *theory* of knowledge that implicitly takes the practical interest as fundamental to all knowledge. From this standpoint one need not deny the usefulness of technical knowledge, but rather one can see this as ultimately based on a shared culture and form of life. Finally, critical theory is a *theory* of knowledge that takes the emancipatory interest as fundamental. It recognizes the other types of knowledge but attempts to show how they too have their basis in human interests. In a sense, then, critical theory is pluralistic in that it allows a legitimate place for each of the other two types of knowledge in its own scheme. However, it suggests that the emancipatory interest defines a higher or broader standpoint from which one can critique the other two theories of knowledge. In other words, while the other two cognitive interests, the technical and the practical, are accepted as real species interests, the *theories* of knowledge that take these interests and their related object domains and standards as fundamental are not. What the critical theorist rejects are the other *theories* of knowledge, but not knowledge constituted by the technical or the practical interests.

For the critical theorist knowledge and value are fundamentally interrelated, since knowledge is constituted by interests. The researcher is never just a passive observer telling us how the world is; he or she is a participant in the very act of maintaining and reconstructing the social life-world. A useful example of this is the explanation of inequalities in educational achievement for those of different social groups. As we noted in the Introduction, one approach to research on this issue has involved an analysis of learning in terms of inputs and outputs. Variables such as student social backgrounds and IQ test scores, along with various school-related inputs, are used to predict differences in student learning. The consistent outcome of this research has been the finding that school input factors are poor predictors of differences in achievement relative to student input factors. The instrumental conclusion to be drawn from this is that schools as they currently are can do relatively little to equalize achievement. The moral conclusion that is easily drawn is then that those groups who do badly have only themselves to blame. A second approach to the same issue, which adopts an interactional perspective similar to that taken in the research articles in Part Two of this volume, sees learning as an interactive process involving interpretation and not just as one-way transmission: those who are members of one culture must attempt to understand those who belong to another. The frustration of misunderstanding due to cultural differences can result in developing reified, stereotypical conceptions of the other that then lock them into certain (negatively valued) social identities and related types of treatment. In this view, the cause of failure is neither with the student nor with the teacher but is rather rooted in cultural differences and in a particular interactional history. Here the instrumental conclusion is that things can be done differently, as in multicultural education. The likely moral conclusion to be drawn is that it is primarily the schools, with their monocultural orientation, that are at fault, rather than the students.

Contrasting the two streams of research makes it clear that these research efforts are largely constituted by different interests or methodological orientations. The first tradition of research has been almost totally positivisticly oriented while the second has generally utilized an interpretive approach. The conclusions that each reaches, with their very different moral implications, are often arrived at as the results of rigorous research as rigor is determined by these competing forms of inquiry. Whatever their personal values, the researchers end up taking very different implicit political stances merely by following the logic of their respective methodologies. For the critical theorist, an example like this is evidence that knowledge can never be disinterested, however rigorously one follows particular methodological canons. To claim that one's knowledge is value free is in fact to begin to distort that knowledge.

What the critical theorist seeks rather than value- or interest-free knowledge is knowledge representing universal rather than special interests. This is one reason why so much emphasis is placed on the nature of species interests, or on the interests of human beings in general. For the critical theorist knowledge is distorted knowledge when it claims to be universal (as much knowledge does) but when it is in fact related to special interests that are disguised by its universal claims. Various school tests such as IQ tests or college entrance exams, for instance, are treated as though they were meritocratic, and yet it appears to be impossible to develop such tests without relying on implicit culturally learned background knowledge to provide the context needed to answer the test questions. What is egalitarian treatment at the formal level is thus frequently not egalitarian at a practical level; nevertheless, as long as such tests are thought to be "value free" the special interests that they serve remain hidden. For the critical theorist the knowledge generated by such tests is distorted knowledge because of the implicit claim of universality when in fact some are systematically better served by them than others.

This conception of the relation between knowledge and value does not exactly deny the distinctions drawn in the other theories of knowledge, but it does place them on a different footing. It suggests that while knowledge may indeed be generated independent of one's personal values, as the positivist would have it, such "objective" knowledge is nonetheless not interest-free knowledge. It also suggests that while relevant knowledge must always be practically related to the norms of some community, and so must always be normative, as the interpretivist would have it, such "correct" knowledge may nonetheless be oriented to either more specialized or more universal interests. Thus critical theory both agrees and disagrees with these other two conceptions of the relation of knowledge and value. It suggests that knowledge is always interested, but that when this is recognized it can aspire to a kind of purity by self-consciously serving more universal rather than more specialized interests.

Explanation in Critical Theory

Critical theory also differs from the other two theories of knowledge in its approach to explanation. The critical theorist rejects an exclusive emphasis on either external "causal" explanation or on internal "reason" explanation.[6] Instead, these two types of explanation are seen as dialectically interrelated, with their interplay serving to provide grounds for a third type of explanation. This third type of explanation, termed "explanatory understanding" by Habermas, serves to combine elements of both of the other two types of explanation.

What the critical theorist attempts to explain are, of course, systematic distortions in communication, both on the individual and on the social level. These are the "facts" that critical theory seeks to account for, although they are by no means bare, uninterpreted facts. The principal form of distortion with which critical theory is concerned occurs when concepts and procedures that are applicable to one level in the hierarchy of contexts are overextended by applying them to a different level.[7] To approach social-relational problems as merely technical problems would be one such type of distortion. What such distortion does is in effect to mistake the part for the whole. It takes a limited domain of knowledge, and, failing to recognize the context in which this knowledge fits, considers this knowledge to be all that there is. In mistaking the part for the whole, such an approach in effect fails to recognize its own partiality.

How does such partiality in learning and communication occur? As Gouldner argues, ideologies mobilize those whose interests would be served by the programs that the ideologies legitimize in large part because there are strong tendencies for people's sentiments to be consistent with their interests.[8] Thus, those whose sentiments incline them towards a particular ideology tend, on the average, to be those whose interests would be served by the ideology. This is only roughly true, however, and to varying degrees. (In chapter 17 aspects of this theme are developed in relation to the work of social science.) Some people may be attracted to an ideology only because they are disenchanted with the current social reality that the ideology opposes and not because of strong acceptance of the ideology's implicit program. A narrower group may have their interests served by having the implicit program pushed forward to some degree, but not to its ultimate conclusion. Finally, an even narrower group may be well served by a relatively extreme and purist consistency of action with the ideology. The Iranian revolution might be considered an example of this kind of differentiation of interests.

If this is often true, then successful social movements will often overshoot the mark and institute policies that serve the interests of few of their members. Their very success will create conditions that promote disaffection since some of their adherents will be satisfied simply by the overthrow of the old regime, but not necessarily by the program of the new. As a result, an ideology that had live roots in widely shared interests and sentiments can come to be dissonant with the sentiments an ever-increasing number of prior supporters. The outcome of this decline in support commonly is that those whose interests continue to be served by the ideology, and whose attitudes remain consonant with it, respond by ideological entrenchment. The ideology is ever more fitting for them, with the result that they tend to take its truths as universal truths that are fitting for all. Here, then, we have a case of an ideology that initially provided many people with an intellectually and emotionally satisfying understanding of their practical world and its possibilities but that comes to be absolutized and removed from that context. The result is communicative distortion.

In brief, critical theory attempts to explain communicative distortion in terms of a history of events in which people's interests were involved: it recognizes that this historical context gives meaning to present communicative distortions and can be used to reveal the partial interests behind current ideologies. That is, by seeing how current ideologies made sense in their earlier lively days when they fitted their practical social contexts and the ways in which those social contexts changed, the critical theorist can better understand current distortions and the limited interests that they serve.

This discussion of ideological rigidity helps show how reasons can become causes. That is, it shows how feelings that are allowed expression by a social movement in its early phases come to be eliminated from the realm of legitimate discourse later on. The result is that they must be communicated in inexplicit, subterranean fashion as in private backbiting and denigration, symbolic expressions of disaffection, crime, and violence. From the perspective of the now dominant ideology, such behavior is irrational and senseless behavior, which can only be explained in terms of causes rather than reasons. The aim of the critical theorist is to participate in reversing this process— that is, to try to enable causes to become reasons so that problem situations can be dealt with more rationally on a collective basis. This is done first by a critique of ideology so as to loosen the grip of the ideology as definitive of rationality. Secondly, the critical theorist also tries to show how seemingly senseless action can be rationally understood when placed in a broader historical-developmental context.

Habermas discusses these issues in the context of a consideration and reinterpretation of psychoanalysis, where in the initial encounter between the client and the therapist the client narrates his past history within a causal, deterministic ideology. Communicative distortion at this level is considered in terms of a divergence between motives and intentions, where the latter are considered to be conscious. When people systematically act in ways that are inconsistent with their intentions, they may be said to have a distorted self-understanding. The role of the therapist is to facilitate the overcoming of this distortion.

To see how this might work, take a client whose actions are self-defeating and who initially sees them as caused by forces external to himself or herself. Inappropriate responses seem to have a life of their own and to be determined by situational stimuli independent of the client's acknowledged intentions. As long as situations are defined as they are, such stimuli do indeed serve as causes of behavior. Yet part of the therapits's role is to help the client see that past events maintain their causal status precisely because the client defines situations in a particular way. In other words, the client's narrative must come to be perceived not simply as the factual reporting of causes and effects, but as the reporting of situations in which the client's interpretation itself helped to deny certain motives and to give events an external, causal status. Eventually, events that are initially perceived as externally related to one another can come to be perceived as internally related through the total framework in which they are given the meaning that they have. When the framework is brought to consciousness and perceived to function in the way that it does, events can be placed in a different perspective and steps taken to break the hold that they have on the individual, to emancipate him from an old and rigid framework. These steps serve not just as new ways of seeing but as moments towards a new way of being, as steps towards a new set of internal relationships. Although not identified as a critical theorist, Alisdair MacIntyre treats many of these issues in his criticism of Peter Winch. We have therefore included that essay by MacIntyre as Chapter 14.

Whether in the social or in the individual case of distorted communication, the type of explanation offered differs from, but does not entirely supplant, those offered by positivists and by interpretivists. Where the positivist explains events by showing that they can be logically deducible from empirical generalizations, and the interpretivist explains actions by showing that they are consistent with following a rule (i.e., that they have their reasons), the critical theorist explains them in the context of social or individual development. However, these three types of explanation all work together in complex fashion. If empirical-analytic explanations are to be valid and adequate they must take into account both interpretive and critical knowledge, for otherwise they will result either in the meaningless counting of different things as the same or in ideologically distorted knowledge. Hermeneutic or interpretive knowledge must also take into account the outcomes of critical research or end up with accounts of inherently contradictory behavior that presuppose coherent motivation. At the same time, it must take account of empirical-analytic research, so that it can judge whether behavior that is inconsistent with intentions as the researcher understands them is the result of external interference with effective action or arises because of a misunderstanding about intentions. Finally, critical explanations, to be valid, must be based, first, on adequate interpretations of conscious intentions and, second, on empirical research into unintended but motivated behavioral regularities. Thus all three types of explanation and of inquiry are needed, although the critical theorist sees his type of inquiry as "higher," in that it involves inquiry at the level of the broadest context in which the other types of knowledge function. One of the gaps in critical theory has been the articulation of a well-developed method of gaining these insights, especially on a wider social scale. Donald Comstock, in Chapter 18, provides an attempt to develop the methodological implications of critical theory.

Communicative Competence and the Ideal Speech Situation

To observe distorted understanding the critical theorist must have anticipations of undistorted or authentic communication that form the background against which distortions may be seen, and to judge the validity of particular accounts he or she must rely on communication that itself approximates an ideal of undistorted communication. Thus both the observational and the explanatory aspects of critical theory, not to speak of its critical and emancipatory potential, are based on an ideal of undistorted communication. In his more recent work, Habermas has attempted to work out a theory of communicative competence, or what he calls a "universal pragmatics," which serves to define undistorted communication theoretically and to suggest some of the situational conditions that may make it possible.[9] This work might be seen as an attempt to provide legitimating grounds for critical theory that are more specific to the domain of communication than is the appeal to the evolutionary history of the human species.

Habermas' aim in this theory is to propose an expanded conception of rationality that encompasses both technical and practical reason. He seeks to synthesize these two types of rationality, the first of which corresponds to the positivistic conception of rationality and the second to the interpretive conception, just as he also sought to develop a new synthesis of fact and value and of explanation and understanding.[10] He

281

attempts to do this by developing a theory of communication that retains a place for the positivists' concerns about the "report" aspects of communication and for the interpretivists' concerns with the "command" aspects of communication, while putting both on a different footing. By adopting a pragmatic approach to communication, Habermas again attempts to provide a broader context that embraces concerns of both of these aspects and that also suggests a third, neglected, aspect. His strategy in considering various theories of communication is to point out the linguistic functions they have overlooked, and hence their incompleteness, or to show how they erroneously attempt to reduce different functions to a single function—for example, to reduce the relational or command aspect of an utterance to just another content message. By developing a universal pragmatics, Habermas attempts to focus on the universal functions that language always serves, rather than its particular functions in a particular institutional context, and thus in effect to find a universal grammar of rationality. By showing that this grammar or set of rules is implicit in language itself, he hopes to show that a certain conception of rationality is also part of the very nature of communication and hence is by no means arbitrary.

In this view of communication, speech has a double structure. Every speech act has a content and a relational aspect. That is, it says something and it proposes or establishes a social relationship. The interrelation between these two levels of communication serves to create a third level of communication that communicates the intentions of the speaker.[11] Every speech act thus has three aspects or levels at which it communicates: a report or content level that communicates about the "objective" world; a relational level that implies that a certain social relationship has been or should be adopted between speaker and listener; and an expressive level that shows certain feelings and intentions on the part of the speaker.

In Habermas' view every act of communication presupposes that certain validity claims related to these three levels of communication have been fulfilled. These presuppositions form a background consensus within which ordinary communication is understood. When one says something in a particular situation and before a particular audience one in effect claims: (1) that the propositional content of what is said is true; (2) that one has the right to adopt the social position that one adopts (i.e., that one has the right to speak in this way in this situation); and (3) that the expressive aspects of the utterance are genuine (i.e., that one is neither self-deceived nor deceiving of others). These three validity claims, then, refer to the truth, legitimacy, and veracity of the utterance and its speaker. A fourth claim, to which Habermas gives less attention, involves the use of language itself. This is the claim that the utterance was in fact comprehensible and not just gibberish, a claim also not given much emphasis here.

One makes these claims in ordinary communication only implicitly because in such communication none of these aspects of the utterance are bracketed and singled out for explicit examination. However, if any of these elements of the background consensus are disturbed or called into question, then second-order speech about the earlier speech becomes necessary to restore the consensus. Habermas terms this second-order communication about communication "discourse," a usage that is somewhat idiosyncratic. Such discourses thematize or focus on aspects of the earlier communication that were problematic. The aim of such discourses is to create a *rational* consensus where there was at best only an *accepted* consensus. There are, then, three principal types of "discourse" that serve the function of questioning and resolving validity issues concerning each of the three principal levels of communication. The first focuses on the propositional content of previous utterances, the second on the relational claims implicit in the way the utterance was performed, and the third on expressive claims implicit in the utterance. The first involves the purely cognitive use of language; it is what on does in *theoretical* discourse. The second involves the regulative use of language; it is what one does in *practical* discourse. And the third involves the expressive use of language, and is presumably what one does in critical discourse (although Habermas does not say as much).[12]

While each of these types of validity claims may be made problematic and so become the subject of a discourse (i.e., one can talk about the truth of the propositions advanced, about the legitimacy of the mode of speech adopted, or about the authenticity of the intentions expressed), the ensuing discourse itself depends, of course, on the tacit acceptance of certain validity claims. Thus the discursive justification of any validity claim will itself be based on the presupposition of a variety of other claims that will not at that time be subject to question. Are there then any criteria for deciding when a validity claim has been met—for example, for deciding when a statement is true? In this view there are none outside of the process of argumentation itself, where this presumably involves communicatively competent persons.

In discourse it is implied that the only basis on which validity claims are redeemed is argumentation itself. The practice of discourse thus implies an idealized form of communication in which matters can be resolved on their merits and not on the basis of any form of pressure, coercion, or suppression. Since this ideal is implied in discourse, it is also implied, albeit indirectly, in ordinary communication itself. Thus Habermas claims that an "ideal speech situation" is both presupposed and anticipated in communicative action itself. Such an ideal situation would involve conditions such as (1) no violence, (2) permeable boundaries between public and private speech, (3) allowance of traditional symbols and rules of discourse to be made problematic, and (4) insistence on equal opportunities to speak.[13] Since such situations do not presently exist, or exist only locally and fleetingly, they remain an ideal, but one that we can attempt to approximate.

While claims about the truth of propositions, or the rightness of utterances, or the veracity of speakers, are ultimately dependent upon discursive argumentation, the full rationality of such discourse is itself likely to depend upon the extent to which it is conducted under conditions approximating the ideal speech situation. At the present time some types of discourses seem to be able to take place under conditions more nearly approximating this ideal than others. Thus it is often easier to question freely the truth of propositions than to question the legitimacy of the utterance or the veracity of the speaker.

By grounding rationality in conditions that are seen to be both presupposed and anticipated in communicative action itself, "is" and "ought" are merged. The nature of communication as it is implies the way in which communication ought to be conducted if claims are to be rationally validated. This view of rationality, then, involves more than the view of it as purely logical induction or deduction. It goes beyond the view of rationality that sees it as persuasion within some taken-for-granted set of premises. It accepts the two related functions of reason—namely, to validate truth claims and the situational correctness of utterances. However, it also adds a third function—namely, to validate claims of authenticity or veracity. Thus, the view of rationality implicit here is one that embraces three different types or aspects of reason, the theoretical, the practical, and the critical. Most importantly, it is one that insists that full rationality requires the implicit validity claims underlying any communication to be themselves freely subject to questioning and to free discursive consideration. An adequate conception of human rationality must then include the possibility and indeed the necessity of such self-reflection.

The insights of critical theory have not frequently been applied to education. With Jon Hellesnes' essay, however, we have one explicit attempt to develop the implications of this movement for educational theory. Both Pierre Bourdieu and Paul Willis continue to address this theme of inequality. Bourdieu, in a manner consistent with critical theory, shows how the wishes and aspirations held by working and lower middle class parents for their children are shaped by "objective" social and economic structures. Willis, with a somewhat different twist, examines the meaning system of a group of rebellious working class students and shows how, in interaction with the formal meaning system of the school, the class position of the youngsters is maintained.

Criticisms of Critical Theory

A number of scholars have offered a variety of criticisms of Habermas' approach to critical theory. Three of the more important of these criticisms will be considered here: first, a criticism of the categorical nature of the cognitive interests and thus of the different types of sciences; second, a criticism of the "quasi-transcendental" status of these interests; third, a criticism of the practical politics implied by critical theory.

The first of these criticisms is raised particularly forcefully by Richard Bernstein.

> Habermas wants to preserve the central claim of transcendental philosophy that there are *categorically* distinct object domains, types of experience, and corresponding forms of inquiry. But he has not succeeded in establishing this central thesis. . . . His typical strategy in criticizing previous thinkers is to show that they confuse categorically distinct levels of action. . . . But the validity of these criticisms is itself dependent on the acceptance of Habermas' categorical distinctions. The tables can be turned on Habermas by arguing that he seeks to introduce hard and fast distinctions where there is really only continuity. We can see this most clearly when he uses the distinctive cognitive interests and their corresponding object domains to demarcate categorically distinct types of inquiry. Despite his protestations, it begins to look as if Habermas is guilty of the type of hypostatization that he so brilliantly exposes in others.[14]

Bernstein goes on to support this criticism by arguing that recent philosophy and history of science tend to show close analogs in the fundamental disputes occurring in both the natural and the social sciences. For example, observe the parallel between Kuhn's views on theory-governed observation in the natural sciences and Taylor's views on intersubjective meaning and constituted practice in the social sciences. Thus, in this example, interpretation is vital in very different types of sciences. Similarly, critical self-reflection is also both necessary and practiced in different sciences. By implication Habermas is wrong in trying to confine these interests to one science or another. Moreover, when one looks at the actual methodological procedures used in different sciences one finds great variation. There are *quantitative* historians and *qualitative* economists. As a result, one cannot say that particular methodologies apply to particular fields.

While one can agree with these points, it is not clear that they are really relevant to what Habermas is proposing. Habermas is not claiming that description, interpretation, and critique each only occur or should occur in separate types of sciences. All sciences require all three of these types of discourse. Rather, he claims that the *object domains* of the different sciences are constituted in different ways. The natural scientist, for example, need not worry about the way atoms interpret events, and as a result his object domain is not constituted through the use of intersubjective meanings. Furthermore, Habermas' points about methodological procedure are normative rather than descriptive of current practice. If researchers currently constitute their objects of research in inappropriate ways, Habermas would presumably be interested in seeing how their research distorted their inquiry. Thus the fact that researchers currently do things one way or another is in a sense irrelevant to his point.

A more telling point is Bernstein's original one that Habermas has absolutized as differences in kind what may be only differences in degree. In the case of the distinction between the technical and the practical interest this question is analogous to asking how rigorously one can distinguish between content and structure, between elements and relations, or between individual and collective phenomena. It seems possible to make clear conceptual distinctions between these, however the problem arises when one attempts to apply these distinctions to particular cases. Consider the difficulty that we often have in deciding whether a problem is to be taken as an individual one or as a social one. While there is a discrete conceptual distinction between the two kinds of problems, in actual practice the interdependencies that occur among individuals and that create social problems may be continuously variable in extent. Thus, while Habermas is right that one must keep these levels of analysis conceptually straight in practice there is no discrete point at which a problem moves from being one type to being the other. The application of these distinctions, like others, is a matter calling for judgment and interpretation.

The second criticism is that the status of the cognitive interests—that is, the claim that they are "quasi-transcendental"—is ambiguous. What is involved here is the suggestion that the very grounding of critical theory is unclear. McCarthy makes this point as follows:

> In other words, the question, How is critical theory itself to be justified? cannot be answered merely negatively, by pointing to distortion. It demands that we specify positively the "legitimating grounds" (Rechtsgründe) of critique. But under the presupposition of universal distortion any such positive specification would itself be suspect. The radical critic, like the radical skeptic, appears to be condemned to silence.[15]

To elaborate on this criticism, it is unclear whether the legitimating grounds of critical theory are to be found in the natural history of social evolution or in an internal reflection on the categorical nature of different types of knowledge. McCarthy seems to be raising this problem when he says that

> in attempting to combine a "transcendental" with a "naturalistic" approach to the subjective conditions of knowledge, Habermas appears to be caught in a dilemma: either nature has the transcendental status of a constituted objectivity and cannot, therefore, be the ground of the constituting subject; or nature is the ground of subjectivity and cannot, therefore, be simply a constituted objectivity. Habermas wants, paradoxically, to hold to both horns.[16]

If it is true, as McCarthy suggests, that this dilemma is unresolved in Habermas' work, then it would seem to follow that critical theory, like the theories it criticizes, also cannot adequately account for itself. In a way this should not be surprising given either Gödel's proof or the facts of perception (where the latter suggest that each higher stage of reflection must leave its own standpoint unobserved). However, this does not take away from the value of the criticisms that critical theory allows one to make of positivistic or interpretive approaches. That is, critical theory allows us to comprehend those approaches within a more comprehensive context and to see how their respective categorical distinctions can be transcended. In the end this conclusion suggests once again that there are no ultimate grounds to be found for knowledge; learning is a part of a continuous process of growth. Just as the consistent relativist must hold his own theory relativistically, so the consistent critical theorist must hold his own theory critically.

The third criticism of critical theory is that its practical political implications are absent or at least confused. While such a criticism might not be damaging to other theories, it is very damaging to one that promises greater relevance of theory to practice. A criticism of this sort is suggested by Gouldner, but only after he first defends critical theory against the harsher version of this criticism made by critics on the left who do not see how critical theory, with its emphasis on communicative forms of domination, fits into their analysis of revolutionary struggle. As Gouldner puts it:

> From the standpoint of the left, this will be taken to mean that Habermas has "no" politics or no "serious" politics. In truth, however, such a judgment may simply mean that the Left has a very limited concept of politics. . . . Habermas' theory will be judged apolitical by those operating with a historically limited Leninist conception of politics-as-revolution-via-vanguard party, for whom the paradigm of revolution is the October Revolution of 1917. From *that* statement and in *that* interpretation of what is politically relevant, Habermas' theory will seem politically unproductive. But such a critique is limited by its own truncated historical perspective.[17]

In contrast to this, Gouldner sees critical theory as having practical political implications that are very relevant to contemporary society, in which mass communications have become such an important element. After defending critical theory in this way, however, Gouldner offers a criticism of his own: while accepting the relevance of critical theory and the importance of an emphasis on communication, he finds it to have contradictory practical implications.

In Gouldner's view freedom and equality are two independent dimensions along which one can describe contemporary ideologies. Habermas' conception of an ideal speech situation is one that emphasizes freedom of access but that seems to presuppose equality of communicative competence. The ideal speech community is one in which everyone has equal access to the conversation while the ideal of communicative competence suggests the possibility that some people may be better able than others to employ the norms governing successful communication. As Gouldner sees it, there is a potential conflict between these two norms that Habermas does not acknowledge, for greater competence could be used as a legitimate reason to provide greater access. That is, once we recognize that there may well be different levels of communicative competence, then there seems to be something problematic about an ideal speech community that does not recognize this. To recognize it, however, may force us to mitigate the idea of equal access in a direction that would lead us to accommodate variations in competence. The task that remains for Habermas to complete is to show just how this can be done while minimizing domination.

Gouldner develops this problem through the issue of state censorship, which he thinks may be necessary to achieve equality. He writes:

> This, then, is a dilemma of a Habermasian theory. If it does what it must to foster the equality necessary for communicative competence, it inevitably undermines the freedom it so prizes. The doctrine of communicative competence seeks to mute this contradiction by developing, at the level of *theory*, so abstract a conception of communicative distortion that the place of *state* censorship and the growing domination of the modern state over communication is hidden.[18]

In other words, by not facing up to this practical dilemma, critical theory ends up emphasizing one important aspect of communication while neglecting another. Critical theory emphasizes communicative freedom and in effect concentrates its attention on the kinds of communicative distortions that arise from market forces and the influence of large corporations in restricting access to and topics of legitimate communication. In other words, it focuses on the kinds of communicative distortion prevalent in the capitalist West. As a result, Gouldner believes that the theory defocalizes or remains silent about the kinds of distortion that are prevalent in the socialist East, namely, state censorship: "His critique of the public, then, has a profound political spillover, impugning the legitimacy of electoral institutions and political democracy where they already exist, and forestalling struggle to institute them where they do not."[19] For Gouldner, then, what is needed is an approach that recognizes the potential distorting effects on communication of both property, on the one hand, and the state, on the other, and whose political implications work to ensure communicative autonomy from both of these threats. By focusing on one set of threats to authentic communication and downplaying the other, he believes that critical theory runs into the danger of itself becoming ideological and failing to recognize the interests that it may serve. In the selection included in this volume Gouldner suggests some of the considerations—both personal and professional—that the social scientist might keep in mind in order to minimize this danger.

Gouldner's criticism is valuable. It reminds one that in the search for new freedoms one should not forget or too readily take for granted the value of old freedoms already won (at least by some). Gouldner was writing this critique at a time when the free press was doggedly challenging systematic attempts at manipulation by the Nixonian White House.

The visibility of the threat of state manipulation was clear, as was the value of an independent press. The other side of the coin, not stressed by Gouldner, is the scarcity of news that is critical of matters of corporate interest and, in this comparison, the relative value and freshness of state-supported public radio and television. Thus, an acceptance of Gouldner's critique of critical theory should also not blind one to the relevance of critical theory to our current situation, even while it serves as a healthy corrective to an absolutizing of critical theory itself. In effect, this criticism seems to place critical theory in just the sort of perspective that one would want in the practice of critique.

Notes

1. Martin Jay, *The Dialectical Imagination: A History of the Frankfurt School and the Institute of Social Research* (Boston: Little Brown, 1973).
2. Jürgen Habermas, *Knowledge and Human Interests* (Boston: Beacon, 1971).
3. Jürgen Habermas, "Towards a Reconstruction of Historical Materialism," *Communication and the Evolution of Society* (Boston: Beacon, 1979), ch. 4.
4. This view of social evolution differs, first, from nondialectical theories of social progress. It sees progress as neither merely technical advance divorced from cultural values nor as the articulation of cultural values divorced from technical advance. Instead, progress is seen as involving both of these dimensions and in a dialectical interplay rather than a linear extrapolation. This view also differs from some other dialectical theories. Its divergence from orthodox Marxism, in Habermas' interpretation, lies in its emphasis on the relative autonomy of communicative action and the independent logic of learning in this dimension.
5. Russell Keat and John Urry, *Social Theory as Science* (London: Routledge and Kegan Paul, 1975), p. 223.
6. We are using this terminology, which contrasts "causes" with "reasons," because it is a familiar one. In our own view the concept of cause needs to be broadened to include "having a reason" as a possible cause of someone's behavior. See also McIntyre's article in this part of the present volume.
7. It is interesting to note that this conception of distortion is different from that which interpretivists see as likely to be created by positivisticly oriented research. While interpretivists see positivists as making a category mistake, that is, as applying a particular conceptual scheme to the wrong domain, they are less likely to see distortion as a confusion of logical levels. For instance, one could apply concepts to the wrong domain—that is, a domain to which they are inapplicable, but one that was at the same logical level as the appropriate domain. This suggests that there is a difference in the conceptions of reification adopted by interpretivists and critical theorists. The error of mistaking the part for the whole, which is of primary concern to critical theorists, is a special case of the error of mistaking one domain for another.
8. Alvin W. Gouldner, "Interests, Ideologies, and the Paleo-Symbolic," *The Dialectic of Ideology and Technology* (New York: Seabury, 1976), ch. 10.

9. Habermas, "What Is Universal Pragmatics," *Communication and the Evolution of Society*, ch. 1.
10. Richard J. Bernstein, *The Restructuring of Social and Political Theory* (Philadelphia: University of Pennsylvania Press, 1978), p. 205.
11. Habermas also tends to neglect this third level of communication. However, it is developed in Gregory Bateson's article, "Towards a Theory of Play and Fantasy," included in the readings in Part Two of this volume.
12. See p. 64 of Habermas, "What Is Universal Pragmatics."
13. Gouldner, *Dialectic of Ideology and Technology*, p. 142.
14. Bernstein, *Restructuring of Social and Political Theory*, pp. 220–21.
15. Thomas A. McCarthy, *The Critical Theory of Jürgen Habermas*, (Cambridge: MIT Press, 1978), p. 108.
16. Ibid., pp. 110–11.
17. Gouldner, "Toward a Media Critical Politics," *Dialectic of Ideology and Technology*, p. 147.
18. Ibid., p. 151.
19. Ibid., p. 164.

CHAPTER 14

The Idea of a Social Science

Alasdair MacIntyre

I

My aim in this paper is to express dissent from the position taken in
Mr. Peter Winch's book whose title is also the title of this paper.[1] Winch's
book has been the subject of a good deal of misunderstanding, and he has
been accused on the one hand of reviving familiar and long-refuted views[2]
and on the other of holding views so eccentric in relation to social science
as it actually is that they could not possibly have any practical effect on the
conduct of that science.[3] In fact, however, Winch articulates a position
which is at least partly implicit in a good deal of work already done,
notably in anthropology, and he does so in an entirely original way. He
writes in a genre recognizable to both sociologists and philosophers.
Talcott Parsons and Alain Touraine have both found it necessary to
preface their sociological work by discussions of norms and actions and
have arrived at rather different conclusions from those of Winch; the
importance of his work is therefore undeniable.

"Wittgenstein says somewhere that when one gets into philosophical
difficulties over the use of some of the concepts of our language, we are
like savages confronted with something from an alien culture. I am simply
indicating a corollary of this: that sociologists who misinterpret an alien
culture are like philosophers getting into difficulty over the use of their
own concepts." This passage epitomizes a central part of Winch's thesis
with its splendid successive characterizations of the figure baffled by an
alien culture; a savage at one moment, he has become a sociologist at the
next.[4] And this is surely no slip of the pen. According to Winch the
successful sociologist has simply learnt all that the ideal native informant
could tell him; sociological knowledge is the kind of knowledge possessed

Reprinted with the permission of the Editor of The Aristotelian Society from *Aristotelian Society Supplement*, XLI (1967), 93–114. © 1967 The Aristotelian Society.

in implicit and partial form by the members of a society rendered explicit and complete.[5] It is not at first entirely clear just how far Winch is at odds in this contention with, for example, Malinowski, who insisted that the native Trobriander's account of Trobriand society must be inadequate, that the sociologists' account of institutions is a construction not available to the untutored awareness of the native informant.[6] For Winch of course is willing to allow into the sociologist's account concepts "which are not taken from the forms of activity which he is investigating; but which are taken rather from the context of his own investigation," although he adds that "these technical concepts will imply a prior understanding of those other concepts which belong to the activities under investigation." Perhaps this might seem sufficient to remove the apparent disagreement of Winch and Malinowski, until we remember the conclusion of Malinowski's critique of the native informant's view. The sociologist who relies upon that view, he says, "obtains at best that lifeless body of laws, regulations, morals and conventionalities which *ought* to be obeyed, but in reality are often only evaded. For in actual life rules are never entirely conformed to, and it remains, as the most difficult but indispensible part of the ethnographers' work, to ascertain the extent and mechanism of the deviations."[7] This makes two points clear.

First, Malinowski makes a distinction between the rules acknowledged in a given society and the actual behavior of individuals in that society, whereas Winch proclaims the proper object of sociological study to be that behavior precisely as rule-governed. The second is that in the study of behavior Malinowski is willing to use notions such as that of mechanism which are clearly causal; whereas Winch warns us against comparing sociological understanding with understanding in terms of "statistics and causal laws" and says of the notion of function, so important to Malinowski, that it "is a quasi-causal notion, which it is perilous to apply to social institutions."[8]

It does appear therefore that although Winch and Malinowski agree in seeing the ideal native informant's account of his own social life as incomplete by comparison with the ideal sociologist's account, they do disagree about the nature of that incompleteness and about how it is to be remedied. My purpose in this paper will be to defend Malinowski's point of view on these matters against Winch's, but this purpose can only be understood if one reservation is immediately added. It is that in defending Malinowski's views on these points I must not be taken to be endorsing Malinowski's general theoretical position. I have in fact quoted Malinowski on these matters, but I might have quoted many other social scientists. For on these matters Malinowski speaks with the *consensus*.

II

A regularity or uniformity is the constant recurrence of the same kind of event on the same kind of occasion; hence statements of uniformities presuppose judgments of identity. But . . . criteria of identity are necessarily relative to some rule: with the corollary that two events which count as qualitively similar from the point of view of one rule would count as different from the point of view of another. So to investigate the type of regularity studied in a given enquiry is to examine the nature of the rule according to which judgments of identity are made in that enquiry. Such judgments are intelligible only relatively to a given mode of human behaviour, governed by its own rules.[9]

This passage is the starting point for Winch's agrument that J. S. Mill was mistaken in supposing that to understand a social institution is to formulate empirical generalizations about regularities in human behavior, generalizations which are causal and explanatory in precisely the same sense that generalizations in the natural sciences are. For the natural scientist makes the relevant judgments of identity according to *his* rules, that is the rules incorporated in the practice of his science; whereas the social scientist must make his judgments of identity in accordance with the rules governing the behavior of those whom he studies. *Their* rules, not *his*, define the object of his study. "So it is quite mistaken in principle to compare the activity of a student of a form of social behaviour with that of, say, an engineer studying the working of a machine. If we are going to compare the social student to an engineer, we shall do better to compare him to an apprentice engineer who is studying what engineering—that is, the activity of engineering—is all about."[10]

What the type of understanding which Winch is commending consists in is made clearer in two other passages. He says that although prediction is possible in the social sciences, it "is quite different from predictions in the natural sciences, where a falsified prediction always implies some sort of mistake on the part of the predictor: false or inadequate data, faulty calculation, or defective theory."[11] This is because, "since understanding something involves understanding its contradictory, someone who, with understanding, performs X must be capable of envisaging the possibility of doing not-X."[12] Where someone is following a rule, we cannot predict how he will interpret what is involved in following that rule in radically new circumstances; where decisions have to be made, the outcome "cannot be *definitely* predicted," for otherwise "we should not call them decisions."

These points about prediction, if correct, reinforce Winch's arguments about the difference between the natural sciences and the social sciences. For they amount to a denial of that symmetry between explanation and prediction which holds in the natural sciences.[13] But when we consider what Winch says here about decision, it is useful to take into account at the same time what he says about motives and reasons. Winch treats these as similar in this respect: that they are made intelligible by reference to the rules governing the form of social life in which the agent participates. So Winch points out that "one can act 'from considerations' only where there are accepted standards of what is appropriate to appeal to" and argues against Ryle that the "law-like proposition" in terms of which someone's reasons must be understood concerns not the agent's disposition "but the accepted standards of reasonable behaviour current in his society."[14]

From all this one can set out Winch's view of understanding and explanations in the social sciences in terms of a two-stage model. An action is *first* made intelligible as the outcome of motives, reasons, and decisions; and is then made *further* intelligible by those motives, reasons, and decisions being set in the context of the rules of a given form of social life. These rules logically determine the range of reasons and motives open to a given set of agents and hence also the range of decisions open to them. Thus Winch's contrast between explanation in terms of causal generalizations and explanations in terms of rules turns out to rest upon a version of the contrast between explanations in terms of causes and explanations in terms of reasons. This latter contrast must therefore be explored, and the most useful way of doing this will be to understand better what it is to act for a reason.

Many analyses of what it is to act for a reason have written into them an incompatibility between acting for a reason and behaving from a cause, just because they begin from the apparently simple and uncomplicated case where the action is actually performed, where the agent had one and only one reason for performing it and where no doubt could arise for the agent as to why he had done what he had done. By concentrating attention upon this type of example a basis is laid for making central to the analyses a contrast between the agent's knowledge of his own reasons for acting and his and others' knowledge of causes of his behavior. For clearly in such a case the agent's claim that he did X for reason Y does not seem to stand in need of any warrant from a generalization founded upon observation; while equally clearly any claim that one particular event or state of affairs was the cause of another does stand in need of such a warrant. But this may be misleading. Consider two somewhat more complex cases than that outlined above. The first is that of a man who has several quite different reasons for performing a given action. He performs the action; how can he as agent know whether it was the conjoining of all the different reasons that was sufficient for him to perform the action or whether the action was over-determined in the sense that there were two or more reasons, each of which would by itself alone have been sufficient? The problem arises partly because to know that one or other of these possibilities was indeed the case entails knowing the truth of certain unfulfilled conditionals.

A second case worth considering is that of two agents, each with the same reasons for performing a given action; one does not in fact perform it, the other does. Neither agent had what seemed to him a good reason or indeed had any reason for not performing the action in question. Here we can ask what made these reasons or some sub-set of them productive of action in the one case, but not in the other? In both these types of case we need to distinguish between the agent's having a reason for performing an action (not just in the sense of there being a reason for him to perform the action, but in the stronger sense of his being aware that he has such a reason) and the agent's being actually moved to action by his having such a reason. The importance of this point can be brought out by reconsidering a very familiar example, that of post-hypnotic suggestion.

Under the influence of post-hypnotic suggestion a subject will not only perform the action required by the hypnotist, but will offer apparently good reasons for performing it, while quite unaware of the true cause of the performance. So someone enjoined to walk out of the room might on being asked why he was doing this, reply with all sincerity that he had felt in need of fresh air or decided to catch a train. In this type of case we would certainly not accept the agent's testimony as to the connection between reason and action, unless we are convinced of the untruth of the counter-factual, "He would have walked out of the room, if no reason for doing so had occurred to him," and the truth of the counter-factual, 'He would not have walked out of the room, if he had not possessed some such reason for so doing." The question of the truth or otherwise of the first of these is a matter of the experimentally established facts about post-hypnotic suggestion, and these facts are certainly expressed as causal generalizations. To establish the truth of the relevant generalization would entail establishing the untruth of the second counter-factual. But since to establish the truth of such causal generalizations entails consequences concerning the truth or untruth of generalizations about reasons, the question inevitably arises as to whether *the possession of a given reason* may not be the cause of an action in precisely the same sense in which hypnotic suggestion may be the cause of an action. The chief objection to this view has been that the relation of reason to action is internal and conceptual, not external and contingent, and cannot therefore be a casual relationship; but although nothing could count as a reason unless it stood in an internal relationship to an action, *the agent's possessing a reason* may be a state of affairs identifiable independently of the event which is *the agent's performance of the action*. Thus it does seem as if the possession of a reason by an agent is an item of a suitable type to figure as a cause, or an effect. But if this is so then to ask whether it was the agent's reason that roused him to act is to ask a causal question, the true answer to which depends upon what causal generalizations we have been able to establish. This puts in a different light the question of the agent's authority as to what roused him to act; for it follows from what has been said that this authority is at best *prima facie*. Far more of course needs to be said on this and related topics; but perhaps the argument so far entitles us to treat with skepticism Winch's claim that understanding in terms of rule-following and causal explanations have mutually exclusive subject-matters.

This has obvious implications for social science, and I wish to suggest some of these in order to provide direction for the rest of my argument. Clearly if the citing of reasons by an agent, with the concomitant appeal to rules, is not necessarily the citing of those reasons which are causally effective, a distinction may be made between those rules which agents in a given society sincerely profess to follow and to which their actions may in fact conform, but which do not in fact direct their actions, and those rules which, whether they profess to follow them or not, do in fact guide their acts by providing them with reasons and motives for acting in one way rather than another. The making of this distinction is essential to the notions of *ideology* and of *false consciousness*, notions which are extremely important to some non-Marxist as well as to Marxist social scientists.

But to allow that these notions could have application is to find oneself at odds with Winch's argument at yet another point. For it seems quite clear that the concept of ideology can find application in a society where the concept is not available to the members of the society, and furthermore that the application of this concept implies that criteria beyond those available in the society may be invoked to judge its rationality; and as such it would fall under Winch's ban as a concept unsuitable for social science. Hence there is a connexion between Winch's view that social science is not appropriately concerned with causal generalizations and his view that only the concepts possessed by the members of a given society (or concepts logically tied to those concepts in some way) are to be used in the study of that society. Furthermore it is important to note that Winch's views on those matters necessarily make his account of rules and their place in social behavior defective.

III

The examples which Winch gives of rule-following behavior are very multifarious: games, political thinking, musical composition, the monastic way of life, an anarchist's way of life, are all cited. His only example of non-rule-governed behavior is "the pointless behaviour of a beserk lunatic," and he asserts roundly "that all behaviour which is meaningful (therefore all specifically human behaviour) is *ipso facto* rule-governed."[15] Winch allows for different kinds of rules; what he does not consider is whether the concept of a rule is perhaps being used so widely that quite different senses of *rule-governed* are being confused, let alone whether his account of meaningful behavior can be plausibly applied to some actions at all.[16]

If I go for a walk, or smoke a cigarette, are my actions rule-governed in the sense in which my actions in playing chess are rule-governed? Winch says that "the test of whether a man's actions are the application of a rule is . . . whether it makes sense to distinguish between a right and a wrong way of doing things in connection with what he does." What is the wrong way of going for a walk? And, if there is no wrong way, is my action in any sense rule-governed? To ask these questions is to begin to bring out the difference between those activities which form part of a coherent mode of behavior and those which do not. It is to begin to see that although many actions must be rule-governed in the sense that the concept of some particular kinds of action may involve reference to a rule, the concept of an action as such does not involve such a reference. But even if we restrict our attention to activities which form part of some coherent larger whole, it is clear that rules may govern activity in quite different ways. This is easily seen if we consider the variety of uses to which social scientists have put the concept of a role and role-concepts.

Role-concepts are at first sight peculiarly well-fitted to find a place in the type of analysis of which Winch would approve. S. F. Nadel wrote that "the role concept is not an invention of anthropologists or sociologists but is employed by the very people they study," and added that "it is the existence of names describing classes of people which make us think of roles." It would therefore be significant for Winch's thesis if it were the case that role-concepts had to be understood in relation to causes, if they were to discharge their analytic and explanatory function.

Consider first a use of the notion of role where causal questions do not arise. In a society such as ours there are a variety of roles which an individual may assume or not as he wills. Some occupational roles provide examples. To live out such a role is to make one's behavior conform to certain norms. To speak of one's behavior being governed by the norms is to use a sense of "governed" close to that according to which the behavior of a chess-player is governed by the rules of chess. We are not disposed to say that the rules of chess or the norms which define the role of a head-waiter constrain the individual who conforms to them. The observation of the rules constitutes the behavior as what it is; it is not a causal agency.

Contrast with this type of example the enquiry carried on by Erving Goffman in his book *Asylums*.[17] One of Goffman's concerns was to pose a question about mental patients; how far are the characteristic patterns of behavior which they exhibit determined, not by the nature of the mental disorders from which they suffer, but by the nature of the institutions to which they have been consigned? Goffmann concludes that the behavior of patients is determined to a considerable degree by institutional arrangements which provide a severely limited set of possible roles both for patients and for the doctors and orderlies with whom they have to deal. Thus the behavior of individual patients of a given type might be explained as the effect of the role-arrangements open to a person of this type. In case it is thought that the role-structure of mental hospitals only has a causal effect upon the patients because they are *patients* (and the implication might be that they are not therefore rational agents but approach the condition of the exception Winch allows for, that of the beserk lunatic) it is worth noting that Goffman's study of mental hospitals is part of a study of what he calls "total institutions." These include monasteries and armed services as well as mental hospitals. A successful terminus to his enquiry would therefore be the formulation of generalizations about the effects upon agents of different types of character of the role-structure of such different types of institution.

If Winch were correct and rule-governed behavior was not to be understood as causal behavior, then the contrast could not be drawn between those cases in which the relation of social structure to individuals may be correctly characterized in terms of control or constraint and those in which it may not. Winch's inability to make this contrast adequately in terms of his conceptual scheme is the counterpart to Durkheim's inability to make it adequately in terms of his; and the resemblance of Winch's failure to Durkheim's is illuminating in that Winch's position is roughly speaking that of Durkheim turned upsidedown. Durkheim in a passage cited by Winch insisted first "that social life should be explained, not by the notions of those who participate in it, but by more profound causes which are unperceived by consciousness" and secondly "that these causes are to be sought mainly in the manner according to which the associated individuals are grouped."[18] That is, Durkheim supposes, just as Winch does, that an investigation of social reality which uses the concept available to the members of the society which is being studied and an investigation of social reality which utilizes concepts not so available and invokes causal explanations of which the agents themselves are not aware are mutually exclusive alternatives. But Durkheim supposes, as Winch does not, that the latter alternative is the one to be preferred. Yet his acceptance of the same dichotomy involves him in the same inability to understand the different ways in which social structure may be related to individual action.

Durkheim's concept of *anomie* is the concept of a state in which the constraints and controls exercised by social structure have been loosed and the bonds which delimit and contain individual desire have therefore been at least partially removed. The picture embodied in the Durkheimian concept is thus one according to which the essential function of norms in social life is to restrain and inhibit psychological drives. For Durkheim, rules are an external imposition upon a human nature which can be defined independently of them; for Winch, they are the guidelines of behavior which, did it not conform to them, could scarcely be human. What is equally odd in both is the way in which rules or norms are characterized as though they were all of a kind. Durkheim is unable to recognize social structure apart from the notions of constraint and control by the structure; Winch's concept of society has no room for these notions.

Just as Winch does not allow for the variety of relationships in which an agent may stand to a rule to which his behavior conforms, so he does not allow also for the variety of types of deviance from rules which behavior may exhibit. I quoted Malinowski earlier on the important gap between the rules professed in a society and the behavior actually exhibited. On this Winch might well comment that his concern is with human behavior as rule-following, not only with mere professions of rule-following, except in so far as profession to follow rules is itself a human and (for him) *ipso facto* a rule-following activity. Moreover he explicitly allows that "since understanding something involves understanding its contradictory, someone who, with understanding, performs X must be capable of envisaging the possibility of doing not-X." He makes this remark in the context of his discussion of predictability; and what he does not allow for in this discussion is that in fact the behavior of agents may exhibit regularities of a Humean kind and be predictable just as natural events are predictable, even although it can also be characterized and in some cases must also be characterized in terms of following and deviating from certain rules. That this is so makes it possible to speak not only, as Malinowski does in the passage quoted earlier, of mechanisms of deviation, but also of mechanisms of conformity. Of course those who deviate from the accepted rules may have a variety of reasons for so doing, and in so far as they share the same reasons their behavior will exhibit rule-following regularities. But it may well be that agents have a variety of reasons for their deviance, and yet deviate uniformly in certain circumstances, this uniformity being independent of their reasons. Whether in a particular case this is so or not seems to me to be an empirical question and one which it would be well not to attempt to settle *a priori*.

I can put my general point as follows. We can in a given society discover a variety of systematic regularities. There are the systems of rules which agents professedly follow; there are the systems of rules which they actually follow, there are causal regularities exhibited in the correlation of statuses and forms of behavior, and of one form of behavior and another, which are not rule-governed at all; there are regularities which are in themselves neither causal nor rule-governed, although dependent for their existence perhaps on regularities of both types, such as the cyclical patterns of development exhibited in some societies; and there are the inter-relationships which exist between all these. Winch concentrates on some of these at the expense of the others. In doing so he is perhaps influenced by a peculiarly British tradition in social anthropology and by a focus of attention in recent philosophy.

The anthropological tradition is that centered on the work of Professor E. E. Evans-Pritchard, work which exemplifies the rewards to be gained from understanding a people first of all in their own terms. Winch rightly treats Evans-Pritchard's writing as a paradigm case of a social scientist knowing his own business, but neglects the existence of alternative paradigms.[19] Edmund Leach, for example, has remarked how ecological factors do not in fact genuinely figure in the explanatory framework of Evans-Pritchard's *The Nuer*.[20] Now it is clear that such factors may affect the form of social life either in ways of which the agents are conscious (by posing problems to which they have to formulate solutions) or in ways of which they are unaware. This elementary distinction is perhaps not given its full weight in a recent discussion by Walter Goldschmidt in which the very problems discussed by Winch are faced from the standpoint of an anthropologist especially concerned with ecological factors.[21] Goldschmidt offers the example of the high correlation between agnatic segmentary kinship systems and nomadic pastoralism as a form of economy. He argues that nomadic pastoralism, to be a viable form of economy, has to satisfy requirements which are met most usually by segmentary lineages, but "age-sets can perform some of the same functions—especially those associated with the military—with equal effectiveness." Goldschmidt's claim is at least superficially ambiguous. He might be read (at least by a critic determined to be captious) as asserting that first there are economic forms; these pose problems of which the agents become aware and segmentary or age-set patterns are constructed as solutions by the agents. Or he might be read (more profitably, I imagine) as moving towards a theory in which social patterns (including kinship patterns) represent adaptations (of which the agents themselves are not aware) to the environment, and to the level of technology prevailing. It would then in principle be possible to formulate causal laws governing such adaptations, and work like Leach's on Pul Eliya or Goldschmidt's on East Africa could be placed in a more general explanatory framework. This type of project is at the opposite extreme from Evans-Pritchard's concern with conceptual particularity.

Secondly, on Winch's account the social sciences characterize what they characterize by using action-descriptions. In his stress upon these Winch follows much recent philosophical writing. It is on what people *do* and not what they *are* or *suffer* that he dwells. But social scientists are concerned with the causes and effects of *being unemployed, having kin-relations of a particular kind, rates of population change*, and a myriad of conditions of individuals and societies the descriptions of which have a logical character other than that of action descriptions. None of this appears in Winch's account.

IV

The positive value of Winch's book is partly as a corrective to the Durkheimian position which he rightly castigates. But it is more than a corrective because what Winch characterizes as the whole task of the social sciences is in fact their true starting-point. Unless we begin by a characterization of a society in its own terms, we shall be unable to identify the matter that requires explanation. Attention to intentions, motives, and reasons must precede attention to causes; description in terms of the agent's concepts and beliefs must precede description in terms of our concepts and beliefs. The force of this contention can be brought out by considering and expanding what Winch says about Durkheim's *Suicide*.[22] Winch invites us to notice the connection between Durkheim's conclusion that the true explanation of suicide is in terms of factors outside the consciousness of the agents themselves such that the reasons of the agents themselves are effectively irrelevant and his initial decision to give the term "suicide" a meaning quite other than that which it had for those agents. What is he inviting us to notice?

A number of points, I suspect, of which one is a central insight, the others in error. The insight is that Durkheim's particular procedure of giving to "suicide" a meaning of his own *entails* the irrelevance of the agents' reasons in the explanation of suicide. Durkheim does in fact bring forward independent arguments designed to show that reasons are either irrelevant or inaccessible, and very bad arguments they are. But even if he had not believed himself to have grounds drawn from these arguments, he would have been unable to take reasons into account, given his decision about meaning. For Durkheim arbitrarily equates the concept of *suicide* with that of *doing anything that the agent knows will bring about his own death* and thus classifies as suicide both the intended self-destruction of the Prussian or English officer who shoots himself to save the regiment the disgrace of a court-martial and the death of such an officer in battle who has courageously headed a charge in such a way that he knows that he will not survive. (I choose these two examples because they both belong to the same category in Durkheim's classification.) Thus he ignores the distinction between *doing X intending that Y shall result and doing X knowing that Y will result*. Now clearly if these two are to be assimilated, the roles of deliberation and the relevance of the agent's reasons will disappear from view. For clearly in the former case the character of Y must be central to the reasons the agent has for doing X, but in the latter case the agent may well be doing X either in spite of the character of Y, or not caring one way or the other about the character of Y, or again finding the character of Y desirable, but not desirable enough for him for it to constitute a reason or a motive for doing X. Thus the nature of the reasons *must* differ in the two cases and if the two cases are to have the same explanation the agent's reasons can scarcely figure in that explanation. That is, Durkheim is forced by his initial semantic decision to the conclusion that the agent's reasons are in cases of what agents in the society which he studies would have called suicide (which are included as a sub-class of what he calls suicide) *never* causally effective.

But there are two further conclusions which might be thought to, but do not in fact, follow. It does not follow that all such decisions to bring actions under descriptions other than those used by the agents themselves are bound to lead to the same *a priori* obliteration of the explanatory role of reasons; for this obliteration was in Durkheim's case, as I have just shown, a consequence of certain special features of this treatment of the concept of suicide, and not a consequence of any general feature of the procedure of inventing new descriptive terms in social sciences. Secondly, from the fact that explanation in terms of reasons ought not to be excluded by any initial decision of the social scientist, it does not follow that such explanation is incompatible with causal explanation. Here my argument in the second section of this paper bears on what Winch says about Weber. Winch says that Weber was confused because he did not realize that "a context of humanly followed rules . . . cannot be combined with a context of causal laws" without creating logical difficulties, and he is referring specifically to Weber's contention that the manipulation of machinery and the manipulation of his employees by a manufacturer may be understood in the same way, so far as the logic of the explanation is concerned. So Weber wrote, "that in the one case 'events of consciousness' do enter into the causal chain and in the other case do not, makes 'logically' not the slightest difference." I also have an objection to Weber's argument, but it is in effect that Weber's position is too close to Winch's. For Weber supposes that in order to introduce causal explanation he must abandon description of the social situation in terms of actions, roles, and the like. So he proposes speaking not of the workers being paid, but of their being handed pieces of metal. In so doing Weber concedes Winch's point that descriptions in terms of actions, reasons, and all that falls under his term "events of consciousness" cannot figure in causal explanations without a conceptual mistake being committed. But in this surely he is wrong.

Compare two situations: first, one in which managers minimize shop-floor trade union activity in a factory by concentrating opportunities of extra overtime and of earning bonuses in those parts of the factory where such activity shows signs of flourishing; and then one in which managers similarly minimize trade union activity by a process of continual transfers between one part of the factory and another or between different factories. In both cases it may be possible to explain the low level of trade union activity causally by reference to the manager's policies; but in the former case the reasons which the workers have for pursuing overtime and bonuses can find a place in the explanation without it losing its causal character and in both cases a necessary condition of the managers' actions being causally effective may well be that the workers in question remain ignorant of the policy behind the actions. The causal character of the explanations can be brought out by considering how generalizations might be formulated in which certain behavior of the managers can supply either the necessary or the sufficient condition or both for the behavior of the workers. But in such a formulation one important fact will emerge, namely, that true causal explanations cannot be formulated— where actions are concerned—unless intentions, motives, and reasons are taken into account. That is, it is not only the case as I have argued in the second section of this paper that a true explanation in terms of reasons must entail some account of the causal background; it is also true that a causal account of action will require a corresponding account of the intentions, motives, and reasons involved. It is this latter point that Durkheim misses and Winch stresses. In the light of this it is worth returning to one aspect of the explanation of suicide.

In modern cities more than one study has shown a correlation between the suicide rate for different parts of the city and the proportion of the population living an insolated single-room apartment existence. What are the conditions which must be satisfied if such a correlation is to begin to play a part in explaining why suicide is committed? First it must be shown that at least a certain proportion of the individuals who commit suicide live in such isolated conditions: otherwise (unless, for example, it was the landlord of such apartments who committed suicide) we should find the correlation of explanatory assistance only in so far as it pointed us towards a common explanation of the two rates. But suppose that we do find it is the individuals who live in such isolated conditions who are more likely to commit suicide. We still have to ask whether it is the pressure on the emotions of the isolation itself, or whether it is the insolubility of certain other problems in conditions of isolation which leads to suicide. Unless such questions about motives and reasons are answered, the casual generalization "Isolated living of a certain kind tends to lead to acts of suicide" is not so much an explanation in itself as an additional fact to be explained, even although it is a perfectly sound generalization, and even although to learn its truth might be to learn how the suicide rate could be increased or decreased in large cities by changing our local authority housing policy.

Now we cannot raise the questions about motives and reasons, the answers to which would explain why isolation has the effect which it has, unless we first of all understand the acts of suicide in terms of the intentions of the agents and therefore in terms of their own action-descriptions. Thus Winch's starting-point proves to be the correct one, provided it is a starting-point. We could not even formulate our initial causal generalization about isolation and suicide, in such a way that the necessary question about motives and reasons could be raised later, unless the expression "suicide" and kindred expressions which figured in our causal generalizations possessed the same meaning as they did for the agents who committed the acts. We can understand very clearly why Winch's starting-point must be substantially correct if we remember how he compares sociological understanding with understanding a language.[23] The crude notion that one can first learn a language and then secondly and separately go on to understand the social life of those who speak it can only flourish where the languages studied are those of people whose social life is so largely the same as our own that we do not notice the understanding of social life embodied in our grasp of the language; but attempts to learn the alien language of an alien culture soon dispose of it. Yet the understanding that we thus acquire, although a necessary preliminary, is only a preliminary. It would be equally harmful if Winch's attempt to make of this preliminary the substance of social science were to convince or if a proper understanding of the need to go further were not to allow for the truth in his arguments.

V

These dangers are likely to be especially inhibiting in the present state of certain parts of social science. Two important essays by anthropologists, Leach's *Rethinking Anthropology* and Goldschmidt's *Comparative Functionalism*, focus upon problems in which adherence to Winch's conclusions would preclude any solution.[24] At the outset I contrasted Winch with Malinowski, but this was in respects in which most contemporary social scientists would take the standpoint quoted from Malinowski for granted. We owe also to Malinowski, however, the tradition of what Goldschmidt calls "the detailed internal analysis of individual cultures" with the further comparison of institutional arrangements in different societies resting on such analysis. This tradition has been criticized by both Leach and Goldschmidt; the latter believes that because institutions are defined by each culture in its own terms, it is not at the level of institutions that cross-cultural analyses will be fruitful. The former has recommended us to search for recurrent topological patterns in, for example, kinship arrangements, with the same aim of breaking free from institutional ethnocentrism. I think that both Leach and Goldschmidt are going to prove to be seminal writers on this point, and it is clear that their arguments are incompatible with Winch's. It would therefore be an important lacuna in this paper if I did not open up directly the question of the bearing of Winch's arguments on this topic.

Winch argues, consistently with his rejection of any place for causal laws in social science, that comparison between different cases is not dependent on any grasp of theoretical generalizations, and he sets limits to any possible comparison by his insistence that each set of activities must be understood solely in its own terms.[25] In so doing he must necessarily reject for example all those various theories which insist that religions of quite different kinds express unacknowledged needs of the same kind. (No such theory needs to be committed to the view that religions are and do no more than this.) Indeed in his discussion of Pareto he appears to make such a rejection explicit by the generality of the grounds on which he rejects Pareto's comparison of Christian baptism with pagan rites.[26] I hold no brief for the theory of residues and derivations. But when Winch insists that each religious rite must be understood in its own terms to the exclusion of any generalization about religion, or that each social system must be so understood to the exclusion of any generalization about status and prestige, he must be pressed to make his grounds precise. In his later discussion of Evans-Pritchard, one aspect of Winch's views becomes clear, namely, the implication of his remarks that "criteria of logic are not a direct gift of God, but arise out of, and are only intelligible in the context of, ways of living or modes of social life."[27] Winch's one substantial point of difference with Evans-Pritchard in his treatment of witchcraft among the Azande is that he thinks it impossible to ask whether the Zande beliefs about witches are true. [28] We can ask from within the Zande system of beliefs if there are witches and will receive the answer "Yes." We can ask from within the system of beliefs of modern science if there are witches and will receive the answer "no." But we cannot ask which system of beliefs is the superior in respect of rationality and truth; for this would be to invoke criteria which can be understood independently of any particular way of life, and on Winch's view there are no such criteria.

This represents a far more extreme view of the difficulties of cultural comparison than Goldschmidt, for example, advances. Both its extreme character and its error can be understood by considering two arguments against it. The first is to the effect that on Winch's view certain actual historical transitions are made unintelligible; I refer to those transitions from one system of beliefs to another which are necessarily characterized by raising questions of the kind that Winch rejects. In seventeenth-century Scotland, for example, the question could not but be raised, "But are there witches?" If Winch asks, from within what way of social life, under what system of belief was this question asked, the only answer is that it was asked by men who confronted alternative systems and were able to draw out of what confronted them independent criteria of judgment. Many Africans today are in the same situation.

This type of argument is of course necessarily inconclusive; any historical counter-example to Winch's thesis will be open to questions of interpretation that will make it less than decisive. But there is another important argument. Consider the statement made by some Zande theorist or by King James VI and I, "There are witches," and the statement made by some modern skeptic, "There are no witches." Unless one of these statements denies what the other asserts, the negation of the sentence expressing the former could not be a correct translation of the sentence expressing the latter. Thus if we could not deny from our own standpoint and in our own language what the Azande or King James assert in theirs, we should be unable to translate their expression into our language. Cultural idiosyncracy would have entailed linguistic idiosyncracy and cross-cultural comparison would have been rendered logically impossible. But of course translation is not impossible.

Yet if we treat seriously, not what I take to be Winch's mistaken thesis that we cannot go beyond a society's own self-description, but what I take to be his true thesis that we must not do this except and until we have grasped the criteria embodied in that self-description, then we shall have to conclude that the contingently different conceptual schemes and institutional arrangements of different societies make translation difficult to the point at which attempts at cross-cultural generalization too often become little more than a construction of lists. Goldschmidt and Leach have both pointed out how the building up of typologies and classificatory schemes becomes empty and purposeless unless we have a theory which gives point and criteria to our classificatory activities. Both have also pointed out how, if we compare for example marital institutions in different cultures, our definition of "marriage" will either be drawn from one culture in terms of whose concepts other cultures will be described or rather misdescribed, or else will be so neutral, bare, and empty as to be valueless.[29] That is, the understanding of a people in terms of their own concepts and beliefs does in fact tend to preclude understanding them in any other terms. To this extent Winch is vindicated. But an opposite moral to his can be drawn. We may conclude not that we ought not to generalize, but that such generalization must move at another level. Goldschmidt argues for the recommendation: Don't ask what an institution means for the agents themselves; ask what necessary needs and purposes it serves. He argues for this not because he looks for functional-ist explanations of a Malinowskian kind, but because he believes that different institutions, embodying different conceptual schemes, may be illuminatingly seen as serving the same social necessities. To carry the argument further would be to raise questions that are not and cannot be raised within the framework of Winch's book. It is because I believe writers such as Goldschmidt are correct in saying that one must transcend such a framework that I believe also that Winch's book deserves close critical attention.

Notes

1. Peter Winch, *The Idea of a Social Science and Its Relation to Philosophy* (London: Routledge and Kegan Paul, 1958; rpt. New York: Humanities Press). I have in this paper focused attention upon Winch's arguments in such a way that, although it will be obvious that I am either indebted to or at odds with various other philosophers, I have not usually made this explicit. But I ought to acknowledge that in arguing with Winch I shall also be arguing with myself, and that the arguments of section II of this paper entail the falsity of some assertions in section II of "A Mistake about Causality in the Social Sciences," *Philosophy, Politics and Society*, ed. Peter Laslett and W. C. Runciman (2nd ser.; Oxford: Blackwell, 1963).
2. See, for example, Richard Rudner, *The Philosophy of Social Sciences* (London: Prentice-Hall, 1966), pp. 81–83.
3. See A. R. Louch's review in *Inquiry*, Vols. 5–6. 1963, p. 273.
4. Winch, *Idea of a Social Science*, p. 114.
5. Ibid., p. 88.
6. Bronislaw Malinowski, *The Sexual Life of Savages* (N.Y.: Harcourt, Brace and World), pp. 425–429.
7. Ibid., pp. 428–429.
8. Winch, *Idea of a Social Science*, p. 116.
9. Ibid., pp. 83–84.
10. Ibid., p. 88.
11. Ibid., pp. 91–92.
12. Ibid., p. 91.
13. It has been argued often enough that this symmetry does not hold in the natural sciences; Professor Adolf Grünbaum's arguments in chapter 9 of the *Philosophical Problems of Space and Time* (Boston: Reidel, 1973) seem a more than adequate rebuttal of these positions.
14. Winch, *Idea of a Social Science*, pp. 82, 81.
15. Ibid., p. 53.
16. Ibid., p. 52.
17. Erving Goffman, *Asylums: Essays on The Social Situation of Mental Patients and Other Inmates* (New York: Doubleday Anchor Books, 1961; Harmonds-worth: Penguin Books, 1968).
18. Emile Durkheim, review of A. Labriola's *Essays on Historical Materialism*.

Part Three: The Critical Approach

19. Peter Winch, "Understanding a Primitive Society," *Rationality*, ed. Brian R. Wilson (Oxford: Blackwell, 1970), pp. 78–111.
20. E. R. Leach, *Pul Eliya, a Village in Ceylon* (Cambridge University Press: Cambridge Eng., 1961).
21. Walter Goldschmidt, *Comparative Functionalism* (Berkeley, California: University of California Press, 1966), pp. 122–124.
22. Winch, "Understanding a Primitive Society," p. 110.
23. Winch, *Idea of a Social Science*, p. 115.
24. Edmund Leach, *Rethinking Anthropology* (London: Athlone Press, 1966); Goldschmidt, *Comparative Functionalism*.
25. Winch, *Idea of a Social Science*, pp. 134–136.
26. Ibid., pp. 104–111.
27. Ibid., p. 100.
28. Winch, "Understanding a Primitive Society," pp. 79 ff.
29. See Kathleen Gough, "The Nayars and the Definition of Marriage," *Culture and Social Anthropology*, ed. P. B. Hammond (London and New York: Collier-Macmillan, 1964); E. R. Leach, "Polyandry, Inheritance and the Definition of Marriage with Particular Reference to Sinhalese Customary Law," *Rethinking Anthropology*; Goldschmidt, *Comparative Functionalism*, pp. 17–26.

CHAPTER 15

On Systematically Distorted Communication

Jürgen Habermas

1. Where difficulties of comprehension are the result of cultural, temporal, or social distance, we can say in principle what further information we would need in order to achieve understanding: we know that we must decipher the alphabet, become acquainted with lexicon and grammar, or uncover context-specific rules of application. In attempting to explain unclear or incomprehensible meaning-associations we are able to recognize, within the limits of normal communication, what it is that we do not—yet—know. However, this "hermeneutic" consciousness of translation difficulties proves to be inadequate when applied to systematically distorted communication. For in this case incomprehensibility results from a faulty organization of speech itself, Obvious examples are those clearly pathological speech disturbances to be observed, for example, among psychotics. But the more important occurrences of the pattern of systematically distorted communication are those which appear in speech which is not conspicuously pathological. This is what we encounter in the case of pseudo-communication, where the participants do not recognize any communication disturbances. Pseudo-communication produces a system of reciprocal misunderstandings which, due to the false assumption of consensus, are not recognized as such. Only a neutral observer notices that the participants do not understand one another. However, as long as we communicate in a natural language there is a sense in which we can never be neutral observers, simply because we are always participants. That is, and as I have argued elsewhere,[1] any attempt to locate misunderstanding in communication is itself part of a further (or

Reprinted with the permission of the author and Universitetsforlaget from *Inquiry* 13 (1970): 205–18.

possibly the same) process of reciprocal communication, and therefore not the result of "observing" such processes. The critical vantage-point can never be better than that of a partner in the communication. Consequently we have no valid criterion at our disposal for determining in general whether we are laboring under the mistaken conviction of normal understanding, and thus wrongly considering difficulties to be hermeneutically explicable when they actually require systematic analysis.

Freud dealt with the occurrence of systematically deformed communication in order to define the scope of specifically incomprehensible acts and utterances. He always envisaged the dream as the standard example of such phenomena, the latter including everything from harmless, everyday pseudo-communications and Freudian slips to pathological manifestations of neurosis, psychosis, and psychosomatic disturbance. In his essays on cultural theory, Freud broadened the range of phenomena which could be conceived as being part of systematically distorted communication. He employed the insights gained from clinical phenomena as the key to the pseudo-normality, that is to the hidden pathology, of collective behavior and entire social systems. In our discussion of psychoanalysis as a kind of linguistic analysis pertaining to systematically distorted communication, we shall first consider the example of neurotic symptoms.

Three criteria are available for defining the scope of specific incomprehensible acts and utterances. (a) On the level of language, distorted communication becomes noticeable because of the use of rules which deviate from the recognized system of linguistic rules. Particular semantical contents or complete semantical fields—in extreme cases the syntax too—may be affected thereby. Using dream texts, Freud examined, in particular, condensation, displacement, absence of grammaticalness, and the use of words with opposite meaning. (b) On the behavior level, the deformed language-game appears in the form of rigidity and compulsory repetition. Stereotyped behavior patterns recur in situations involving stimuli which cause emotionally loaded reactions. This inflexibility is symptomatic of the fact that the semantical content has lost its specific linguistic independence of the situational context. (c) If, finally, we consider the system of distorted communication as a whole, we are struck by the discrepancy between the levels of communication; the usual congruency between linguistic symbols, actions, and accompanying gestures has disintegrated. The symptoms, in a clinical sense, offer nothing but the most recalcitrant and tangible proof of this dissonance. No matter on which level of communication the symptoms appear, whether in linguistic expression, in behavioral compulsion, or in the realm of gestures, one always finds an isolated content therein which has been excommunicated from the public language-performance. This content expresses an intention which is incomprehensible according to the rules of public communication, and which as such has become private, although in such a way that it remains inaccessible even to the author to whom it must, nevertheless, be ascribed. There is a communication obstruction in the self between the ego, which is capable of speech and participates in intersubjectively established language-games, and that "inner foreign territory" (Freud), which is represented by a private or a primary linguistic symbolism.

2. Alfred Lorenzer has examined the analytical conversation between physician and patient from the standpoint of psychoanalysis as analysis of language.[2] He considers the process by which the meanings of specific incomprehensible manifestations are decoded as an understanding of scenes linked by analogy to those in which the symptoms occur. The purpose of analytical interpretation is to explain the incomprehensible meaning of the symptomatic manifestations. Where neuroses are involved, these manifestations are part of a deformed language-game in which the patient "acts": that is, he plays an incomprehensible scene by violating role-expectations in a strikingly stereotyped manner. The analyst tries to make the symptomatic scene understandable by associating it with analogous scenes in the situation of transference. The latter holds the key to the coded relation between the symptomatic scene, which the adult patient plays outside the doctor's office, and an original scene experienced in early childhood. In the transference situation the patient forces the doctor into the role of the conflict-defined primary reference person. The doctor, in the role of the reflective or critical participant, can interpret the transference situation as a repetition of early childhood experiences; he can thus construct a dictionary for the hidden idiosyncratic meanings of the symptoms. "Scenic understanding" is therefore based on the discovery that the patient behaves in the same way in his symptomatic scenes as he does in certain transference situations; such understanding aims at the reconstruction, confirmed by the patient in an act of self-reflection, of the original scene.

2.1. The re-established original scene is typically a situation in which the child has once suffered and repulsed an unbearable conflict. This repulse is coupled with a process of desymbolizaion and the formation of a symptom. The child excludes the experience of the conflict-filled object from public communication (and at the same time makes it inaccessible to its own ego as well); it separates the conflict-laden portion of its memory of the object and, so to speak, desymbolizes the meaning of the relevant reference person. The gap which arises in the semantic field is then closed by employing an unquestionable symbol in place of the isolated symbolic content. This symbol, of course, strikes us as being a symptom, because it has gained private linguistic significance and can no longer be used according to the rules of public language. The analyst's scenic understanding establishes meaning equivalences between the elements of three patterns—the everyday scene, the transference scene, and the original scene—and solves the specific incomprehensibility of the symptom; thus it assists in achieving resymbolization, that is, the re-entry of isolated symbolic contents into public communication. The latent meaning of the present situation becomes accessible when it is related to the unimpaired meaning of the original infantile scene. Scenic understanding makes it possible to "translate" the meaning of the pathologically frozen communication pattern which had been hitherto unconscious and inaccessible to public communication.

2.2. If we consider everyday interpretation within the range of ordinary language or translation from one language into another, or trained linguistic analysis in general, all of them leading to hermeneutic understanding of initially incomprehensible utterances, then scenic understanding differs from that hermeneutic understanding because of its explanatory power. That is, the disclosure of the meaning of specific incomprehensible acts or utterances develops to the same extent as, in the course of reconstruction of the original scene, a clarification of the genesis of the faulty meaning is achieved. The What, the semantic content of a systematically distorted manifestation, cannot be "understood" if it is not possible at the same time to "explain" the Why, the origin of the symptomatic scene with reference to the initial circumstances which led to the systematic distortion itself. However, understanding can only assume an explanatory function, in the strict meaning of the word, if the semantic analysis does not depend solely on the trained application of the communicative competence of a native speaker, as is the case with simple semantic analysis, but is instead guided by theoretical propositions.

Two considerations indicate that scenic understanding is based on hypotheses which are in no way to be derived from the natural competence of a native speaker. In the first place, scenic understanding is linked to a special design of communication. The fundamental analytic rule introduced by Freud ensures a standard relationship between the physician and his patient, a relationship which meets quasi-experimental conditions. Suspension of the usual restraints of social reality and free association on the part of the patient, along with purposively restrained reactions and reflective participation on the part of the doctor, assure the achievement of a transference situation, which can then serve as a framework for translation. Secondly, the analyst's pre-understanding is directed at a small sampling of possible meanings, at the conflict-disturbed early object-relationships. The linguistic material which results from conversations with the patient is classified according to a narrowly circumscribed context of possible double meanings. This context comprises a general interpretation of early-childhood patterns of interaction. Both considerations make it obvious that scenic understanding—in contrast to hermeneutic understanding, or ordinary semantic analysis—cannot be conceived as being a mere application of communicative competence, free from theoretical guidance.

3. The theoretical propositions on which this special kind of language analysis is implicitly based can be elicited from three points of view. (1) The psychoanalyst has a preconception of the structure of nondistorted ordinary communication; (2) he attributes the systematic distortion of communication to the confusion of two developmentally following phases of prelinguistic and linguistic symbol-organization; and (3) to explain the origin of deformation he employs a theory of deviant socialization which includes the connection between patterns of interaction in early childhood and the formation of personality structures. I would like to consider these three aspects briefly.

3.1. The first set of theoretical propositions concerns the structural conditions which must be met if normal communication is to obtain.

(*a*) In the case of a nondeformed language-game there is a congruency on all three levels of communication. Linguistic expressions, expressions represented in actions, and those embodied in gestures do not contradict one another, but rather supplement one another by metacommunication. Intended contradictions which have some informational content are normal in this sense. Furthermore, ordinary communication implies that a particular portion of extraverbal meanings must be convertible into verbal communication.

(*b*) Normal communication conforms to intersubjectively recognized rules; it is public. The communicated meanings are identified for all members of the language community. Verbal utterances are constructed according to the valid system of grammatical rules and are conventionally applied to specific situations. For extraverbal expressions, which are not grammatically organized, there is likewise a lexicon which varies socioculturally with certain limits.

(*c*) In the case of normal speech the speakers are aware of the categorical difference between subject and object. They differentiate between outer and inner speech and separate the private from the public world. The differentiation between being and appearance depends, moreover, on the distinction between the language-sign, its significative content (*significatum*), and the object which the symbol denotes (referent, *denotatum*). Only on this basis is it possible to apply situationally nondependent language symbols (decontexualization). The speaking subject will master the distinction between reality and appearance to the same extent as speech attains a distinct reality for him, distinct, that is, from the denoted objects and their meanings, as well as from private experiences.

(*d*) In normal communication an intersubjectivity of mutual understanding, guaranteeing ego-identity, develops and is maintained in the relation between individuals who acknowledge one another. On the one hand, the analytic use of language allows the identification of objects (thus, the categorization of particular items, the subordination of elements under classes, and the inclusion of sets). On the other hand, the reflexive use of language assures a relationship between the speaking subject and the language community which cannot be sufficiently presented by the analytic operations mentioned. For a world on the level of which subjects maintain mutual existence and understanding solely by virtue of their ordinary communications, intersubjectivity is not a universal according to which the individuals could be classified in the same way as elements are subordinated to their classes. On the contrary, the relation between I (ego), you (alter-ego), and we (ego and alter -ego) is established only by an analytically paradoxical achievement: the speaking persons identify themselves at the same time with two incompatible dialogue-roles and thereby ensure the identity of the I (ego) as well as of the group. The one being (ego) asserts his absolute nonidentity in relation to the other being (alter-ego); at the same time, however, both recognize their identity inasmuch as each acknowledges the other as being an ego, that is, a nonreplaceable individual who can refer to himself as "I." Moreover, that which links them both is a mutual factor (we), a collectivity, which in turn asserts its individuality in relation to other groups. This means that the same paradoxical relationship is established on the level of intersubjectively linked collectives as holds between the individuals.

The specific feature of linguistic intersubjectivity exists in the fact that individuated persons communicate on the basis of it. In the reflexive use of language we present inalienably individual aspects in unavoidably general categories in such a way that we meta-communicatively comment upon and sometimes even revoke direct information (and confirm it only with reservations). We do this for the purpose of an indirect representation of the nonidentical aspects of the ego, aspects which are not sufficiently covered by the general determinations and yet cannot be manifestly represented other than by just these determinations. The analytical use of language is necessarily embedded in the reflexive use, because the intersubjectivity of mutual understanding cannot be maintained without reciprocal self-representation on the part of the speaking subjects. Inasmuch as the speaker masters this indirect information on the meta-communicative level, he differentiates between essence and appearance. The understanding we come to about objects can be direct, but the subjectivity we encounter when we speak with one another remains, in direct information, only at the level of appearance. The categorial meaning of this kind of indirect communication, in which the indefinable individualized aspect of a person is expressed and his claim upon individuality is maintained, is something we merely reify in the ontological concept of essence. In fact this essence exists only in its appearances.

(*e*) Finally, normal speech is distinguished by the fact that the sense of substance and causality, of space and time, is differentiated according to whether these categories are applied to the objects within a world or to the linguistically constituted world itself, which allows for the mutuality of speaking subjects. The interpretational schema, "substance," has a different meaning for the identity of items which can be clearly categorized analytically from that which it has for speaking and interacting subjects themselves, whose ego-identity, as has been shown, just cannot be grasped by analytically clear-cut operations. The interpretational schema of causality, when applied to observable events, leads to the concept of "cause"; when it is applied to an association of intentional actions it leads to the concept of "motive." In the same way "space" and "time" undergo a different schematism when viewed in regard to physically measurable properties of observable events from that which they undergo when viewed according to experienced interactions. In the first case the categories serve as a system of coordinates for observation controlled by the success of instrumental action: in the latter case the categories serve as a frame of reference for the experience of social space and historical time from a subjective point of view.

3.2 The second set of postulates concerns the connection between two genetically successive phases of human symbol-organization.

(*a*) The archaic symbol-organization, which resists the transformation of its contents into grammatically regulated communication, can only be disclosed on the basis of the data of speech pathology and by means of the analysis of dream material. Here we mean symbols which control interactions, and not just signs, for these symbols already represent interactional experiences. Otherwise, however, the level of palaeosymbols lacks all the characteristics of normal speech.[3] Palaeosymbols do not fit into a system of grammatical rules. They are not classifed elements and do not appear in sentences which could be transformed grammatically. For this reason, the way in which these symbols function has been compared to the functional manner of analog computers in contrast to that of digital computers. Freud had already noticed the lack of logical connections in his dream analyses. He draws attention particularly to the use of words with opposite meaning, a remnant of the linguistic level of the genetically earlier peculiarity of combining logically incompatible meanings. Prelinguistic symbols are emotionally loaded and remain fixed to particular scenes. There is no dissociation of linguistic symbol and bodily gesture. The connection to a particular context is so strong that the symbol cannot vary independently of actions. Although the palaeosymbols represent a prelinguistic basis for the intersubjectivity of mutual existence and shared action, they do not allow public communication in the strict sense of the word. For the identity of meaning is not yet granted and the private meaning-associations still prevail. The privatism of prelinguistic symbol-organization, so striking in all forms of speech pathology, originates in the fact that the usual distance between sender and addressee, as well as the differentiation between symbolic signs, semantic content, and items of reference, has not yet been developed. The distinction between reality and appearance, between the public and the private sphere, cannot yet be clearly differentiated with the help of palaeosymbols (adualism).

Finally, prelinguistic symbol-organization does not allow an analytically satisfying categorization of the objects experienced. Two types of deficiencies are found in the communication and thought disturbances of psychotics; namely "amorphous" and "fragmented" speech disorders.[4] In both cases the analytic operations of classification are disturbed. In the first, a fragmentation of structure is apparent which does not allow disintegrated single elements to be compiled into classes according to general criteria. In the second, an amorphous structure appears which does not allow aggregates of superficially similar and vaguely compiled things to be analyzed. Symbol usage is not altogether destroyed, but the inability to form class hierarchies and to identify elements of classes offers, in both cases, proof of the breakdown of the analytical use of language. However, the second variation allows the possibility of achieving an archaic class-formation with the aid of prelinguistic symbols. And in any case we find so-called primary classes on early ontogenetic and historical levels, as well as in pathological cases; that is, classes that are not formed on the abstract basis of their identify of properties, but where the aggregates contain concrete items which, irrespective of their identifiable properties, are coordinated within an all-embracing association of motives, interpreted on the basic of subject plausibility Animistic *Weltanschauungen*, for example, are formed in accordance with such primary classes.

(*b*) The symbol-organization described here, which precedes language genetically, is a theoretical construct. We cannot observe it anywhere. But the psychoanalytical decoding of systematically distorted communication presupposes such a construction, because the special type of semantic analysis introduced here as "scenic understanding" resolves confusions of ordinary speech by interpreting them either as forced regression back to an earlier level of communication, or as the breakthrough of the earlier form of communication into language. On the basis of the analyst's experience with neurotic patients, we can, as has been shown, recognize the function of psychoanalysis as language analysis, in so far as it allows separated symbolic contents, which lead to a private narrowing of public communication, to be reintegrated into common linguistic usage. The performance of the analyst in putting an end to the process of inhibition serves the purpose of resymbolization; inhibition itself can therefore be understood as a process linked to desymbolization. The defense mechanism of inhibition, which is analogous to flight is revealed by the patient in his resistance to plausible interpretation made by the analyst. This mechanism is an operation carried on with and by language; otherwise it would not be possible to reverse the process of repulsion hermeneutically, i.e. precisely by means of a special type of semantic analysis. The fleeing ego, which has to submit to the demands of outer reality in a conflict situation, hides itself from itself by eliminating the symbolic representation of unwanted demands of instinct from the text of its everyday consciousness. By means of this censorship the representation of the prohibited object is excommunicated from public communication and banished to the archaic level of palaeosymbols. Moreover, the assumption that neurotic behavior is controlled by palaeosymbols, and only subsequently rationalized by a substitutive interpretation, offers an explanation for the characteristics of this behavior pattern: for its pseudo-communicative function, for its stereotyped and compulsive form, for its emotional load and expressive content, and, finally, for its rigid fixation upon particular situations.

If inhibition can be understood as desymbolization, then it follows that there must be a correspondingly linguistic interpretation for the complementary defense mechanism, which does not turn against the self but rather against outer reality, i.e. for projection and denial. While in the case of inhibition the language-game is deformed by the symptoms formed in place of the excommunicated symbols, the distortion in the case of this defense mechanism results directly from the uncontrolled penetration of palaeosymbolic derivatives into language. In this case the therapeutic type of language analysis doesn't aim at re-transforming the desymbolized content into linguistically articulated meaning, but aims rather at a consciously achieved excommunication of the intermingled prelinguistic elements.

In both cases the systematic distortion can be explained by the fact that palaeosymbolically fixed semantic contents have encysted themselves, like foreign bodies, into the grammatically regulated use of symbols. Language analysis has the duty of dissolving this syndrome, i.e. of isolating the two language levels. There is, however, a third case: the processes of the creative extension of language. In this case a genuine integration is accomplished. The palaeosymbolically fixed meaning-potential is then brought into the open and is thus made available for public communication. This transfer of semantic contents from the pre-linguistic into the common stock of language widens the scope of communicative action as it diminishes that of unconsciously motivated action. The moment of success in the use of creative language is a moment of emancipation.

The joke, although a different case, sheds light upon this process of creative language-extension. The laugh with which we react almost compulsively to what is comic in the joke contains the liberating experience which results when one moves from the level of palaeosymbolic thought to the level of linguistic thought. It is the revealed ambiguity of a text which is funny, an ambiguity which exists because it tempts us to regress to the level of prelinguistic symbolism, i.e. to confuse identity and similarity, and at the same time convinces us of the mistake of this regression. The laugh is one of relief. The joke lets us repeat virtually and experimentally the dangerous passage across the archaic border between prelinguistic and linguistic communication. In our reaction to it we assure ourselves of the control which we have attained over the dangers of a developmental stage of consciousness which we have overcome.

3.3. Psychoanalysis, which interprets the specific incomprehensibility of systematically distorted communication, can no longer strictly speaking be conceived according to the translation model which applies to simple hermeneutic understanding or ordinary semantic analysis. For the obscurities which controlled "translation" from prelinguistic symbolism to language does away with are ones which arise not within the scope defined by a given language-system, but rather within language itself. Here it is the very structure of communication, hence the basis of all translation, that we are concerned with. Semantic analysis of this special type therefore needs a systematic pre-understanding which pertains to language and linguistic communication as such, while on the other hand our ordinary semantic analysis proceeds *ad hoc* from a traditionally determined pre-understanding which is tested and revised within the process of interpretation. The theoretical propositions deal, as described, with the preconditions of normal communication, with two levels of symbol organization, and with the mechanism of speech disorder. These theoretical assumptions can be organized in the structural model.

The constructions of "ego" and "id" interpret the analyst's experiences in his encountering the resistance of his patients. "Ego" is the instance which fulfills the function of reality-testing and of censorship. "Id" is the name given to those parts of the self that are isolated from the ego and whose representations become accessible in connection with the processes of repression and projection. The "id" is expressed indirectly by the symptoms which close the gap which develops in everyday language when desymbolization takes place; direct representation of the "id" is found in the illusory palaeosymbolic elements dragged into the language by projection and denial. Now, the same clinical experience which leads to the construction of an ego- and id-instance, shows also that the defense mechanisms usually work unconsciously. For this reason Freud introduced the category of "superego": an ego-foreign instance which is formed out of detached identifications with the expectations of primary reference persons. All three categories—ego, id, and super-ego—reflect fundamental experiences typical of a systematically distorted communication. The dimensions established by id and superego for the personality structure correspond to the dimensions of deformation of the intersubjectivity of mutual understanding in informal communication. So the structural model which Freud introduced as the categorial frame of metapsychology can be reduced to a theory of deviant communicative competence.[5]

4. I have chosen psychoanalysis as my example in order to differentiate between two types of interpretation and two forms of communication.

From the viewpoint of a logic of explanation, this example of the semantic analysis of specific incomprehensible manifestations is of interest because, in a unique way, it affords simultaneous hermeneutic understanding and causal explanation. The analyst's understanding owes its explanatory power—as we have seen—to the fact that the clarification of a systematically inaccessible meaning succeeds only to the extent to which the origin of the faulty or misleading meaning is explained. The reconstruction of the original scene makes both possible at the same time: the reconstruction leads to an understanding of the meaning of a deformed language-game and simultaneously explains the origin of the deformation itself. Of course, the connection between semantic analysis and causal explanation doesn't become evident until one shows that the categorial framework of the theory used—in our case the Freudian metapsychology—is based on an at least implicitly underlying language theory. I have outlined only some of the assumptions which extend to the structure of normal communication and to the mechanisms of systematic distortion of communication. These assumptions would have to be developed within the framework of a theory of communicative competence, which is lacking as of now.

I can sum up my thesis as follows. The common semantic analysis of incomprehensible utterances, which leads to hermeneutic understanding, makes use of the nonanalyzed communicative competence of a native speaker. On the other hand, the special type of semantic analysis which deals with manifestations of a systematically distorted communication and affords an explanatory understanding, presupposes a theory of communicative competence. It is only in virtue an at least implicit hypothesis concerning the nature and the acquisition of communicative competence that explanatory power can be accorded to this (particular) semantic analysis. . . .*

Notes

1. See Jürgen Haberma , ' Zur Logik der Sozialwissenschaften," *Philosophische Rundschau*, supp. 5 (Tübingen: C. B. Mohr, 1967), pp. 101 ff. The problem is discussed at length in A. V. Cicourel, *Method and Measurement in Sociology* (Glencoe, Ill.: Free Press, 1964), pp. 21 ff.

*Editors' deletion.

2. A. Lorenzer, *Symbol und Verstehen im psychoanalytischen Prozess: Vorarbeiten zu einer Metatheorie der Psychoanalyse* (Frankfurt am Main: Suhrkamp Verlag, 1970).
3. Cf. S. Arieti, *The Intrapsychic Self* (New York: Basic Books, 1967); also H. Werner and B. Kaplan, *Symbol Formation* (New York: John Wiley, 1967); P. Watzlawick, J. H. Beavin, and D. D. Jackson, *Pragmatics in Human Communication* (New York: W. W. Norton, 1967), esp. chs. 6 and 7.
4. See L. C. Wynne, "Denkstörung und Familienbeziehung bei Schizophrenen," *Psyche*, May 1965, pp. 82 ff.
5. For further elaboration see Jürgen Habermas, *Erkenntnis und Interesse* (Frankfurt am Main: Suhrkamp Verlag, 1968), chs. 10 and 11.

CHAPTER 16

Sociology: Contradictions and Intrastructure

Alvin Gouldner

Background and Domain Assumptions

Deliberately formulated social theories, we might say with deliberate oversimplification, contain at least two distinguishable elements. One element is the explicitly formulated assumptions, which may be called "postulations." But they contain a good deal more. They also contain a second set of assumptions that are unpostulated and unlabeled, and these I will term "background assumptions." I call them background assumptions because, on the one hand, they provide the background out of which the postulations in part emerge and, on the other hand, not being expressly formulated, they remain in the background of the theorist's attention. Postulations are brought into focalized attention, while background assumptions are part of what Michael Polanyi calls the theorist's "subsidiary attention."[1] Background assumptions are embedded in a theory's postulations. Operating within and alongside of them, they are, as it were, "silent partners" in the theoretical enterprise. Background assumptions provide some of the bases of choice and the invisible cement for linking together postulations. From beginning to end, they influence a theory's formulation and the researchers to which it leads.

Background assumptions also influence the *social* career of a theory, influencing the responses of those to whom it is communicated. For, in some part, theories are accepted or rejected because of the background assumptions embedded in them. In particular, a social theory is more

From *The Coming Crisis of Western Sociology* by Alvin W. Gouldner. © 1970 by Alvin W. Gouldner. By permission of Basic Books, Inc., Publishers, New York, and of Heinemann Educational Books Ltd.

likely to be accepted by those who share the theory's background assumptions and find them agreeable. Over and above their stipulated connotations, social theories and their component concepts contain a charge of surplus meanings derived in part from their background assumptions, and these may congenially resonate the compatible background assumptions of their hearers or may generate a painful dissonance.

Commitment to a social theory, in this view, occurs through a process rather different, and certainly more complex, than is supposedly the case in the canons of scientific method. The latter conceives of the process of commitment to a theory, or withdrawal from it, very largely in cerebral and rational terms: it emphasizes that the rejecting or accepting process is governed by a deliberate inspection and rational appraisal of the theory's formal logic and supporting evidence. That sociologists content themselves with such a limited view testifies to their readiness to explain their own behavior in a manner radically different from that by which they explain the behavior of others. It testifies to our readiness to account for our own behavior as if it were shaped solely by a willing conformity to the morality of scientific method.

That sociologists content themselves with such a view testifies to the fact that we have failed to become *aware* of ourselves and to take our own *experience* seriously. For as anyone who has ever dealt with theories knows, some are in fact accepted as convincing and others are rejected as unconvincing, long before the supporting evidence is in hand. Students do this frequently. Some theories are simply experienced, even by experienced sociologists, as *intuitively* convincing; others are not. How does this happen? What makes a theory intuitively convincing?

One reason is that its background assumptions coincide or are compatible with, consensually validate or bring to psychic closure the background assumptions held by the viewer. The theory felt to be intuitively convincing is commonly experienced as *déjà vu*, as something previously known or already suspected. It is congenial because it confirms or complements an assumption already held by the respondent, but an assumption that was seen only dimly by him precisely because it was a "background" assumption. The intuitively convincing theory or concept is one that "sensitizes" the viewer, as Herbert Blumer suggests; but it sensitizes him not merely to some hidden part of the world outside, but also to some hitherto obscured part of the world *inside* himself. We do not know how much of what we now regard as "good" social theory is favored for these reasons. We can be sure, however, that it is a great deal more than those with scientific pretensions assume.

Background assumptions come in different sizes; they govern domains of different scope. They are arranged, one might say, like an inverted cone, standing on its point. At the top are background assumptions with the largest circumference, those that have no limited domain to which alone they apply. These are beliefs about the world that are so general that they may, in principle, be applied to any subject matter without restriction. They are, as Stephen Pepper calls them, "world hypotheses."[2] Being primitive presuppositions about the world and everything in it, they serve to provide the most general of orientations, which enable unfamiliar experiences to be made meaningful. They provide the terms of reference by which the less general assumptions, further down the cone, are themselves limited and influenced. World hypotheses are the most pervasive and primitive beliefs about what is real. They may involve, for example, an inclination to believe that the world and the things in it are "really" *one* or are "truly" *many*. Or, again, they may involve a disposition to believe that the world is "really" highly integrated and cohesive (regardless of whether it is one or many), or only loosely stranded together and dispersive. World hypotheses—the cat may as well be let out of the bag—are what are sometimes called "metaphysics."

Background assumptions of more limited application, for example, about man and society, are what I shall call "domain assumptions." Domain assumptions are the background assumptions applied only to members of a single domain; they are, in effect, the metaphysics of a domain. Domain assumptions about man and society might include, for example, dispositions to believe that men are rational or irrational; that society is precarious or fundamentally stable; that social problems will correct themselves without planned intervention; that human behavior is unpredictable; that man's true humanity resides in his feelings and sentiments. I say that these "might" be examples of domain assumptions made about man and society, because whether they are or not is a matter that can be decided finally only by determining what people, including sociologists, believe about a given domain.

Domain assumptions are of less general application than world hypotheses, although both are background assumptions. We might say that world hypotheses are a special or limiting case of domain assumptions, the case is which no restrictions are applied to the subject matter to which its assumptions refer. Domain assumptions are the things attributed to all members of a domain; in part they are shaped by the thinker's world hypotheses and, in turn, they shape his deliberately wrought theories. They are an aspect of the larger culture that is most intimately related to the postulations of theory. They are also one of the important links between the theorist's work and the larger society.

There are at least two different questions that may be raised about the role of background assumptions, whether world hypotheses or domain assumptions, in social science. One is whether social science must, for logical reasons, rest inescapably on some such assumtpions. Whether social theories *unavoidably* require and must rest *logically* on some background assumptions is a question that simply does not concern me here. It is, I think, an important problem, but one primarily for logicians and philosophers of science. Another question does, however, interest me. This is whether social scientists do, in point of fact, tend to commit themselves to domain assumptions about man and society, with significant consequences for their theory. I think it probable and prudent to assume that they do.

What I am saying, then, is that the work of sociologists, as of others, is influenced by a sub-theoretical set of *beliefs*, for that is what background assumptions are: beliefs about all members of symbolically constituted domains. I am not saying that the work of sociologists should be influenced by background assumptions; this is a problem for methodological moralists. Nor am I saying that sociology logically requires and necessarily rests upon background assumptions; this is a problem for philosophers of science. What I am saying is that sociologists *do* use and are influenced by background assumptions; this is an empirical matter that sociologists themselves can study and confirm.

I think it is in the essential nature of background assumptions that they are not originally adopted for instrumental reasons, the way, for example, one might select a statistical test of significance or pick a screwdriver out of a tool kit. In short, they are not selected with a calculated view to their utility. This is so because they are often internalized in us long before the intellectual age of consent. They are affectively laden cognitive tools that are developed early in the course of our socialization into a particular culture and are built deeply into our character structure. They are therefore likely to change with changes in modal or "social character," to vary with changes in socialization experiences and practices, and therefore to differ with different age or peer groups.

We begin the lifelong process of learning background assumptions while learning our first language, for the language gives us categories that constitute the domains to which the domain assumptions refer. As we learn the categories and the domains that they demarcate, we also acquire a variety of assumptions or beliefs about all members of the domain. In simple truth, all of these domain-constituting categories derive from and function in much the same manner as "stereotypes." Thus, as children are taught the category of Negro, they also learn certain background assumptions—and "prejudices"—about Negroes. Certain *existential* background assumptions are learned about what Negroes presumably *are*, for example, "lazy and shiftless." We also learn *normative* background assumptions, that is, beliefs about their moral value, their goodness or badness. Indeed, normative and existential assumptions are so closely intertwined as to be inseparable, except analytically. In a similar way, we learn linguistic categories such as man, society, group, friend, parent, poor, women; accompanying each of these are background assumptions, dispositions to attribute certain things to all members of the constituted domain. For example, friends are helpful, or will betray you; man is a weak, or a strong, animal; society is powerful, or precarious; the poor are deserving, or undeserving.

The domains that come to be constituted vary with the languages learned and used, and the background assumptions accompanying them vary with the cultures or subcultures in which they are learned and use. To suggest that they operate in much the same manner as racial stereotypes and prejudices entails a set of strong and specifiable assumptions: (1) there is a disposition to believe that there are certain attributes that will be manifested by *all* members of the domain, which (2) is acquired well before the believer has had a personal experience with anything like a true sample of the members of the domain, and perhaps even before he has had any, but which (3) may, nonetheless, entail the strongest feelings about them, (4) shape his subsequent encounters with them, and that (5) are not at all easily shaken or changed, even when these encounters produce experiences discrepant with the assumptions. In short, they are often resistant to "evidence." To say, then, that sociology is shaped by the background assumptions of its practitioners is only to say that they have a human vulnerability to prejudice. These prejudices, however, may be even more difficult to escape than racial prejudice, insofar as they do not manifestly impair the interests of special groups whose struggle against the prejudice may heighten public awareness of it.

It would seem to be one implication of Charles Osgood's work on the "semantic differential" that certain kinds of background assumptions will be made *universally*, about all linguistically constituted domains.[3] For example, they may always be judged in terms of their weakness or strength, their activity or passivity; most importantly, they will always be defined in terms of their "goodness" or "badness." In short, if linguistic categories constitute domains and thus define reality, they inescapably entail an imputation about moral worth and value. As in the realm of physics, where there is no quality without some quantity, so in the social realm, there is no reality without value; the real and the ideal are different dimensions, but they are simultaneously constituted by and inseparably fused in the linguistic categories that constitute social domains.

In brief, to understand the character of Academic Sociology we have to understand the background assumptions, the world hypotheses and domain assumptions, with which it works. These may be inferred from the stipulated social theories with which it operates. The theories thus constitute part but not all of the data by which we can glean a theorist's background assumptions. I say "part but not all" of the data, because theorists leave other tracemarks than their formal publications; they write letters, have conversations, give informal lectures, and take political positions. In short, they do not merely write technical articles; they live in all the revealing ways that other men do. Indeed, they may even submit to interviews.

Background assumptions provide the inherited intellectual "capital" with which a theorist is endowed long before he becomes a theorist, and which he later invests in his intellectual and scientific roles, fusing it to his technical training. Sub-theoretical in character, background assumptions endow the stipulated theory with its appeal, its power, its reach; they establish its maneuver ground for technical development. At some point in this development, however, old background assumptions may come to operate in new conditions, scientifically or socially unsuitable, and thus create an uncomfortable dissonance for the theorist. They then become boundaries which confine and inhibit the theory's further development. When this occurs, it is no small technical rectification that is required; rather, a basic intellectual shift impends. Again, a new generation may arise with new background assumptions, ones that are not resonated congenially by theories based on older assumptions which the young generation feels to be wrong or absurd. It is then we can say that a theory, or the discipline based on it, verges on crisis.

The most basic changes in any science commonly derive not so much from the invention of new research techniques but rather from new ways of looking at data that may have long existed. Indeed, they must neither refer to nor be occasioned by "data," old or new. The most basic changes are in theory and in conceptual schemes, especially those that embody new background assumptions. They are thus changes in the way the world is seen, in what is believed to be real and valuable. To understand the impending crisis in sociology, therefore, it is necessary to understand its dominant intellectual schemes and theories; it is necessary to see the ways in which their background assumptions, by no means new, are being brought to a painful dissonance by new developments in the larger society.

It is an essential element in my theory about sociology that its articulated theories in part derive from, rest on, and are sustained by the usually tacit assumptions that theorists make about the domains with which they concern themselves. Articulate social theory, I shall hold, is in part any extrusion from, and develops in interaction with, the theorist's tacit domain assumptions. Believing this to be the case for other theorists, I shall be obliged at various points in the discussion to present my own domain assumptions, for reasons of candor as well as of consistency.

It is of the essence of domain assumptions that they are intellectually consequential, which is to say, they are theory-shaping, not because they rest on evidence nor even because they are provable; a social domain defined as real is real in its consequences for theory-making. In setting out one's domain assumptions, however, there is considerable danger that one will dissemble precisely because one wants to be "reasonable." One does not want to acknowledge as one's own an assumption for which one can give no "good" reason, and there is a great disposition to adorn or disguise a domain assumption in a reasonable argument, even if that is not the reason one holds it. And it is an almost overpowering temptation, particularly for those sociologists who need to think of themselves as scientists, to present their domain assumptions as if they were empirically substantiated "facts."

Yet the presentation of one's domain assumptions may provide an occasion when the theorist may glimpse whether or not he has a right to believe in them. The point, then, at which the theorist sees the importance of and attempts to present his domain assumptions is an ambiguous moment. It has the contradictory potential of increasing his self-awareness or his self-deception, of disclosing or dissembling, of activating growth-inducing forces or foreclosing the possibilities of basic intellectual development. It may be a fruitful but always is a dangerous moment in the lives of theorists.

Two things are needed to grasp it productively. First, the theorist must recognize that what is at issue here is not only what is in the world but also what is in himself; he must have a capacity to hear his own voice, not simply those of others. Second, he must have the courage of his convictions, or at least courage enough to acknowledge his beliefs as his, whether or not legitimated by reason and evidence. Unless he delivers his domain assumptions from the dim realm of subsidiary awareness into the clearer realm of focal awareness, where they can be held firmly in view, they can never be brought before the bar of reason or submitted to the test of evidence. The theorist lacking in such insight and courage is in the wrong business.

The important thing in setting forth one's domain assumptions is to have the insight to see what one believes and the courage to say what one sees. And since insight and courage are scarce moral resources, the important thing in reading someone else's account of his domain assumptions is to be continually aware that at some point you are going to be deceived.

One of the reasons that domain assumptions have importance as part of the entire sub-theoretical matrix on which theory rests is that they provide foci for feelings, affective states, and sentiments, although they are by no means the only structures around which sentiments come to be organized. To say, for example, that someone "believes" Negroes are lazy and also "believes" this is bad, is not entirely correct. For, those viewing this as "bad" do more than *believe* it; they *feel* it and may indeed feel it strongly. They may have sentiments of disgust and avoidance, or a wish to punish, associated with their assumptions about what the Negro is and with their devaluation of him. Sentiments entail a hormone-eliciting, muscle-tensing, tissue-embedded, fight-or flight disposition of the total organism. While sentiments often may be organized around or elicited by domain assumptions, they are not the same thing. And they may, of course, be organized around or elicited by a great many things other than domain assumptions, for instance, individual persons or concrete situations.

Furthermore, people may have sentiments that are not conventionally called for by the domain assumptions that they have learned, but they are not for that reason any the less powerful and body-gripping. There may, in brief, be various forms of dissonance between the existential and normative beliefs that people learn in connection with domain-constituting categories, and the sentiments that they feel toward members of that category. Thus, for instance, a white woman may *feel* sexually aroused and attracted to a black man, even though she also believes that blacks are "dirty" and "disgusting." A man may *feel* pessimistic and despairing, resigned and quiescent, even though he also believes that men are good and that society progresses, simply because he himself is ill or aging. Correspondingly, a man may, when young, feel optimistic and energetically activistic, even though he may believe that the world is on a collision course with disaster and that there is little that can be done about it.

I am, of course, not suggesting that young men are invariably more optimistic than old ones, but what I am intimating, using age only as an example, is that people may feel things at variance with their domain assumptions, with their existential beliefs or normative values; feelings emerge from people's experience with the world, during which they often come to need and learn things that are somewhat different from what they are supposed to need or were deliberately taught to learn. If Freud and other psychologists are right about the Oedipal Complex, many men in Western societies feel hostility toward their fathers even though they have never been taught to do so, and in fact have been taught to love and honor them. In short, men may have feelings at variance with those of their culturally prescribed "languages" that is, with the domain assumptions conventional to their group of society. Such sentiments may be idiosyncratic to an individual and derive from his unique experience, or they may be shared by large numbers and derive from an experience common to them, even if not culturally prescribed for them. Thus, at least since about the early nineteenth century, many young people in Western countries seem to be subjected to a common experience that induces them to be somewhat more anti-authoritarian, rebellious, or critical of the political and cultural status quo than were their elders.

The prescribed domain assumptions, then, are one thing; the sentiments men have may be quite another. When they diverge, when the things men feel are at variance with their domain assumptions, there is a dissonance or tension between the two levels. Sometimes this is dealt with simply by giving ritualistic "lip service" to the domain assumptions required and taught in the culture; sometimes men may openly rebel against them, adopting or seeking new domain assumptions more consonant with the feelings they actually have. But there is likely to be an intrinsic difficulty in such an open and active rebellion: first, unless there are already alternatives formulated, men may find it easier to live with the old uncomfortable assumptions than with none at all; second, men often experience their own deviant feelings as "wrong" and as perilous to their own security, and consequently may conceal their unprescribed feelings even from themselves; third, as a consequence of this, they may not openly communicate their deviant feelings to others who might share and therefore encourage and support them.

In consequence, then, when a gap opens between the sentiments men feel and the domain assumptions they have been taught, their most immediate response may be to suppress or privatize the experienced dissonance. They may allow the tension to fester; or they may begin a kind of sporadic, cultural, guerrilla warfare against the prevailing domain assumptions, in which their dissatisfaction is intermittently expressed in squeaks of black humor or by an inertial apathy. This situation, very much like the attitude of some young radicals today toward academic sociology, begins to change importantly when domain categories and assumptions emerge that are more consonant with what people feel. When resistance to established assumptions lacks alternatives, it may at first be manifested socially among those who, while lacking a new language, do nonetheless recognize their common possession of deviant sentiments, and therefore may enter into informal solidarities with one another against those who they commonly feel share other sentiments. The current "generation gap" seems a case in point. When, however, the new sentiments begin to find or create their own appropriate language, the possibilities of larger solidarities and of rational public discussion are extended.

It is in part because social theories are shaped by and express domain assumptions that they are also sentiment-relevant: reactions to social theories involve the sentiments of the men who read and write them. Whether a theory is accepted or rejected, whether it undergoes change or remains essentially unchanged, is not simply a cerebral decision; it is in some part contingent upon the gratifications or tensions that it generates by dint of its relation to the sentiments of those involved. Social theories may be sentiment-relevant in various ways and to varying degrees may inhibit or arouse the expression of certain sentiments. As a limiting case, the degree to which they impinge upon sentiments may be so small that, for all practical purposes, they may be said to be "neutral" in their sentiment-relevance. Yet even this last case is consequential for reactions to the theory, for the sentiment-neutral theory may simply be eliciting apathetic or disinterested responses, the feeling that the theory is somehow "irrelevant," and thus induce avoidance of, if not active opposition to, it. Moreover, reactions to a social theory may also depend upon the *kinds* of sentiments that are aroused directly or by association. The activation of particular sentiments may at some times and for some people be enjoyable, or it may be discomfiting and painful.

Max Weber's theory of bureaucracy, for example, stressing, as it does, the inevitable proliferation of bureaucratic forms in the increasingly large and complex modern social organizations, tends to elicit and resonate sentiments of pessimism concerning the possibilities of large-scale social change that could successfully remedy human alienation. Those committed to efforts at such change will experience such sentiments as dissonant and may therefore react critically to the theory, attempting to change it in ways that strip it of such consequences, or they may reject it altogether. Conversely, those who never had—or who once had but then relinquished—aspirations for social change, or whose inclination is to seek limited intra-system reforms, may for their part not experience the Weberian theory as inducing an unpleasant pessimism.

In one case, then, a theory may have a coherence-inducing or integrating effect, while in another it may have a tension- or conflict-inducing effect; each has different consequences for the individual's ability to pursue certain courses of *action* in the world and has different implications for different lines of political conduct. It is thus through its sentiment-relevance as well as through its domain assumptions that a social theory takes on political meanings and implications quite apart from whether these were knowingly intended or recognized by either those who formulated or those who accepted it. In the example mentioned above, concerning Weber's theory of bureaucracy, it is commonly understood that the theory has strongly anti-socialist implications, for it implies that change toward socialism will not prevent bureaucratization and alienation.

Personal Reality and Social Theory

If every social theory is thus a tacit theory of politics, every theory is also a personal theory, inevitably expressing, coping, and infused with the personal experience of the individuals who author it. Every social theory has both political and personal relevance, which, according to the technical canons of social theory, it is not supposed to have. Consequently, both the man and his politics are commonly screened out in what is deemed the proper presentation of presumably "autonomous" social theory.

Yet, however disguised, an appreciable part of any sociological enterprise devolves from the sociologist's effort to explore, to objectify, and to universalize some of his own most deeply personal experiences. Much of any man's effort to know the social world around him is prompted by an effort, more or less disguised or deliberate, to know things that are personally important to him; which is to say, he aims at knowing himself and the experiences he has had in his social world (his relationship to it), and at *changing* this relationship in some manner. Like it or not, and know it or not, in confronting the social world the theorist is also confronting himself. While this has no bearing on the validity of the resultant theory, it does bear on another legitimate interest: the sources, the motives, and the aims of the sociological quest.

Whatever their other differences, all sociologists seek to study something in the social world that they take to be real; and, whatever their philosophy of science, they seek to explain it in terms of something that they *feel* to be real. Like other men, sociologists impute reality to certain things in their social world. This is to say, they believe, sometimes with focal and sometimes only with subsidiary awareness, that certain things are truly attributable to the social world. In important part, their conception of what is "real" derives from the domain assumptions they have learned in their culture. These culturally standardized assumptions are, however, differentiated by personal experience in different parts of the social structure. Individually accented by particular sentiment-generating experiences, the common domain assumptions in time assume personal arrangements; they become part of a man's personal reality.

For simplicity's sake, I suggest that there are two kinds of "reality" with which sociologists must come to terms. One consists of "role realities," the things they learn as sociologists; these include what they believe to be the "facts" yielded by previous researchers, whether conducted by themselves or others. The "facts," of course, entail imputations made by men about the world. To assign factuality to some imputation about the world is also to express a personal conviction about its truth, as well as about the propriety of the process by which it was made. To believe an imputation to be "factual" is to assign a high value to it, setting it above such things as "opinions" or "prejudices."

Inevitably, to assign factuality to an imputation is to make it an anchor point in the self's relation to the world, to make it or claim it should be central to the self. To assign factuality to an imputation is to invoke an obligation and duty upon the self: one must "take the facts into account" under certain conditions. There is the further obligation to inspect severely and to examine critically (in short to defend against) attacks on one's "factual" beliefs; a denial of beliefs previously thought to be factual is thus a self-mobilizing "challenge." Within scientific communities, therefore, men engage in committed personal efforts—through contest, conflict, struggle, and negotiation—to establish and maintain the facts. The facts are not automatically produced by the impersonal machinery of research. To assign factuality to a belief is a self-involving commitment; the person makes a claim upon the credence of another, or himself lends credence to the claim of another. In these and other ways, the factual becomes part of the sociologist's personal reality.

In particular those imputations that a sociologist makes about the factuality of beliefs based on research tend to become aspects of his reality, part of his *focal awareness* as a *sociologist*. Deemed relevant to his work as a sociologist and derived in accordance with methodological decorum, the sociologist commonly feels that he may with propriety publicly endorse such beliefs. Indeed, these *must* explicitly be attended to by him under certain conditions. In short, he must not ignore them, and he need not conceal his belief in them.

A second order of conceptions about reality held by sociologists consists of the "personally real." These are imputations about "realities" in the social world that sociologists make, not because of "evidence" or "research," but simply because of what they have seen, heard, been told, or read. While these beliefs differ from "facts" systematically gathered and scientifically evaluated, the sociologist nonetheless *experiences* them as no less real—and it is well for his sanity that he does. Still, while these are every bit as real to him as facts garnered through research, if not more so, the sociologist *qua* sociologist is not supposed to credit or attend to them in the same way that he treats "facts"; indeed, he may feel obliged as a sociologist to subject them to systematic doubt. Imputations about the world that are part of the sociologist's *personal* reality may therefore sink into his subsidiary awareness rather than remaining consciously available to him, when he acts as a conforming sociologist. But this, of course, is very far from saying that they thereby cease to have consequences for his work as a sociologist or social theorist. In practice, the sociologist's role realities and his personal realities interpenetrate and mutually influence one another.

During the 1940s and 1950s, largely under the influence of Talcott Parsons, many sociologists stressed the importance of theory in structuring research. Starting from the commonplace that sociologists did not view all parts of the social world as equally important, but rather focused their attention upon it selectively, they concluded that this perceptual organization was largely the result of the "theories," tacit or explicit, which were held. "Facts" were thus seen as the product of an effort to pursue the inferences of theories and, indeed, as being constituted by the conceptual schemes embedded in the theories. Facts were seen, at least primarily, as interacting with theories, confirming or disproving them, and thus as cumulatively shaping theoretical development; perceptual selectivity, and hence the focus of research, was largely accounted for in terms of the sociologist's theoretical commitment.

This emphasis tended to deprecate the earlier tradition of methodological empiricism, which had stressed the primary value of data and research. If the empiricists had stressed that sociologists are or should be guided by the facts yielded by properly conducted research, theory-stressing sociologists tended to reply that sociologists are or should be guided by articulate, explicit, and hence testable theory. From the standpoint presented here, however, both seem to have been at least partially mistaken.

Those who emphasized theory tended unduly to deprecate the self-implicating, perception-anchoring, and stabilizing role of "facts" (as distinct from their validity-testing function); the empiricists tended to miss the importance of previously held theoretical assumptions. Both, in addition, made a common error in limiting themselves to only one order of the imputably real, namely, the "factual." What both missed is that scientific factuality is only a special case of a larger set of beliefs, those imputing reality; both failed to see that whether an aspect of "role reality" or "personal reality," the imputably real has a special force in structuring the perception of the sociologist and shaping his subsequent theorizing and research. The theorists in particular failed to see the importance of the sub-theoretical level, including the "personally real," as consequential for theory and research. A situation defined as real is real in its consequences, for sociologists as for other men.

Whether part of his role reality or his personal reality, things to which the sociologist imputes reality play a role in his work in several ways. They may be elements that he is concerned to explain, in short, as "dependent variables" or effects; they may be part of his explanatory effort, serving as "independent variables" or possible "causes"; or, again, they may be used as explicit models or tacit paradigms that he employs to clarify the nature of what he wants to explain or the factors that explain it.

To amplify the latter point: the imputably real enters importantly into theory construction by being regarded as possessed of *generalizable* significance, by being treated as an example or case of, or a model or paradigm of, a larger set of things. Sociologists assume that things they have researched or with which they have otherwise become personally acquainted and hence "know," are like (and may be used to understand) other things with which they are unacquainted at first hand or have not yet researched. Thus, while aiming to account for a set of events that extend beyond the sociologist's facts or personal realities, social theories are at the same time also influenced by his prior imputations about what is real in the world, whether these are his facts or personal realities. For example, Max Weber's general theory of bureaucracy was influenced both by his historical, scholarly researches and by his first-hand acquaintance with German bureaucracy and, in particular, with governmental rather than private bureaucracy. The German governmental bureauc-

337

racy, both as experienced social structure and as cultural ideal, constituted for Weber a personal reality that served as his central paradigm for all bureaucracies; it provided a framework for organizing and assimilating the facts yielded by his scholarly researches.

If personal reality shapes scholarly research, scholarly research is also a source of personal reality, not only of role reality. A man's research or work is commonly more than just a way he spends time: it is often a vital part of his life and a central part of the experience that shapes his personal reality. If this were not so, then all relevant research would be equally significant to a sociologist. But the truth is that researchers and discoveries made by the scholar himself have a special importance for him; a man's own researches become a part of his personal reality in ways that the work of his colleagues usually does not. If nothing else, they become personal commitments that he wishes to defend.

The limited parts of the social world with which a sociologist's research bring him into contact are endowed with a compelling reality precisely because they are part of his personal experience. Limited though they are, they often come to be used as paradigms for other, unknown parts, and serve as the basis for generalizing about larger wholes. Thus, for example, *one* reason Malinowski's theory of magic differed from that of A. R. Radcliffe-Brown was because the different kinds of magic each had first closely studied came to stand for all other kinds of magic. Although Malinowski had focused on work- and subsistence-getting magic, and Radcliffe-Brown on childbirth magic, each treated his limited experience as a paradigm, exemplary of and essentially akin to other kinds of magic. Evidence incorporated into personal experience became part of a permeating personal reality to which the larger world was assimilated and by which it was shaped.

Sociologists, of course, are familiar with these dangers, at least *en principe*, and they seek to use systematic sampling as a way of obviating them. Nonetheless, systematic sampling cannot fully avoid the problem, for it provides a basis for testing a theory only subsequent to its formulation. Disciplined research entails the use of a systematic sample in order to test inferences from a theory, but, in the nature of the case, the theory must be formulated prior to the sample. Indeed, the more the sociologist stresses the importance of articulate theory, the more this is likely to be the case. The theory will therefore tend to revolve around, and consequently be shaped by, the limited facts and personal realities available to the theorist, and *in particular by those imputed realities that he treats as paradigms*.

Systematic sampling serves primarily as a restraint on unjustified generalization from "facts"; but it does not similarly restrain the influence of "personal realities." Since the latter commonly remains only at the fringes of subsidiary awareness, being deemed scientifically irrelevant, it is often (and mistakenly) assumed that it is scientifically inconsequential. In point of fact, the personally real and problematic often enough becomes the starting point for systematic inquiry—and, indeed, there is no scientific reason this should not be so.

What is personally real to men is real, frequently though not always, primarily because it is not unique to them—in the sense of idiosyncratic to, or uniquely different for, then—but rather is socially and collectively true. Since the sense of the reality of things often depends on mutual agreement or consensual validation, collectively held notions of reality are among the most firmly constituted components of an individual's personal reality. Yet the personally real does not entirely consist of or derive from collective definitions of social reality. It may also emerge from recurrent personal experience, whether unique to the person or shared with a few others. What becomes personally real to one individual, then, need not be personally real to others. But whether derived from collective definitions or from recurrent personal experiences, a man believes that some things are real; and these imputed realities are of special importance to the kinds of theories that he formulates, even if he happens to be a sociologist.

The Infrastructure of Social Theory

From this perspective all social theory is immersed in a subtheoretical level of domain assumptions and sentiments which both liberate and constrain it. This sub-theoretical level is shaped by and shared with the larger culture and society, at least to some extent, as well as being individually organized, accented, differentiated, and changed by personal experience in the world. I call this sub-theoretical level the "infrastructure" of theory.

This infrastructure is important not because it is the ultimate determinant of the character of social theory, but because it is part of the most immediate, local surround from which the theory-work eventuates in theory-performances and theory-products. Theory-work is surely linked to, even if not solely determined by, the character of the theorist doing it. This infrastructure can never really be left behind, even in the most isolated and lonely moments of theory-work, when a man finally puts pen to paper in a room where there is no one but himself. The world is, of course, there in the room with him, in him; he has not escaped it. But it is not *the* world, not *the* society and *the* culture that is there with him, but *his* limited version and partial experience of it.

However individual a work of theory is, nonetheless, some (and perhaps much) of its individuality is conventional in character. The individuality of theory-work is, in part, a socially sanctioned illusion. For there are the assistants who have helped the theorist do his research and writing; there are the colleagues and the students, the friends and the lovers, on whom he has informally "tested" his ideas; there are those from whom he has learned and taken and those whom he opposes. All theory is not merely influenced but actually produced by a group. Behind each theory-product is not only the author whose name appears upon the work, but an entire shadow group for whom, we might say, the "author" is the emblem; in a way, the author's name serves as the name of an intellectual team.

Yet the "author" is not merely the puppet of these group forces, because to some extent he selects his team, recruits members of and eliminates them from his theory-working group, responds selectively to the things they suggest and the criticisms thay make, accepting some and ignoring others, attending to some more closely than others. Thus, while authorship is always in some measure conventional, it is also in some measure the expression of the real activities and initiatives of an individual theorist whose "infrastructure" helps shape both the ideas and the shadow group whose tacit collaboration eventuates in theoretical performances.

A concern with sub-theory or the infrastructure of theory is not the expression of an inclination to psychologize theory and is certainly not a form of psychological reductionism. It is, rather, the outcome of a concern for empirical realism, an effort to come close to the human systems to which any theoretical work is most visibly and intimately linked. It is an effort that is peculiarly necessary for those working within a sociological tradition that tends to obscure and to cast doubt upon the importance and reality of persons, and to view them as the creatures of grander social structures. For those, such as myself, who have lived within a sociological tradition, the importance of the larger social structures and historical processes is not in doubt. What is intellectually in question, when the significance of theoretical infrastructure is raised, is the analytic means by which we may move between persons and social structures, between society and the local, more narrowly bounded environments from which social theory discernibly derives. My own view is that any sociological explanation or generalization implies (at least tacitly) certain psychological assumptions; correspondingly, any psychological generalization tacitly implies certain sociological conditions. In directing attention to the importance of the theoretical infrastructure, I have sought not to psychologize social theory and remove it from the larger social system, but rather to specify the analytic means by which I hope to *link it more firmly* with the larger social world.

Theoretical Infrastructure and Ideology

Rooted in a limited personal reality, resonating some sentiments but not others, and embedded in certain domain assumptions, every social theory facilitates the pursuit of some but not of all courses of *action*, and thus encourages us to change or to accept the world as it is, to say yea or nay to it. In a way, every theory is a discreet obituary or celebration for some social system.

The sentiments resonated by a social theory provide an immediate but privatized mood, an experience that inhibits or fosters anticipated courses of public and political conduct, and thus may exacerbate or resolve internal uncertainties or conflicts about the possibilities of successful outcomes. Similarly, domain assumptions entail beliefs about what is real in the world and thus have implications about what it is possible to *do*, to *change* in the world; the values they entail indicate what courses of action are desirable and thus shape conduct. In this sense, every theory and every theorist ideologizes social reality.

The ideologizing of sociology is not an archaism manifested only by long-dead "founding fathers" but absent from more truly modern sociologists. Indeed, it is fully manifest in the school of thought that has been most insistent on the importance of professionalizing sociology and of maintaining its intellectual autonomy, namely, that developed by Talcott Parsons. This may be noted even in a recent collection of essays on *American Sociology*, edited by Parsons in 1968.[5] The dominant mood of this volume, published in the midst of the ongoing war in Vietnam and written during a period when hostilities between the black and white communities in American cities had reached the point of recurrent summer violence and rioting, was, despite this, one of self-congratulatory celebration.

One convenience of this volume is that, being intended for popular consumption—indeed, originally prepared for the Voice of America broadcasts—its essays are swathed in fewer layers of gauzy jargon. One can more readily see the domain assumptions on which they rest, the sentiments that they resonate, the politics they imply. S. M. Lipset, in his essay, for example, remarks that "basic structural changes while maintaining traditional legitimacy in political institutions would appear to be the best way to avoid political tensions."[6] But is the avoidance of political tensions always best, for whom? If I can fathom Mr. Lipset's meaning here, he is saying that political stability would be achieved if efforts at social change prudently stopped short of changing established ways of allocating and justifying power. I doubt this, for it seems to me that the clinging to established legitimations of political power is one of the ways in whch elites seek to block all other "basic structural changes." Moreover, what of countries where political legitimacy itself is based on revolution? One also wonders whether Lipset would apply his assumptions about continuity to Soviet Russia and tell Soviet liberals that they too should adapt their reform impulses to their nation's traditional mode of legitimating political power, thus maintaining its autocratic political traditions. Politically, Lipset's argument is the classical conservative brief against abrupt tensionful change which might disrupt legitimacy, continuity, and gradualism.

The self-congratulatory tone of this volume is raised to patriotic pitch when Mr. Lipset argues that exceptional grace was bestowed on American society when George Washington, for reasons unexplained, refused the crown. This triumphal theme is carried forward by Albert Cohen, who implicitly answers those who call America a sick society by maintaining that, to the contrary, "the United States is a dynamic, growing, prosperous, more or less democratic society."[7] The celebration continues: Thomas Pettigrew recounts the story of black progress in the United States, where, he holds, "one out of every three Negro Americans today can be sociologically classified . . . as middle class."[8] He reassures us that racial violence today, far from being a symptom of societal malaise, is, to the contrary, proof of the "rapid social progress taking place."[9] "Rapid" from whose standpoint?

Reinhard Bendix also assures us that, in modern society, the words "ruler" and "ruled" no longer have "clear meaning."[10] Presumably this is so, because the people now exercise "control through periodic elections . . . [and] the fact that every adult has the vote is a token of the regard in which he is held as an individual and a citizen."[11] The franchise, Bendix tells us, has been "extended." One wonders if that is how the matter would be put by those who were arrested, beaten, and killed in the struggle during the 1960s to enfranchise blacks in the American South: would *they* see what had happened as an "extension" of the franchise?

In all this, a very selective, one-sided picture of American society is made persuasive by a number of techniques. One is to call the partly filled glass of water half-filled, rather than half-empty; for example, American blacks are described as one-third middle class, rather than as two-thirds miserable. There is also the strategy of the Great Omission. In this volume there is scarcely anything about war, not an echo of the new revisionist historiography; indeed, the word "imperialism" does not appear in the book's index, and there is nothing about the relation between democracy, affluence, and war. Furthermore, we may note how myths are woven into the total view of social reality, deeply but invisibly, by the entire structure of language and conceptualization. When, for instance, the bloody struggle to register blacks in the South is rendered as the mechanical "extension" of the franchise, a much larger view of social change and of men is implicitly communicated.

Methodology as Ideology

Domain assumptions concerning man and society are built not only into substantive social theory but into methodology itself. Charles Tilly's essay on urbanization, in Parsons' volume, presents an interesting case of the latter, revealing the manner in which research methods predicate domain assumptions and how, at the same time, these methods generate dispositions of political relevance. "No country," complains Tilly, "has a social accounting system allowing the quick, reliable detection of changes in organizational membership, kinship organization, religious adherence, or even occupational mobility."[12] From Tilly's standpoint as a research-oriented sociologist, this is a bad thing. Yet what kind of country would it be that would have such a relentless, "quick, reliable" all-embracing system of information about its population? Surely it would be a nation in which the potentialities (at least) for the most complete totalitarianism were at hand. Undoubtedly Tilly would reject such a society as quickly as I. Yet he and many other sociologists fail to see that the conventional methodologies of social research often premise and foster a deep-going authoritarianism, a readiness to lie to and manipulate people: they betray a bureaucratic numbness.

As Chris Argyris has put it (but not in Parsons' *American Sociology*) conformity to "rigorous research criteria would create a world for the subject in which his behavior is defined, controlled, evaluated, manipulated, and reported to a degree that is comparable to the behavior of workers in the most mechanized assembly-line conditions." Stated otherwise, information-gathering systems or research methods always premise the existence and use of some system of social control. It is not only that the information they yield may be used *by* systems of social control, but that they themselves *are* systems of control.

Every research method makes some assumptions about how information may be secured from people and what may be done with people, or to them, in order to secure it; this, in turn, rests on certain domain assumptions concerning *who and what people are.* To the degree that the social sciences are modeled on the physical sciences, they entail the domain assumption that people are "things" which may be treated and controlled in much the same manner that other sciences control their nonhuman materials: people are "subjects" which may be subjected to the control of the experimenter for purposes they need not understand or even consent to. Such social science will thoughtlessly drift into buying increments of information at the cost of human autonomy and dignity.

When viewed from one standpoint, "methodology" seems a purely technical concern devoid of ideology; presumably it deals only with methods of extracting reliable information from the world, collecting data, constructing questionnaires, sampling, and analyzing returns. Yet it is always a good deal more than that, for it is commonly infused with ideologically resonant assumptions about what the social world is, who the sociologist is, and what the nature of the relation between them is.

The Autonomy of Social Structure as Domain Assumption

It is not only in its basic methodological conceptions, however, that sociology is embedded in domain assumptions having ideological resonance, but also in its most fundamental conceptions of what its subject matter is and what the characteristics are of the distinctive domains it studies. For example, in Peter Blau's contribution to Parsons' *American Sociology*, there is the conventional but unexamined assumption that, "once firmly organized," an organization tends to assume an identity of its own which makes it independent of the people who have founded it or of those who constitute its membership."[13] Although flatly asserted as fact, Blau's statement is, being a characterization of *all* formal organizations, clearly a domain assumption. The evidence that would allow *all* formal organizations to be thus characterized is trivial in comparison to the scope of the generalization. But there is nothing novel in this; it is the common way of men with domain assumptions.

Whether Blau's statement is actually a fact or only a domain assumption parading as one, there is still a consequential choice of how to view it. It makes a substantial difference whether one views the autonomy or alienation of social structures from people as a normal condition to be accepted or as an endemic and recurrent disease to be opposed. It is inherent in the very occupational ideology of many modern sociologists, faced as they are with the professional task of distinguishing their own from competing academic disciplines, not only to stress the potency and autonomy of social structures—and therefore the dependence of persons—but also to accept this as normal, rather than asking: Under what conditions does it occur? Are there not differences in the degree to which social structures get out of hand and live independently of their members? What accounts for these differences?

In short, then, from the substantive domain assumption that human beings are the raw materials of independent social structures, to the methodological domain assumption that men may be treated and studied like other "things," there is a repressive technocratic current in sociology and the other social sciences, as well as in the general society. It is a current that has great social importance because it congenially resonates the sentiments of any modern elite in bureaucratized societies who view social problems in terms of technological paradigms, as a kind of engineering task.

The domain assumptions of sociological analysis are embedded in—both expressed and concealed by—its most central programmatic concepts, its most elemental vision of "society" and "culture." The *focal* implications of these concepts stress the manner in which men are shaped and influenced by their groups and group heritage. Yet since the social sciences emerged in the secularized world of the "self-made" bourgeoisie that surfaced after the French Revolution in nineteenth-century Europe, these concepts also tacitly imply that man *makes* his own societies and cultures. They imply the potency of man. But this vision of the potency of man, in contrast to that of society and culture, tends to be confined to the merely subsidiary attention of Academic Sociology rather than to its focal concerns.

Academic Sociology's emphasis on the potency of society and the subordination of men to it is itself an historical product that contains an historical truth. The modern concepts of society and of culture arose in a social world that, following the French Revolution, men could believe they themselves had made. They could see that it was through their struggles that kings had been overthrown and an ancient religion disestablished. Yet at the same time men could also see that this was a world out of control, not amenable to men's designs. It was therefore a grotesque, contradictory world: a world made by men but, despite this, not *their* world.

No thinker better grasped this paradoxical character of the new social world than Rousseau. It was central to his conception that man was corrupted by the very advance of the arts and sciences, that he had lost something vital in the very midst of his highest achievements. This paradoxical vision also underlies his conception of man as born free but now living everywhere in chains: man creates society through a willing contract but must then subject himself to his own creation.

Culture and society thus emerged as ambiguous conceptions, as being man's own creations but also having lives and histories of their own. It is precisely this ambiguity to which the central conceptions of sociological analysis, "culture" and "society," give continued expression. Both culture and society are seen, in sociological analysis, as having a life apart from the men who create, embody, and enact them. The concepts of culture and society tacitly predicate that men have created a social world from which they have been alienated. The germinal concepts of the social sciences, then, are imprinted with the birth trauma of a social world from which men saw themselves alienated from their own creations; in which men felt themselves to be at once newly potent and tragically impotent. The emerging academic social sciences thus commonly came to conceive of society and culture as *autonomous* things: things that are independent and exist for themselves. Society and culture were then amenable to being viewed like any other "natural" phenomena, as having laws of their own that operated quite apart from the intentions and plans of men, while the disciplines that studied them could be viewed as natural sciences like any other. Method, then, follows domain assumption. In other words, sociology emerged as a "natural" science when certain domain assumptions and sentiments became prevalent: when men felt alienated from a society that they thought they had made but could not control. Whereas European men had once expressed their estrangement from themselves in terms of traditional religion and metaphysics, they now began to do so through academic social science, and scientism became, in this way, a modern substitute for a decaying traditional religion.

The concepts of society and culture, which are at the very foundation of the academic social sciences, are in part based upon a reaction to an historical defeat: man's failure to possess the social world that he created. To that extent, the academic social sciences are the social sciences of an alienated age and alienated man. From this standpoint the possibility of "objectivity" in, and the call to "objectivity" by, the academic social sciences has a rather different meaning than that conventionally assigned. The "objectivity" of the social sciences is not the expression of a dispassionate and detached view of the social world; it is, rather, an ambivalent effort to accommodate to alienation *and* to express a muted resentment of it.

In one part, then, the dominant expressions of the academic social sciences embody an accommodation to the alienation of men in contemporary society, rather than a determined effort to transcend it. The core concepts of society and culture, as held by the social sciences, entail the view that their autonomy and uncontrollability are a normal and natural condition, rather than intrinsically a kind of pathology. It is this assumption that is at the heart of the *repressive* component of sociology.

At the same time, however, the social sciences' accommodation to alienation is an ambivalent and resentful one. It is in this muted resentment that there is the suppressed *liberative* potential of sociology. And it is this total conception of man—the dominant focal view of him as the controlled product of society and culture, combined with the subsidiary conception of man as the maker of society and culture—that shapes the unique contradiction distinctive of sociology.

It is not simply that one or another "school" of sociology embodies these contradictory domain assumptions about men and society, but that these dwell in the basic charter of Academic Sociology as a discipline. These assumptions resonate certain sentiments about the grotesqueness of the social world that began to emerge during the nineteenth century, and they are rooted in a contradictory personal reality widely shared by men who, then as now, felt that they were somehow living in a world that they made but did not control.

The Contradiction of Autonomy

When sociologists stress the autonomy of sociology—that it should (and, therefore, that it can) be pursued entirely in terms of its own standards, free of the influences of the surrounding society—they are giving testimony of their loyalty to the rational credo of their profession. At the same time, however, they are also contradicting themselves as sociologists, for surely the strongest general assumption of sociology is that men are shaped in countless ways by the press of their social surround. Looked at with bland innocence, then, the sociologists' claim to autonomy entails a contradiction between the claims of sociology and the claims of reason and "profession."

In large measure, this contradiction is hidden, in daily practice, by sociologists who premise a dualistic reality in which their own behavior is tacitly held to be different from the behavior of those they study. It is hidden by employing the focal sociological assumption, that men are shaped by culture and social structure, when sociologists study *others*, yet tacitly employing the assumption that men make their own cultures, when sociologists think about *themselves*. The *operating* premise of the sociologist claiming autonomy for his discipline is that he is free from the very social pressures whose importance he affirms when thinking about other men. In effect, the sociologist conjugates his basic domain assumptions by saying: *they* are bound by society; *I* am free of it.

The sociologist thus resolves his contradictory assumptions by splitting them and applying each to different persons or groups: one for himself and his peers, another for his "subjects." Implicit in such a split is an image of self and other, in which the two are assumed to be deeply different and thus to be differentially evaluated, the "self" tacitly viewed as a kind of elite, the "other" as a kind of mass.

One reason for this split is that the focal sociological assumption about the governing influence of the social surround violates the sociologist's own sense of personal reality. He, after all, *knows* with direct inner certainty that his own behavior is *not* socially determined; but the freedom of the others whom he studies is an aspect only of their personal reality, not of his own. When he premises that their behavior is socially determined, the sociologist is not violating *his* sense of personal reality, but only *theirs*.

The methodological dualism by which the sociologist keeps two sets of books, one for the study of "laymen" and another when he thinks about himself, evidences one of the most profound ways in which the sociologist's personal reality shapes his methodological and theoretical practice. It cannot be stressed too strongly that in everyday practice the sociologist believes himself capable of making hundreds of purely rational decisions—the choice of research problems, sites, question formulations, statistical tests, or sampling methods. He thinks of these as free technical decisions and of himself as acting in autonomous conformity with technical standards, rather than as a creature molded by social structure and culture. If he finds he has gone wrong, he thinks of himself as having made a "mistake." A "mistake" is an outcome produced not by any social necessity, but by a corrigible ignorance, a lack of careful thought or rigorous training, a hasty assessment.

When this inconsistency is called to the sociologist's attention, he will acknowledge that his behavior, too, is influenced by social forces. He will acknowledge, for example, that there is or can be such a thing as a sociology of knowledge or a sociology of sociology, in which even the sociologist's own behavior may be shown to be socially influenced. But such acknowledgments are usually made *en principe*; they are begrudging concessions; they are formally acknowledged for reasons of consistency; but, not being consistent with his own feelings of freedom and personal reality, they are not deeply convincing to the sociologist. In short, they are not really an operating part of his normal way of thinking about his own everyday work.

Another way in which this inconsistency is maintained is through the use of "self-obscuring" methodologies. That is, they obscure the sociologist from himself. The more prestigious and "high science" these methodologies are, the less likely it is that the sociologist will recognize himself as implicated in his research or will see his findings as having implications about himself. Not being constrained to see his research as having a bearing upon his own life, he can more readily maintain a different set of assumptions concerning it.

More specifically, a high science methodology tends to distill the complexity of social situations into a search for the effects of a few highly formalized and specially defined "variables," whose presence often cannot be gauged by direct inspection but requires special instruments employed under special conditions. Thus the "variables" sociologists study often do not exist for laymen; they are not what laymen see when they look about themselves. High science methodologies, in effect, create a gap between what the sociologist as sociologist deals with and what he (like others) confronts as an ordinary person, experiencing his *own* existence. Thus even when he undertakes studies in the sociology of knowledge, exploring, say, the effects of "class position," "reference groups," or "income levels" on intellectual activities, it is easy for him to feel that he is talking about someone else, perhaps some other sociologist, not about himself and his own life.

It is a function of high science methodologies to widen the gap between what the sociologist is studying and his own personal reality. Even if one were to assume that this serves to fortify objectivity and reduce bias, it seems likely that it has been bought at the price of the dimming of the sociologist's self-awareness. In other words, it seems that, at some point, the formula is: the more rigorous the methodology, the more dimwitted the sociologist; the more reliable his information about the social world, the less insightful his knowledge about himself.

A concern with the problem of the sociologist's autonomy clearly must confront the manifold ways in which the sociologist's own social surround affects his work. But if we do not talk about this in ways enabling the sociologist to recognize this surround as his own, he will never recognize himself in it. When, however, an exploration of this problem is informed by a sensitivity to the importance of the sociologist's personal reality, it can then lead him to a view of "society," not as exotic and external to him, but as his familiar practice and mundane experience. A concern with his personal reality leads to an insistence on the unusual importance of the most mundane experience for the sociologist. It can lead to a concern with the recognizable *texture* of his experienced situation rather than with only a few sifted-out, technically defined 'variables." Awareness of textured reality enables "variables" to be seen as *self*-experience and allows them to be mobilized for self-understanding. The sociologist is not what he eats; but the sociologist is what he sees, does, and wants every day, in all his activities, morning, noon, and night, whether as sociologist or not. To understand him and his personal reality we must see how he lives as well as how he works.

To take a few singular examples: some sociologists I know conceive of themselves as gentlemen-professors. They invest considerable energies not merely in their work but in their total style of life. One I know starts his day by breakfasting in his luxury apartment, and then, donning his smoking jacket, returns to bed where he reads or writes in presumably unruffled serenity until noon, when, as is his unvarying habit, he goes to the university. To indicate that matters cannot be simplified, I should also add that he holds relatively radical views about the value of peasant revolutions. Still other sociologists I know are gentlemen-farmers and gentlemen-ranchers. Most live suburban existences; not a few have summer homes; many do extensive traveling. Most of the sociologists I know seem to have little interest in "culture" and are rarely in evidence at galleries, concerts, or plays.

Like other men, sociologists also have sexual lives, and "even this" may be intellectually consequential. In loyalty tinged with bitterness, most stick it out to the end with the wives who saw them through graduate school, while others practice serial polygamy. And a few are hidden homosexuals, often tensely preoccupied by the dangers of self-disclosure in a "straight" world. My point is not that this is especially important, but that even this remote sexual dimension of existence reaches into and is linked with the sociologist's world of work. For example, it is my strong but undocumented impression that when some sociologists change their work interests, problems, or styles, they also change mistresses or wives. Again, and while I do not know why it is so, I also believe that some well-known "schools" of American sociology—both the people whom they produce and the teachers who produce them—seem to be dominantly "masculine" and even "studsy" in group tone; others, however, seem to be more "feminine" in their personal behavior and in the more aesthetically refined sensibility that their work manifests.

Some sociologists I know are deeply involved in the stock market, and have been for quite a while. When they gather together they will often proudly inform one another of their recent triumphs or bemoan their losses and pass on current gossip about promising stocks. Sometimes they are making money from the very wars that, as liberals, they denounce. They are also much interested in who is making how much money as a sociologist, or how much money it took to lure someone from his old to a new university.

Many sociologists are also much interested in political power and in being close to men of power. It is not simply the academicians who were stockpiled at the Kennedy Center of Urban Affairs, and not simply Harvard men, who tied their careers to political outcomes in the years preceding the American election of 1968. Some had pinned their hopes on the election of Robert Kennedy, and, when the latter was assassinated, it was for them not only a national tragedy but also a career calamity. Being close to power also involves being close to funds, funds for research, of course; and despite protestations to the contrary, this is also linked to appreciable increments in professional prestige and personal income.

Nor is it simply the pull of larger, distant things and great public events but the press of smaller, nearer things that punctuates the rhythm of academic days: the Byzantine conniving about the chairmanship of departments; the upward and onward press toward promotion and keeping up with those with whom one had been at graduate school; the daily exposure to young, still unshaped minds, and the wallowing in their admiration, or the bitterness at their ingratitude when it is not forthcoming; the comparing of the size of class enrollments at the beginning of each semester, while pretending not to care about something as vulgar as that; the careful noting of who has been invited to whose home and the pain of being excluded.

These and countless other things comprise the texture of the sociologist's world, which is probably not altogether different from other worlds. It is really quite impossible to imagine that men who care as much about the world as sociologists do will be untouched by it. It is fantasy to believe that a man's work will be autonomous from his life or that his life will not be profoundly consequential for his work. The daily texture of the sociologist's life integrates him into the world as it is; more than that, it makes this world, and indeed its very problems, a source of gratification. It is a world in which the sociologist has moved onward and upward, with increasing access to the corridors of power, with growing public acknowledgement and respect, and with an income and a style of life increasingly like that of comfortably privileged strata (or, if a younger man, with considerable prospects). Sociologists have, in short, become men with a very substantial stake in society.

Their own personal experience of success suffuses with congenial sentiment their conception of the society within which this happened. It colors their personal reality with a tacit conviction of the opportunity in and viability of the status quo. At the same time, however, the sociologist's work often brings him to a first-hand acquaintance with suffering. The complacency and yea-saying born of the sociologist's personal success thus often conflicts with what he sees as a sociologist.

This tension is neither casual nor accidental, but is the inevitable outcome of his contradictory role in the world. The sociologist's value to his social world depends in substantial measure upon its failures and its consequent need for ideas and information that will enable it to cope with them. The sociologist's personal opportunities thus grow as the crisis of his society deepens. His very efforts to fulfill his social mandate, the studies for which he is rewarded and the rewards that link him to the status quo thus also bring him closer to society's failures. His awareness of these failures, however, is largely seen from his perspective of realized personal ambitions. The failures of society, that is, do not resonate the sociologist's *own* sense of personal failure; they are seen through the softening lens of a personal reality that *knows* success to be possible within this society.

The tension between the sociologist's personal reality of success and his occupationally induced awareness of societal failure often finds its resolution in political liberalism, for this is an ideology that allows him to seek remedies for the failures of society without challenging its essential premises. It is an ideology that allows him to seek change in his society while still working within and, indeed, for it. The ideology of liberalism is the political counterpart of the contemporary sociologist's claim to autonomy. Liberalism is the politics toward which the conventional professional ideology of autonomy is disposed to drift.

In the end, however, a critique of the ideology of autonomy, as of liberalism, must recognize that it does serve as a brake upon the sociologist's full assimilation into his society. The ideology of autonomy involves partial acquiescence, but it is better by far than an ideology sanctioning total submission to society. "Autonomy" is the timid form of the verb "to resist." Like liberalism, it means: accept the system, work within it, but also try to maintain some distance from it. A critique of the ideology of autonomy must show what autonomy means in practice, that it entails a measure of contradiction with the very claims of sociology itself. Yet such a critique does not make the most fair case if it merely affirms that autonomy is a myth. For autonomy is still a regulative ideal, even if it (like others) can never be perfectly fulfilled. Rather, the problem is that autonomy is too often given only ritualistic lip service by successful men comfortable within the status quo, and frequently is not pursued even to its achievable potentialities.

From one perspective, to affirm the value of autonomy is to insist that the story the sociologist tells be his own story, that it be an account in which *he* truly believes and to which *he* commits himself. Autonomy is, in one form, an insistence upon authenticity. It says that if a man can never tell the "whole truth," then at least he should strive to tell his own truth. It may be that this is the closest we can get to "objectivity" within the framework of liberal assumption. At any rate, the claim to autonomy may provide leverage for those who believe that there can, even now, be a great deal more of it than one presently finds. The claim to autonomy at least legitimates efforts to know more about the textured reality that is part of the sociologist's daily surround, for it says to him: you must find out what it is that actually limits your autonomy and makes you and your work less than you want it to be. Such analysis can lead us to begin to know the larger implications of what the sociologist is doing in the world and to extend his self-awareness.

The object of a critique of the ideology of autonomy, then, is not to unmask the sociologist but, by confronting him with the frailty and ambiguity of his own professions, to stir his self-awareness. Its object is not to discredit his efforts at autonomy but to enable these to be realized more fully by heightening awareness of the social forces that, surrounding and penetrating the sociologist, subvert his own ideals.

Notes

1. M. Polanyi, *Personal Knowledge* (New York: Harper and Row, 1964).
2. Stephan C. Pepper, *World Hypotheses: A Study in Evidence* (Berkeley: University of California Press, 1942).
3. Charles E. Osgood, George Suci, and Percy Tannenbaum, *The Measurement of Meaning* (Urbana: University of Illinois Press, 1957).
4. See J. T. Sprehe, "The Climate of Opinion in Sociology: A Study of the Professional Value and Belief Systems of Sociologists," Ph.D. diss., University of Washington, Jan. 1967. [No test citation in original.]

5. *American Sociology*, ed. T. Parsons, (New York: Basic Books, 1968).
6. S. M. Lipset, "Political Sociology," *American Sociology*, ed. Parsons, p. 159.
7. *American Sociology*, ed. Parsons, p. 237.
8. Ibid., p. 263.
9. Ibid., p. 270.
10. Ibid., p. 278.
11. Ibid., p. 279.
12. Charles Tilly, "The Forms of Urbanization," *American Sociology*, ed. Parsons, p. 77.
13. Peter Blau, "The Study of Formal Organization," *American Sociology*, ed. Parsons, p. 54.

CHAPTER 17

Education and the
Concept of Critique

Jon Hellesnes

Scientism in theory is authoritarianism in practice.

Education and emancipation concentrated to an isolated, spiritual domain confirm the concrete social practice as something different from spirit and human intentions, as something necessarily being the way it actually is. To withdraw from society is a way of letting oneself be overpowered by society, and pure philosophy falls an easy prey to the unpure forces of society. In other words, self-sufficient philosophy turns ideological. Ideology is a kind of systematic misunderstanding which is producing as well as produced by false consciousness. False consciousness means that the rationality of society, not being transparent to the members of society, appears as causality and natural forces.

On the other hand, human and social science isolated or abstracted from philosophy also turns ideological and confirms the existing social conditions. Philosophical reflection is a necessary but insufficient condition for their ability to conceive rightly the social reality. The dialectical unity of philosophy and human or social science constitutes this kind of science as "critical."

This essay will mainly consider the relation between theory and practice in *one* human discipline, namely *education*. To a large extent the argumentation will be dependent on Jürgen Habermas, and to a lesser degree on the philosophy of Karl-Otto Apel. The latter is not to be classified as a member of the Frankfurt school, but he has much in common with Habermas.

First, some general comments on the relation of theory and practice in "noncritical," empirical-analytical science.[1] The procedure of a natural

Reprinted by permission of Justus George Lawler from *Continuum* 8, no. 1 (spring-summer 1970).

scientist is hypothetico-deductive. The scientist forms hypotheses, deduces consequences from the hypotheses, and checks that the deduced consequences correspond to the experimental results. A hypothesis confirmed by observation, i.e., observation made under conditions systematically controlled by the observer, assumes the status of a theory. The scientist can continue to deduce consequences from it and now present them as predictions. When a class of phenomena is theoretically explained, we are able to predict phenomena belonging to this class. A theory giving no basis for prediction is not an explanatory theory, but only a hypothesis.

The possibility of experimental observation, e.g. the possibility of keeping one variable constant while varying another, refers to a special kind of relationship between the experimenting observer and the phenomena observed. This relationship we might describe as a subject-object-relation wherein the subject is controlling the object and its condition of behavior.

The object is "historically resting," while the subject is "historically moving." The object or the universe of physical phenomena has been "resting," e.g. from the time of Aristotle to our time; i.e. Aristotle and the present scientists are facing the *same* nature, but the scientific approach to this same nature has changed very much. The unchangeability of nature is a presupposition for saying that we in one sense have better explanations of natural processes than Aristotle had. If Aristotle and present day science explained different natures, we couldn't say this. The unchangeability of nature is also a presupposition for establishing experimental techniques giving the same results at the time t_1 as t_n. The repeatability of experiments is a presupposition for establishing physical knowledge. On the basis of established natural laws we are able to predict and to control.

The control is facilitated by our ability to predict what happens under such and such conditions, conditions which we are technically able repeatedly to produce.

Saying that empirical-analytical science descriptively conceives the facts of nature, we must remember that the facts in question are constituted as empirical facts in a context defined by technique or instrumental action; i.e., instrumental action organizes the kind of experience which empirical-analytical science represents. Following Habermas we have to say that the basic propositions of empirical-analytical theories are no direct representations of facts. They express rather the results of our instrumental or technical operations. If nature made up her mind to behave in another way, made up her mind to get "historically moving," our experiments would not be repeatable as experiments giving the same results. The concept of experiment and the concept of technique would at the same time have been very problematic indeed (as they are in social science). We had to suppress nature in order to make her react according to the established laws of nature. Then techniques would change to authoritarian practice and experiments imply a moment of power.

The main point here is that technique or instrumental action is not something secondary or external in relation to empirical-analytical science in the sense of only being its practical application. Experimental observation refers to and presupposes technique. Technique is so to speak a presupposition for the possibility of empirical-analytical science. Empirical-analytical theories reveal regularities in nature which we can take advantage of. When we are able systematically to take advantage of regularities in nature, we have technology. In technology the "cunning consciousness" turns the laws of nature against nature herself.[2] In technology we talk about ends and means. To know the means to an end E is to know that causing factors of E. Ends and means, effects and causes, go together.

Educational Practice as Technique

Is educational practice a kind of technology? If educational theories are analogical to empirical-analytical theories, the answer to this question has to be in the affirmative. Educational theories conceived as analogical to empirical-analytical theories are primarily something which makes prediction and control of educational processes possible. The educational aims indicate for what the ability to predict and to control is going to be used. The concept of aim or end is a technological category and refers to a complete mastery over the factors affecting the aim.

D. J. O'Connor compares the educational practice to the practice of medicine and engineering: "Education like medicine and engineering, is a set of practical activities and we understand better how to carry them out if we understand the natural laws that apply to the material with which we have to work."[3] The material with which the educationist has to work is human beings, and the laws that apply to this material are "the laws of human nature." O'Connor, having no objections to speaking of the laws of human nature, conceives psychology and sociology as sciences discovering such laws.[4] Consequently O'Connor regards the constitutive interest of psychology as the interest of control. "So also modern psychological theory has arisen, partly at least, to meet the requirements of administrators for whom the problems offered by industry, mental health and education were rapidly outgrowing the crude psychological opinions common to intelligent men."[5]

In order to administer effectively, the administrating subjectivity must have complete control over the processes to be administered. Psychological theory structured according to the paradigm of empirical-analytical science facilitates this control. O'Connor thus conceives psychological theory as the know-how of effective administration. The psychologist and the educationist are conceived as persons able "to play at" the laws of human nature. Alluding to Habermas we can say that according to O'Connor they represent the "cunning consciousness," being able to turn the laws of human nature against human nature herself, thus mastering her.

Alternative conceptions of educational practice are not discussed by O'Connor because of his empirical-analytical paradigm of science. Educational practice, as the practical application of empirical-analytical science, is technique. Nontechnological educational practice is pre-scientific and to be replaced when the level of a well-established science has been reached in educational theory and psychology. Accordingly, O'Connor considers the difference between human and natural science not as qualitative difference, but as a difference of developmental level. Referring to T. H. Huxley's definition of natural history, he places social science in its present state at the level of natural history: "It [natural history] falls roughly into two parts: (a) careful and exact observation and recording of facts; (b) the intelligent classification of these facts to reduce them to a manageable and comprehensible order."[6]

The level which the human and social sciences have not yet reached is exemplified by biology—"when the whole of the plant world and its environment is understood by the biologists as a complex system of interacting causes and effects."[7] O'Connor does not see any fundamental hindrance to reaching this level. It is true, he says, that the difficulties in varying social conditions on a large scale are great. He also considers contemporary mores as a hindrance to experimenting with human beings. But these are accidental, not fundamental hindrances. Social cooperation and better techniques should enable us to reach the high level of a well-established natural science.

The position I have sketched here, I will call "scientism." Against scientism I will argue for the fundamental difference between social/human science and natural science. I have already described the relationship between the natural scientist and his theme as a subject-object-relation. The relationship between, e.g., the educationist and his theme cannot be described in this way. As far as his theme of inquiry is concerned, the educationist is involved in a reciprocal relationship, a subject-subject-relation.[8] In other words, the educationist belongs to the same order as his theme of inquiry. This is not the case with the natural scientist.

Reducing his theme of inquiry to another order than that to which he himself belongs, i.e., when the educationist transforms the subject-subject-relation to a subject-object-relation, a relation of control wherein techniques are involved, the educationist behaves authoritarianly and confirms the authoritarian conditions of society. Scientism in theory is authoritarianism in practice. I repeat, if one of the subjects in a subject-subject-relation treats it as a subject-object-relation, he acts authoritarianly. Authoritarianism is determining on behalf of others without justifying the determination rationally. The objectification of the Other is necessarily irrational, since rational justification presupposes the recognition of the Other as subject.[9]

Politics is not only involved in the discussion of "the aims of education"; the determination of education as an empirical-analytical discipline *is* political.

To say that education is a social and historical process, a process of "the lived world" (*Lebenswelt*), and that "it is happening" in a community of subjects, is to say something to which it is possible to give some, but not complete, sense in terms of "ordinary language philosophy."

Language and the Social Reality

The meaning of a word being its use in a practical context, "a form of life," much insight into social phenomena is attainable by analysis of meaning. Analysis of the meaning or "the job" of words is, so to speak, an analysis of the social reality also. Human behavior is embedded in conceptual frames and is conceivable as meaningful moves in social games. Between language and social reality there is no "gap" to be empirically bridged. Peter Winch seems to identify language and social reality completely.[10] Accordingly, he believes that sociological concepts have to be related to the conceptual frames in which the social agents understand themselves, their actions and their internal relationships. Language constitutes, as it were, the social phenomena, and society is "something we can" in a fashion similar to the way in which we can speak our language. But this is not the case with natural phenomena.

An apple falls to the ground. By the notion of gravitation we conceive this fall. But the behavior of the apple is not dependent on this physical concept. If no physical concepts existed, apples would still fall to the ground. The existence of natural phenomena is thus independent of the concepts we have formed of them. The existence of social phenomena, on the other hand, is dependent on the concepts we have formed of them. The phenomenon of greeting is an example. To say that the people of the X-society are greeting each other daily without knowing about it themselves, without having any concept of it, is to say something absurd. Without the concept of greeting the act of greeting would disappear from the social universe, being only a physical movement of the body.

This is certainly true. But the thesis that the universe of social phenomena is a universe one-sidedly constituted by the conceptual frames of the social agents is, however, an overstatement. The primacy of language which Winch is advocating has an idealistic air about it.[11] Criticizing[12] Winch's use of Wittgenstein's concept of the language game, Habermas presents arguments from two traditions of thought, mediating them in his criticism; one is the tradition of transcendental philosophy wherein the question of self-justification and reflection is central; the other is the historical materialism of Karl Marx.

The first objection to Winch has to do with the relation between language and the user of language, the speaking subject. The synthesis of the speaking subject is eliminated to the benefit of the grammar of language games. "Die Vieldeutigkeit der Umgangssprache und die Ungenauigkeit ihrer Regeln ist Schein; jedes Sprachspiel gehorcht einer vollkommenen Ordnung."[13] This order is so to speak engulfing the speaking subject and the possibility of self-justification and reflection. Following Habermas (and Apel), I will try to elaborate this point.

When we say that the meaning of a word is its use in a certain language game, the relation between language games has the marks of family resemblance, and constitutes a theory of meaning, and we have to justify what has been said to accord with this theory of meaning. The theory of meaning has in other words to express the possibility of theory of meaning. If the philosopher's talk about language as different forms of life is totalizing talk, if it expresses reflection over language *as such*, then the talking philosopher is not taking part in a *particular* language game, and his talk is not meaningful according to his theory of meaning. On the other hand, if to theorize about the problem of meaning is to take part in a definite, isolated language game, the language game of philosophy, then what is presented is no general theory of meaning, and therefore is no theory of meaning at all. In other words, to talk about games is not to make a move in a game, to make a move in a game is not to talk about games.

The conception of language as a plurality of language games is not justifiable in terms of the conception itself. Habermas formulates the objection in the following way: "Wenn jede Aussage nur im Kontext ihres Sprachspiels sinnvoll ist, wenn aber andererseits die Sprachanalyse die monadischen Sprachspiele durch Abwägen ihrer Familienähnlich-keiten durchsichtig macht, dann fragt sich: welchen Sprachspiels diese Analyse selber sich bedient."[14] Questions are meaningful in a language game which has rules for "question moves" as for "answer moves." "What is meaning?" is, however, a general question and does not belong to any particular question-answer game. To ask in a general way is to commit a category mistake. It is like asking how to move the chessboard after having been told how to move the queen.[15]

According to Winch people do what they understand, and under-stand what they are doing. Social reality is transparent in the way lan-guage is transparent. What is hidden is hidden in the sense of being implicit. But this raises another objection. "Eine verstehende Soziologie, die Sprache zum Subjekt der Lebensform und der Überlieferung hypos-tasiert, bindet sich an die idealistische Voraussetzung, dass das sprachlich artikulierte Bewusstsein das materielle Sein Der Lebenspraxis bestimmt."[16] To conceive the actual "self-understanding of society" as exhausting the social reality, is to postulate the post-revolutionary utopia as realized now. Because such postulation contributes to the maintenance of unarticulated and unjustified social authority, it has an ideological function. In this way the philosophy and "die verstehende Soziologie" of Peter Winch is ideological. Man, in his reproduction of social life, actu-ally does not understand all of what he is doing, and does not do all of what he understands. In other words, language is not to be completely identified with social reality as determining this reality.

A description of a social situation can in principle be a moment changing the situation, and a misinterpretation of a situation which is widespread among the agents constituting the situation contributes to the perverson of it. To say that everybody always lies is to say something absurd; it is possible to lie only because we do not lie always. To say that everybody misinterprets his situation is a fundamental way is to say something different and not absurd. The former case is a case of "pure logic" which the latter case is not. This is so because language does not "exhaust" social reality.

In a social situation there are authority-relations mediated by the material relations of the situation. That the material of society is not everybody's property is an important factor, and a misinterpretation of what is "everybody's interest" is constitutive for the way people behave in relation to the material and to the authority involved in the ownership of it. Ordinary language legitimates the status quo by not articulating the material and authoritarian mediation of social relationships. What is unsaid and repressed contributes in a negative way to the definition of the situation. Accordingly, to say the unsaid is often an important form of critique, contributing to a redefinition of the situation. If language were identifiable with social reality in the sense of determining this reality, to say the unsaid would be an expansion of social reality itself; but to say the unsaid is only to expand the *understanding* of social reality.

Language is the medium of understanding. Language and social practice mutually refer to and presuppose each other. Practice is mediated by the material. Accordingly, language is constitutive, but language *alone* is not constitutive.

The relation between language and social practice being mediated by material relations, the material relations are also constitutive. An abstraction of either language or the material as the primary constituent of social reality, the reality of practice, generates philosophical misinterpretations, e.g., "idealism" or "mechanistic materialism."

Sprache ist auch ein Medium von Herrschaft und sozialer Macht. Sie dient der Legitimation von Beziehungen organisierter Gewalt. Soweit die Legitimationen das Gewaltverhältnis, dessen Institutionalisierung sie ermöglichen, nicht aussprechen, soweit dieses in den Legitimationen sich nur ausdrückt, ist Sprache *auch* ideologisch. Dabei handelt es sich nicht um Täuschungen in einer Sprache, sondern um Täuschungen mit Sprache als solcher. Die hermeneutische Erfahrung, die auf eine solche Abhängigkeit des symbolischen Zusammenhangs von faktischen Verhältnisse stösst, geht in Ideologiekritik über.[17]

The actual communication of speaking subjects is not free; it is obstructed by social authority, confirming at the same time the obstruction by not thematizing the authority and its material basis. The communicating and interacting subjects are not autonomous; by understanding themselves as undergoing social processes conceived as analogical to natural processes, they confirm their heteronomy. The social processes are "going behind the backs" of the communicating and interacting subjects, being autonomous to the same degree as the subjects themselves are without autonomy.

Interpersonal relationships are essentially reciprocal or dialogical subject-subject-relations in a situation of material equality. The way in which capitalist and state-capitalist society actually mediates these relations perverts them. The ideological self-understanding of the subjects confirms what is perverting. Alluding to the Hegelian distinction between "Eurscheinungen" and "Wesen," we can say that the historical "appearance" of subject-subject-relations is not in accordance with their "essence." To take this seriously is to take the concept of critical and emancipatory science seriously.

In order to be adequate the scientific study of a theme has to accord with the essence of the theme studied. We may formulate the fault of Peter Winch as his identification of appearance and essence, thus making critique unnecessary. Discussing "realism" as contrasted to "nominalism" moves us in the right direction. A Humean discussion of the relation between normative and descriptive statements will certainly miss the point.

When Habermas and Apel determine the constitutive knowledge-interest of human and social science as the interest of emancipation, they do not appeal to any extra-disciplinary and irrational values. What they are hinting at *cannot* be formulated in the following way: "The social and human sciences ought not to be used for suppression. They ought to be used for the benefit of mankind, for the emancipation of man!"

Apel and Habermas are not appealing to any abstract "oughts." They are saying that the scientific study of a theme has to be in accordance with the essence of the theme studied. Moreover, social and human science, adequately pursued, is not "usable" and cannot be "applied." The kind of insight it facilitates is self-understanding and enlightenment which makes autonomy and self-determination possible. "Social engineering," applied empirical-analytical sociology and educational technology, presupposing the heteronomy of the people in society, is ruled out. Social science, before being a question of administration and technological expertise, is a question of political theory and practice.

Critical science sets human consciousness free from hypostatizing forces, by making these "forces" appear as they are, as social authority problems connected with material relations, and demanding political, not technological solutions. The maintenance of technological solutions in the political domain is "technological fascism." Only unmasked authority gives us authority problems, i.e., political problems, but such problems are essential for our social mode of being. When authority gives us no conscious problems, it is because we have disposed of authority, either to the benefit of "the mechanism of the market," of the administration of the state with its experts, or to the benefit of "der Führer." The disappearance of authority problems is at the same time their reappearance as something different, as problems belonging to another category. Ideologically repressed social authority reappears as "natural catastrophies of society," as economic crises, as wasting of natural resources, etc.

Psychoanalysis teaches us that repressed motives are perverted to causality. The repression makes the motive reappear, e.g. as physical symptoms. In a similar way the ideological repression of authority and its material basis perverts it to social causality. Psychoanalysis, expanding the consciousness of the analysand, enables him to take a conscious attitude to problems previously concealed. In an analogical way critical science, by unmasking and enlightening social authority, and its material basis, makes political discussion and self-determination possible. This is so *sub specie rationis*. Presented as a political strategy in a primarily political discussion, however, this analogy is misleading.

In spite of his "resistance" the analysand going through a psychoanalytical treatment, is fundamentally interested in the unmasking of psychic "forces." But, maintaining the analogy, it is reasonable to presuppose the capitalist's fundamental interest in the unmasking of social "forces"? Is it possible to transcend the class-determined antagonism of interests by means of a critical theory provoking reflection?

Education as a Critical Discipline

A discipline which is empirical without being empirical-analytical is a critical discipline. The nature of a discipline, as either empirical-analytical or as critical, is constituted by the theme of the discipline. The theme of educational study is the educational situation and what is constitutive of such a situation. The educational situation is, among other things, constituted by the dialogue between teacher and student. This dialogue is not free and socratic. It is obstructed by the unarticulated authority relations in the particular educational situation as well as by the power relations of society in its totality. By not thematizing and enlightening these obstructive relations, the obstructed educational dialogue contributes to the confirmation of them.

"Dialogue" we can take in a broad sense, conceiving written text-books as constituents of it. Text-books on modern history and constitution present our societies one-sidedly as democratic and parliamentary. They are one-sided because our societies to a large extent are "extra-parliamentary" in the sense that authority often is conceived as necessary, social causality, and not subject to political discussion in the parliament or elsewhere. They are "extra-parliamentary" in the sense that there are centers of decision like monopolistic, supernational business and industrial enterprises and military organizations, whose fatal decisions are not under parliamentary control.

By their lack of discussion of extra-parliamentary and undemocratic centers of political decision and by defining politics as something primarily going on in the parliament, text-books mask the extra-parliamentary power.

Education, being a critical discipline, is essentially interested in revealing what obstructs the educational dialogue in order to set it free. This essential interest of emancipation constitutes education primarily as critical sociology of education. According to Klaus Mollenhauer the children of the working class do not have the same chance to succeed in the educational system as the children of the bourgeoisie have. What is the point of establishing this empirical fact?

Die empirisch zu sichernde Feststellung, dass die Chancengleichheit im Bildungswesen nicht verwiklicht ist, is überhaupt nur bedeutungsvoll in einer Kommunikationsgemeinschaft, in der eine Interesse an Chancengleichheit mindestens vorkommt. Sonst wäre solche Feststellung nicht interessanter als die, dass es Menschen mit blonden und Menschen mit schwarzen Haaren gibt.[18]

Empirical-analytical science is the paradigm of science discovering laws. To the same degree that people react to each other without communicative understanding of each other, to the same degree that people are determined by social processes, "going behind the backs" of the social agents and thus have a kind of autonomy because of the agents' lack of autonomy, the methods of empirical-analytical science *seem* to be adequate. They grasp what actually is *but not* what might be. By its concentration on the positively given, the historicity and thereby the changeability of actual conditions are bracketed out. This way of conceiving what actually is sanctions it for eternity.

I have described the relation between "the historically moving, scientific subjectivity" and "the historically resting object of scientific explanation" as typical of the natural sciences. In the social and human sciences the "object" is historically moving too, at least it is potentially so. To describe it as "historically resting," analogical to natural objects, is to describe it in an ideological way. To *keep* it resting, e.g., by means of social technology, is to act in an authoritarian way.

There are regularities in society appearing as natural laws. By discovering these regularities, critical science is *nomothetic*. But the regularities discovered by critical science are not be be conceived as eternal in the sense in which the law of gravitation is eternal. The discovery of regularities here in question is a *prologomena* to the elimination of them.

Education and Interest

We are not interested in educating the younger generation merely because we are living here and now on a certain cultural level. The interest in education refers to the interest in understanding and in being understood, and this interest we cannot abdicate and still be human beings. In a discussion of what education and the relation between theory and practice in education is, the concept of interest as developed by Habermas is important. Interest as understood by Habermas is not something which does and does not occur empirically. It is not empirical research that reveals the fundamental interests of man.

The fundamental interests are revealed by the epistemological study into the preconditions for the possibility of science. This kind of study reveals, e.g., that experimental observation belongs to the preconditions for the possibility of natural science, and that experimental observation presupposes a knowledge-subject which is bodily and working. A rationality without body would not be able to carry out experiments. A rationality without body would not find any point in prediction and control either. Moreover, a bodiless rationality would not be able to identify particulars or to communicate. When there are no points of view, there is no communication. To put it briefly: a bodiless rationality would not be a subjectivity.

As far as natural science is concerned, scientific progress is merely the progress of the knowledge-subject which is increasing its ability to predict and to control. It is not "a progress of nature herself." Ahistorical nature is a transcendental precondition for instrumental action, but is not in any sense "beyond" that for which it is a precondition, and therefore is not "beyond" the dialectic of subject and object. The ahistorical nature is constituted by as well as constitutive of "the technical knowledge-interest."

Instrumental action is embedded in intersubjectivity and presupposes communication. A scientist cannot explain anything exclusively for himself. In order for it to be an explanation it has to be explanatory for more than one person. The scientist is taking part in "the language game of scientific explanation" which includes a plurality of subjects. The communication of the scientists cannot be "improved" by instrumental action, for instrumental action and its improvement presupposes communication. The problem of communication is, in other words, not a technical problem to which there are technical solutions.

Instrumental action is an action in the lived-world and presupposes a public discussion in order to be rational. The scientific discussion in "the community of investigators" which makes experimental techniques possible presupposes public language and the community of the lived-world; and the increased ability of prediction and control concerns this community in which "the community of investigators" is a moment. The solipsistic abstraction from the public discussion is unjustifiable because public discussion is a presupposition for all justification of scientific research.

To educate is to enable the educand to take part in the public discussion which guarantees, e.g., that scientific research and technology is a moment in "the good life" as well as a material guarantee of it. The educand has, accordingly, to be taught about scientific research and technology as well as to be enlightened about the social context in which science and technology are embedded. The project of education includes the project of reestablishing the partly repressed public discussion. This project constitutes critical sociology of education.

Progress in education is therefore radically different from progress in the ability to predict and to control. The wish to predict and control educational processes is incompatible with the essence of education. Education refers to the principal equality of human beings in the same sense as natural science and technology refer to the principal inequality in the relation between man and nature. This principal equality is claimed and presupposed by every utterance of language. The linguistic utterance presupposes the "other" as an autonomous co-subject just as the instrumental act presupposes a heteronomous object. By speaking I claim and confirm myself as a subject and the "other" as an autonomous co-subject.

When we argue from the Habermasian theory of interests that education roots in another interest than natural science and technology, our view is not far from Wittgenstein's argument against the possibility of private language. It is, as I have tried to show, possible to talk about an interest of communication and emancipation which co-appears with the linguistic utterance. This is also the interest governing education when education is in accordance with its own essence.

Die Idee der Wahrheit, die im ersten gesprochenen Satz schon impliziert war, lässt sich nämlich allein am Vorbild der idealisierten, in herrschaftsfreier Kommunikation erzielten Übereinstimmung bilden. Insofern ist die

Wahrheit von Aussagen an die Intention eines wahren lebens gebunden. Nicht mehr als dieses in alltäglicher Rede Implizierte, aber auch nicht weniger nimmt Kritik ausdrücklich in Anspruch.[19]

To the same degree as the actual situation contradicts the autonomy of the speaking subjects, the activity of critique and the struggle for political change is justified. This kind of contradiction is a contradiction between the *appearance* and the *essence* of intersubjectivity. By language intersubjectivity is claimed, but not realized. By language the project of realizing the uncompelled communication is launched. In speaking we are anticipating a state of intersubjectivity and equality which is not yet materially realized.

Notes

1. For a more thorough discussion of empirical-analytical science see Karl-Otto Apel, "Scientistik, Hermeneutik, Ideologiekritik," *Wiener Jahrbuch für Philosophie* 1 (1968).
2. Jürgen Habermas, "Arbeit und Interaktion," *Technik und Wissenschaft als "Ideologie,"* pp. 26–27.
3. D. J. O'Connor, *An Introduction to the Philosophy of Education* (London, 1957), p. 94.
4. Ibid., p. 95.
5. Ibid., p. 96.
6. Ibid., p. 103.
7. Ibid.
8. Cf. Hans Skjervheim, *Objectivism and the Study of Man* (Oslo, 1959).
9. In this statement I do not include the kind of objectification of the Other which serves his own self-understanding as well as our understanding of him, i.e., the kind of objectification which is represented by psychoanalysis. "To the models of psychoanalysis given here corresponds the model of 'critique of ideologies.' Here, too, human 'self-understanding' is undoubtedly corrected by objective methods. But the result of these latter methods—e.g., the uncovering of economic interests—can always be incorporated in principle into a more profound understanding of oneself. And in regard to the above-mentioned criterion of an 'objective explanation' we can say this much: The sociologist, just like the psychoanalyst, cannot completely separate his own descriptive 'objective-language' from the language of his 'objects,' who are his 'co-subjects.' (For this reason the assumption that human attitudes are ideological can never be 'total,' because in that case it either loses its function as critique—as it does in fact in the works of K. Mannheim—or it becomes applicable to the language of sociology itself, thus invalidating its own truth-claim)" (Karl-Otto Apel, *Analytic Philosophy of Language and the Geisteswissenschaften* [Dordrecht, Holland, 1967], p. 27). The kind of objectification discussed here is rationally justifiable in terms of that widened dialogue which this objectification serves.

368

10. Peter Winch, *The Idea of a Social Science and Its Relation to Philosophy* (London, 1958).
11. The "idealism" of Peter Winch is discussed by Karl-Otto Apel in connection with the german conception of "Geisteswissenschaften" (*Analytic Philosophy of Language and the Geisteswissenschaften*). Much of the criticism later presented by Jürgen Habermas is implicit in this study. One aspect of this criticism has also been explicated and elaborated by Apel himself in "Sprache und Reflexion," *Proceedings of the XIV Congress of Philosophy*, vol. 3 (Vienna, 1969).
12. Jürgen Habermas, "Zur Logik der Sozialwissenschaften," *Philosophische Rundschau*, supp. 5 (Tübingen, 1967), p. 134 et seq.
13. Ibid., p. 155. "The ambiguity of Everyday language and the imprecision of its rules is an illusion; every language game is part of a perfect order" (trans. Gabriele Lakomski).
14. Ibid., p. 142. "If each utterance makes sense only within the context of its language game, and if language analysis explains monadic language games by pointing out their family resemblances, then one has to ask which language game analysis itself is using" (trans. Gabriele Lakomski).
15. Objections of this kind are presented by Ernest Gellner, *Words and Things* (London, 1959). They are, I think, objections to peter Winch, who is presenting a "verstehende Soziologie." I am not sure that they eliminate the subtleties of Ludwig Wittgenstein, who is able to imagine a language game in which we create the rules as we go along.
16. Habermas, "Zur Logik der Sozialwissenschaften," p. 179. "A reflexive sociology which posits language as the subject of a form of life and of tradition ties itself to the idealist presupposition that consciousness expressed through language determines the material existence of everyday life" (trans. Gabriele Lakomski).
17. Ibid., p. 178. "Language is also a medium of domination and social power. It serves to legitimate relations of organized power. In so far as these legitimations do not express power relations (whose institutionalization they make possible) language is also ideological. This does not mean deceptions in langage but deceptions with language as such. The hermeneutic experience which recognizes the dependence of the symbolic context on material relations becomes ideology-critique" (trans. Gabriele Lakomski).
18. Klaus Mollenhauser, *Erziehung und Emanzipation* (Munich, 1968), pp. 15–16. "The empirically ascertainable fact that educational equality has not been realized only makes sense in a community in which at least the interest in equality exists. Otherwise this fact would be as interesting as the observation that some people have blond and others black hair" (trans. Gabriele Lakomski).
19. Jürgen Habermas, "Odysse der Vernunft in die Nature," *Die Zeit*, no. 37 (1969), p. 4. "The idea of truth, being already implied in the first spoken sentence, can only be formed on the basis of an ideal consensus achieved through domination-free communication. To this extent the truth of statements is tied to the intention of the good life. Nothing more and nothing less is claimed by critique" (trans. Gabriele Lakomski).

CHAPTER 18

A Method for Critical Research

Donald E. Comstock

Take the ideas of the masses (scattered and unsystematic ideas) and concentrate them (through study turn them into concentrated and systematic ideas), then go to the masses and propagate and explain these ideas until the masses embrace them as their own, hold fast to them and translate them into action, and test the correctness of these ideas in such action. Then once again concentrate ideas from the masses and once again go to the masses. . . . And so on, over and over again in an endless spiral, with the ideas becoming more correct, more vital and richer each time. Such is the Marxist theory of knowledge.—Mao Tsetung[1]

In the last decade there has been a remarkable number of books and articles intended to familiarize American sociologists with the critical theories of society associated with the Frankfurt Institute for Social Research. However, partly because of considerable ambivalence by the members of the "Frankfurt school" toward empirical research, and partly because, since the 1930s, they have been isolated from political practice, limited attention has been given to research methods appropriate to a critical social science.[2] In this paper I outline such a method with the hope of stimulating a reconsideration of research activities which are appropriate to a social science of *praxis*. Following a brief discussion of the need for such a method, I will point out several distinctions between positive social science and critical social science which are relevant to research methods. In the final section of the paper I will present a sequence of steps which outline a critical method of research. In this context "method" is not to be confused with specific research techniques involved in data collection and analysis. Rather, I use the term to refer to the general procedure by which we go about studying society, including selecting research problems, constructing and evaluating theories, and disseminating our findings.

Printed with the permission of the author.

370

I. The Necessity for a Critical Method of Research

The central argument of this paper is that the development of critical theories of contemporary social institutions requires a critical research method. We cannot simply apply the investigative logic developed by the positive social sciences to new topics and expect to develop a truly critical social science. Moreover, most critical theory, and neo-Marxist analysis in general, is presently far removed from the people and class it purports to enlighten and is of very little use to those engaged in concrete struggles for progressive change. Despite the best intentions of its practitioners radical theory remains entrapped in the academic practice of theory building. The questions it addresses are theoretical questions and the answers it supplies are meant to advance theoretical knowledge, not political practice. This is because both mainstream social science and radical analysis is practiced almost entirely in academic settings and because the first has consciously and the second has unconsciously adopted the epistemology of positive science.[3]

The function of a critical social science is to increase the awareness of social actors of the contradictory conditions of action which are distorted or hidden by everyday understandings. It is founded on the principle that all men and women are potentially active agents in the construction of their social world and their personal lives: that they can be the subjects, rather than the objects, of socio-historical processes. Its aim is self-conscious practice which liberates humans from ideologically frozen conceptions of the actual and the possible. The method of research appropriate to this endeavor cannot be adopted from positive social or natural sciences. The method of positive social science reflects the empiricist assumption that society is a neutral datum for a systematic observation. This is both a reflection of, and a contribution to, the reification of monopoly and state capitalist societies. This method objectifies the human subjects of an investigation by treating their behavior as raw data which is external to the scientific enterprise. The positive research method reifies social processes by naturalizing social phenomena, addressing them as eternal to our understandings, and denying their socio-historical constructedness. The consequence is to reinforce the alienaton of the subjects of social science research from their social, political, and economic institutions.

A consistent critical method which treats society as a human construction and people as the active subjects of that construction would be based on a *dialogue* with its subjects rather than the observation or experimental manipulation of people. A critical social science must directly contribute to the revitalization of moral discourse and revolutionary action by engaging its subjects in a process of active self-understanding and collective self-formation. In this way, science becomes a method for self-conscious action rather than an ideology for the technocratic domination of a passive populace.

II. Some Differences between Critical Social Science and Positive Social Science

The roots of scientific thought lie in the Enlightenment belief that genuine knowledge is the most effective means for the liberation of humans. Yet modern positive science has excluded, on epistemological and methodological grounds, any such interest. Instead, science is viewed as a neutral means equally utilizable for liberation or oppression. The specific use to which knowledge will be put is excluded from the province of scientific understanding itself. The self-image of contemporary social science is dominated by the epistemology and methodology of the natural sciences which assumes a fundamental separation of the knower from the known, of the subject from the object.

Critical theory is the historical contradiction to this scientistic self-image of modern society. Critical theory expressly denies the view that humans and society can be understood via the assumptions and methods of the natural sciences that deny the self-creative character of human thought and action. A brief comparison of positive and critical social sciences will cover four points of divergence: (1) their different images of society and human nature, (2) the constitution of our knowledge of social processes, (3) the form that scientific explanations of social processes must take, and (4) the role of the social scientist.[4]

1. Images of Society and Human Nature

Positive social science sees society as an objective phenomenon which can be described as a set of ahistoric forces which constrain human behavior. Critical social science, on the other hand, views society as a human construction which is altered through people's progressive understanding of historically specific processes and structures. Positive social science takes human nature as a constant datum while the critical perspective argues that humans change themselves by reconstituting their society. By attributing a "thing-like" quality to society, positive social sciences endow social processes with what Barry Smart calls pseudo-concreteness.[5] Reflecting the common sense objectifications of the alienated individual in capitalist society, positive social science fails to analyze society as a human construction. This approach may have predictive validity in the short run so long as the reificatory power of ideology remains unchallenged. However, since it fails to see the social processes and structures it studies as historically specific, positive social science can neither account for nor serve as a guide for fundamental social change.[6]

In contrast, a critical social science, which self-consciously participates in the reconstruction of social structures and collective meanings, is an immediately historical project. Rather than an exclusive concern with naive descriptions of what exists, critical social science directs attention to the *possibilities* immanent in the historical development of social processes created by human understanding and action. As Horkheimer wrote, "the critical theory of society . . . has for its objective men as producers of their own historical way of life in its totality."[7] This quite different view of society and human nature has profound implications for the constitution of social science knowledge.

The Constitution of Social Science Knowledge

For a positive social science, knowledge is constituted by the theoretical ordering of empirical observations of an objective reality. The data are descriptions of social behaviors and the subjective beliefs, attitudes, and values of individuals.[8] These are assumed to exhaust the field of enquiry and to provide an external or objective datum for testing theoretical models. Positive social science attempts to model parts of this reality through the use of value-neutral concepts. According to Habermas, "in this way the naive idea that knowledge describes reality itself becomes prevalent."[9] Objectivism and the value-neutrality of concepts become guiding principles of positive social science such that facts are sharply distinguished from values and theory from practice. Although unacknowledged, the intention that has justified and legitimated positive science has been the prediction and instrumental control of nature.[10] Thus, as Fay shows, when this interest is applied to the study of humans, the result is the manipulation of social relationships, the enthronement of technical means over moral ends, the impoverishment of political discussion, and the support of dominant classes.[11]

From the perspective of a critical social science, knowledge may fulfill two human interests, in addition to technical control. Since human life is social life and is governed by normative principles and moral precepts, a second interest consists of the practical requirement for intersubjective understanding and agreement on norms, values, and meanings. The social sciences are therefore ineluctably hermeneutic: they rest on an interpretation of the intersubjective meanings and practices which order everyday life. In turn, they contribute to the maintenance or change of those meanings and practices. For this reason, it becomes necessary to recognize a third human interest and a third type of knowledge: that which frees participants from outmoded and reified conceptions of reality. This emancipatory interest is the basis for a critique of ideology and for knowledge that informs fundamental social change.

A critical social science refuses to accept current social practices as the final context of validation. Both meanings and actions at any historical moment are transitory manifestations of changing social structures. A critical social science must analyze these in light of their arrested and denied possibilities.[12] Under conditions of domination, actors' understandings are historically frozen by ideologies which legitimate and attempt to perpetuate existing relations of power. Yet social action continues to change the social structure in ways that contradict these meanings. Possibilities for different understandings and actions remain hidden from view only so long as the powerful and their agents can maintain distorting ideas.

The intention which constitutes a critical social science is the emancipation of its subjects from ideologically frozen conceptions and the development of self-sustaining processes of enlightenment and self-conscious political action. Critical knowledge is never neutral; it is always for some particular subject. The validity of its concepts, data, and theory is related to the historical aims and purposes of that subject.[13] Thus instead of simply describing a particular historical formation, a critical social science attempts to elucidate the possible courses of action and meanings which are immanent in the development of the present order. To do this it must combine a theory of structural change with a critique of its subjects' ideologically distorted understandings. In this way a critical understanding of society mediates theory and practice.

3. The Form of Scientific Knowledge

Positive social science assumes that a single form of explanation is appropriate to all sciences. The deductive nomological or covering-law is paradigmatic, even if rarely achieved in the social sciences. The heart of this form of explanation lies in the appeal to ahistoric laws or nomological statements of deterministic or probablistic relations between phenomena. Explanation is symmetrical with prediction: the deduction of an event *post factum* from laws and empirical conditions is identical in form to the prediction of future events. The validity of these laws rests on their capacity to conditionally predict future events. All positive scientific activities—collecting and refining data, discovering correlations, and formulating empirical generalizations, hypotheses, and models—is directed toward the growth of testable and well-confirmed laws which are ordered by logically coherent theories.

A critical social science challenges both the possibility of this model of explanation and the advisability of its function as a paradigm for the social sciences. While positive social science studies human *behavior*, critical social science studies human *action* and seeks to make manifest the processes by which social structures are constructed by human action and ordered by intersubjective meanings. Critical accounts relate social conditions to the subjects' actions, not directly or mechanically, but as they are interpreted and ordered by their understandings and motives. Since all human actions are consequences of socially interpreted sets of conditions, we cannot predict behavior directly from social conditions. Instead, critical explanations must recognize the mediation of meanings by which members make sense of their own and others' acts. Once we assume that social processes are constituted through meaningful action, the prediction of social action is possible only so long as constitutive meanings do not change. Since humans are self-defining agents who reflect on and interpret their actions, and since all fundamental social change is the product of innovation in both meanings and social practices, future conditions and regularities are not predetermined. Moreover, as Taylor notes, even the categories and concepts we use today are likely to be superseded in the future.[14] (Curiously, positivists assume this in the development of their own scientific disciplines but exclude it from their considerations on other social processes.)

If all social processes must be understood as the product of meaningful human actions, then all critical accounts must begin from the intersubjective meanings, values, and motives of historically specific groups of actors. Interpretive accounts of action, in contrast to causal explanations, take the form of practical inferences whereby acts are deduced from a knowledge of the actors' intentions and conceptions of what must be done to accomplish those intentions.[15] Moreover, these meanings, values, and motives must be related to social processes in a way which clearly demonstrates how they have been constructed by human action and reflection.

Critical explanations include a theory of basic structural change and an account of the genesis of meanings, values, and motives which arise in consequence of structural changes. They must also reveal the contradictory consequences in social structure which result from acting in accordance with dominant meanings—consequences which render actors' intentions unachievable in the context of changed circumstances. For example, the idea of social mobility may have been supported by the personal experiences of a visible and vocal minority during the early development of capitalist social relations—especially in the United States. However, since that time continued interpersonal competition has solidified the position of an elite and severely reduced the possibility of significant personal mobility. A critical social science would endeavor to show both how the intention of individual mobility is unrealizable under present social conditions and how the ideology of mobility serves to reinforce the existing inequalities of opportunity and achievement which are experienced by actors as a frustration of personal values.

Critical explanations explicate the historical dialectic between subjective and objective factors whereby historically preformed social structures and processes set the conditions for human action and these conditions are, in turn, negated by social actions. Actors interpret social and natural conditions, they act to achieve certain intersubjectively valid intentions, and they thereby alter the conditions of action. Under conditions of ideologically frozen understandings—the tendency in any hierarchical social formation—the objective conditions of action come to contradict the intersubjective meanings attributed to them. In this way, the unanticipated consequences of action bring about changes in social conditions which render ideologies less and less able to account for actors' experiences.

Radical changes occur because of crises that result from emerging contradictions in social processes. These are revealed in the divergence of social conditions from ideologies. A fundamental contradiction will exist when the changed social conditions give rise to contradictory action imperatives which cannot be integrated and legitimated by the old ideology (for example, state regulation and protection of monopolies versus laissez faire competition). Eventually a crisis threatens when actors experience these changes as both critical for their continued material existence and threatening to their social identity.[16] One or more new meaning systems arise and contend with the old and some of these new meanings will express progressive possibilities immanent in the contradictory social conditions. A group or class that is dominated and frustrated by current conditions will organize for political struggle and social change.

The outcome of these political struggles depends upon the degree to which social conditions have changed as well as the relative effectiveness of progressive interests vis-à-vis the old power holders. If fundamental contradictions have not yet matured, adjustments in the ideology or power structure may suffice to temporize dissatisfactions while competing leaders are coopted, isolated, or expelled. At some point a crisis arises which cannot be resolved through adjustment and cooptation and a radical change must occur in both the social structure and the system of meanings. The timing of such radical changes cannot be predicted from knowledge of the contradictions immanent in a social structure because human action is not the mechanical result of natural forces but the product of conscious choice based on varying degrees of social awareness by the participants. Thus, the aim of a critical theory is not to predict social change, but to explicate the immanent tendencies in the historical development of a social formation so that the participants may create social change. This implies a radically different role for the social scientist than the one idealized by positive social science.

4. The Role of the Social Scientist

Horkheimer noted that traditional, that is, positive and interpretive, social sciences, in an attempt to deny the political aspects of knowledge, separate the role of the social scientist, *qua* scientist from her or his role as a political actor.[17] In a contemporary manifestation of Marx's distinction between *bourgeois* and *citoyen*, the scientist is divided into two beings: a nonpolitical, value-free observer and theorizer on the one hand, and a political person who expresses values and interests on the other. The positivist injunction is to always keep these roles separate: to cultivate a disinterested attitude when investigating social phenomena and only as a private citizen to bring one's tentative knowledge to bear on vital issues of the day. According to this, the task of the social scientist is to describe and explain the facts, not to make prescriptive statements about what ought to be.[18]

Critical social science recognizes that social scientists are participants in the socio-historical development of human action and understanding. As such, they must decide the interests they will serve. Since all knowledge is rooted in social practices and social practices are informed and ordered, in part, by social science explanations, theory and action are inseparable and all facts and theories are warranted as valid from a particular framework of social practices. The only legitimate activity of a critical social scientist is to engage in the collective enterprise of progressive enlightenment with the aim of showing how his or her accounts are valid in light of the subjects' oppressive social position and the specific values and actions possible in that position.

In summary, a critical social science sees society as humanly constructed and, in turn, human nature as a collective self-construction. This emphasizes the historicity of social structure, processes, and meanings

377

and directs attention to the possible world immanent in present formations. Social science knowledge is, like all reflexive understanding of social practice, constituted by the understandings, values, and goals of particular individuals, groups, or classes. Critical social science is distinguished by its interest in the emancipation of those groups and classes that are presently dominated. This makes it a science of *praxis* in which action serves as both the source and the validation of its theories. It rejects the criterion of prediction as reifying social practices and alienating humans from their social products. In aim and method it must be self-consciously de-alienating in order to enable humans, as subjects, to reappropriate the world they have constructed. The form of its explanations is historical. It traces the dialectic between preformed structural conditions, human understandings, and social action while endeavoring to reveal how ideological distortions have masked contradictions between intentions and structural possibilities. It tries to show its subjects how they can emancipate themselves by conceiving and acting upon the social order in new ways.

The criterion for the truth of critical theorems is the response of the theory's subjects. Because it begins from the meanings its subjects attribute to social processes and attempts to rectify ideologically distorted meanings and values, its method of investigation and validation is based on *dialogue* with its subjects. It does not simply observe humans as objects but endeavors to *engage* them in self-conscious action. In the next section I will outline a method of research which rests on the paradigm of dialogue and participation rather than observation and manipulation.

III. The Method of Critical Research

Critical social research begins from the life problems of definite and particular social agents who may be individuals, groups, or classes that are oppressed by and alienated from social processes they maintain or create but do not control. Beginning from the practical problems of everyday existence it returns to that life with the aim of enlightening its subjects about unrecognized social constraints and possible courses of action by which they may liberate themselves. Its aim is enlightened self-knowledge and effective political action. Its method is dialogue, and its effect is to heighten its subjects' self-awareness of their collective potential as the active agents of history. Practically, this requires the critical investigator to begin from the intersubjective understandings of the participants of a social setting and to return to these participants with a program of education and action designed to change their understandings and their social conditions. Analytically, critical research must, first, provide an account of the dynamics of the social situation of its subjects, that is, a theory of the genesis and maintenance of both social conditions and intersubjective understandings, and, second, must offer a critique of ideologies based on a comparison of the social structure with participants' understandings of it. Critical research links depersonalized social processes to its subjects' choices and actions with the goal of eliminating unrecognized and contradictory consequences of collective action.[19]

A similar logic of investigation applies at any level of analysis from the political struggles of a ghetto neighborhood to the class struggles of world capitalism. The method outlined in this section is phrased in terms of the struggles of local groups and movements—the arena of most progressive action today. However, it is intended, at least in broad outline, as a logic of investigation equally applicable at the societal or world-system levels. Its repeated movement through four phases—interpretive, empirical-analytic, critical-dialectical, and practical—is intended as a fair reading of the method Marx used in his critique of liberal capitalism. Critiques of advanced capitalism must similarly combine structural analyses with critiques of the ideologies that command contemporary thought. Only in this way will radical analysis encourage self-conscious revolutionary action.

Research for local struggles must begin from a dialectical view of the totality of advanced capitalism, however limited our understanding may be at the present. This view of the totality will guide the selection of progressive issues and movements, the interpretation of ideologies, and the selection and analysis of empirical data. In turn, micro-analyses of particular struggles will serve to modify and elaborate macro-theories of advanced capitalism. Critical micro- and macro-analyses thus proceed in dialectical tension . . . and unity.

In the following paragraphs I will present a critical research method in seven steps. While this may seem a bit programmatic and mechanical, my intention in setting out this method so explicitly is to clearly display the necessary differences between the critical method and the method of positive social research. This critical method is summarized and contrasted with the positive method in Figure 18-1 located at the end of this chapter.

1. Identify Movements or Social Groups Whose Interests Are Progressive

Critical research is not *about* a social process but rather is *for* particular social groups—groups that represent progressive tendencies currently obscured and dominated. Abstract categories such as mankind, the people, the working class, women, or minorities cannot be agents of social change. Instead, we must identify organizations, parties, and movements that represent these categories and that are not only able but also willing to put the research findings into practice.[20]

The identification of such groups is not a simple matter and ultimately relies on critical theories of the totality of advanced capitalism. Contemporary commentators do not agree on this totality. For example, Sandberg suggests these will be primarily organizations of the working class while Piccone goes so far as to argue that the Marxist notion of class is no longer useful for identifying progressive movements.[21] I wish to propose that groups are progressive insofar as they express interests, purposes, or human needs which cannot be satisfied within the context of a social order characterized by material and ideological domination. In other words, their interests require more or less fundamental changes in the direction of increased participation in the collective and self-conscious control of social institutions.

Appropriate subjects for critical research would include organizations of the trade union movement including rank and file movements to restore democracy, but it would also include groups not always identified as working class movements such as associations of neighborhood residents, environmental groups, organizations representing the needs of women, minorities, poor people, and other such unpopular peoples' movements. In each case the investigator must determine if the group is both willing and able to participate in the investigation and put the findings into practice.

2. Develop an Interpretive Understanding of the Intersubjective Meanings, Values, and Motives Held by All Groups of Actors in the Subjects' Milieu

Critical research begins with a study of the subjects' own life world—the constitutive meanings, social rules, values, and typical motives which govern action in their particular setting. Social action is dominated by models of what the world is like so that what people are and what they do is determined by the understandings that penetrate their thought and action.[22] This requires that critical accounts be grounded in the meanings and values held by its subjects and those with whom they interact. The second step of critical research is thus hermeneutic: the investigator seeks, through dialogue with the participants, to construct a coherent account of the understandings they have of their world.[23] The resulting accounts will present the practical inferences the actors use to warrant their own actions and the conduct of others.[24] Thus both typical motives and intentions as well as conceptions of conditions will be explicated. These accounts will serve both as a basis for empirical-analytic studies and as a corrective to the investigator's preconceptions regarding the subjects' life-world and experiences.

The critical investigator must determine if meanings are differentiated, that is, if the understandings of some subjects differ from the dominant ideology. Such a differentiation of meaning will provide clues to the contradictions immanent in the dominant system of action and indicate the maturity of the resistance by the dominated group. Moreover, a differentiation of meaning *within* the dominated group may indicate emerging contradictions within the movement itself which must be addressed by the members. The possiblity of ideologically distorted self-understandings within progressive movements must not be discounted.

The accuracy of these interpretive accounts is to be judged by the degree to which the investigator and the subjects come to talk about the latter's actions and beliefs in the same way.[25] Only in dialogue with the subjects can the investigator determine if his or her understanding of their world is adequate for further analysis and critique. In this dialogue the investigator must learn and use the subjects' language and must avoid esoteric mainstream or Marxist social science terms. Only later, in the pedagogical step of the investigation, should the researcher introduce critical concepts and theories.

Meanings, values, and motives are not reducible to individual psychological attributes. The failure of positive social science to consider subjectivity as *inter*subjectivity, that is, as a socio-historical construct and a collective reality, results in an inability to recognize the historical specificity of the particular understandings held by actors.[26] Further, it also leads to the inability to account for crises and fundamental changes which result from attempts to redefine the world and hence reconstitute social practices.[27] Human actions and interpretations are historical; "they take place within a context preconditioned by the sedimentations of the past."[28] The critical study of intersubjective meanings makes sense of what the subjects do by reference to the structural bases of present meanings, values, and motives.

3. Study the Historical Development of the Social Conditions and the Current Social Structures That Constrain the Participants' Actions and Shape Their Understandings

Social reality is not limited to the intersubjective understandings of historically specific groups or classes. Under conditions of domination, these are, to a greater or lesser extent, mystifying and distorting ideologies. In order to critically engage the participants in dialogue about their world, the researcher must also carry out empirical studies of social structures and processes. These studies will elucidate the specific determinants of the participants' beliefs and the existing constraints on social practices.[29] According to Adorno the task for a critical social science is "to confront all its statements on the subjective experience . . . of human beings and human groups, with the objective factors determining their existence." This means, "it will emphasize . . . those determining factors that are connected with the subjective thoughts, feelings and behaviors of those whom it is investigating."[30] These determining factors will be found in historically constructed social structures.

While eschewing the epistemological assumptions of positivism, the critical researcher may fruitfully use empirical findings of past research as well as conduct his or her own empirical studies. Especially important will be studies of the macro-structures of advanced capitalism—structures that form the context for the dominated group's actions and interpretations. For example, in working with progressive labor union movements, it is crucial to confront their anti-communism with accounts of the innumerable red-scare tactics used by capitalists to purge labor of its best organizers. Similarly, the critical researcher working with an anti-nuclear power group will find it necessary to use or develop analyses of the economic and political structure of the energy industry, while a group opposing banks that red-line neighborhoods will need empirical studies of the banking industry. What is important here is to present such empirical findings and analytic theories in ways that clearly show the historicity and constructedness of social conditions. Conditions must be shown, not to be the consequences of immutable laws, but to be structures and processes constructed by elites with specific interests and intentions. Only in this way can oppressed groups see social structures both as constraints and as processes subject to conscious direction.

These empirical analyses of social structures must be referred to the specific experiences of the study's subjects. They must appear to the group to recount real events, issues, and processes which the participants or their predecessors have experienced—even though the subjects may differ from the investigator in the significance or importance they attribute to certain events and processes. In these analyses the origins of specific ideologies must be distinguished from the social processes which serve to maintain them. It is in the latter that we will find immanent contradictions which will lead to crises. It si also in the processes by which ideologies are maintained that we will find the specific social conditions which must be targeted for change. These empirical and historical analyses, along with the interpretive accounts developed in step two, are the basic components of the dialectical and critical steps which follow.

4. Construct Models of the Determinate Relations between Social Conditions, Intersubjective Interpretations of Those Conditions, and Participants' Actions

All critical accounts are based on an understanding of the historical dialectic by which social processes and intersubjective meanings have developed. The aim is to show how the meanings are the product of specific historical conditions and, further, to show how social conditions have changed in such a way as to render these meanings partially or wholly invalid. We must keep in mind that neither social conditions nor intersubjective meanings alone constitute the whole of social reality. Rather, in contrast to both positive and phenomenological approaches, a critical social science focuses on the dialectical tension between the historically created conditions of action and the actors' understandings of these conditions. This requires that the intersubjective meanings, values, and intentions, which may be false or distorting ideologies, be linked to the social processes and structures that create and maintain them. In this way, the critical investigator prepares the way for the comparison of objective social conditions, with intersubjective understandings in the way Adorno suggested in the passage quoted above.

This phase of the investigation takes the form of describing the social processes and structures that gave rise to particular understandings and that presently serve to reinforce or maintain meanings, values, and motives. For example, the meaning of being a university professor today includes the necessity of carrying out well-funded research programs. This is maintained by the historically developed university dependence on government and foundation support. At least in part, the ideology of research productivity and graduate education has developed to legitimate the university's dependence upon this support. Without an understanding of the historical development of both the structures of dependence and the legitimating meaning systems, it would be difficult to account for the frenzied search for grants and contracts which characterizes most faculty activity today. Such a dialectical account lays bare particular relationships between social conditions, ideologies, and actions and provides the foundation for the critique which follows.

5. Elucidate the Fundamental Contradictions Which Are Developing as a Result of Current Actions Based on Ideologically Frozen Understandings

Under conditions of domination and ideologically frozen understandings, many actions are the result of social conditions over which actors have no conscious control.[31] As Giddens notes, "the production or constitution of society is a skilled accomplishment of its members, but one that does not take place under conditions that are wholly intended or wholly comprehended by them."[32] The critical investigator studies the historical consequences of actions in order to uncover the unanticipated and contradictory social conditions which result from ideologically determined actions. Thus, in the university large numbers of graduate students are recruited to work on funded research projects. Many of these students eventually graduate and, in increasing numbers, join private research organizations which compete with university faculty for grants and contracts. The result is a reduction in support for funded research at universities—a consequence surely not intended and one which contradicts present efforts in the universities to maintain research activity. Thus, actions to increase funding for research create the conditions which contradict both the ideology of research productivity and the administrative structure and social practices of the university which have been built up over the past few decades. The ensuing crisis may result in a minor adjustment, such as university research centers adopting organizational forms of private organizations and greatly reducing graduate education, or it may result in more radical changes both in social conditions and in the meanings, values, and motives for research. The outcome of such crises depends upon the critical awareness of groups of scientists and administrators with varying degrees of power and differing interests in either maintaining or changing present relations of power.

The search for fundamental contradictions follows what Adorno called immanent analysis, or the "analysis of the internal consistency or inconsistency of the opinion itself and of its relationship to its object . . . the social structure that undergirds it."[33] This analysis sets the stage for a critique of the dominating ideology which prevents the participants from recognizing the possibilities immanent in the present. Such a critique must proceed from the progressive elements of current understandings (e.g., the desirability and possibility of socially useful research at universities) to show how such possibilities are frustrated by other intentions and practices. In this way the elements of truth in an ideology are extracted from their context of falsity.

Against the background of an historical account and an analysis of the relations between social conditions, ideology, and actions, the critical researcher helps the participants to see why past social conditions cannot be recaptured. The researcher must show how present intentions are unrealizable in the context of changed circumstances (e.g., the return to days of large and numerous research grants or, in other struggles, the return to laissez faire capitalist economy) or, alternatively, must show how the ideology was internally contradictory and therefore never did accurately interpret social conditions (for example, relations of equal exchange between workers and capitalists).

At this point, having initiated the interpretive, empirical, and dialectical phases of critical research, investigator must participate in a program of education and provide assistance in developing strategies for change. The final two steps in this research method demonstrate the *practical intent* of critical research.

6. *Participate in a Program of Education with the Subjects That Gives Them New Ways of Seeing Their Situation*

Critical social science is distinguished fundamentally from positive social science by its goal of involving the actors it studies. According to Fay the aim is to enlighten subjects so that, coming to see themselves and their social situation in a new way, they *themselves* can decide to alter the conditions which they find repressive.[34] A program of education links social conditions to the subjects' actions by explicating the contradictions that have developed historically. Moreover, it shows how conditions have changed and how they can be changed in the future given increased understanding and self-awareness. Finally, a program of education encourages the participants to develop new understandings and actions which are appropriate and possible under changed conditions.

The model of education which is appropriate is not the familiar one of formal schooling but, rather, a model of dialogue in which the critical researcher attempts to either problematize certain meanings, motives, or values accepted by his or her subjects or to respond to issues which are already perceived by them as problematic. The impetus to search for new understandings and new actions must come from the subjects, not from the researcher. In response, the researcher must express his or her critical accounts in the subjects' own language and in terms of acting *agents* rather than in terms of impersonal social processes.[35] These accounts must show them how they can *act* to change the situation that frustrates them rather than merely showing them how that situation came to exist. It must point to theoretically and empirically warrantable *possibilities* immanent in the development of social conditions. The pegagogy of Paulo Freire provides a model for such an education.[36] Freire's image of critical education has been characterized as "the process in which people, not as recipients, but as knowing subjects, achieve a deepening awareness both of the sociohistorical reality which shapes their lives and of their capacity to transform that reality."[37]

A critical education program provides one criterion of the validity of critical accounts: the response which its subjects make to its claims. This is one reason why education, as well as political action, are not simply "tacked on" at the end of the critical research program but is central to testing and improving its accounts. Dialogic education is integral to every research program which treats subjects as active agents instead of objectifying them and reifying their social conditions. The aim of critical research, however, is not simply to enlighten but also to inform and initiate political action.

7. Participate in a Theoretically Grounded Program of Action Which Will Change Social Conditions and, in Addition, Will Engender New Less Alienated Understandings and Needs

The purpose of critical research and theory is to initiate action by providing an adequate knowledge of the historical development of social conditions and meanings and a vision of a desirable and possible future.[38] This final step of political action links the subjects' actions back to social conditions in order to reduce or eliminate the irrational construction of contradictory social conditions. Action becomes conscious and reflective through critical education while social conditions become intentional constructions through action informed by a critical analysis. What is objective—social structure and process—becomes subjective or meaningful comprehended and what is subjectively comprehended becomes objectified in social process and structure. The subjects' existence and their self-understandings are brought into theoretical and practical unity and critical thought becomes an active social force. Through critical action the subjective and objective factors of revolutionary change are united. Despite the dangers to theoretical independence which inhere in too great an identification with a progressive or revolutionary movement (for example, subordination to the party), the validity of critical theorems can only be tested in practice and this requires the involvement of the researchers in the subjects' political activity.

Another major reason for continuing involvement in political action carried on by the subjects of a critical investigation is the necessity to combat tendencies for groups to become reformist. If the researcher merely responds to the felt needs and frustrations of dominated groups as Fay suggests, she or he may only help to satisfy immediate needs and intentions within the context of a fundamentally unchanged social structure.[39] Since the needs of members of society are generated by the concretely existing and alienating social conditions, the critical researcher must encourage political action which constructs new social conditions conducive to nonalienated needs such as participation, love, creativity;, and collective control.[40] The challenge for the researcher as participant is to continually broaden and deepen the participants' awareness of the meaning and probable outcome of their political action. The aim is the subject's progressive movement toward an understanding of the totality of historical circumstances that affect them. This requires participation in a continuous cycle of critical analysis, education, and action.

Critical researchers do not, therefore, enter progressive groups on an episodic basis to solve clearly defined problems. Since their aim is to stimulate a self-sustaining process of critical analysis and enlightened action, it becomes necessary for critical researchers to ally themselves with progressive groups and work wih them for considerable periods of time. This increases the problems of selecting a group willing and able to participate in critical research for it requires that they become progressively more self-critical and willing to analyze their own values, motives, and understandings as well as critically evaluate the results of their political actions. The role of the critical researcher is, through dialogue and analysis, to return the group's attention to their understandings and intentions (Step 2) and to re-initiate the critical analysis of actions (Step 4) in light of the further development of historical forces (Step 3). The aim here is to develop the group's own capacity to discover the contradictions which may be developing as a result of their actions (Step 5) and to educate themselves for more enlightened and self-conscious political action (Steps 6 and 7).

IV. Conclusion

A look at Figure 18-1 will highlight the differences between positive and critical social research. Positive social research begins with the iden-

Figure 18-1 Steps in the Research Methods of Positive and Critical Social Sciences.

Positive Social Science	Critical Social Science
1. Identify a scientific problem by studying the results of past empirical and theoretical work.	1. Identify social groups or movements whose interests are progressive.
2. Develop empirically testable hypotheses which promise to improve the theory's explanatory and predictive power.	2. Develop an interpretive understanding of the intersubjective meanings, values, and motives held by all groups in the setting.
3. Select a setting (community, group, organization, etc.) which is suitable to the scientific problem.	3. Study the historical development of the social conditions and the current social structures that constrain actions and shape understandings.
4. Develop measures and data-gathering strategies based on: Previous research Observations and interviews in the setting The investigator's own "common-sense" Knowledge of social processes	4. Construct models of the relations between social conditions, intersubjective interpretations of those conditions, and participants' actions.
5. Gather data through: Experiments Existing documents and texts Surveys and interviews Observations	5. Elucidate the fundamental contradictions which are developing as a result of actions based on ideologically frozen understandings: Compare conditions with understandings Critique the ideology Discover immanent possibilities for action
6. Analyze data to test hypotheses.	6. Participate in a program of education with the subjects that gives them new ways of seeing their situation.
7. Alter laws and theory in light of findings and restate scientific problem to be addressed by subsequent research.	7. Participate in a theoretically grounded program of action which will change social conditions and will also engender new, less alienated, understandings and needs.
Return to Step 1.	Return to Step 2.

tification of a scientific problem, proceeds through data gathering and hypothesis testing, and returns to confirm or revise theoretical understandings. Critical research begins from the practical problems and ideologically distorted understandings of groups that are dominated and frustrated by present social conditions. It proceeds through interpretive, empirical, and dialectical phases of analysis with the intent to inform the emancipatory practices of these groups. It is a method of *praxis* for it combines disciplined analysis with practical action. It is aimed not merely at understanding the world, but at changing it. Instead of objectifying people and society, it enables its subjects to reappropriate their life-world and become self-conscious agents of socio-historical progress. It is democratic, rather than elitist and it is enlightening instead of mystifying. Such a critical research method is the basis for critical theories which have practical utility in the political struggle for freedom.

Notes

Acknowledgments. I would like to thank Richard Appelbaum, Walter Feinberg, and T. R. Young for their comments on earlier drafts of this paper. I hope the present version fairly reflects many of their suggestions while maintaining enough of our original differences to prompt further dialogue.

1. Mao Tsetung, "Some Questions Concerning Methods of Leadership," *Selected Readings from the Works of Mao Tsetung* (Peking: Foreign Language Press, 1943), pp. 287–94.
2. Martin Jay, *The Dialectical Imagination* (Boston: Little, Brown, 1973); Perry Anderson, *Considerations on Western Marxism* (London: New Left Books, 1976).
3. Anderson, *Considerations on Western Marxism.*
4. Cf. John H. Sewart, "Critical Theory and the Critique of Conservative Method," *American Sociologist* 13 (1978): 15–22.
5. Barry Smart, *Sociology, Phenomenology and Marxist Analysis* (Boston: Routledge and Kegan Paul, 1976).
6. Max Horkheimer, *Critical Theory: Selected Essays* (New York: Herder and Herder, 1972).
7. Ibid., p. 244.
8. Charles Taylor, "Interpretation and the Sciences of Man," *Review of Metaphysics* 25, no. 3 (1971): 1–51.
9. Jürgen Habermas, *Knowledge and Human Interests* (Boston: Beacon, 1971), p. 69.
10. Ibid.: Richard J. Bernstein, *The Restructuring of Social and Political Theory* (New York: Harcourt, Brace and Jovanovich, 1976).
11. Brian Fay, *Social Theory and Political Practice* (New York: Holmes and Meier, 1976), p. 57.
12. James Farganis, "A Preface to Critical Theory," *Theory and Society* 2 (1975): 467–482.
13. Paul Piccone, "Phenomenological Marxism," in *Towards a New Marxism*, ed. B. Grahl and P. Piccone (St. Louis, Mo.: Telos Press, 1973).
14. Taylor, "Interpretation."
15. Georg Henrik von Wright, *Explanation and Understanding* (Ithaca, N.Y.: Cornell University Press, 1971).
16. Jürgen Habermas, *Legitimation Crisis* (Boston: Beacon, 1975).
17. Horkheimer, *Critical Theory.*
18. Bernstein, *Restructuring of Social and Political Theory*, p. 44.
19. Ake Sandberg, *The Limits to Democratic Planning* (Stockholm: Liber Förlag, 1976), p. 45.
20. Ibid., p. 227.

Part Three: The Critical Approach

21. Piccone, "Phenomenological Marxism," p. 157.
22. Bernstein, *Restructuring of Social and Political Theory*, p. 63.
23. Hans-Georg Gadamer, "The Historicity of Understanding," in *Critical Sociology*, ed. P. Connerton (New York: Penguin, 1976), pp. 117–133.
24 .Von Wright, *Explanation and Understanding*
25. Fay, *Social Theory and Political Practice*, p. 82.
26. Friedrich Pollock, "Empirical Research into Public Opinion," in *Critical Sociology*, ed. Connerton, pp. 225–236.
27. Taylor, "Interpretation."
28. Piccone, "Phenomenological Marxism," p. 141.
29. Richard P. Appelbaum, "Marxist Method: Structural Constraints and Social Praxis," *American Sociologist* 13 (1978): 73–81.
30. Theodor W. Adorno, "Sociology and Empirical Research," in *Critical Sociology*, ed. Connerton, pp. 237–257.
31. Fay, *Social Theory and Political Practice*, p. 95.
32. Anthony Giddens, *New Rules of Sociological Method* (New York: Basic Books, 1976), p. 102.
33. Adorno, "Sociology and Empirical Research," p. 256.
34. Fay, *Social Theory and Political Practice*, p. 102.
35. Sandberg, *Limits to Democratic Planning*, p. 227.
36. Paulo Freire, *Pegagogy of the Oppressed* (New York: Seabury, 1970); Paulo Freire, *Cultural Action for Freedom* (Cambridge, Mass.: Center for the Study of Development and Social Change, 1970).
37. Freire, *Cultural Action*, p. 27 n.
38. Fay, *Social Theory and Political Practice*.
39. Agnes Heller, "Theory and Practice: Their Relation to Human Needs," *Social Praxis* 1 (1973): 359–373.

CHAPTER 19

The School as a Conservative Force: Scholastic and Cultural Inequalities

Pierre Bourdieu

(translated by J. C. Whitehouse)

It is probably cultural inertia which still makes us see education in terms of the ideology of the school as a liberating force ("l'école libératrice") and as a means of increasing social mobility, even when the indications tend to be that it is in fact one of the most effective means of perpetuating the existing social pattern, as it both provides an apparent justification for social inequalities and gives recognition to the cultural heritage, that is, to a *social* gift treated as a *natural* one.

As processes of elimination occur throughout the whole of the period spent in education, we can quite justifiably note the effects they have at the highest levels of the system. The chances of entering higher education are dependent on direct or indirect selection varying in severity with subjects of different social classes throughout their school lives. The son of a manager is eighty times as likely to get to university as the son of an agricultural worker, forty times as likely as the son of a factory worker, and twice as likely as even the son of a man employed in a lower-salaried staff grade.[1] It is striking that the higher the level of the institution of learning, the more aristocratic its intake. The sons of members of managerial grades and of the liberal professions account for 57 percent of students at the Polytechnique, 54 percent of those at the École Normale Supérieure (noted for its "democratic" intake), 47 percent of those at the École Normale and 44 percent of those at the Institut d'Études Politiques.

Reprinted with the permission of the author from *Contemporary Research in the Sociology of Education* edited by J. Eggleston (London: Methuen and Co., 1974).

However, simply stating the fact of educational inequality is not enough. We need a description of the objective processes which continually exclude childen from the least privileged social classes. Indeed, it seems that a sociological explanation can account for the unequal achievement usually imputed to unequal ability. For the most part, the effects of cultural privilege are only observed in their crudest forms—a good word put in, the right contacts, help with studies, extra teaching, information on the educational system, and job outlets. In fact, each family transmits to its children, indirectly rather than directly, a certain *cultural capital* and a certain *ethos*. The latter is a system of implicit and deeply interiorized values which, among other things, helps to define attitudes towards the cultural capital and educational institutions. The cultural heritage, which differs from both points of view according to social class, is the cause of the initial inequality of children when faced with examinations and tests, and hence of unequal achievement.

Choice of Options

The attitudes of the members of the various social classes, both parents and children, and in particular their attitudes towards school, the culture of the school, and the type of future the various types of studies lead to, are largely an expression of the system of explicit or implied values which they have as a result of belonging to a given social class. The fact that different social classes send, despite equal attainment, a different proportion of their children to *lycées* is often explained by such vague terms as "parental choice." It is doubtful whether one can meaningfully use such expressions except metaphorically, as surveys have shown that "in general there is a massive correlation between parental choice and options taken"—in other words, parental choice is in most cases determined by real possibilities.[2] In fact, everything happens as if parental attitudes towards their children's education—as shown in the choice of sending them either to a secondary school or leaving them in the upper classes of an elementary school, and of sending them to a *lycée* (and thus accepting the prospect of prolonged studies, at least, to the *baccalauréat*) or to a *collège d'enseignement général* (and thus accepting a shorter period of education, until the *brevat*, for example)—were primarily the interiorization of the fate objectively allotted (and statistically quantifiable) as a whole to the social category to which they belong. They are constantly reminded of their fate by a direct or indirect intuitive grasp of the statistics of the failures or partial successes of children of the same kind, and also less directly, by the evaluation of the elementary school teacher who, in his role as a counsellor, consciously or unconsciously takes into account the social origin of his pupils and thus, unwittingly and involuntarily, counterbalances the over-theoretical nature of a forecast based purely on performance. If members of the lower middle and working classes take reality as being equivalent to their wishes, it is because, in this area as elsewhere, aspirations and demands are defined in both form and content by objective conditions which exclude the possibility of hoping for the unobtainable. When they say, for example, that classical studies in a *lycée* are not for them, they are saying much more than that they cannot afford them. The formula, which is an expression of internalized necessity, is, we might say, in the imperative indicative as it expresses both an impossibility and a taboo.

The same objective conditions as those which determine parental attitudes and dominate the major choices in the school career of the children also govern the children's attitude to the same choices and, consequently, their whole attitude towards school, to such an extent that parents, to explan their decision not to let the child go to secondary school, can offer as a close runner-up to the cost of study the child's wish to leave school. But, at a deeper level, as the reasonable wish to get on through education will not materalize as long as the real chances of success are slim, and although working class people may well be unaware of their children's 2 in 100 chance of getting to university, their behavior is based on an empirical evaluation of the real hopes common to all individuals in their social group. Thus it is understandable that the lower middle class—a transitional class—lays more emphasis on educational values as the school offers them reasonable chances of achieving all they want by mixing the values of social success and cultural prestige. In comparison with working class children, who are doubly disadvantaged as regards facilities for assimilating culture and the propensity to acquire it, middle class children receive from their parents not only encouragement and exhortation with regard to their school work but also an ethos of "getting on" in society and an ambition to do the same at and by means of school, which enables their keen desire for the possession of culture to compensate for cultural poverty. It also seems that the same self-denying ethos of social mobility which gives rise to the prevalence of small families in certain sections of the lower middle classes also underlies their attitude toward the school.[3]

In the most fertile social groups, such as agricultural workers, farmers, and factory workers, the chances of going into the *sixième* decrease clearly and regularly as a further unit is added to the family, but they fall drastically for less fertile groups such as artisans, small tradesman, clerks, and lower-salaried personnel, in families of four and five children (or more)—i.e., in families distinguished from others in the group by their high fertility—so that instead of seeing in the number of children the causal explanation of the sharp drop in the percentage of children attending school, we should perhaps suppose that the desire to limit the number of births and to give the children a secondary education are a sign, in groups where *both* those traits are noted, of the same inclination to make sacrifices.[4]

In general, children and their families make their own choices by reference to the constraints which determine them. Even when the choices seem to them to follow simply from taste or vocational sense, they nevertheless indicate the roundabout effects of objective conditions. In other words, the structure of the objective chances of social mobility and, more precisely, of the chances of a social mobility by means of education, conditions attitudes to school (and it is precisely these attitudes which are most important in defining the chances of access to education, of accepting the values of norms of the school and of succeeding within the framework and thus rising in society) through subjective hopes (shared by all individuals defined by the same objective future, and reinforced by the group's pressure for conformity), which are no more than objective chances intuitively perceived and generally internalized.[5]

A description of the logic of the process of internalization, at the end of which objective chances have become subjective hopes or lack of hope, would seem necessary. Can that fundamental dimension of class ethos, the attitude to the objective future, be in fact anything but the internalization of the objective future course of events which is gradually brought home to and imposed on every member of a given class by means of the experience of successors and failures? Psychologists have observed that the level of aspiration of individuals is essentially determined by reference to the probability (judged intuitively by means of previous successes or failures) of achieving the desired goal.

"A successful individual," writes Lewin, "typically sets his next goal somewhat, but not too much, above his last achievement. In this way he steadily raises his level of aspiration. . . . The unsuccessful individual on the other hand, tends to show one of two reactions: he sets his goal very low, frequently below his past achievement . . . or he sets his goal far above his ability."[6] It is quite clear that a circular process occurs: "If the standards of a group are low an individual will slacken his efforts and set his goals far below those he could reach. He will, on the other hand, raise his goals if the group standards are raised."[7] If we also accept that "both the ideals and the action of an individual depend on the group to which he belongs and upon the goals and expectation of that group,"[8] it can be seen that the influence of peer groups—which is always relatively homogeneous from the point of view of social origin as, for example, the number of children going to *collèges d'enseignement général, collèges d'enseignement technique* and *lycées*, (and, within these, their spread through the various types of education offered by each) is very much a function of the social class of the children—reinforces, among the least privileged children, the influence of the family milieu and the general social environment, which tend to discourage ambitions seen as excessive and always somewhat suspect in that they imply rejection of the individual's social origins. Thus, everything conspires to bring back those who, as we say, "have no future" to "reasonable" hopes (or "realistic" ones, as Lewin calls them) and in fact, in many cases, to make them give up hope.

The cultural capital and the ethos, as they take shape, combine to determine behavior in school and the attitude to school which make up the differential principle of elimination operating for children of different social classes. Although success at school, directly linked to the cultural capital transmitted by the family milieu, plays a part in the choice of options taken up, it seems that the major determinant of study is the family attitude to the school which is itself, as we have seen, a function of the objective hopes of success at school which define each social category. M. Paul Clerc has shown that, although both scholastic attainment and the rate of entry into the *lycée* depend closely on social class, the overall inequality in the rate of entry to the *lycée* depends more on the inequality in the proportion of those of equal attainment who enter the *lycée* rather than on inequality of attainment itself.[9]

That means in fact that the handicaps are *cumulative*, as children from the lower and middle classes who overall achieve a lower success rate must be more successful for their family and their teachers to consider encouraging further study. The same method of double selection also comes into operation with the age criterion: children from peasant and working class homes, usually older than children from more privileged homes, are more severely eliminated, at an equal age, than children from the latter. In short, the general principle which leads to the excessive elimination of working and middle-class children can be expressed thus: the children of these classes, who because of a lack of cultural capital have less chance than others of exceptional success, are nevertheless expected to achieve exceptional success to reach secondary education. But the process of double selection becomes increasingly important as one rises to the higher levels of secondary establishments and ascends the socially selective hierarchy of subject departments within them. There, once again, given equal achievement, the children of privileged classes go more often than others both to the *lycée*, and the classics side of the *lycée*, the children of underprivileged strata mostly having to pay for their entry to the *lycée* by relegation to a *collège d'enseignement général*, while the children of well-to-do classes who are not clever enough to go to a *lycée* can find a suitable alternative in a private school.

It will be seen that here too advantages and disadvantages are cumulative, because the initial choices (of school and subject department) determine the school future irreversibly. Indeed, one survey has shown that results obtained by arts students over a series of exercises aimed at measuring the comprehension and manipulation of language and in particular of the language of education were directly related to the type of secondary establishment attended and to knowledge of Greek and Latin. Choices made when entering the *lycée* thus close the options once and for all so that the child's part of the cultural heritage is determined by his previous school career. In fact, such choices, which are a commitment of a whole future, are taken, with reference to varying images of that future. Thirty-one percent of the parents of children at *lycées* want their children to go on to higher education, 27 percent to the *baccalauréat*, only a tiny proportion of them wanting the children to proceed to a technical diploma (4 percent) or to BEPC (2 percent): 27 percent of parents of children at *collèges d'enseignement général* on the other hand want to see them obtain a technical or professional diploma, 15 percent the BEPC, 14 percent the *baccalauréat*, and 7 percent want them to go on to higher education.[10]

Thus, overall statistics which show an increase in the percentage of children attending secondary school hide the fact that lower class children are obliged to pay for access to this form of education by means of a considerable diminution in the area of their choices for the future.

The systematic figures which still separate, at the end of their school career, students from different social milieus owe both their form and their nature to the fact that the selection that they have undergone is not equally severe for all, and that *social* advantages or disadvantages have gradually been transformed into *educational* advantages and disadvantages as a result of premature choices which, directly linked with social origin, have duplicated and reinforced their influence. Although the school's compensating action in subjects directly taught explains at least to some extent the fact that the advantage of upper class students is increasingly obvious as the areas of culture directly taught and completely controlled by the school are left behind, only the effect of compensation

396

combined with overselection can explain the fact that for a behavioral skill such as the scholastic use of scholastic language, the differences tend to lessen to an overwhelming extent and even to be inverted, since highly selected students from the lower classes obtain results equivalent to those of the higher social classes who have been less vigorously selected and better than those of the middle classes, who are also penalized by the linguistic atmosphere of their families, but are also less rigorously selected.[11]

Similarly, all the characteristics of a school career, in terms of schools attended or subjects taken, are indices of the direct influence of the family milieu, which they reflect within the logic of the scholastic system proper. For example, if greater mastery of language is always encountered, in our present state of pedagogical traditions and techniques among arts students who have studied classical languages, this is because pursuit of a classical education is the medium through which other influences are exerted and expressed, such as parental information on subjects of study and careers, success in the first stages of a school career, or the advantage conferred by entry into those classes in which the system recognizes its elite.

In seeking to grasp the logic by which the transformation of the social heritage into a scholastic heritage operates in different class situations, one would observe that the choice of subjects or school and the results obtained in the first year of secondary education (which themselves are linked to these choices) condition the use which children from different milieux can make of their heritage, be it positive or negative. It would no doubt be imprudent to claim to be able to isolate, in the system of relations we call school careers, determining factors and, *a fortiori*, a single predominant factor. But, if success at the highest level of a school career is still very closely connected to the very earliest stages of that career, it is also true that very early choices have a great effect on the chances of getting into a given branch of higher education and succeeding in it. In short, crucial decisions have been taken at a very early stage.

The Functioning of the School and Its Role as a Socially Conservative Force

It will be easy—perhaps too easy—to accept what has been said so far. To stop there, however, would mean not questioning the responsibility of the school in the perpetuation of social inequalities. If that question is seldom raised, it is because the Jacobin ideology which inspires most of the criticism leveled at the university system does not really take inequality with regard to the school system into account, because of its attachment to a formal definition of educational equity. If, however, one takes socially conditioned inequalities with regard to schools and education seriously, one is obliged to conclude that the *formal* equity, which the whole education system is subject to, is in reality unjust and that in any society which claims to have democratic ideals it protects privileges themselves rather than their open transmission.

In fact, to penalize the underprivileged and favor the most privileged, the school has only to neglect, in its teaching methods and techniques and its criteria when making academic judgments, to take into account the cultural inequalities between children of different social classes. In other words, by treating all pupils, however unequal they may be in reality, as equal in rights and duties, the educational system is led to give its *de facto* sanction to initial cultural inequalities. The formal equality which governs pedagogical practice is in fact a cloak for and a justification of indifference to the real inequalities with regard to the body of knowledge taught or rather demanded. Thus, for example, the "pedagogy" used in secondary or higher education is, objectively, an "arousing pedagogy," in Weber's words, aimed at stimulating the "gifts" hidden in certain exceptional individuals by means of certain incantatory techniques, such as the verbal skills and powers of the teacher. As opposed to a rational and really universal pedagogy, which would take nothing for granted initially, would not count as acquired what some, and only some, of the pupils in question had inherited, would do all things for all and would be organized with the explicit aim of providing all with the means of *acquiring* that which, although apparently a natural gift, is only *given* to the children of the educated classes, our own pedagogical tradition is in fact, despite external appearances of irreproachable equality and universality, only there for the benefit of pupils who are in the *particular position* of possessing a cultural heritage conforming to that demanded by the school. Not only does it exclude any questions as to the most effective methods of transmitting to all the knowledge and the know-how which it demands of all and which different social classes transmit very unequally; it also tends to disparage as "elementary" (with undertones of "vulgar") and, paradoxically, as "pedantic" pedagogical methods with such aims. It is not by chance that higher elementary education, when it was in competition with the *lycée* in its traditional form, unsettled working class pupils less and attracted the scorn of the elite precisely because it *was* more explicitly and technically methodical. We have here two concepts of culture and of the techniques of transmitting it which, in the form of corporate interests, are still visible in the clash between teachers emerging from the elementary schools and those following the more traditional route through the secondary system.[12] We should also have to examine the role played for teachers by the pious horror of cramming for examinations as opposed to "general education." Cramming is not an absolute evil when it consists simply of realizing that pupils are being prepared for an examination and of making them aware of this. The disparagement of examination techniques is merely the corollary of the exaltation of intellectual prowess which is structurally akin to the values of culturally privileged groups. Those who have by right the necessary *manner* are always likely to dismiss as laborious and laboriously acquired values which are only of any worth when they are innate.

Teachers are the products of a system whose aim is to transmit an aristocratic culture, and are likely to adopt its values with greater ardor in proportion to the degree to which they owe it their own academic and social success. How indeed could they avoid unconsciously bringing into play the values of the milieu from which they come, or to which they now belong, when teaching and assessing their pupils? Thus, in higher education, the working or lower middle class student will be judged according to the scale of values of the educated classes which many teachers owe to their social origin and which they willingly adopt, particularly, perhaps, when their membership of the elite dates from their entry into the teaching profession. As soon as the lower middle class ethos is judged from the point of view of the ethos of the elite, and measured against the dilettantism of the well-born and well-educated man, the scale of values is reversed and, by means of a change of sign, application becomes pedantry and a respect for hard work grinding, limited pettiness, with the implication that it is intended to compensate for a lack of natural talents. On the other hand, of course, the dilettantism of students from privileged social classes, which is apparent in many aspects of their behavior and in the very style of their relationship with a culture which they never owe exclusively to school, corresponds to what—often unconsciously—is expected of them by their teachers and even more by the objective and explicit demands of the school. Even minor signs of social status such as "correct" dress and bearing and the style of speech and accent are minor class signs and—again most often without their knowledge—help to shape the judgment of their teachers.[13] The teacher who, while appearing to make judgments on "innate gifts," is in fact measuring by reference to the ethos of the cultivated elite conduct based on a self-sacrificing ethos of hard and painstaking work in setting one type of relationship to culture against another, and all children are born into one or the other. The culture of the elite is so near to that of the school that children from the lower middle class (and *a fortiori* from the agricultural and industrial working class) can only acquire with great effort something which is *given* to the children of the cultivated classes—style, taste, wit—in short, those attitudes and aptitudes which seem natural in members of the cultivated classes and naturally expected of them precisely because (in the ethnological sense) they are the *culture* of that class. Children from the lower middle classes, as they receive nothing from their family of any use to them in their academic activities except a sort of undefined enthusiasm to acquire culture, are obliged to expect and receive everything from school, even if it means accepting the school's criticism of them as "plodders."

What the education system both hands on and demands is an aristocratic culture and, above all, an aristocratic relationship with it.[14] This is particularly clear in the relationship of teachers to language. Moving to and fro between charismatic use of the word as a lofty incantation whose function is to create in the pupil a suitable receptivity to grace, and a traditional use of university language as the consecrated vehicle of a consecrated culture, teachers assume that they already share a common language and set of values with their pupils, but this is only so when the system is dealing with its own heirs. By acting as if the language of teaching, full of allusions and shared understanding, was "natural" for "intelligent" and "gifted" pupils, teachers need not trouble to make any technical checks on their handling of language and the students' understanding of it, and can also see as strictly fair academic judgments which in fact perpetuate cultural privilege. As language is the most important part of the cultural heritage because, as syntax; it provides a system of transposable mental postures which themselves completely reflect and dominate the whole of experience, and as the gap between university language and that spoken in fact by the different social classes varies greatly, it is impossible to have pupils with equal rights and duties towards university language and use of language without being obliged to hold the gift responsible for a number of inequalities which are primarily social. Apart from a lexis and a syntax, each individual inherits from his milieu a certain attitude towards words and their use which prepares him, to a greater or lesser extent, for the scholastic games which are still to some extent, in the French tradition of literary studies, games with words. This relationship with words, whether reverent or emancipated, assumed or familiar, thrifty or extravagent, is never more obvious than in oral examinations, and teachers consciously or unconsciously distinguish between "natural" ease of expression composed of fluency and elegant lack of constraint, and "forced" ease, common among lower middle and working class students, which reflects the effort to conform, at the price of not getting quite the right note, to the norms of university discourse, indicating some anxiety to impress, and too evidently an attempt to create the right impression to be free of all taint of self-seeking vulgarity. In short, the teachers' *certitudo sui*, which is never more clearly seen than in the high eloquence of a lecture, is based on class ethnocentrism which authorizes both a given usage of academic language and a certain attitude to the use which students made of language in general and of academic language in particular.

Thus, implicit in these relationships with language, there can be seen the whole significance allotted by the educated classes to learned culture and the institution responsible for transmitting it—the latent functions which they give to educational institutions, i.e. the task of organizing the cult of a culture which can be offered to all because in fact it is reserved for the members of the class whose culture it is, the hierarchy of intellectual values which gives the impressive manipulators of words and ideas a higher rank than the humble servants of techniques, and the inner logic of a system whose *objective* function is to *preserve* the values which are the basis of the social order. More deeply, it is because traditional education is objectively addressed to those who have obtained from their social milieu the linguistic and cultural capital that it *objectively* demands that it cannot openly declare its demands and feel itself obliged to give everyone the means of meeting them. Like common law, the university tradition merely specified infringements and punishments without ever openly stating the principles underlying them. Thus, to take examinations as an example, it is quite clear that the more vaguely what they ask for is defined, whether it be a question of knowledge or of presentation, and the less specific the criteria adopted by the examiners, the more they favor the privileged. Thus, the nearer written examinations come to the more traditional kind of "literary" exercise, the more they favor the exhibition of imponderable qualities in style, syntax of ideas, or knowledge marshaled, the *dessertatio de omni re scribili* which dominates the great *concours* in literary subjects (and still plays an important part in scientific ones), the more clearly they divide candidates of differing social classes. In the same way, the "inheritors" are more favored in oral examinations than in written ones, particularly when the oral becomes *explicitly* the test of distinguished and cultivated manners which it always *implicitly* is.[15] It is quite clear that such a system can only work perfectly as long as it can recruit and select students capable of satisfying its objective demands, that is, as long as it can be directed towards individuals possessing a cultural capital (and able to make it pay off) which it presupposes and endorses without openly demanding it or transmitting it methodically. The only test to which it can really be put is not, it is clear, that of numbers, but that of the *quality* of students. "Mass education," about which we talk so much nowadays, is the opposite of both education reserved for a small number of inheritors of the culture demanded by the school and of education reserved for any small number of students of any *kind whatever*.

In fact, the system can take in an increasingly large number of pupils, as happened during the first half of this century, without having to change profoundly, provided that the newcomers are also in possession of the socially acquired aptitudes which the school traditionally demands.

On the other hand, it is bound to experience crises (which it will describe as "a lowering of standards") when it takes in an increasingly large number of pupils who have not acquired the same mastery as their predecessors of the cultural heritage of their social class (as happens when there is a continuous increase in the percentage of children undergoing secondary and higher education from the classes which have traditionally enjoyed it, if there is a similar drop in the rate of selection) or who, coming from culturally underprivileged classes, have no cultural heritage. A number of changes now taking place within the education system can be ascribed to determining factors which can properly be described as *morphological*. It is therefore clear that they affect nothing essential, and that there is very little question, either in programs of reform or in the demands of teachers and students, of anything affecting specifically the traditional system of education or its working. It is true that enlarging the social basis of recruitment to the *sixième* would no doubt be a decisive test entailing very probably major changes in the functioning of the system in its most specific form, if the segregation of children according to the hierarchy of types of schools and "sides" (ranging from the *collèges d'enseignement général* or the *collèges d'enseignement technique* to the classical "sides" of the *lycées*) did not afford the system a protection tailored to its own inner logic, in that lower class children, who do not bring to their school work either the keenness to learn of lower middle class children or the cultural capital of upper class children, take refuge in a kind of negative withdrawal which upsets teachers, and is expressed in forms of disorder previously unknown. It is of course obvious that in such cases it is enough to let matters take their own course to bring crude social handicaps into play and for everything to return to normal. To meet this challenge in a really effective way, the education system should have at its disposal the means to carry out systematic and widespread educational priority programs of the kind that it can dispense with as long as it is aimed at children from the privileged classes.[16]

It would therefore be ingenuous to expect that, from the very way of working of a system which itself defines its methods of recruitment by imposing demands which are all the more effective for being implicit, there should arise the contradictions capable of determining a basic change in the logic of its own working and of preventing the institution responsible for the conservation and transmission of culture from carrying out its task of social conservation. By giving individuals educational aspirations strictly tailored to their position in the social hierarchy, and by operating a selection procedure which, although apparently formally equitable, endorses real inequalities, schools help both to perpetuate and legitimize inequalities. By awarding allegedly impartial qualifications (which are also largely accepted as such) for socially conditioned aptitudes which it treats as unequal "gifts," it transforms *de facto* inequalities into *de jure* ones and *economic and social* differences into *distinctions of quality*, and legitimates the transmission of the cultural heritage. In doing so, it is performing a confidence trick. Apart from enabling the elite to justify being what it is, the *ideology of giftedness*, the cornerstone of the whole educational and social system, helps to enclose the underprivileged classes in the roles which society has given them by making them see as natural inability things which are only a result of an inferior social status, and by persuading them that they owe their social fate (which is increasingly tied to their educational fate as society becomes more rationalized) to their individual nature and their lack of gifts. The exceptional success of those few individuals who escape the collective fate of their class apparently justifies educational selection and gives credence to the myth of the school as a liberating force among those who have been eliminated, by giving the impression that success is exclusively a matter of gifts and work. Finally those whom the system has "liberated"—teachers in elementary, secondary and higher education—put their faith in *l'école libératrice* at the service of the school which is in truth a conservative force which owes part of its power of conservation to that myth. Thus by its own logic the educational system can help to perpetuate cultural privileges without those who are privileged having to use it. By giving cultural inequalities an endorsement which formally at least is in keeping with democratic ideals, it provides the best justification for these inequalities.

At the end of *The Republic* Plato describes how souls about to start another life had to make their own choice of lots among patterns of lives, all possible animal and human lives, and how, once the choice was made, they had to drink the water of the River of Forgetfulness before returning to earth. The theodicy Plato's myth assumes devolves, in our societies, on university and school examiners. But we can quote Plato further,

> Then a prophet first marshalled them in order, and then taking lots and patterns of lives from the lap of Lachesis, mounted upon a high pulpit and spoke: "The word of the daughter of Necessity, maid Lachesis. Souls of a day, here beginneth another circle that bears the mortal race to death. The angel will not cast lots for you, but you shall choose your angel. Let him whose lot falls first have first choice of a life to which he shall be bound by Necessity. . . . The responsibility is on him that chooseth. There is none on God."[17]

In order to change fate into the choice of freedom, the school, the prophet of Necessity, need only succeed in convincing individuals to rely on its judgment and persuading them that they themselves have chosen the fate that was already reserved for them. From that point there is no questioning the divinity of society. We could consider Plato's myth of the initial choice of lots with that proposed by Campanella in *La Città del Sole:* to set up immediately a situation of perfect mobility and to ensure the complete independence of the position of fathers and sons, one thing only is necessary—the separation of children from their parents at birth.[18]

Statisticians are in fact implicitly invoking the myth of perfect mobility when they refer the empirically observed situation to a situation of total independence between the social position of inheritors and that of parents. We should no doubt allow a critical role to this myth and the clues it enables us to create, as they help to expose the gap between democratic ideals and social reality. But even the most cursory examination would make it clear that considering these abstractions presupposes ignorance of the social costs and of the conditions in which a high degree of mobility would be possible.[19]

But is not the best way of judging to what extent the reality of a "democratic" society conforms to its ideals to measure chances of entering the institutionalized instruments of social elevation and cultural salvation open to individuals of different social classes?[20] If so we are then led to the conclusion that a society which allows the most privileged social classes to monopolize educational institutions—which, as Max Weber would say, hold a monopoly of the manipulation of cultural goods and the institutional signs of cultural salvation—is rigid in the extreme.

Notes

1. Cf. P. Bourdieu and J. C. Passeron, *Les Heririers* (Paris: Éditions de Minuit, 1964), pp. 14–21.
2. Correlation frequently occurs between the wishes expressed by parents with children finishing the *cours moyen*, opinions given later on the choice of a particular school, and the real choice. "By no means all parents want their children to go to a lycée. . . . Only 30 percent of parents with children in *collèges d'enseignement général* or *fin d'études* say yes, whatever the previous achievement of the child may have been" (P. Clerc, "La Famille et l'orientation scolaire au niveau de la sixième: Enquête de juin 1963 dans l'agglomeration Parisienne," *Population* 4 [Aug.-Sept. 1964]: 635–36).
3. Cf. P. Bourdieu and A. Darbel, "La Fin d'un mathusianisme," in Darras, *Le Partage des benefices* (Paris: Éditions de Minuit, 1966) (*Le Sens commun*).
4. Aanalyzing the differential influence (exerted by the dimension of the family in various milieus) on the access to secondary education, A. Girard and H. Bastide write, "Although two-thirds of the children of officeworkers and skilled craftsmen and traders go into the *lycées*, the proportion is highest in the smallest families (i.e., of one or two children). With these groups, however, children from large families (i.e., of four or more) do not enter the *lycée* in greater numbers than those of families of factory workers having only one or two brothers and sisters" (A. Girard and H. Bastide, "La Stratification sociale et la démocratisation de l'enseignement," Vol. 18 *Population*, July-Sept. 1963, p. 458).
5. There is a presupposition in this system of explanation by means of the common perception of objective and collective chances that the advantages or disadvantages perceived are the functional equivalent of the advantages or disadvantages really experienced or objectively verified in that they influence behavior in the same way. This does not imply that we underestimate the importance of objective chances. In fact, every scientific observation, in very different social and cultural situations, has tended to show that there is a close correlation between *subjective hopes* and *objective chances*, the latter tending to effectively modify attitudes and behavior by working through the former (cf. P. Bourdieu, *Travail et travailleurs en Algérie* [Paris: Mouton, 1962], pt. 2, pp. 36–38; Richard A. Cloward and Lloyd E. Oulir, *Delinquency and Opportunity: A Theory of Delinquent Gangs* [New York: Free Press of Glencoe, 1960]; Clarence Schrag, "Delinquency and Opportunity: Analysis of a Theory," *Sociology and Social Research* 46 [Jan. 1962]: 167–75).
6. Kurt Lewin, "Time, Prespective and Morale," in *Resolving Social Conflicts* (New York, 1948), p. 113.
7. Ibid., p. 115.
8. Ibid.
9. Clerc, "La Famille et l'orientation scolaire," p. 646.
10. It is probably by reference to a *social definition* of a reasonably obtainable diploma that individual career projects and hence attitudes to school are determined. This social definition clearly varies from class to class: while, for many of the lower strata of the middle class, the *baccalauréat* still appears to be seen as the normal end of studies—as a result of cultural inertia and lack of information but also probably because office workers and the lower grades of

supervisory personnel are more likely than others to experience the effectiveness of this barrier to promotion—it still appears more to the upper reaches of the middle classes and to the upper classes as a sort of entrance examination to higher education. This image of the scholastic career perhaps explains why a particularly large proportion of the sons of office workers and lower grades of salaried staff do not go on to study after the *baccalauréat*.

11. Cf. P. Bourdieu, J. C. Passeron, and M. de Saint-Martin, In order to have a complete measurement of the effect of the linguistic capital, it would be necessary to find out, by means of experimental studies similar to those carried out by Bernstein, whether there are any significant links between the syntax of the spoken language (e.g., its complexity) and success in fields other than that of literary studies (where the link has been shown)—for example, in mathematics.

12. See V. Isambert-Jamati, "La Rigidité d'une institution: structure scolaire et systèmes de valeur," *Revue française de sociologie* 7 (1966): 306.

13. Similarly elementary school teachers, who have fully absorbed the values of the middle classes from which they increasingly come, always take into account the *ethical coloring* of conduct and attitudes towards teachers and disciplines when making judgments on their pupils.

14. At the heart of the most traditional definition of culture there lies no doubt the distinction between the contents of the culture (in the subjective sense of an interiorized objective culture) or, perhaps, *knowledge*, and the characteristic means of possessing that knowledge, which gives it its whole meaning and value. What the child received from an educated milieu is not only a *culture* (in the objective sense), but also a certain *style* of relationship to that culture, which derives precisely from *the manner of acquiring it*. An individual's relationship with cultural works (and the mode of all his cultural experiences) is thus more or less easy, brilliant, natural, difficult, arduous, dramatic, or tense according to the conditions in which he acquired his culture, the osmosis of childhood in a family providing good conditions for an experience of familiarity (which is the source of the illusion of charisma) which schooling can never completely provide. It can be seen that by stressing the relationship with culture and setting great value on the most aristocratic style of relationship (ease, brilliance) schools favor the most privileged children.

15. The resistance of teachers to *docimology* and their even greater resistance to any attempt to rationalize testing (one has only to think of the indignant protests at the use of closed questionnaires) in unconsciously based on the same aristocratic ethos as the rejection of all pedagogical science, even though a "democratic" excuse for it is found in the ritual denunciation of the danger of technocracy.

16. Can the pressure of economic demand impose decisive changes? It is possible to imagine industrialized societies managing to meet the need for trained personnel without any major widening of the basis of recruitment from secondary, and more particularly from higher, education. If we use only criteria of cost, or rather, of formal rationality, it is perhaps preferable to recruit—in the face of all the claims of educational equality—from those classes whose social culture is the nearest to educational culture, and thus dispense with the need for any educational priority program.

17. Plato, *The Republic*, bk. 10, 617 (N.Y.: Everyman, 1942), p. 322.
18. Cf. Marie Skodak, "Children in Foster Homes: A Study of Mental Development," *Sudies in Child Welfare*, University of Iowa Studies 16, no. 1 (Jan. 1939): 1–56; B. Wellmar, "The Fickle IQ," *Sigma XI Quarterly* 28, no. 2 (1940): 52–60.
19. Apart from the difficulty of obtaining a precise assessment of mobility, and the discussions on the point in the careers of father and son which should be taken to obtain a relevant comparison, mention should be made of the fact that, as Bendix and Lipset have pointed out, "perfect mobility" (in the sense of completely equal chances of mobility) and "maximum mobility" are not necessarily linked, and that a distinction should be made between forced and intentional "rigidity" and "mobility."
20. We should also take into account the differential chances of social elevation given identical use of institutional means. We know that, at an equivalent level of instruction, individuals from different social classes reach varying levels in the social hierarchy.

CHAPTER 20

The Class Significance of School Counter-Culture

Paul Willis

This new type of school . . . is destined not merely to perpetuate social differences but to crystallize them in Chinese complexities.—Antonio Gramsci on "democratic" educational reforms in Italy during the early twenties[1]

The existence of anti-school cultures in schools with a working-class catchment area has been widely commented upon.[2] The raising of the school-leaving age has further dramatized and exposed this culture, often in the form of a "new" crisis: disruption in the classroom. Teachers' unions are calling more and more vehemently for tougher action against "violence" in the classroom, and for special provision for the "unruly" minority. The "reluctant fifth," difficult "RSLA [Raising the School Leaving Age]* classes," and young, "always in tears" (usually female) teachers, have become part of staffroom folklore.

The welter of comment and response, has, however, served to conceal certain crucial features of this culture: the profound significance it has for processes of job selection, and its relation to the wider working-class culture. In what follows I want to draw attention to these omissions. Concretely I want to make two suggestions. (1) Counter-school culture is part of the wider working-class culture of a region and ultimately of the nation, and, in particular, runs parallel to what we might call shop-floor culture. (2) The located anti-school culture provides powerful informal criteria and binding experiential processes which lead working-class lads to make the "voluntary" choice to enter the factory, and so to help to

Reprinted in abridged form with the permission of Routledge & Kegan Paul Ltd. from *Process of Schooling and the Open University: A Sociological Reader* by M. Hammersley and P. Woods. Copyright © 1976 by Routledge & Kegan Paul Ltd.
*Editor's change.

reproduce both the existing class structure of employment and the "culture of the shop floor" as a segment of the over-arching working-class culture. My argument is, then, that the stage of affiliation with the counter-school group carries much more significance than is usually acknowledged. I therefore go on to examine, in the latter part of this chapter, when, how, and why this process occurs. I will conclude with some comments on the meaning and status of this general class culture, of which the school and factory variants are part.

Studies of the transition from school to work, which might have made the connection between the school social system and the world of work, have simply been content to register a failure of the agencies and their rational policies—derived basically from middle-class preconceptions. The matrix of inappropriate middle-class logic—self-development, self-knowledge, matching of lifestyle career profile—overlying the located, informal cultural processes in the institutional practice of the Youth Employment Service and the relentlessly descriptive set of the main writings on the "transition,"[3] has effectively obscured the essential connectedness of working-class experience for the young male proceeding from school to work. Studies of the school[4] have been absorbed by the cultural divisions in the school itself, and have, implicitly at any rate, isolated the school from its surrounding networks. Consequently they have failed to address the central question of the determinancy of counter-school culture—is it the institution or the class context, or what mixture of both, which leads to the formation of this culture? In general the omission of the context in which the school operates would seem to imply that the institution be given primacy in the determination of the social landscape of the school.

My own research suggests that there is a direct relationship between the main features of working-class culture, as it is expressed in shop-floor culture, and school counter-culture. Both share broadly the same determinants: the common impulse is to develop strategies for dealing with boredom, blocked opportunities, alienation, and lack of control. Of course the particular organization of each located culture has its own history and specificity and worked-up institutional forms. The institution of the school, for instance, determines a particular uneven pattern of extension and supression of common working-class themes. In one way a more protected environment than the shop floor, and without the hard logic and discipline of material production, the school is nevertheless a more directly face-to-face repressive agency in other ways. This encourages an emphasis on certain obvious forms of resistance specific to the school. In one sense this is simply a question of inverting the given rules—hence the terrain of school counter-culture: smoking, proscribed dress, truancy, cheek in class, vandalism, and theft.

At any rate, the main cultural and organizational aspects of shop-floor culture (at least in the Midlands industrial conurbation where I did my research), and for the moment ignoring the range of historically and occupationally specific variants, bear a striking similarity to the main features of school counter-culture. . . .*

The really central point about the working-class culture of the shop floor is that, despite harsh conditions and external direction, people do look for meaning and impose frameworks. They exercise their abilities and seek enjoyment in activity, even where most controlled by others. They do, paradoxically, thread through the dead experience of work a living culture which is far from a simple reflex of defeat. This is the same fundamental taking hold of an alienating situation as one finds in counter-school culture and its attempt to weave a tapestry of interest and diversion through the dry institutional text. These cultures are not simply foam paddings, rubber layers between human and unpleasantness. They are appropriations in their own right, exercises of skill, motions, activities applied towards particular ends.

More specifically, the central, locating theme of shop-floor culture—a form of masculine chauvinism arising from the raw experience of production—is reflected in the independence and toughness found in school counter-cultures. Here is a foundry-man talking at home about his work. In an inarticulate way, but for that perhaps all the more convincingly, he attests that elemental, essentially masculine, self-esteem in the doing of a hard job well—and to be known for it.

I work in a foundry . . . you know drop forging . . . do you know anything about it . . no . . . . well you have the factory know the factory down in Bethnall Street with the noise . . . you can hear it in the street . . . I work there on the big hammer . . . it's a six-tonner. I've worked there 24 years now . . and its hot . . . . . . I don't get bored . . there's always new lines coming and you have to work out the best way of doing it . . You have to keep going . . . . and it's heavy work, the managers couldn't do it, there's not many strong enough to keep lifting the metal . . . I earn 80, 90 pounds a week, and that's not bad is it? . . . it ain't easy like . . . you can definitely say that I earn every penny of it . . . you have to keep it up you know. And the managing director, I'd say "hello" to him you know, and the progress manager . . . . they'll come around

*Editors' deletion.

and I'll go . . "all right" (thumbs up) . . . and they know you, you know . . . . a
group standing there watching you . . . . working . . I like that . . . . there's
something there . . . watching *you* like . . working . . . . like that . . you have to
keep going to get enough out.

Here is Joey, this man's son, in his last year at school, and right at the
heart of the counter-culture:

That's it, we've developed certain ways of talking, certain ways of acting and
we developed disregards for Pakis, Jamaicans and all different . . . for all the
scrubs and the fucking ear-'oles and all that (. .) There's no chivalry or
nothing, none of this cobblers you know, it's just . . if you'm gonna fight, it's
savage fighting anyway, so you might as well go all the way and win it
completely by having someone else help ya or by winning the dirtiest
methods you can think of like poking his eyes out or biting his ear and things
like this.

There's a clear continuity of attitudes here, and we must not think that
this distinctive complex of chauvinism, toughness, and machismo is
anachronistic or bound to die away as the pattern of industrial work
changes. Rough, unpleasant, demanding jobs *do* still exist in considerable numbers. A whole range of jobs—from building work, to furnace
work, to deep sea fishing—still involve a primitive confrontation with
exacting physical tasks. The basic attitudes and values developed in such
jobs are still very important in general working-class culture, and particularly the culture of the shop floor; this importance is vastly out of proportion to the number of people involved in such heavy work. Even in
so-called light industries, or in highly mechanized factories where the
awkwardness of the physical task has long since been reduced, the
metaphoric figures of strength, masculinity, and reputation still move
beneath the more varied and richer, visible forms of work-place culture.
Despite, even, the increasing numbers of women employed, the most
fundamental ethos of the factory is profoundly masculine.

The other main, and this time emergent, theme of shop-floor culture—at least in the manufacturing industries of the Midlands—is the
massive attempt to gain a form of control of the work process. "Systematic soldiering" and "gold bricking" have been observed from the particular perspective of management from F. W. Taylor[5] onwards, but there
is evidence now of a much more concerted—though still informal—
attempt to gain control. It does happen, now, sometimes, that the men
themselves actually run production. Again this is effectively mirrored for

us by working-class kids' attempts, with the resources of their counter-culture, to take control of classes, insert their own unofficial timetables, and control their own routines and life spaces.

> JOEY: (. .) of a Monday afternoon, we'd have nothing right? Nothing hardly relating to school work, Tuesday afternoon we have swimming and they stick you in a classroom for the rest of the afternoon, Wednesday afternoon you have games and there's only Thursday and Friday afternoon that you work, if you call that work. The last lesson Friday afternoon we used to go and doss, half of us wagged out o' lessons and the other half go into the classroom, sit down and just go to sleep, and the rest of us could join a class where all our mates are.
>
> WILL: (. .) What we been doing, playing cards in this room 'cos we can lock the door.
>
> PW: Which room's this now?
>
> WILL: Resources Centre, where we're making the frames (*a new stage for the deputy head*), s'posed to be.
>
> PW: Oh! You're still making the frames?
>
> WILL: We should have had it finished, we just lie there on top of the frame, playing cards, or trying to get to sleep.
>
> PW: What's the last time you've done some writing?
>
> WILL: When we done some writing?
>
> FUZZ: Oh ah, last time was in careers, 'cos I writ "yes" on a piece of paper, that broke me heart.
>
> PW: Why did it break your heart?
>
> FUZZ: I mean to write, 'cos I was going to try and go through the term without writing anything. 'Cos since we've cum back, I ain't dun nothing. (*It was half-way through term.*)

Put this against the following account from the father of a boy who was in the same friendship group as the boys talking above. He is a factory hand on a track producing car engines, talking at his home.

> Actually the foreman, the gaffer, don't run the place, the men run the place. See, I mean you get one of the chaps say, "Allright, you'm on so and so today." You can't argue with him. The gaffer don't give you the job, the men on the track give you the job, they swop each other about, tek it in turns. Ah, but I mean the job's done. If the gaffer had gid you the job you would . . . They tried to do it, one morning, gid a chap a job you know, but he'd been on it, you know. I think he's been on all week, and they just downed tools. (. . . .) There's four hard jobs on the track and there's dozens that's . . . you know, a child of five could do it, quite honestly, but everyone has their turn. That's organized by the men.

Of course there is the obvious difference that the school informal organization is devoted to doing nothing, while in the factory culture, at least, "the job's done." But the degree of opposition to official authority *in each case* should not be minimized, and production managers in such shops were quite as worried as deputy heads about "what things were coming to." Furthermore, both these attempts at control rest on the basic and distinctive unit of the informal group. This is the fundamental unit of resistance in both cultures, which locates and makes possible all its other elements. It is the zone where "creative" attempts to develop and extend an informal culture are made, and where strategies for wresting control of symbolic and real space from official authority are generated and disseminated. It is the massive presence of this informal organization which most decisively marks off shop-floor culture from middle-class cultures of work, and the "lads'" school culture from that of the "ear-'oles" (the name used by the "lads" of my research to designate those who conformed to the school's official culture).

. . . *

. . . [In rough humor and] in more detailed ways, from theft, vandalism, and sabotage to girlie books under the tool-bench or desk, it is apparent that shop-floor culture and school oppositional culture have a great deal in common.

The parallelism of these cultures suggests, of course, that they should both be thought of as aspects of the larger working-class culture, though a fuller account would obviously further differentiate regional, occupational, and institutional variations. The fundamental point here is to stress that anti-school culture should be seen in the context of this larger pattern, rather than in simple institutional terms. This wider connection has important and unexamined implications for the school's management of the "disruptive" minority. Put at its most obvious, strategies conceived at the institutional level will not overcome problems arising from a profound class-cultural level. In fact the concerned teacher may be effectively boxed in, since the undoubted level of institutional determinancy—which I am not denying—well may block those strategies which do take into account the wider working-class culture. I mean that the teacher who tries to use working-class themes or styles may be rejected because he's a teacher: "there's nothing worse than a teacher trying to be too friendly," and that a teacher who innovates organizationally—destreaming, mixed ability groupings, etc.—can never prevent the emer-

*Editors' deletion.

gence of oppositional working-class themes *in one form or another.* It is the peculiarly intractable nature of this double determinancy which makes this form of working-class culture present itself as a "crisis." It shows up in high relief some of the unintended consequences and contradictions inherent in the state's ever-expanding attempts to make inroads into located working-class culture.

* . . .

In terms of actual "job choice," it is the "lads' " culture and not the official careers material which provides the most located and deeply influential guides for the future. For the individual's affiliation with the nonconformist group carries with it a whole range of changes in his attitudes and perspectives and these changes also supply over time a more or less consistent view of what sorts of people he wants to end up working with, and what sort of situation is going to allow the fullest expression for his developing cultural skills. The located "lads' " culture supplies a set of unofficial criteria by which to judge not individual jobs or the intrinsic joys of particular kinds of work—indeed it is already assumed that all work is more or less hard and unrewarding—but generally *what kind* of working situation is going to be most relevant to the individual. It will have to be work where he can be open about his desires, his sexual feelings, his liking for "booze," and his aim to "skive off" as much as is reasonably possible. It will have to be a place where people can be trusted and will not "creep off" to tell the boss about "foreigners" or "nicking stuff"—precisely where there were fewest "ear-'oles." Indeed it would have to be work where there was a boss, a "them and us," which always carried with it the danger of treacherous intermediaries. The experience of the division "ear-'ole"/"lads" in school is one of the most basic preparations for the still ubiquitous feeling in the working class proper that there is a "them" and an "us." The "us" is felt to be relatively weaker in power terms, but also somehow more approachable, social, and, in the end, more human. One of the really crucial things about the "us" which the "lads" wanted to be part of was that they were in work where the self could be separated from the work task, and value given to people for things other than their work performance—the celebration of those independent qualities which precisely the "ear-'oles" did not have. Generally, the future work situation would have to be one where people were not "cissies" and could handle themselves, where "pen-pushing" is looked down on in favor of really "doing things." It would have to be a situation where you could speak up for yourself, and where you would not be expected to be subservient. The particular job would have to pay

*Editors' deletion.

good money fairly quickly and offer the possibility of "fiddles" and "perks" to support already acquired smoking and drinking habits. Work would have to be a place, most basically, where people were "all right" and with whom a general culture identity could be shared. It is this human face of work, much more than its intrinsic or technical nature, which confronts the individual as the crucial dimension of his future. In the end it is recognized that it is specifically the cultural diversion that makes any job bearable. Talking about the imminent prospect of work:

> WILL: I'm just dreading the first day like, Y'know, who to pal up with, an er'm, who's the ear-'oles, who'll tell the gaffer.
> JOEY: (. .) you can always mek it enjoyable. It's only you what makes a job unpleasant, . . I mean if you're cleaning sewers out, you can have your moments like. Not every job's enjoyable, I should think. Nobody's got a job they like unless they're a comedian or something, but er'm . . , no job's enjoyable 'cos of the fact that you've got to get up of a morning and go out when you could stop in bed. I think every job's got, has a degree of unpleasantness, but it's up to you to mek . . to push that unpleasantness aside and mek it as good and as pleasant as possible.

The typical division in school between the "lads" and the "ear-'oles" also has a profound influence on thoughts about work. It is also a division between different kinds of future, different kinds of gratification, and different kinds of job that are relevant to these things. These differences, moreover, are not random or unconnected. On the one hand they arise systematically from intra-*school* group oppositions and, on the other, they relate to quite distinct job groupings in the *post-school* situation. The "ear-'oles"/"boys" division becomes the skilled/unskilled and white-color/blue-collar division. The "lads" themselves could transpose the division of the internal cultural landscape of the school on to the future, and on to the world of work outside, with considerable clarity. Talking about "ear-'oles":

> JOEY: I think they're [*the "ear-'oles"*] the ones that have got the proper view of life, they're the ones that abide by the rules. They're the civil servant types, they'll have 'ouses and everything before us (. . .) They'll be the toffs, I'll say they'll be the civil servants, toffs, and we'll be the brickies and things like that.
> SPANKSEY: I think that we . . , more or less, we're the ones that do the hard grafting but not them, they'll be the office workers (. . .) I just want to have a nice wage, that 'ud just see me through.

. . . Altogether, in relation to the basic cultural ground-shift which is occurring, and the development of a comprehensive alternative view of what is expected from life, *particular* job choice does not matter too much to the "lads." Indeed we may see that, with respect to the criteria this located culture throws up, most manual and semi-skilled jobs *are* the same and it would be a waste of time to use the provided middle-class grids across them to find material differences. Considered, therefore, in just one quantum of time—the last months of school—individual job choice does indeed seem random and unenlightened by any rational techniques or end/means schemes. It is, however, confusing and mystifying to pose the entry of working-class youth into work as a matter of *particular* job *choice*—this is, in essence, a very middle-class construct. The criteria we have looked at, the opposition to other more conformist views of work, and the solidarity of the group process, all transpose the question of job choice on to another plane: these lads are not choosing careers or particular jobs, they are committing themselves to a future of generalized labor. Even if it's not explicitly verbalized, from the way many of the kids actually get jobs and their calm expectation that their jobs will change a lot, they do not basically make much differentiation between jobs—*it's all labor*. In a discussion on the jobs they had arranged for when they left:

PERC: I was with my mate, John's brother, I went with 'im to er, . . he wanted a job. Well, John's sister's boyfriend got a job at this place, and he sez to Allan, he sez, "Go down there and they might give you a job there," and he went down, and they sez, "You're too old for training," 'cos he's twenty now, he sez to Allan, he sez, "Who's that out there," and he sez, "One of me mates," he sez, "does he wanna job," and he sez, "I dunno." He sez er'm, "Ask him." He comes out, I went back in and he told me about it and he sez, "Come back before you leave if you want it."
PW:——: What you doing?
PERC: Carpentry, joining. And a month ago I went back and, well, not a month ago, a few weeks ago and I seen him.
PW: Well, that was a complete accident really. I mean had you been thinking of joinery?
PERC: Well, you've only got to go and see me woodwork, I've had it, I ain't done woodwork for years.

In a discussion of their future:

EDDIE: I don't think any of us'll have one job and then stick to it, none of us. We'll swop around.
SPIKE: It just shows in your part-time jobs don't it, don't stick to a part-time job.

416

Shop-floor culture has, as we have seen, an objective dimension which gives it a certain strength and power. Now this quality chimes—unexpectedly for some—with the criteria for acceptable work already thrown up by the counter-school culture. The young adult, therefore, impelled towards the shop floor, shares much more than he knows with his own future. When the lad reaches the factory there is not shock, only recognition. He is likely to have had experience anyway of work through part-time jobs, and he is immediately familiar with many of the shop-floor practices: defeating boredom, time-wasting, heavy and physical humor, petty theft, "fiddling," "handling yourself."

There is a further, perhaps less obvious, way in which the working-class boy who is from the "lads" is drawn in to the factory and confirmed in his choice. This is in the likely response of his new employer to what he understands of the "lads'" culture already generated at school. The reverse side of the "them" and "us" attitude of the "lads" is an acceptance by them of prior authority relations. Although directly and apparently geared to make some cultural interest and capital out of an unpleasant situation, it also accomplishes a recognition of, and an accommodation to, the facts of power and hierarchy. In the moment of the establishment of a cultural opposition is the yielding of a hope for direct, or quasi-political, challenge. The "them" and "us" philosophy is simultaneously a rescue and confirmation of the direct, the human, and the social, and a giving up—at any conscious level—of claims to control the under-workings of these things: the real power relationships. This fact is of central importance in understanding the peculiar density and richness, as well as the limitedness and frequent short-sightedness, of counter-school and shop-floor culture.

Now, curiously enough, those conformist lads who enter the factory unaided by cultural supports, diversions, and typical, habituated patterns of interpretation can be identified by those in authority as more threatening and less willing to accept the established status quo. For these lads still believe, as it were, the rubric of equality, advance through merit and individualism which the school, in its anodyne way, has more or less unproblematically passed on to them. Thus, although there is no surface opposition, no insolent style to enrage the conventional onlooker, there is also no secret pact, made in the reflex moment of an oppositional style, to accept a timeless authority structure: a timeless "us" and "them." Consequently, these kids are more likely to *expect real* satisfaction from their work; to expect the possibility of advance through hard work; to expect authority relations, in the end, to reflect only differences in competence. All these expectations, coupled frequently with a real unhappiness in the individual unrelieved by a social diversion, make the conformist lad very irksome and "hard to deal with." In manual and semi-skilled jobs, then, those in authority often actively prefer the "lads" type to the "ear-'ole" type. Underneath the "roughness" of the "lads" is a realistic assessment of their position, an ability to get on with others to make the day *and production* pass, and a lack of "pushiness" about their job and their future in it. Finally, the "lads" are more likeable because they have "something to say for themselves," and will "stand up for themselves," but only in a restricted mode which falls short of one of the "us" wanting to join the "them." It is precisely this parlous ground upon which the conformist often unwittingly and unhappily stands. For one of the "lads," not only is the shop floor more familiar than he might expect, but he is also welcomed and accepted by his new superiors in such a way that seems to allow for the expression of his own personality where the school had been precisely trying to block it—this is an initial confirming response which further marks up the "transition" from school as a liberation.

What is surprising in this general process of induction into the factory is the voluntary—almost celebratory—nature of the "lads'" choice. The recognition of themselves in a future of industrial work is not a question of defeat, coercion, or resignation. Nor is it simply the result of a managed, machiavellian process of social control. It is a question, at any rate in part and at least at this age, of an affiliation which is seen as joyous, creative, and attractive. This fact is of enormous importance to us in understanding the true complexity of the reproduction of our social order: there is an element of "self-damnation" in the acceptance of subordinate roles.

It is the partly autonomous functioning of the processes we have been considering which surprisingly accomplishes the most difficult task of state schooling: to "direct" a proportion of kids to the unrewarding and basic tasks of industrial production. The word "direct" is carefully chosen here since it need not have connotations of coercion, but it does make the unequivocality of the destination clear.

Pierre Bourdieu[6] argues that it is the exclusive "cultural capital"— among other things, skill in the symbolic manipulation of language and figures—of the dominant groups in society which ensures the success of their offspring and so the reproduction of their class privilege. This is because educational advancement is controlled through the "fair" meritocratic testing of precisely these skills which "cultural capital" provides. We can make a bleak inversion of this hypothesis and suggest that it is the partly "autonomous" counter-cultures of the working class at the site of the school which "behind the back" of official policy ensure the continuity of its own underprivilege through the process we have just been considering. This process achieves the reproduction of underprivilege much more systematically than could any *directed* state policy. Of course state policy *says* it is doing the opposite. In this case, then, "autonomous" working-class processes achieve the "voluntary" reproduction of their own conditions *in spite of* state policy. We cannot unravel this complex knot here, save to observe that the widespread *belief* in the egalitarianism of state policy—not least among teachers themselves—may be an essential prerequisite for the continual functioning of those *actual* processes which are working to the opposite effect.[7]

* . . .

I have been stressing the "cultural level" and the way in which "semi-autonomous" processes at this level have profoundly important material outcomes. In order to do this I have necessarily emphasized the "creative," independent, and even joyous aspects of working-class culture as it is, anyway, for the "lads" during the "transition"—they may well have different views a few years *into* work. Certainly we need to posit the attractiveness of this culture to avoid simple determinist and economist views of what makes kids go to the factory, and the establish properly the level of the "voluntarism" by which these lads go to a future that most would account an impoverished one. However, we should be careful not to lionize or romanticize our concept of working-class culture. School counter-culture and shop-floor culture are fundamentally limited and stop well short of providing any fully worked-out future which is an alternative to the one they oppose. Indeed, in certain fundamental respects, we are presented with the contradiction that they actually—in the end—*do the work of bringing about the future that others have mapped for them.* The basic shortcoming of these cultures is that they have failed to convert *symbolic* power into *real* power. The real power thus still creates the most basic channels along which symbolic meanings run so that the symbolic power is used, in the end, to close the circle the *actual* power has opened up, and so finally to *reinforce* the real power relationships. The insistence of a human meaning which must justify its situation, but which does not have the *material* force to change its situation, can simply operate all too easily to legitimate, *experientially*, a situation which is fundamentally alien to it. To put it more concretely, the school counter-culture, for all its independence, accomplishes the induction of man-

*Editors' deletion.

power "voluntarily" into the productive process, and its mate, shop-floor culture, encourages an accomodation to, rather than a rejection of, the *fundamental* social relations there.

. . .

Key

( )	background information
(inaudible)	part of sentence inaudible
/ /	description relating to collective activity
. . . .	long pause
. . .	pause
. .	
. . ,	phrase incompleted
, . .	phrase completed, then pause
(. .)	phrase edited out
(. . .)	sentence edited out
(. . . .)	passage edited out
—	speaker interrupting or at same time as another speaker
- - -	transcription from a different discussion follows
⸺	name of speaker not identified

Notes

Note. This article is based on the findings of a project at the Centre for Contemporary Cultural Studies between April 1973 and June 1975, financed by the SSRC, on the "transition from school to work" of white working-class average to low ability boys in a Midlands industrial conurbation. It used intensive case-study methods and participant observation based on a number of schools and factories in this region. The "main" case study was of a friendship group of twelve boys as they proceeded through their last four terms in a single-sex secondary modern school (it was twinned with a girls' school of the same name). The school was adapting itself organizationally— mixed ability groupings, timetable blocking, destreaming, etc.—in preparation for an expected redesignation as a comprehensive school which finally occurred only after the case study group had left. All of the parents of the lads were interviewed in depth, and a period of participant observation was spent with each of the lads at some point in the first six months of their respective work situations. The full results of this work will be available to *Learning to Labour: How Working-Class Kids Get Working-Class Jobs*, Saxon House, 1977.

1. A. Gramsci, *Selections from the Prison Notebooks of Antonio Gramsci*, ed. and trans. Q. Hoare and G. Nowell Smith (Lawrence and Wishart, 1971), p. 40.
2. D. H. Hargreaves, *Social Relations in a Secondary School* (London: Routledge and Kegan Paul, 1967); M. D. Shipman, *Sociology of the School* (London: Longman, 1968); Ronald A. King, *School Organization and Pupil Involvement* (London: Routledge and Kegan Paul, 1973); Michael F. D.

Young, *Knowledge and Control: New Directions in the Sociology of Education* (London: Collier-Macmillan, 1971); Colin Lacey, *Hightown Grammar* (Manchester, Eng.: Manchester University Press, 1970).

3. See, for instance, M. P. Carter, *Into Work* (Baltimore: Penguin, 1969); Kenneth Roberts, *From School to Work: Study of the Youth Employment Service* (Newton Abbot, Eng.: David & Charles, 1972).

4. For instance the admirable and pioneering D. H. Hargreaves, *Social Relations in a Secondary School.*

5. F. W. Taylor, *Scientific Management* (Westbury, Ct.: Greenwood Press, 1972; 1st pub. 1947).

6. Pierre Bourdieu and Jean-Claude Passeron, *La Réproduction: éléments pour une théorie du système d'enseignement* (Paris: Éditions de Minuit, 1971).

7. *Learning to Labour* deals more fully with these questions.

Conclusion: Action, Interaction, Self-Reflection

Eric Bredo *and* Walter Feinberg

The essays presented in this volume have suggested the nature of the three principal methodoligical orientations currently guiding social and educational research. As we have introduced each succeeding orientation we have pointed out how it questions the very foundations of the preceding one. This way of presenting the approaches highlights their dialectial interrelations but does not allow for a reply by those who hold the position that has been undercut. In this concluding section we would like to consider how advocates of each of the positions are likely to respond to their critics and thus to initiate a dialogue among them. Our aim in doing so is to further understanding of the interrelationships among the orientations as understood from each vantage point and, ultimately, to draw some tentative conclusions regarding their relative truth, validity, and adequacy. In order to do this without excessive qualification we will have to consider a rather idealized version of each orientation and ignore finer points of difference within them.

The Positivist Response

Knowledge for the positivist is generated in monological fashion. The scientist studies an object and makes observations about it that are then interrelated and checked for their logical consistency with hypothetical, law-like statements. Laws, in turn, are checked for their logical consistency with higher-order theoretical propositions. In the positivistic view, the scientist, not the subject, does the talking, at least insofar as knowledge is concerned. As we have pointed out, this view of knowledge generation is individualistic; it takes both the scientist's and the subject's normative communities for granted as well as the corporate systems of authority in which they are acting. It should not be surprising, then, that the positivistic view is likely to interpret the other approaches in psychological terms. The positivistic response to both interpretative and critical approaches may be conceived of as considering them both as deviations from the ideal of purely cognitive, disinterested, inquiry. Interpretivists let their attitudes get in the way, while critical theorists allow their values to influence their observations. Both fail to maintain the positivistically desired stance of disciplined objectivity.

The interpretivist, in taking the "attitude of the other," or seeking to see things from the viewpoint or worldview of those he or she studies, is seen by the positivist as leaving the objective standpoint and letting subjective factors influence his or her observations, thus threatening the validity and reliability of the observations and the value-neutrality of scientific conclusions. The positivist believes that validity is threatened because the observer will record events from the standpoint of those being studied, who may not use terms in theoretically correct ways. For instance, to say that someone has "power" over another as seen by the subjects being studied might be different from using the term in a more precise technical way. The result is that observations of power relations made in this way would be invalid with respect to the scientific conception of "power." Reliability is also threatened because different observers who examine power relations from different standpoints will be looking for different things, and so will not consistently count the same things as instances of "power." Even a single observer who has no precise operational or criteral definition of the concept will count things in an inconsistent or erratic way. In either case, instances of "power" can thus come to be reported unreliably. Finally, use of the emotive terms that are used in everyday life commonly serves to "smuggle" in value conclusions that cannot legitimately be drawn from scientific research as the positivist conceives of it. To call someone a "bastard" may be factually correct, but it also implies a social evaluation of him and suggests ways in which he is appropriately treated. The positivist objects to such smuggled value statements, recognizing that a purely cognitive approach can, if strictly adhered to, only legitimately tell one *how* to get from A to B, not *whether* one should go there. Smuggled value statements represent a form of deception to the positivist: one is claiming to be a scientist but behaving like an everyday actor. The positivist's solution is to purify scientific language, to use terms that are as abstract and technical and free of everyday evaluative connotations as possible and in this way try to live up to the claim of being an objective, scientific observer.

An interpretive approach fails as science, then, from a positivistic viewpoint, because of gross problems of reliability and validity, and

Action, Interaction, and Reflection

because it is deceptive when it lays claim to being a correct account. An interpretive or "empathetic" attitude may still be seen as useful in that it can help suggest possible hypotheses and can allow one to create questionnaires or experimental situations that are more easily comprehensible to one's subjects. However, its use is limited to the "context of discovery" rather than to the "context of validation." For validation purposes—that is, for really testing hypotheses—one needs systematic observation in terms of standardized criteria that are related to abstract theoretical constructs. An interpretive approach, for the positivist, is much too "subjective" to allow for this.

To be an interpretivist is bad enough, from a positivistic point of view, but to be a critical theorist is worse. While the interpretivist can at least be seen as empathetically taking the attitude of another and seeing things from their existing standpoint, the critical theorist is seen as even more subjective since it is his or her *own* values that strongly determine observations. The critical theorist is a personally committed observer who admits that his or her observations are shaped by interests that he or she serves. As such the critical theorist gives up all pretense of objectivity, at least as the positivist sees it, and thus all claims to being a scientist. Critical theorists seek to find the meaning of distortions or suppressions in communication and to do so must view current communication from the anticipated standpoint of authentic, undistorted communication. As far as the positivist is concerned this means that their observations derive from a comparison of what is real with what is ideal, and since those with different values will view different states of affairs as ideal, their descriptions will be entirely dependent on their individual values. Validity and interobserver reliability are even more threatened in this case than in the interpretive case because here they depend upon comparison with a merely anticipated ideal that is not even as concrete as existing ordinary usage with all its fuzziness and inconsistency. And, needless to say, objectivity goes totally by the board since one's ideals are a direct determinant of one's observations. From a positivistic point of view, such an approach may be valid in a field like aesthetic criticism, and may be an art in itself, but it should not claim the mantle of science.

Both interpretivism and critical theory are thus rejected by the positivist primarily on the grounds of their subjectivity and idiosyncracy. Since positivism emphasizes individual cognition detached from affective or evaluative influences, it is hardly surprising that it rejects its competitors precisely on the grounds that they let attitudinal or value influences affect observations and as such lose their objectivity. This need not mean that both approaches are rejected outright in all human affairs; interpretivism with its "empathy" and critical theory with its "imagination" (of states of affairs other than the status quo) may be useful in the context of discovery or in criticizing existing social arrangements, but they are, respectively, more like a craft and an art than like a science. Arts and crafts may have their uses, but they do not produce tested, generalizable knowledge, or at least so positivists suggest.

The Interpretive Response

From an interpretive point of view, social knowledge is inherently dialogical rather than monological. To understand others' actions one must do more than label them as an outsider would; one must know their meaning to the actors. This does not involve the scientist's confronting a mute object, as the positivist would have it, but rather the interpreter's confronting a "text" that will only make sense if he or she can find the code in which it is written. No amount of external measuring and labeling of such a text will make its meaning clear.

From this point of view the three methodological orientations may be seen as emphasizing three different codes, symbol systems, or types of language games. Positivists implicitly insist that technical languages, languages of elaborated, decontextualized discourse, like logic, are the frameworks in which knowledge should be constructed. To know the real meaning of a concept like "power," for instance, one must see how it is defined in an axiomatic theoretical system. There may be other ordinary usages but they are likely to be vague and inconsistent. The formal, theoretically grounded definitions are what is appropriate in scientific work, it is argued, because they allow for intersubjective agreement among scientists on a unitary meaning of the concept so that hypotheses utilizing it can be tested in the same way in different contexts.

Against this, the interpretivist insists that ordinary language has priority. Social scientists may define "power" in one way, but leaders may *have* power in ways that differ from scientific definition. As Taylor argues in Chapter 9 of this volume, ordinary language is partially constitutive of existing practices; without the language the practices could not be quite as they are. As a result, imposing abstracted definitions on existing practices may result in interrelating things that have no meaningful connection in the pattern of social interaction. It would resemble having someone who knows nothing of the rules of baseball record the timing, frequency, and extent of various behaviors and try to find the laws that predict and explain the associations between various events. No amount of data collection, correlation, and induction will teach him or her the rules of the game and enable the researcher to understand what is happening because the rules define correct and not actual usage.[1]

The interpretivist sees the positivist as trying to force social life into a box in which it does not fit, as trying to apply a language designed for describing "things" to social actors whose language itself helps constitute their patterns of interaction. The positivist is trying to use "thing" language for a purpose to which it is not suited. Rather than taking formal, abstracted definitions as definitive of social practices, interpretivists would turn the equation around. Formal descriptions, to be valid, must be based on ordinary distinctions and usage. Technical discourse may then be seen as a way of codifying aspects of common usage that we might otherwise forget or apply inconsistently (as Winch suggests at the end of Chapter 8). The product of abstract discourse can be thought of as a map serving as a reminder of the interrelation among the roads and allowing a more global calculation of how to get from here to there than would a more localized recognition of familiar landmarks. But to make the formal distinctions definitive of practical usage is as absurd as saying that the map defines where the roads "really" are.

The view of formal definitions, laws, and theories in social science does not suggest that they are wrong or useless, but that they are secondary activities that should be based on the conventions of ordinary usage. For them to be valid they must be applied sensitively and in the correct contexts. If ordinary usage is inconsistent, for instance, then it should be clear that the formal usage that is proposed as a codification of it will only apply in some contexts and not in others. What is also implied is that formal usage, to be correct, must be based on a good translation of informal, ordinary usage. One must know both languages and be able to find terms that mean "the same" in each language. However, this sameness of meaning will not be the sameness the positivist would seek, which would be identical denotations, but rather one in which the connotations or action implications of the terms that are relevant for current purposes are judged to be the same. Something will inevitably be lost in such translation, but something else may also be gained.

A tolerant interpretivist, then, might see the technical language of the positivist as potentially useful, but as subordinate to ordinary usage. When the positivist accuses the interpretivist of allowing "subjective" factors to influence observations, the interpretivist's response is that by seeing things in psychological terms and in terms of a strict subject-object dichotomy the positivist has misconstrued them. Interpreting baseball in the light of its rules is not to base one's interpretation on subjective premises but on *intersubjective* ones. The same is true of understanding

427

other social practices. By failing to understand the difference between subjectivity and intersubjectivity, the positivist misunderstands the interpretive approach and reduces it to psychological terms that do not correctly apply.

The interpretivist's view of the critical theorist is more complex, for while they are allies in their opposition to positivism, they still have reason to be somewhat distrustful of each other's claims. When the interpretivist looks at the critical theorist he or she sees someone who is also engaged in interpretation. However, the critical theorist is engaged in "depth" interpretation; he or she is listening "behind" discourse to find the meanings of the omissions, suppressions, condensations, and the like, of discourse itself. For instance, when the critical theorist is examining some form of speech as ideology, he or she is trying to understand the meaning of the distortions or omissions in that speech and not merely what the speech itself is saying or implying. What the critical theorist is doing is attending to prelinguistic symbolization, in which what might be distinguished in speech is merged, condensed, inverted, and so forth.

To an interpretivist, a critical approach resembles another type of language game, one that is relevant to other areas of action. If positivism uses technical "thing" language, and interpretivism itself the discursive language of everyday moral accountability, then critical theory is based on the interpretation of analog symbolization. It involves the type of language game that we play with those whom we recognize as conscious actors who do not fully know their own minds. It is a game that psychiatrists play with patients, and parents with children, in which one imputes affective states of the actor not on the basis of their self-reports but on the basis of observed distortions in their self-understandings.

The interpretive concern with respect to critical theory is that it, like positivism, may result in inadequate listening to the intended meaning of what is being done or said. The positivist's conversation is only with him or herself, and not with the subject; the critical theorist's focus beyond the intended meaning implies that he or she also may not be in direct dialogue with the subject. Stanton and Schwartz, in a study of a ward in a mental hospital, provide a telling example of what this sort of listening can turn into:

> Restriction of attention to "deep" interpretation was not . . . confined to dealing with patients; on the contrary, many psychiatrists seemed to pride themselves on ignoring the face value of what their colleagues said to them, focusing instead on what they believed to be "really going on." . . . Information was frequently lost . . . particularly when a junior staff member protested

to a senior about certain aspects of the hospital; the protest was likely to be interpreted as a transference rebellion. This interpretation was rarely made when the younger staff member agreed with the older. Because of these pseudo-deep interpretations, communication sometimes became so complex that the situation could almost be summarized by the statement, "If you disagree with me, you need to see a psychiatrist."[2]

If, as the interpretivist believes, we understand our own and others' actions by using and appealing to cultural rules or communicative conventions, then what cultural rules does the critical theorist appeal to when he or she develops a depth interpretation? When we are in doubt in the case of ordinary interpretation we can appeal to authoritative usage or to paradigmatic cases to clarify the nature of the conventions establishing the meaning of an action. But in the case of depth interpretation there can be no such appeal to convention. The standard that is used is that of anticipated ideal speech community, which, since it does not exist at present (except, perhaps, fleetingly or locally), has not codified its practices or developed a repertoire of paradigmatic cases. As a result, the critical theorist's interpretations have no authoritative basis, no tradition to appeal to in deciding whether an interpretation is valid or invalid, and so their interpretations may be regarded as arbitrary. Of course, critical theorists, like psychiatrists, might develop a tradition of language use that labels certain phenomena observed in communication in certain ways, and so develop a set of naming conventions. However, this would not answer the crucial question of whether the meanings attributed to the distortions were meanings for the subject or only for the analyst. In the latter case the critical theorist would simply have become another variety of positivist, busily imposing labels on subjects regardless of meaning for the subjects.

A tolerant interpretivist would again suggest, not that attention to communicative distortion is wrong or useless, but that ordinary language and intentions framed in its terms have priority. Poetry and comedy are examples of a case in which the rules of language or of social interaction are modified; yet despite the surface contradictions that may be apparent in them, both are generally subject to coherent interpretations in terms of the intentions of those creating them. Attention to the exaggerations or distortions present in activities such as these may help make the intended meaning apparent. However, these exaggerations or distortions are, for the interpretivist, better seen as the product of intentions than as productive of them. In short, the intention comes first, and whatever distortions are produced in expressing these intentions are themselves merely in the service of the intention. Ordinary language is once again seen as having priority.

The interpretive response is perhaps best summarized by contrasting the three approaches. All three may be seen as emphasizing different types of symbolization, different regions of language, from the technical language of digital symbolization in the case of positivism, through ordinary language using discursive symbolization in interpretivism, to the prelinguistic analog symbolization emphasized by critical theorists.[3] All three types of symbolization have their uses, and are applicable in different types of activities. However, for the interpretivist the conventions of ordinary language hold priority in understanding social life. When their priority is not recognized, the interpretivist suggests that this leads either to empty irrelevance, as in positivism, or to arbitrary interpretation without authoritative basis, as in critical theory.

The Critical Response

If a positivistic approach to knowledge can be characterized as mono-logical, and an interpretive approach as dialogical, then a critical approach can properly (albeit awkwardly) be characterized as trialogical. What this means is that critical theory takes into account not only the object that is known, as does positivism, nor the interrelation of frameworks in which mutually comprehensible knowledge is con-structed, as does interpretivism, but also the relation between the frameworks of knower and known and the framework supported by dominant authorities or elites. Put more simply, in critical theory the theory of knowledge and the theory of society merge.

In the view of the critical theorist the three methodological orienta-tions are related to three "knowledge-constitutive interests." Positivism is seen as related to a "technical" interest, an interest in prediction and control; interpretivism is seen as related to a "practical" interest, an interest in mutual understanding and normative agreement; and critical theory itself is seen as related to an "emancipatory" interest, an interest in authentic, nonrepressive communication. An orientation towards each of these interests implicitly represents a different stance towards existing authorities or a different political position. To adopt a technical role is to agree to serve as a technician and implicitly to accept a given set of social arrangements when acting as a scientist. One may seek structural change when acting personally, but within a technical understanding of social science there can be no scientific legitimation of such efforts. The adop-tion of an interpretive role puts one in the position of a translator or intermediary, an honest broker between differing communities. One may question particular practices while remaining in such a social scientific role when, for instance, the practices are based on a misunderstanding on the part of one party or another. However, one cannot, as an interpretively oriented scientist, question the conventions of any social group. Finally, the adoption of a critical role creates the possibility for reflective opposition to authorities because one is examining the limitations and omissions of theories that serve to legitimize authorities. Critical theory thus acknowledges its own interestedness and asserts that the other approaches are also related to human interests even though they do not acknowledge it.

Like the other approaches, critical theory naturally views itself in more favorable terms than it views the other approaches. Emancipatory knowledge is considered "higher" than the other forms of knowledge because it is more embracing. It is not so much that knowledge generated from the standpoint of the other interests is wrong *per se*, but that it is limited to one form of knowledge. When this limitation is justified by theories of knowledge that make the one type of knowledge generated definitive of all knowledge, or all legitimate knowledge (as in positivism or interpretivism), then understanding becomes distorted from the standpoint of the more inclusive perspective. The situation is like that depicted in the mathematical classic *Flatland*, in which a being from a one-dimensional world (himself a point) is transported to a two-dimensional world. He can then experience the freedom of moving, and thinking, in two dimensions and can see that he is "really" a two-dimensional being that happened to intersect his previous linear world at one point. However, when he asks his two-dimensional hosts about the next, three-dimensional world, they have elaborate theories explaining why such a world could not possibly exist. Critical theory seeks to add such a third dimension to our view of knowledge and thus to embrace and synthesize knowledge generated from the other two methodological approaches.

Adopting this critical approach in some ways leads to a tolerant acceptance of the other methodological approaches, while in other ways suggesting a powerful critique of hem. What is accepted is the reality of the interests served by the different approaches, and the fact that knowledge serving those interests is a human necessity. The reality of each of the different types of learning produced by the differing methodologies is also accepted, although this is a more difficult issue. It is acknowledged that satisfaction of material human needs requires that an eye be kept to technical matters such as efficient production and coordination of technical activities. Similarly, the need for community and social integration requires that attention be given to intersubjective understanding and to the alignment of action with binding social norms. Finally, there is also a need for self-actualization, for the full development of an autonomous, responsible, self-critical person or society. However, while all three interests are accepted, in their places, *theories* of knowledge that are limited to the "lower" interests are not.

From a critical point of view, the problem with a positivistic understanding of social knowledge is that it does not take into account the way in which the social scientist serves to reinforce or undermine the social practices that create the uniformities that are observed. The positivist moreover confuses social uniformity with natural law. As a result, the social scientist does not understand the way he or she has a hand in maintaining or changing the very phenomena to which the laws apply, thereby affecting the correctiveness or incorrectness of the law. If the social scientist has this effect, it would mean that the positivistic understanding of social science in which laws (if correct) are seen as universal and immutable laws of nature would be wrong.

To see how the social scientist might have this effect, imagine that some new laws purporting to explain social behavior are found and it becomes widely known that they have been accepted by authorities as premises on which policy is based. This will mean that intelligent individuals affected by the policies will calculate their own courses of action taking into account the fact that authorities think that they will behave according to the social scientific "laws." By taking the authorities' use of the laws into account as part of their caluclations, they will then no longer behave purely according to the laws.

A second, closely related point is that preceeding according to a positivistic understanding may not even be a good way to serve the technical interest to which positivism is directed. Since a positivistic approach sees its own precepts as defining all legitimate knowledge, it denies the two other approaches as legitimate ways to gain validated knowledge. The result is that a positivistic approach may be used to deal with problems or issues that are not amenable to the approach itself— that is, in which the approach denies exactly what must be considered in order to solve the problem. The clearest example of this is the attempt to solve problems that are the result of breakdowns in understanding and normative consensus by using technical means. This would be like trying to correct problems in one's love life that are due to inattention to the other's feelings by using more efficient techniques: the more one tries the less it works. This is not to say that a technical approach always fails, for when there is consensus on norms people may agree to act as instruments for some common purpose. However, a technical approach cannot itself determine whether this is the case or bring it about if it is not.

While the first point raised above is a theoretical one concerning the limits of positivistic knowledge, the second point is a practical one. The second point suggests that the use of instrumental knowledge *may* be dysfunctional even in its own terms if it is not used in the right context. In both of these cases positivism may be its own undoing because it fails to take into account the broader context of social relations in which social scientific knowledge works.

Critical theory raises a similar set of issues with respect to the interpretive approach. The problem with an interpretive understanding of social knowledge is that it also does not take into account the way the research may reinforce or undermine existing authorities and interests and may thus make an interpretation wrong or inapplicable that was previously correct. For instance, interpretations that emphasize the rationality of many different cultural groups by showing how each has its own standards of rationality serve, in the end, to undermine authorities indirectly because they make each set of standards appear arbitrary. If such interpretations were widely believed and had this effect, then the practical problem faced by many groups would be that of combatting anarchy and of ensuring commitment to long-run collective goals. In such a situation the old interpretation might appear quite wrong, misplaced, or inappropriate. One can easily imagine new interpretations arising that would stress principles of rationality common to all cultures and would thereby serve to legitimate new authorities. The problem is that as social relations change, in part as a result of proffered interpretations, then the background assumptions of an old interpretation become dissonant with the new conditions, thus making the old interpretation incorrect and calling for a new one. The interpretivist is then struck with the problem of determining which interpretation is "really" correct. Should we believe the first account, before the changes that it helped to bring about, or the second account after the changes? Indeed, if the scientist keeps switching like this why should we ever believe him or her? This problem is particularly apparent in history, where revisionist historians scornfully reject the work of earlier generations of historians not simply because they had their facts wrong but because they based their work on the "wrong" set of presuppositions. The revisionists are then themselves revised, and so on. The problem is that old interpretations are outgrown, but the interpretivist has no way of taking such growth into account within his or her framework.

A second problem that the interpretive approach must face is that it also is *sometimes* a counterproductive way to serve the very interests to which it is directed. If the understandings that are reached through interpretation are generated using a framework of discourse that does not allow for the expression of the real motives of one or another actor, then an overweening emphasis on reciprocal understanding may in fact result in behavior that is even more incomprehensible than that which initially called for interpretation. If active motives cannot be legitimately communicated with a framework, then more communication within that framework further reinforces the illegitimacy of the incommunicable motives and heightens their level of frustration, so that their expression in other ways becomes more urgent. When this expression occurs it will then be all the more surprising and incomprehensible because of the apparent prior understanding. Thus effective communication must take more into account than the communicative conventions or distinctions used by the interactants. What we conclude from this is that both positivistic and interpretive theories of knowledge are incomplete, and that to proceed as though they were adequate understandings is at least sometimes counterproductive.

The two principal criticisms of critical theory raised from the other two positions are that it is value-laden (as seen by positivists) and that its categorical distinctions are arbitrary (as seen by interpretivists). The response from the standpoint of critical theory is partially to acknowledge both criticisms but then to point out how both also represent a misunderstanding of the issues. The positivist's assertion that critical knowledge is value-laden is true as far as it goes, but then so is all knowledge. The very norms of inquiry guiding each methodological orientation represent a particular set of values. In the case of positivism the implicit injunction to maintain an "objective" detached stance towards those one is studying, to view particulars as instances of general uniformities, to describe behavior in terms that have been purged of evaluative connotations, and to separate one's private from one's public (scientific) life represent a particular set of social values. These may be described in terms of Parsons' pattern variables as a value position that is oriented towards affective neutrality, universalism, specificity, and performance. Or, put more simply, they are the values embedded in modern, rationalized, bureaucratic institutions. Thus positivism itself, as a pattern of norms, represents a particular value orientation. Yet because this is not recognized within a positivistic framework the positivist takes his orientation as a given, as simply definitive of rationality itself, and so cannot justify his own value commitments. Positivism asks for a commitment to these values without providing reasons why the value position is itself justifiable.

It is important to recognize that this criticism of positivism does not suggest that the individual positivist's values are of one sort or another. These may vary enormously. Rather it suggests that when a positivist takes on the role commitments of the positivistic scientist, when he or she acts as a scientist as specified by the norms of positivism, he or she acts in accordance with a particular pattern of values even though his or her personal values might differ considerably from those built into the structure of this set of role expectations.

The same point can be made with respect to interpretivism. Here the value pattern is presumably that which is more congruent with the values of "traditional" society—namely, affectivity, particularism, diffuseness, and quality. This is shown, for instance, by the interpretivist's commitment to making sense of a text or text analog as a whole, to valuing the sense of the *particular* test in question, and so forth. Again, these are not necessarily the values of any one interpreter, but are the values embedded in the approach itself. They are standards one must follow to produce a "good" interpretation. Yet these standards also cannot be justified within a relativistic interpretive framework. Thus both positivism and interpretivism call for the adoption of a particular value position, yet neither can justify this commitment within its own framework.

Of course critical theory also has its norms of inquiry and thus its own implicit value commitments. These appear to include, for example, a commitment to the social whole or the common welfare, and to the norms of the ideal speech community. This commitment differs from the commitment of the interpretivist to the semantic whole. Critical theorists would be interested not only in what the "text" says but also in what it conceals, and to what purpose. Another injunction is to look for contradictions, that is, for those cases where theories or ideologies define the situation in a way that is dissonant with practical experience. Bourdieu's analysis (Chapter 19) of the case of students who have less "cultural capital"—that is, who have less fully internalized the code that allows one to decipher school messages, yet who are formally defined as equal to others with more cultural capital—is a case in point. As a formal matter they are equals who presumably have equal chances, but this formal definition simply serves to hide the practical reality that the code used implicitly favors some over others. Another norm guiding critical inquiry is an injunction to be reflective, to apply a critical approach to one's own activity in the attempt to avoid becoming dogmatic or ideological oneself.

While this is surely not a definitive listing or analysis of the norms guiding critical inquiry, it may serve to suggest their nature. The value position implicit in them is that of neither traditional nor modern society but presumably that of some post-modern society in which modernity and tradition, head and heart, have been integrated.

While neither of the other two approaches either fully acknowledges or can justify the value positions they adopt, critical theory acknowledges its own value commitments and at least attempts to justify them. Habermas has attempted to justify the commitments implicit in a critical theory in terms of a theory of communicative competence that he terms a "universal pragmatics." In effect, this theory attempts to specify the nature of nonpathological or authentic communication, and by implication of pathological or inauthentic communication. It suggests that there is a certain set of presumed conditions implicit in all speech. The norms of speech are themselves implicitly modeled after an ideal speech situation in which propositions can be freely tested to see if they are true; actors have full reciprocity of perspectives, and universalized norms are truly universal in their impact. Communicative pathology results when that which it is (implicitly) claimed will stand up to test cannot be redeemed in disputation; when mutuality of perspectives is assumed but does not in fact exist; when norms that are put forth as universal, for the good of all, in fact serve some particular interests. Habermas would claim that the ideal of authentic, undistorted communication is implicit in all speech, including that of positivists or interpretivists, and constitutes a universal set of norms to which one can appeal in grounding one's analysis. Whether this theory will be deemed adequate is still very much open to question. However, it does provide some theoretical justification for the normative position of critical theory and, by making both the value position and its theoretical basis explicit, allows these also to be questioned and put to the test.

The conclusion with respect to the positivist's argument that critical theory is value laden is thus to acknowledge that this is so, but to point out that this is true of positivistic and interpretive approaches as well. This value-ladenness is due not to the values of the individual social scientist but to the pattern of commitments embodied in the norms determining what is "good" research within each tradition. Thus the positivist is partially correct, but has misunderstood the source of the value-ladenness he or she decries. Moreover, the positivist has the further problem of asking for commitment to a set of norms that is not justifiable within his or her own framework.

The other criticism raised against critical theory is that its conventions, presuppositions, or categorical distinctions are arbitrary. The response is first to acknowledge that critical theory, like the other approaches, does consist of a framework of conventions; it involves a viewpoint or worldview just like the others. In this sense all three represent "traditions." However, from the critical perspective it is the other approaches whose conventions or presuppositions are most arbitrary. The positivist is probably in the worst position in this regard for, if "all meaningful statements are either analytic or synthetic," then what kind of statement is this statement itself? The same sort of paradox occurs when one considers any of the other categorical distinctions on which positivism is based, such as that between theory and observation (is this distinction part of a theory or an observation?), fact and value, subject and object. In short, the categorical distinctions of positivism are arbitrary with respect to the positivistic theory of knowledge itself. They are taken-for-granted starting points that cannot be justified within the positivistic approach.

The interpretivist faces a similar problem with respect to his or her presuppositions. In the case of any particular interpretation, the interpretivist can appeal to the conventions of whatever community he or she is dealing with to justify an interpretation. But to what community can interpretivism appeal to justify itself? The attempt is to justify the assumptions of interpretivism itself by appeal to fundamental distinctions in conventional language use. If the grammar of our language games when speaking of *things* is different from the grammar of our speech about *persons*, then the interpretivist concludes that since we are self-interpreting beings who, as actors, are constituted by our speech, there must be a real difference between persons and things. In this way an attempt is made to ground the distinctions between reasons and causes, actions and behaviors, and the like, in linguistic conventions, and so to justify an interpretive approach. The problem, of course, is that the proper way of speaking may represent a confused or distorted way of thinking. In effect the interpretivist is saying that common usage must be right, but how can this assumption be justified? With no other place to appeal to than convention, the interpretivist cannot justify the presuppositions of interpretivism itself.

What this line of reasoning suggests is that the interpretivist is correct in pointing out that critical theory rests upon a set of presuppositions, just as does interpretivism, and that both are in need of validation. However, appeal to the conventions of those one studies does not settle the issue, for why should they be any more adequate than those of social scientists themselves? The interpretivist's attempted validation merely replaces one set of prepositions with another and, in the end, is susceptible to the same charge of being arbitrary that was leveled against critical theory. Apparently the validation of one set of conventions requires more than appeal to another set. The criticism is again partially correct and partially wrong.

But can critical theory justify its own set of presuppositions? The fundamental distinction on which critical theory is based is the contrast between the three knowledge constitutive interests, the technical, the practical, and the emancipatory. Habermas's critique of others' approaches, for instance, is often based on the fact that they either failed to consider one of these "dimensions" of knowledge, or failed adequately to distinguish between them. There is certainly some plausibility to the distinctions that are made between these "levels" of knowledge.[4] One can learn from experience, first, by using a fixed scheme to organize the experience. This is akin to the way in which the positivists suggest all knowledge is generated. It is also the way reinforcement theorists suggest all learning occurs. Secondly, one can use a fixed *set* of conceptual schemes and learn when to apply each in order to make experience comprehensible. Here the task is not so much to map the connections between events defined by a scheme as to judge when a scheme is applicable. This is roughly the interpretivist's view of learning. It is also closely related to gestaltist approaches in psychology. Finally, one can modify the schemes or sets of schemes themselves and significantly change the cognitive structures being used, in the light of their adequacy in facilitating adaptation to problematic situations. This approximates the level of learning considered in critical theory or in emancipatory learning. The three levels of learning would seem to be logically differentiated and are not as *ad hoc* as at least some of Habermas' critics have suggested.[5]

As a practical matter these types of learning blend into one another. We do not treat people either entirely as "things" or as "agents" but as complex intermixtures and in varying ways in between. And sometimes conceptual schemes may change so gradually, in so many small steps, that the line between selecting among and applying old schemes and restructuring them may be impossible to draw. In any event, to justify these distinctions from a critical perspective does not call so much for their logical differentiation as for testing whether critical theory adequately explains communicative distortion and adequately facilitates emancipatory practices. Judgments in this vein must be left up to discursive validation and cannot be demonstrated by the theory itself. For the critical theorist, all social theorizing must be seen as part of a larger process of social evolution which theories can never fully capture. Critical theory thus depicts itself as a potentially limiting theory which will also be outgrown. In the meantime, however, critical theory's critique of positivism and, for that matter, of the whole positivist-interpretivist split, seems a promising and freeing effort, given our current social conditions.

This raises a final question about critical theory that arises from within critical theory itself, namely, is critical theory another partial theory that conceals as much as it reveals and is thereby likely to function as another self-serving ideology? Can an approach that is based on the critique of ideology itself become ideological? The answer is that of course it can. Whether a theory becomes an ideology depends on how it is used. The categorical distinctions in critical theory can be absolutized and used to legitimize a new set of authorities in as unquestionable a fashion as in other ideologies. What can save critical theory from being used in this way is the insistence on reflectivity, the insistence that this theory of knowledge also be applied to those propounding or using the theory. When this is kept in mind, it becomes apparent that our present ability to assess critical theory may be limited by current ideological distortions. While this provides the impetus for reflection on particular aspects of the theory itself, it is important to remember that there is no omniscient standpoint from which to say that critical theory offers an adequate understanding of the present situation. This does not mean that there are no reasonable grounds. However, commitment to critical theory, like commitment to all theories, is making bet on the future.[6] The bet is not made in total ignorance or blindness, but one still has to bet before the most telling results are in. Since critical theory is a theory that we hold of ourselves, the most telling results will be the long-term effects on us if we hold the theory; to that extent these can be known only after the fact. In the meantime nothing would be less consistent with the spirit of critical theory than to adopt it blindly as another "ism," another dogma; nothing would be more consistent with it than to subject it to the same sorts of criticism that it would direct against other approaches, for this would seem to be the best way of ensuring that its legitimate heirs do indeed constitute a more adequate theory of knowledge in society. As Toulmin (who does not consider himself a critical theorist) put it: "A man demonstrates his rationality, not by a commitment to fixed ideas, stereotyped procedures, or immutable concepts, but by the manner in which, and the occasions on which, he changes those ideas, procedures, and concepts."[7]

Conclusion

What does more extended dialogue suggest about the truth, correctness, or adequacy of the different theories of knowledge we have considered? We think it suggests that critical theory may offer a more comprehensive, more adequate basis of understanding educational and social scientific research, though one that is perhaps in need of further elaboration and future modification. Consider what can be learned from each of the evaluative criteria we have discussed.

Truth is the narrowest of the three criteria, but it is the one that is appealed to by each of the three theories. It applies to statements rather than to conceptual systems or communicative practices. To judge the truth of a theory is one way to evaluate it, and since we can take the three approaches we have been discussing as three different theories of knowledge, they may each be evaluated in terms of their truth. If we consider each of these approaches as a set of propositions such as "fact and value are entirely distinct" or "fact and value are always intertwined," we would find that the approaches give logically contradictory sets of statements. They deny each other at every turn. This would suggest that, if one of the theories is true, the others must be false. However, to test the truth of the three theories we must have some facts to appeal to. We must be able to ask which of the three theories best explains (in the sense of logically accounts for) the "same" facts. This is of course a problem because each of the theories is talking about something different even when the same terms are used. As a result, what counts as an instance of the "same" event will differ for the different theories, so that we will not really be testing them against the "same" facts unless we arbitrarily adopt the conventions of one of the theories over the others. It may, however, be a symptom of some broader conception of rightness or adequacy. We may want to reject logically inconsistent theories, but more often we reject or retain them for other reasons and fix up the logic as we go along.

A second and somewhat broader criterion is correctness or rightness.[8] Rightness is something that applies to a whole account rather than to individual statements. The truth of statements may be part of what is used to judge the correctness of an account, but, as Winch puts it, it is not the "court of last appeal." Correctness is a broader matter of the fit of a pattern rather than of the correspondence of any one particular point in the pattern with that to which it is being fitted. Adopting this as a standard, which of the three acounts is more nearly correct? Here it seems possible that each of the three orientations may be judged to be relevant or appropriate at different times.

Sometimes the dominant concern is with efficiency or productivity or effectiveness. At other times it is with equity, with sensitivity to local situations and differences, with maintaining community. Finally, at still other times, the dominant concern may be with the legitimacy of existing authorities and the adequacy of prevailing ideologies. In the first case a positivistic approach, or something structurally very much like it, is likely to be "right," in the second an interpretive approach, or something like it, and in the third case a critical approach or its near equivalent. The trouble is that this segregation to different contexts does nothing to resolve the issue as to the relative merits of the three approaches. And it leaves the problem that what is deemed to be correct from the standpoint of one group or community may seem incorrect from the standpoint of another.

Perhaps we can segregate or partition the three approaches and apply each only when it is appropriate. There is something to be said for this; however, the difficulty is that standards of rightness come from within a tradition and often give little hint of how they could be used comparatively, across traditions. Thus what is a technical problem for one person, or one community, is a communicational problem for another. As a result, we can neither segregate the approaches and proclaim them all "correct" (though at different times) nor ultimately decide that one is more correct than the others. Rightness may be a test for some broader characteristic of desirable theories, but it is also too narrow to be definitive.

The final and broadest criterion to be applied in evaluating a theory is its adequacy. By this we mean the ability to better meet specifically *human* needs through the use of the theory. Inadequate theories gives a distorted understanding of the practical-functional nature of the world. We have argued that a belief in postivism or in interpretivism may, at times, produce results that are dysfunctional from the standpoint of the very needs or interests these orientations attempt to serve. For instance, approaching breakdowns in relationship in positivistic terms is merely asking for more of the same. Similarly, approaching such breakdowns as matters of pure communication between equals when in fact one or another framework is supported by authorities and dominant institutions is to ask for pseudocommunication and ultimately for disagreement and miscomprehension. This suggests that the other approaches may at times be less flexible than critical theory. Since critical theory does not deny the interests served by the other approaches (though it does deny their *theories* of knowledge), it essentially captures the adaptive potential of both others while adding another dimension that needs to be considered.

Conclusion

That is, from a critical standpoint, one sometimes needs to be instrumental; at other times one needs to be sensitive to the application of schemes; at still other times one needs to take account of the inadequacy of present schemes. Just as a three-dimensional view does not deny the first and second dimensions (although it does deny theories that collapse everything to one or two dimensions), so critical theory does not deny the interests or procedures used in the other approaches, but rather their theories of knowledge and the conditions under which their procedures are appropriately applied. As Taylor puts it (in Chapter 9):

> The superiority of one position over another will consist in this, that from the more adequate position one can understand one's own stand and that of one's opponent, but not the other way around. It goes without saying that this argument can only have weight for those in the superior position.

By this criterion, critical theory would seem to be in a good position since, as we have attempted to show, it can understand the other two approaches, while they tend to collapse the critical perspective into either psychological or interactional terms. While the overall verdict is still out on critical theory, from the present standpoint it appears to offer a promising new basis for understanding the nature of social and educational knowledge and for helping to create a society that is better fit for all of its members.

Notes

1. This goes back to Winch's point (in Chapter 8) that one can tell that an activity is rule governed when there are right and wrong ways to do it.
2. Alfred H. Stanton and Morris S. Schwartz, *The Mental Hospital* (New York: Basic Books, 1954), p. 203. Quoted in Anselm L. Strauss, *Mirrors and Masks* (San Francisco: Sociology Press, 1969), p. 54.
3. See Nelson Goodman's *Languages of Art* (Indianapolis: Hackett Press, 1972) for an instructive analysis of the three major types of symbolic systems (digital, discursive, and analog) and of differing modes of symbolization (denotation, exemplification, representation, and expression).
4. An interesting and closely related analysis can be found in Gregory Bateson's "The Logical Categories of Learning and Communication" in *Steps to an Ecology of Mind* (New York: Ballantine, 1972).
5. E.g., Richard Bernstein, *Restructuring Social and Political Theory* (Philadelphia: University of Pennsylvania Press, 1976).
6. Stephen Toulmin, *Human Understanding* (Princeton, N.J.: Princeton University Press, 1972).
7. Toulmin, *Human Understanding*, Preface.
8. Nelson Goodman, *Ways of Worldmaking* (Indianapolis, Indiana: Hackett Press, 1978).